# The East Asian Development Experience
# The Miracle, the Crisis and the Future

## Ha-Joon Chang

**TWN**
Third World Network
Penang, Malaysia

**Zed Books**
London and New York

**The East Asian Development Experience
The Miracle, the Crisis
and the Future**
is published by
Zed Books Ltd.,
7 Cynthia Street, London N1 9JF, UK and
Room 400, 175 Fifth Avenue, New York, NY 10010, USA
and
Third World Network,
131 Jalan Macalister, 10400 Penang, Malaysia

Distributed exclusively in the USA on behalf of Zed Books
by Palgrave Macmillan,
a division of St Martin's Press, LLC
175 Fifth Avenue,
New York, NY 10010, USA

Copyright © Ha-Joon Chang,
Third World Network 2006

The right of Ha-Joon Chang to be identified as the author of this work has
been asserted by him in accordance with the Copyright, Designs and
Patents Act, 1988

All rights reserved

No part of this publication may be reproduced, stored in a retrieval system
or transmitted, in any form or by any means, electronic or otherwise,
without the prior permission of the publisher.

ISBN-13: 978-1-84277-141-9
ISBN-10: 1-84277-141-8

Transferred to Digital Printing 2008

A catalogue record for this book is available from the British Library
US CIP data is available from the Library of Congress

# Contents

## PART IV: LOOKING INTO THE FUTURE OF EAST ASIA

**Chapter 9**
**EVALUATING THE POST-CRISIS CORPORATE RESTRUCTURING IN KOREA** 279

## ACKNOWLEDGEMENTS

**Chapter 1**: 'The East Asian Model of Economic Policy' was originally published in E. Huber (ed.), *Models of Capitalism and Latin American Development* (2002, The Pennsylvania State University Press). I thank the Social Science Research Council, New York, and the Pennsylvania State University Press for the permission to reprint the chapter.

**Chapter 2:** 'The Political Economy of Industrial Policy in Korea' was originally published in *Cambridge Journal of Economics*, 1993, vol. 17, no. 2. I thank the Academic Press for its permission to reprint the article.

**Chapter 3:** 'Explaining "Flexible Rigidities" in East Asia' was originally published in T. Killick (ed.), *The Flexible Economy* (1995, Routledge). I thank the Overseas Development Institute for its financial support and Routledge for its permission to reprint the article.

**Chapter 4:** 'How Important were the "Initial Conditions" for Economic Development?: East Asia vs. Sub-Saharan Africa' is a revised version of the paper 'The "Initial Conditions" of Economic Development – Comparing the East Asian and the Sub-Saharan African Experiences', prepared as a background paper for the *Trade and Development Report, 1998* of UNCTAD (United Nations Conference on Trade and Development). I thank UNCTAD for its financial support.

**Chapter 5:** 'The Hazard of Moral Hazard – Untangling the Asian Crisis' was originally published in *World Development*, 2000, vol. 28, no. 4. I thank Elsevier Science Ltd. for its permission to reprint this article.

**Chapter 6:** 'Interpreting the Korean Crisis – Financial Liberalisation, Industrial Policy and Corporate Governance' (co-authored with Hong-Jae Park and Chul Gyue Yoo) was originally published in *Cambridge Journal of Economics*, 1998, vol. 22, no. 6. I thank Oxford University Press for its permission to reprint the article.

**Chapter 7:** 'Industrial Policy and East Asia – The Miracle, the Crisis and the Future' is a revised version of the paper presented at the World Bank workshop on 'Re-thinking East Asian Miracle', San Francisco, 16-7 February, 1999. I thank the World Bank for its financial support.

**Chapter 8:** 'The Triumph of the Rentiers?' was originally published in *Challenge*, 2000, vol. 43, no. 1. I thank M.E. Sharpe for its permission to reprint the article.

**Chapter 9:** 'Evaluating the Post-Crisis Corporate Restructuring in Korea' (co-authored with Jang-Sup Shin) is an updated version of the paper of the same title published in *Seoul Journal of Economics*, 2002, vol. 15, no. 2.

# INTRODUCTION

THE socio-economic transformation of East Asia – by which I mean Japan and the four first-tier NICs, or newly industrialising countries, of South Korea (henceforth Korea), Taiwan, Hong Kong, and Singapore, unless specified otherwise[1] – in the last few decades has been truly spectacular. In the early 1960s, the richest economy in the region (Japan) was on a par with South Africa and Chile in terms of per capita income, while the poorest one (Korea) had a per capita income less than half those of Ghana and Honduras.[2] Today East Asia is literally the richest part of the world outside the old industrial centres of Western Europe and North America. Moreover, the achievements of the region's economies do not stop at income growth. Their records in terms of improvements in infant mortality, life expectancy, educational achievements, and other indicators of 'human development' have also been very impressive, even considering their rapid income growth.

Of course, this is not to say that everything has been rosy in East Asia. Political authoritarianism, human rights violations, corruption, repression of labour unions, gender discrimination, mistreatment of ethnic minorities, and so on, have all been problems to one degree or

---

[1]  The definition of East Asia is itself a contested issue, with different definitions resulting in different theoretical and policy implications. This issue is addressed in Chapters 1 and 7 of this book.

[2]  In 1961, Japan's per capita income in current US dollars was $402, compared to $396 for South Africa and $377 for Chile. In the same year, Korea's per capita income was $82, compared to $179 for Ghana and $182 for Honduras. The figures are from Kindleberger (1965: pp. 12-3, Table 1.1), except for Korea, which is from its National Accounts statistics.

another in the East Asian economies. However, these economies have made good progress by historical standards even on these accounts. And despite these blemishes, it would be fair to say that, during the second half of the twentieth century, the citizens of the East Asian economies experienced improvements in income and general well-being that are so far unparalleled in human history.

What makes the East Asian development experience even more interesting is that their policies and institutions have often significantly diverged from what many people, including many East Asians themselves, regard as the 'best practice' ones. Instead of pursuing the so-called Washington Consensus policies of inflation-focused macroeconomic policy, liberalised international trade and investment, deregulation, and privatisation, the East Asian economies, with the exception of Hong Kong, used interventionist trade and industrial policies, often through a large public-enterprise sector, backing it up with pro-investment macroeconomic policy. They used institutions and policies such as business groups with interlocking ownership, lifetime employment, relation-based contracting, and the bank-based financial system, which do not conform to the Anglo-American ideal of free-standing enterprise ruthlessly pursuing shareholder values (therefore lacking room for features such as lifetime employment or relation-based contracting) in a stock-market-based financial system.

Given the combination of the spectacular records and the unorthodox methods through which they have been achieved, it is not surprising that the development experiences of the East Asian economies have been at the centre of numerous academic and policy controversies since the 1960s. And a very emotionally charged and intellectually turbulent debate it has been, as many of the chapters that follow testify.

The essays collected in this volume try to shed light on this debate by unearthing new facts, applying unorthodox theories to re-interpret many of the widely-accepted 'facts', and coming up with often unconventional policy suggestions. Consequently, the essays will sometimes shock, confuse, or intrigue people, but I hope that after reading some, if not all, of them, the reader will begin to see the East Asian experience, and economic development in general, with some fresh perspectives.

Chapter 1, which constitutes the scene-setting Part I, 'The East Asian Model of Economic Policy', provides an overview of the debate on East Asian development experience by analysing the East Asian model of economic policy in comparative perspective.

After the discussion of the comparative context and the discussion of the definition of the East Asian model, three areas of economic policies are examined – investment policy, trade policy, and industrial policy (including technology policy). In the process, the chapter highlights some policies which have received inadequate attention even by those who are sympathetic to the East Asian model. These include, among others: (i) the pro-investment, rather than anti-inflationary, macroeconomic policy; (ii) the control on luxury consumption, which served both economic *and* political functions; (iii) the strict control on foreign direct investment (FDI), which is contrary to the popular impression that the East Asian economies (perhaps except Japan) have had an 'open' FDI policy; (iv) the integrated pursuit of infant industry protection and export promotion; (v) the use of export as a tool to exploit scale economy and thus to accelerate the maturation of infant industries; and (vi) the productivity-oriented (as opposed to allocation-oriented) view of competition.

Then the chapter discusses whether replicating the East Asian model in other countries is feasible. While acknowledging that a wholesale replication of any economic model is neither feasible nor desirable, the chapter argues that those who are sceptical about the replicability of the East Asian model tend to base their arguments on partial (and often misleading) information and dubious theories. This theme is more fully taken on in Chapters 2 and 4. This discussion is followed by a short commentary on whether the 1997 financial crisis in some of the NICs and the decade-long stagnation in Japan signify the end of the East Asian model. The chapter argues that, if anything, the recent economic troubles in the region can be attributed to departures from the traditional East Asian model, rather than to adherence to it.

In Part II, a set of three essays present my interpretation of the East Asian miracle, based on some unorthodox theories and drawing on numerous formerly ignored or distorted facts.

The title of Chapter 2, 'The Political Economy of Industrial Policy in Korea', may make it sound rather narrow, being about one country (Korea), and one aspect of economic policy (industrial policy). However, the chapter goes well beyond Korea. While it may start by drawing mainly on the Korean case until the late 1980s, it soon develops its arguments in relation to the whole region. Korea was chosen not simply because it is my own country but also because it shows the best and the worst of the East Asian model as the most 'extreme' variety of it. While it may start off with a relatively narrow discussion of industrial policy, the chapter also eventually goes into a wide range of factors affecting economic development, including the role of the state in general, class structure and politics, international political economy, and institution building.

After reviewing a variety of the mainstream interpretations of the Korean developmental process, the chapter provides some detailed theoretical and empirical criticisms of them. It then discusses how industrial policy, and state intervention in general, works in Korea and why, emphasising the importance of historical, social, and political factors in determining the effectiveness of state intervention.

There are four key conclusions to the chapter. First, development strategy is a complex set of interrelated policies rather than a simple matter of trade policy (the whole literature on 'openness'), as is often implied by the mainstream literature. Second, economic development requires a constant upgrading of the industrial structure based on the development of local technological and managerial capabilities, with the help of appropriate import protection, government subsidies, and institution building. Third, the conduct of industrial policy in East Asia casts serious doubts on the conventional wisdom that more competition is always better. Fourth, some 'unique' institutions that we see in Korea and other East Asian countries need not mean that other countries cannot learn from them. Indeed, there are many examples in history, both inside and outside East Asia, which show the importance of institutional learning and adaptation.

Chapter 3, 'Explaining "Flexible Rigidities" in East Asia', is a rather unconventional essay, even by the standards of the present book. It tries to explain how the East Asian economies are full of 'rigidities' in the short run, particularly at the micro-level, but exhibit a surprising degree of 'flexibility' in the long run at the national level – a phenomenon aptly named 'flexible rigidities' by Ronald Dore in his

classic 1986 book.[3] And it does so by employing an institutionalist
theoretical framework that develops the notion of bounded rationality, first pioneered by Herbert Simon.

The chapter argues that there are good theoretical reasons to
believe that all complex modern economies with specific assets and
non-off-the-shelf technology require institutional rigidities so as to
socialise risk in specific investments and provide a stable environment for learning. In such a world, it is argued there is an inherent
conflict between short-run and long-run flexibilities, as short-run
flexibilities may discourage productivity-enhancing investments,
which are likely to increase long-run flexibility by providing a larger
resource base and increased technological capabilities. The chapter
also argues that, in a world which has more than one national economy
and has assets with different degrees of mobility, allowing total flexibility for individuals may lead to a reduction in the flexibility of the
national economy. This is because it may reduce the resource base
and hamper productivity growth of the national economy. In short,
the chapter argues that the neoliberal ideal of a regulation-free and
collusion-free economy is, even if it can be obtained, not desirable in
a world where the agents have bounded rationality and where productivity growth requires specific investments and learning.

The East Asian economies provide ample examples that support these arguments. The explanations for these 'flexible rigidities'
of the East Asian economies are found in the ability of their states and
private sector agents to develop institutions to enhance long-run national flexibilities at the cost of short-run individual flexibilities. It is
also argued that, by acknowledging the inherently political nature of
the resource re-allocation process and thereby incorporating political
considerations in their industrial policy, these economies could facilitate the industrial restructuring process.

Chapter 3 ends with an appendix which provides some detailed
technical criticisms of the World Bank's *East Asian Miracle* report. A
more theoretical criticism is offered later in the volume, in Chapter 7.
While the appendix is not essential for the arguments advanced in the
chapter, at the time of writing (1993/4), it was felt necessary for the

---

[3]    The book is R. Dore, *Flexible Rigidities: Industrial Policy and Structural Adjustment in the Japanese Economy 1970-80*. London: The Athlone Press.

chapter to respond to the report, given its influence at the time.

Chapter 4, 'How Important were the "Initial Conditions" for Economic Development?: East Asia vs. Sub-Saharan Africa', is a revised and updated version of a previously unpublished paper, 'The "Initial Conditions" of Economic Development – Comparing the East Asian and the Sub-Saharan African Experiences', which was written as a background paper for the 1998 *Trade and Development Report* of the United Nations Conference on Trade and Development (UNCTAD).

The chapter addresses the increasingly-popular literature on the 'initial conditions' of development, which argues that factors like natural resource endowment, human capital stock, and infrastructure at the beginning of a country's economic development effort have extremely strong effects on its subsequent growth path. This literature particularly emphasises how some regions like East Asia have benefited from their favourable initial conditions, while others, notably Sub-Saharan Africa, have been crippled by poor initial conditions.

While questioning some of the 'initial conditions' argument (especially the 'resource curse' thesis, which argues that countries with more natural resources grow more slowly), the focus of the chapter is in showing that, contrary to the conventional wisdom, the East Asian countries did not have exceptionally favourable initial conditions, especially if we take the 1940s or the 1950s as the starting point. The chapter takes a particularly close look at the differences in initial conditions between East Asia and Sub-Saharan Africa, a region which is supposed to have been most disadvantaged by its poor initial conditions. When relevant, it also looks at other country groups such as Latin America, Southeast Asia, and the advanced countries. The initial conditions examined in the chapter are human resource endowments, natural resource endowments, physical and social infrastructure, previous industrial experiences, and foreign aid.

The chapter shows that, while somewhat ahead of most Sub-Saharan African countries, the East Asian countries at the time did not have a huge advantage in terms of initial conditions. Particularly in the case of Korea, the least developed in the region, a substantial number of Sub-Saharan African countries were more favourably positioned in relation to most indicators examined in the chapter. These findings imply that policies and other conscious human actions are more important than historically-inherited or structurally-determined 'initial conditions' in determining the developmental outcome.

The two chapters in Part III discuss the 1997 Asian financial crisis and its implications for our understanding of the preceding miracle and the future of East Asia.

The first of the two chapters, that is, Chapter 5, 'The Hazard of Moral Hazard – Untangling the Asian Crisis', criticises various mainstream explanations of the recent Asian crisis that put emphasis on the political and institutional deficiencies that are supposed to have created 'moral hazard' for the investors by over-protecting them (e.g., crony capitalism, industrial policy, deposit insurance, and government guarantees accorded to banks and industrial firms that are considered too important to fail). The chapter also discusses the international dimension of the moral hazard argument in the context of International Monetary Fund (IMF) bailouts.

After putting the problem of moral hazard into historical perspective by pointing out that, contrary to the popular perception, moral hazard has historically been an integral part of the development of modern capitalism, the chapter critically examines the validity of the mainstream moral hazard arguments. It finds that some of the arguments are conceptually too ill-defined. For example, cronyism, by definition, has to be selective, but many of those who use this concept assume that it had extended to more or less all major business transactions (including foreign borrowings) in Asian countries. The chapter also finds that some of the arguments patently mis-specify the problem. For example, in the deposit insurance argument and the IMF bailout argument, lender-of-last-resort facilities are identified as the source of moral hazard, when it is really the deficiency of the incentive mechanism for the (national and international, respectively) bank managers that is at the heart of the problem. Last but not least, the chapter finds that many facts simply do not fit the moral hazard arguments.

The chapter concludes that, while the explanations of the Asian crisis built around the notion of moral hazard contain some germs of truth (some more than others), they are conceptually ill-defined, mis-specify the problems, and are empirically unconvincing. By pointing out the fundamental weaknesses in the moral hazard arguments, the chapter strengthens the arguments that put emphasis on domestic financial regulation and the international financial architecture.

In Chapter 6, 'Interpreting the Korean Crisis – Financial Liberalisation, Industrial Policy and Corporate Governance', I and my co-authors Hong-Jae Park and Chul Gyue Yoo delve deeper into the Korean case in order to understand how this once-mighty economy could fall so dramatically.

Written in the very early days of the Korean financial crisis (spring of 1998), the chapter critically examines the three most contentious issues regarding the origins of and the solutions to the 1997 Korean crisis – namely, financial liberalisation, industrial policy, and corporate governance. It argues that it was the dismantling of the traditional mechanisms of industrial policy and financial regulation, rather than their perpetuation, that generated the crisis in Korea. It also points out that Korea's allegedly pathological corporate governance system was neither a main cause of the crisis on its own, nor something that needed radical restructuring in the Anglo-American direction before the country can resume its growth.

Looking back, I am saddened to note that the mis-diagnosis of the causes of the crisis that I and my co-authors criticise in the chapter became the basis for the 'reforms' that followed. As a result, investment and growth have fallen, employment has become much more insecure for more workers, income inequality and poverty have increased, and the economy as a whole has become much more unstable and undynamic, as the chapters in the last part of the book (Chapters 7-9) show.

The three essays in Part IV try to look into the future of East Asia, and in particular Korea, through the examination of the events that followed the 1997 crisis.

Chapter 7, 'Industrial Policy and East Asia – The Miracle, the Crisis and the Future', critically examines the roles of industrial policy in East Asia during the miracle years, in the making of the recent economic troubles, and the likely future.

The chapter starts by reviewing the negative verdict on East Asian industrial policy advanced by the World Bank's *East Asian Miracle* report. Some technical aspects of the report's discussion of East Asian industrial policy are already criticised in the appendix to Chapter 3 of this book, but the present chapter focuses on more theoretical criticisms. Next, the chapter critically examines the currently popular view that industrial policy was behind the downfall of the East Asian model and exposes the weaknesses of this view. The chapter also tries to look into the future and discusses whether the more recent economic, political, and institutional changes (both at the national and international levels) have made the use of industrial policy less feasible and/or less desirable for the region as well as for the rest of the world.

The chapter comes up with a number of conclusions that go against conventional wisdom. First, it argues that the debate on industrial policy is hardly closed: there is little evidence for the argument that the recent economic troubles in East Asia are due to industrial policy; there are more theoretical justifications for industrial policy than is normally acknowledged; and better ways to test the true effects of industrial policy need to be developed. Second, the chapter argues, while it is important to design industrial policies in line with the government's administrative capabilities, it is wrong to dismiss the relevance of East Asian-style industrial policy on the ground that most other developing countries do not have the high administrative capabilities that the East Asian countries had. Industrial policy does not necessarily require a better bureaucracy than other policies do, and, more importantly, bureaucratic capabilities can always be built up, which is what the East Asians had done. Third, the chapter argues that, while factors like industrial maturity, democratisation, and the rise of the private sector have made the execution of industrial policy in East Asia more complicated, their effects on the feasibility and the desirability of industrial policy are not necessarily negative.

Chapter 8, 'The Triumph of the Rentiers?', co-authored with Chul Gyue Yoo, one of my co-authors for Chapter 6, is an early assessment of the post-crisis reform in Korea, written in the summer of 1999.

The chapter argues that the 1997 crisis and the reform that followed it signify an important watershed in modern Korean economic history. First, the crisis was the result of a growing disintegration of the traditional economic system, in which industrial interests were put before financial rentier interests. Second, the management of the crisis has been in the interests of the rentiers in the sense that it has ended the traditional dominance of industry over finance through changes in the institutions of corporate governance, financial regulation, and industrial policy.

The chapter argues that the new system that is emerging after the 1997 crisis in Korea does not look very promising. The recovery, while quite impressive in absolute terms, has been slower than the recoveries from the two earlier financial crises (1970-2 and 1980), while unemployment and income inequality have increased as never before. And this was despite the fact that the external conditions were much more favourable than in the cases of the two earlier crises – following the earlier crises, Korea had to struggle with the First Oil Shock in 1973-4, on the one hand, and the Second Oil Shock and the subsequent monetarist recession in the early 1980s, on the other hand. More worrying, the chapter argues, are the economy's future prospects. The chapter argues that the institutional changes that followed the crisis are likely to dampen the economy's investment dynamism by making the financial system much more volatile and 'conservative' than before, and consequently making long-term, patient capital much more scarce.

In writing Chapter 9, 'Evaluating the Post-Crisis Corporate Restructuring in Korea', in the summer of 2002, I and my co-author Jang-Sup Shin had the benefit of being able to watch the new Korean system unfold for longer, compared to when I wrote Chapters 6 or 8. Unfortunately, the events have confirmed my worst fears about Korea's decision to completely ditch the traditional East Asian model following the 1997 crisis.

The chapter critically assesses Korea's post-1997 reform programme, focusing on the reform of the corporate sector. After critically reviewing the economic analyses that informed the country's post-crisis reform programme, it looks at the country's key corporate reform measures, which essentially set out to dismantle what remained of the traditional economic system of the country after the liberalisation exercise in the 1990s and replace it with an Anglo-American-style system.

The chapter argues that Korea's new economic system is mainly geared towards ensuring the stability and the profitability of the financial sector. It shows that, while the post-crisis reform programme has introduced some positive elements (e.g., increased corporate transparency), it has been implemented at substantial 'transition costs' and has reduced the long-run dynamism of the economy by negatively affecting the corporate financing system and forcing the managers to become extremely defensive in their management style. To make it even worse, the new system has even failed to reduce financial risk of the corporate sector, a key goal of the corporate reform programme.

The chapter argues that the biggest challenge for the country will be to figure out a way to forge a second-stage catching-up system, which revitalises investment dynamism while managing systemic financial risk. The chapter outlines some elements of this alternative strategy.

The essays in the book are attempts to dispel some of the myths, misunderstandings, and factual distortions that plague the literature on East Asia. They also try to put some of the well-known 'facts' into fresh perspective, which often results in very unconventional interpretations of the past and very unorthodox policy recommendations for the future. I do not claim to have monopoly over the truth, but I hope this book helps the reader to understand arguably what is the most dramatic development experience in human history in a more balanced and sophisticated way.

## Bibliography

Dore, R. (1986). *Flexible Rigidities: Industrial Policy and Structural Adjustment in the Japanese Economy 1970-80.* London: The Athlone Press.
Kindleberger, C. (1965). *Economic Development.* New York: McGraw-Hill.

# Chapter 1

# THE EAST ASIAN MODEL OF ECONOMIC POLICY

## 1. Introduction: The Belated Interest in the Diversity of Capitalism

THE last two decades have witnessed the rise of neoliberalism as the dominant vision of how our economies should be organised (for some critical reviews of the neoliberal doctrine, see Chang, 1994a: Chapters 1 and 2, and essays in Chang and Rowthorn (eds.), 1995[1]). In this revival of the old doctrine of *laissez-faire*, the early postwar consensus that capitalism has to be 'tamed' in order to be saved from itself (Shonfield, 1965, is a classic statement of this early consensus) has been overturned, and the virtues of the 'invisible hand' are endlessly praised. Countries which do not conform to this doctrine are constantly chastised for being 'backward-looking', and (the idealised version of) Anglo-Saxon capitalism, characterised by reactive (if not completely non-interventionist) governments and arm's-length contractual relationships, is promoted as the 'best practice' model of capitalism that every country should emulate.

During the same period, however, there have been a number of debates which focused on the differences between different 'models' of capitalism with different goals, institutional structures, and policy tools. These debates were prompted by the very divergent economic performances of different economies, both developed and developing, which can all be described as 'capitalist' in the sense that they rely heavily (although by no means exclusively) on private property,

---

[1]   The first two chapters of Chang and Rowthorn (eds.) (1995) appear in Spanish translation in Chang (1996b).

profit motives, and market-type coordination of activities. Prominent debates in this vein include: (a) the debate on financial systems and corporate governance, especially contrasting the Anglo-Saxon model and the German-Japanese model[2]; (b) the debates on industrial relations, which include the debate on (mainly) Scandinavian social corporatism and the debate on the Japanese employment system[3]; (c) the debate on industrial policy, especially, although not exclusively, in relation to the East Asian experience[4]; (d) the debate on industrial districts, especially based on the experiences of Central Italy (Emilia-Romagna) and Southern Germany (Baden-Württemberg)[5].

Collectively, these debates have demonstrated how there are many different ways to organise production and distribution even within a basically *capitalist* institutional framework, and how these differences matter for economic performance. The common message from these debates is that economies which have the institutional mechanisms to generate more effective long-term-oriented cooperative arrangements regarding (technological and organisational) learning and investments (in human and physical assets) are likely to outperform the countries that predominantly rely on classic free-market mechanisms, which depend on short-term-oriented, individualistic competitive forces that work through arm's-length contracts (for a theoretical discussion on the institutional diversity of capitalism, see Chang, 1997a).

---

[2]   Zysman (1983) and Cox (ed.) (1986) are important earlier works in this literature. More recent influential works include Albert (1991) and Dore (1993).

[3]   On social corporatism, see Goldthorpe (ed.) (1984), Schott (1984), Bruno and Sachs (1985), and Pekkarinen *et al.* (eds.) (1992). On the Japanese employment system, see Dore (1987), Koike (1987), Aoki (1990), and Aoki and Dore (eds.) (1994).

[4]   It was not just in East Asia where industrial policy played an important role. Before the 1980s, France conducted a very 'East Asian style' industrial policy (Cohen, 1977; Hall, 1987). Some other European economies, especially Austria and Finland, are also known to have put emphasis on sectoral industrial policy (Vartiainen, 1995). However, it is true that the debate of the 1980s was largely prompted by the success of East Asia. Summaries of the debate can be found in Johnson (ed.) (1984: Introduction), Thompson (ed.) (1989: Introduction), and Chang (1994a: Chapter 3). The more recent phase of the debate revolved around the so-called 'East Asian Miracle Report' by the World Bank (1993). See Section 5 for further details on the debate surrounding this report.

[5]   For example, see Brusco (1982), Piore and Sabel (1984), Murray (1987), Castells *et al.*(eds.) (1989), and Dei Ottati (1994).

One interesting thing is that this diversity in the institutional structure of capitalism has been there all the time since the history of 'late development' began, that is, when the backward nations started their attempts to adapt the institutions of the first industrial nations to their own economic, political, and social conditions in order to industrialise (Gerschenkron, 1966, is the classic work on this). The institutional diversity of capitalism persisted even through the height of *laissez-faire* capitalism, namely the period between 1870 and 1913, and has increased in many ways throughout the postwar period, although more recently there are increasing questions about the corroding effect of globalisation on it (see essays in Berger and Dore (eds.), 1996). However, it is only recently that the issue has received proper attention. What are the reasons for this?

Firstly, during the first three decades of the postwar period, all advanced capitalist economies performed very well by historical standards, thus bestowing the name of the 'Golden Age of Capitalism' to the period (Marglin and Schor (eds.), 1990, Cairncross and Cairncross (eds.), 1992). Certain countries did so well as to deserve the title of 'miracle' (such as Japan and Germany), but even the under-performers, such as the US and the UK, did well enough not to make their under-performance a matter of serious political concern. Accordingly, there was relatively little interest in explaining why some countries were doing better than others, and consequently finding out how the better-performing countries organised their economies, until the 'Golden Age' ended (in the mid-1970s).

Secondly, at least until the onset of their stagnation in the 1970s, the socialist economies seemed to pose a serious competitive threat to capitalism, and in the face of such a challenge, the differences between capitalist economies probably seemed less important. And given the Cold War, there was a certain political interest on the part of the advanced capitalist economies in underplaying the perceived differences between themselves.[6]

---

[6]  So, for example, the early postwar attempt by the US to re-mould the German institutional structure in its own image (or the propagandistic version of it) was quickly watered down and consequently the German model allowed to develop, as soon as the Cold War became serious in the 1950s. However, the American-style 'free market' rhetoric has remained very strong in German political discourse, especially during the early postwar years (Shonfield, 1965).

Thirdly, its vast economic superiority during the early postwar years made it possible for the United States, the standard bearer of *laissez-faire* doctrine in the postwar world order (although not before the war when it was itself a 'catching-up' economy relying heavily on infant-industry protection), to ignore what it later perceived as non-level playing fields created by 'abnormal' institutions of its trading partners (normality here being defined by the US model). Various recent attempts led by the US to standardise the institutional structure across different countries in the name of securing a level playing field, and all the intellectual trappings that go with such attempts, can be seen as a belated and somewhat pathological acknowledgement that such 'abnormal' institutions have been important competitive assets of its trading partners.

Lastly, the underdevelopment of institutionally-conscious economic theories until the 1980s may have been one reason behind the neglect of the institutional diversity of capitalism. The orthodox, that is neoclassical, economic theory is a theory about (very narrowly and peculiarly defined) markets, and is not able to adequately deal with other economic institutions of modern capitalism such as firms, unions, or government regulatory regimes. This made it naturally difficult to discuss the institutional diversity of capitalism in a way that was acceptable to the academic establishment. The rise of institutional economics during the last two decades has prompted a wide range of empirical studies of diverse economic institutions, utilising better analytical tools, and thus bestowing more 'respectability' to comparative institutional analysis (e.g., see essays in Langlois (ed.), 1986 and Aoki *et al.* (eds.), 1990).

Whatever the exact weight that we assign to each of the above-mentioned factors in apportioning the blame for the relative absence of interest in the diversity of capitalism until recently, the fact remains clear that now, compared to even, say, 10 years ago, there is a much more widespread recognition of the issue. Moreover, there are now much richer theoretical and empirical literatures to draw upon in discussing the issue. In addition, there is a growing interest in the application of certain successful 'models' to less successful countries. Needless to say, such desire to learn from the successful countries has been the essence of 'late development' efforts since the 19th century, but what makes this current phase interesting is that, for the first time in many years, the Anglo-Saxon model's status as the 'best practice' model is being seriously challenged – although the recent crisis in Asia generated a degree of Anglo-Saxon triumphalism (see Section 7 for further discussion). It is in this context that I want to place my discussion of the East Asian model of economic policy.

## 2. Does the East Asian Model Exist?

The spectacular economic performance of certain East Asian countries during the postwar period, first that of Japan and then those of the first-tier newly industralising countries (NICs) (namely, Korea, Taiwan, Singapore, and Hong Kong), has naturally generated a lot of interest in the East Asian 'model'. During the postwar period, these countries have grown at roughly 6% per annum in per capita terms, which puts the growth records of the first industrial nations during the 'Industrial Revolution' (1-1.5% p.a.) to shame and even overshadows their records during the 'Golden Age' (around 3% p.a.), thus making their postwar experience *literally the fastest economic transformation in human history*. And given the (belatedly acknowledged) differences in the institutions and policies of many East Asian countries from those found in the Anglo-Saxon economies which (rightly or wrongly) have set the international norms, the model has been regarded by many as providing an obvious, and probably superior, alternative to the dominant Anglo-Saxon model.

As is well known, talk of the East Asian model has generated many heated debates, and as in the case of debates involving other economic models, such as Scandinavian corporatism or Latin American import-substitution industrialisation, these debates have involved questioning the desirability, sustainability, and replicability of the model. What makes the debate on East Asia unique, however, is that it has also involved the questioning of the very *existence* of the model.

The classic example of this is the early mainstream argument that the East Asian countries succeeded on the basis of free-market, free-trade policies, namely, the kinds of policies and institutions that constitute the Anglo-Saxon model. Adopting this interpretation, there is no point in talking about the East Asian model, because it is essentially the same as the Anglo-Saxon one. Although the fallacy of this interpretation has been widely exposed recently, it still has remarkable staying power in popular policy discourse.

Later, other commentators have questioned the existence of the East Asian model from a different angle, namely, on the ground that the East Asian countries differ from each other in terms of their institutions and policies, and therefore that we cannot talk of a region-wide model. This is at one level a correct argument, as the East Asian countries show important differences between themselves. However, at another level, it is not a very useful argument, because this way we will never be able to talk about a model that applies to more than one country. At least when we exclude the two city-states (Hong Kong and Singapore) and look only at the 'Big Three' (Japan, Korea, and Taiwan), we can identify enough commonalities between them to warrant the talk of a model.

The World Bank (1993) has recently muddied the waters in this debate even further by arguing that there are really two East Asian models – the Northeast Asian one (the 'Original Five', viz., Japan plus the first-tier NICs) and the Southeast Asian one (the second-tier NICs, viz., Malaysia, Indonesia, and Thailand). The Bank then goes on to argue that the Southeast Asian model is more suitable for other developing countries because it is more market-oriented and therefore institutionally less demanding. Although the differences between the two groups are less than what the Bank makes them out to be, it is true that there are considerable differences in terms of institutions and policies between the Original Five (or, more pertinently, the Big Three) and the second-tier NICs. However, this is really diverting our attention from the real issue, because the original usage of the term 'East Asian model' essentially referred to the Big Three, and certainly did not imply that all the countries in (the very broadly defined) East Asia are practising one model (for further criticisms of this point, see Akyuz et al., 1998).

So when we talk about the East Asian model in this book we are referring to the Big Three, that is, Japan, Korea, and Taiwan. Being an 'ideal type', not all the details of the model match the real-life experiences of even these three countries, but we hold on to this model, because we believe that some degree of generalisation is necessary in any social-science discourse. We will try to bring out the differences between these countries whenever they bring out important points, but will ignore the differences when they do not.


## 3.   Investment Policy

The first area of economic policy that we want to look at is investment policy. The role of physical investments as one of the main determinants of growth is theoretically central in many economic models and is empirically very well established by now. And it is well known that the East Asian countries have maintained very impressive investment ratios during their high-growth period. Less well understood is how this has been possible.

The most conventional explanation of high investments in the East Asian countries is that they could invest a lot because they saved a lot. As for the cause of high savings, some believe that it was due to their Confucian culture that emphasises frugality and abstinence from instant gratification, but the critical limitation of this interpretation is that, like many other simplistic 'cultural' explanations, it attributes a recent phenomenon (i.e., high savings) to a millennium-old cause (Confucian culture) (on the criticism of the simplistic version of 'cultural' explanations of the East Asian success, see Dore, 1987). Alternatively, it has been argued that high savings in these countries were due to high real interest rates, but by now there is a rather widespread consensus that this explanation is not supported by evidence (e.g., see Stiglitz, 1998).

In the end, it is doubtful whether it is high savings that is causing high investments, rather than the other way around. Although there is an ongoing theoretical dispute on the relationship between savings and investments, there is a growing opinion that investment, rather than savings, is the prime mover in the savings-investment-growth dynamic (see Studart, 1995). Therefore, while we should not dismiss the important role that certain 'savings policies' played in raising savings in East Asia (e.g., tax benefits for savers, postal savings system that gave access to banking facilities to those in rural areas), we wish to concentrate our attention on how high and productive investments were made possible in the East Asian model.

## 3.1    Maintaining 'stability', East-Asian-fashion

Many commentators emphasise the importance of political and economic stability in encouraging investments, a position that probably has a particularly strong appeal in Latin America. Political and/or economic instabilities obviously shrink potential investors' time horizon, and discourage commitments of resources to projects whose returns are far in the future and often uncertain but which may be crucial for modern industrial development. The Keynesian notion of 'animal spirit' and the notion of 'investors' confidence' frequently used in policy discussions (if not in academic debates) reflect such concern.

More recently, however, there has been a tendency among the mainstream economists to interpret this issue of stability very narrowly and basically reduce it to the achievement (or otherwise) of very low inflation (say, below 5%).[7] And in this context the East Asian countries have been often paraded as examples of the investment-boosting effect of low inflation.

However, the East Asian experiences, especially those of Japan and Korea during their earlier periods of development, do not lend much support to this argument. At least until the late 1970s, the Japanese and the Korean states have pursued what can be called a 'pro-investment macroeconomic policy' (the term is due to Chang, 1993), which puts emphasis on maintaining high levels of investment, if necessary at the cost of moderate inflation.[8] For example, average rates of inflation (measured by the average annual growth of the consumer price index) in Korea were 17.4% in the 1960s and 19.8% in the 1970s, which were higher than the inflation rates found in many Latin Ameri-

---

[7]    Some recent studies show, however, there is no statistical correlation between growth and the inflation rate if the latter is moderate (say, less than 40%; see Bruno and Easterly, 1994).

[8]    The Kuomintang government that had until recently ruled Taiwan from 1949 had a much greater aversion to inflation, as it regarded its failure to control inflation as one reason why it lost mainland China to the Communists.

can countries, for whose 'troubles' inflation is often blamed, during the same period.[9] Even when they pursued 'stabilisation' programmes (e.g., Korea in the early 1980s), their macroeconomic policy was fine-tuned to ensure that it did not kill off investors' confidence (and thus investments), if necessary at the cost of allowing more inflation – a policy pattern that has obviously been broken in Korea recently due to the International Monetary Fund (IMF) conditionality on low in-flation and budget balancing following the 1997 crisis (for some criti-cisms of this policy, see Stiglitz, 1998; Wade and Veneroso, 1998; and Chang, 1998a).

## 3.2  Controlling capital outflows and inflows

In any country, especially in the early stages of development, capital flight has to be prevented in order to ensure that whatever investible surplus that is generated in the economy at least stays in the country, before one can contemplate having it re-invested in pro-ductive projects. However, capital flight was an even more serious problem for the East Asian countries, because of the constant (real and imagined) threats from their Communist neighbours. So the East Asian states have maintained very strict regimes of capital control until recently. Every economic transaction involving foreign exchange had to be made through the banks under government ownership and/ or control, and there were heavy punishments for those who attempted major capital flight (they could be punished with the death sentence in Korea).

How important it can be to have an effective means of prevent-ing capital control is particularly dramatically demonstrated by the case of Korea during the 1980s. In the build-up to the debt crisis of the early 1980s, there was virtually no capital flight out of Korea, which was then the fourth-largest debtor country in the world, while many other major debtor countries in Latin America suffered from

---

9    In the 1960s, the Korean inflation rate was higher than those of Venezuela (1.3%), Bolivia (3.5%), Mexico (3.6%), Peru (10.4%), and Colombia (11.9%), and was not much lower than that of Argentina (21.7%). In the 1970s, it was higher than those found in Venezuela (12.1%), Ecuador (14.4%), and Mexico (19.3%), and was not much lower than those found in Colombia (22.0%) or Bolivia (22.3%). See Singh (1995: Table 5) for further information.

## Table 1.1: The Ratio of FDI Inflows to Gross Domestic Capital
1971 - 98

|  | 1971-75 | 1976-80 |
|---|---|---|
| **All Countries** |  | n.a. |
|  |  |  |
| **Developed** | n.a. | n.a. |
| European Union | n.a. | n.a. |
| USA | 0.9% | 2.0% |
| Canada | 3.6% | 1.7% |
| Japan | 0.1% | 0.1% |
|  |  |  |
| **Developing** | n.a. | n.a. |
| Africa | n.a. | n.a. |
|  |  |  |
| Latin America | n.a. | n.a. |
| Argentina | 0.1% | 2.1% |
| Brazil | 4.2% | 3.9% |
| Chile | -7.3% | 4.2% |
| Mexico | 3.5% | 3.6% |
|  |  |  |
| Asia | n.a. | n.a. |
| China | 0.0% | 0.1% |
| Hong Kong | 5.9% | 4.2% |
| India | 0.3% | 0.1% |
| Indonesia | 4.6% | 2.4% |
| Korea | 1.9% | 0.4% |
| Malaysia | 15.2% | 11.9% |
| Pakistan | 0.5% | 0.9% |
| Philippines | 1.0% | 0.9% |
| Singapore | 15.0% | 16.6% |
| Taiwan | 1.4% | 1.2% |
| Thailand | 3.0% | 1.5% |
|  |  |  |
| Eastern Europe | n.a. | n.a. |

**Source**: UNCTAD, *World Investment Report (WIR), 1993,* Annex Table 3 (for 1971-80) *WIR, 2000* (for 1998)

**Formation for Various Regions and Selected Countries,**
(annual average)

| 1981-85 | 1986-90 | 1991-95 | 1996-98 |
|---------|---------|---------|---------|
| 2.3% | 4.1% | 4.3% | 8.2% |
| 2.2% | 4.6% | 3.7% | 7.4% |
| 2.6% | 5.9% | 6.0% | 10.2% |
| 2.9% | 6.9% | 4.2% | 9.7% |
| 1.0% | 5.8% | 5.8% | 12.7% |
| 0.1% | 0.0% | n.a. | n.a. |
| 3.3% | 3.2% | 6.4% | 10.1% |
| 2.3% | 3.5% | 5.8% | 8.3% |
| 4.1% | 4.2% | 7.5% | 15.1% |
| 5.0% | 11.1% | 15.8% | 12.1% |
| 4.3% | 1.7% | 2.2% | 12.5% |
| 6.7% | 20.6% | 13.6% | 26.8% |
| 5.0% | 7.5% | 11.8% | 14.5% |
| 3.1% | 2.8% | 5.9% | 8.4% |
| 0.9% | 2.1% | 11.1% | 13.8% |
| 6.9% | 12.9% | 8.0% | 17.0% |
| 0.1% | 0.3% | 1.2% | 3.3% |
| 0.9% | 2.1% | 4.7% | 5.1% |
| 0.5% | 1.2% | 0.7% | 2.9% |
| 10.8% | 11.7% | 19.3% | 12.8% |
| 1.3% | 2.3% | 4.5% | 7.2% |
| 0.8% | 6.7% | 7.4% | 8.9% |
| 17.4% | 35.0% | 30.7% | 22.7% |
| 1.5% | 3.7% | 2.4% | 2.5% |
| 3.0% | 6.5% | 3.9% | 11.7% |
| 0.0% | 0.1% | 8.4% | 10.2% |

*WIR, 1995,* Annex Table 5 (for 1981-92), *WIR, 1999,* Annex Table B.5 (for 1993-97),

massive capital flight, which was estimated by Sachs (1984) to have been sometimes as big as the total debt of the country. While strict capital control did not save Brazil from being bogged down in a downward macroeconomic spiral after the debt crisis (there was also very little capital flight from Brazil during the period), thus showing that capital control is only part of the story, it would be hard to deny that it was central to Korea's escape from a similar fate.

However much a government controls capital outflows, if it cannot control capital inflows, its control over the direction and pattern of investment will be diminished. In terms of their relations with foreign capital, the experiences of the East Asian countries during their high-growth years diverged considerably, except that, contrary to some popular perception, none of them relied heavily on foreign direct investment (FDI) (more on this in Section 5.4). Japan during this period did not rely on any form of foreign capital inflow – little aid, no loans, virtually no FDI. Taiwan received a relatively large amount of foreign aid in the earlier stages of development (but not as much as Korea did), but did not borrow very much from abroad. While its reliance on FDI was higher than that of Japan or Korea, it was rarely above the international average (see Table 1.1). Korea received a lot of aid in the 1950s and the 1960s (but much less than countries like Chile did), borrowed a lot (but only under strict government control), but strictly controlled FDI. Although more recently these countries have relaxed many of these controls (with disastrous consequences in the case of Korea), it is important to note that controls on capital inflows constituted a main pillar in the East Asian countries' investment policy (see Chang *et al.*, 1998, and Chang and Yoo, 2000 for further details on the role of capital-account liberalisation in the 1997 Korean crisis).

## 3.3  Luxury-consumption control

Securing the maximum possible amount of investible surplus by controlling capital inflows and outflows may be the first step towards guaranteeing its re-investment, but there is still a long way to go before it is actually invested. One obvious hurdle is that the potential investor classes who control such surplus may consume it in 'luxury' goods, rather than investing it – a problem that has been an exceptionally emotive issue in the Latin American development discourse, at least until recently.

Of course, the economics behind luxury consumption is not so simple as to allow us to say that higher luxury consumption necessarily reduces investments (think about Malthus or Keynes) nor that restraint of such consumption necessarily requires government intervention[10], but the issue is more than a 'moralistic' one, contrary to what many mainstream economists believe (for a more detailed discussion, see Chang, 1997b). Especially in many developing countries where imports of luxury goods (or the parts and components needed to produce them) usually have to chase after scarce foreign exchange in competition with the capital goods that are necessary for investment (given the lack of a viable capital goods sector), control of luxury consumption becomes even more important for investment.

The East Asian countries, accordingly, have imposed heavy tariffs and domestic taxes on, and sometimes even banned the domestic production as well as the import of, certain 'luxury' products especially in the earlier stages of their development. Table 1.2 shows one example of how effective these controls have been. Korea and Japan have had literally the two lowest numbers of passenger cars per capita than what any of the advanced and developing countries have achieved at comparable levels of development.[11] For another example, in Korea, foreign tourism was banned until the early 1980s, and since then was heavily controlled, until it was (almost) fully liberalised in 1988 (there are still restrictions on the amount of money that one can take abroad for tourism purposes) (for more details, see Chang, 1997b). The interesting thing is that, after the liberalisation in 1988, Korea's foreign tourism expenditure increased five-fold in three years, thus suggesting that the low expenditure before the liberalisation was not really due to a 'cultural' aversion to spending, as is sometimes asserted, but was a result of government control.

---

[10] For example, following Max Weber's classic work, it is widely accepted that the Protestant Ethic restrained luxury consumption by the entrepreneurial class in the early phases of capitalist development in Western Europe. I thank Chung H. Lee for reminding me of this important point.

[11] Unfortunately, comparable data on Taiwan is not available after the mid-1960s, but until then, it showed a similar, although somewhat milder, pattern to those of Korea and Japan.

| Table 1.2: Number of Passenger Cars per 1,000 People (real GDP per capita in constant dollars, | | | | | | |
|---|---|---|---|---|---|---|
| | | **Germany** | **France** | **Italy** | **Japan** | **Korea** |
| $1,000 | year | | | | 1950[a] | 1963-4 |
| | cars | | | | < 1 | 1 |
| $2,000 | year | | | | 1955 | 1973 |
| | cars | | | | 2 | 2 |
| $3,000 | year | | | 1951-2 | 1960 | 1978 |
| | cars | | | 10 | 5 | 5 |
| $4,000 | year | 1951 | 1950 | 1958 | 1963-4 | 1984 |
| | cars | 16 | 36 | 30 | 15 | 12 |
| $5,000 | year | 1954-5 | 1956 | 1961 | 1966 | 1987 |
| | cars | 33 | 69 | 48 | 29 | 20 |
| $6,000 | year | 1958-9 | 1961 | 1966 | 1968 | 1989 |
| | cars | 62 | 133 | 121 | 52 | 37 |
| $7,000 | year | 1962-3 | 1964 | 1968-9 | 1969-70 | 1990-1 |
| | cars | 116 | 182 | 169 | 76 | 56 |

**Source**: Summer and Heston, Penn World Table (for income and population
**Note**: Sometimes it is not possible to identify a single year as the point when
could pass a certain threshold between two consecutive years. In such cases
two years. In some other cases, a country's income could pass a certain
such cases, a range of years is given, which starts from the year when the
country's income does not go below the threshold again (or at least until the
is also given as a range.

a. The relevant income level was reached before the earliest year for which
b. Income did not reach the level until the last year for which the data are

| **for Selected Countries at Fixed Levels of Per Capita Income** expressed in 1985 international prices) | | | | | | |
|---|---|---|---|---|---|---|
| **Thailand** | **Malaysia** | **Argentina** | **Brazil** | **Chile** | **Mexico** | **S. Africa** |
| 1962-3 | 1955[a] | | 1950[a] | | | |
| 2 | < 8 | | < 6 | | | |
| 1979 | 1960-70 | | 1967-8 | 1950[a] | 1950[ɛ] | 1953 |
| 9 | 22 | | 20 | < 7 | < 7 | 35 |
| 1989 | 1977 | | 1972-3 | 1961-76 | 1963 | 1970-90 |
| 21 | 39 | | 29 | 7-27 | 14 | 65-95 |
| 1992[b] | 1981-7 | 1950-4 | 1978-91 | 1987 | 1970 | |
| 24 | 61-91 | 17-19 | 64-80 | 49 | 23 | |
| | 1990 | 1965-89 | | 1992[b] | 1977-8 | |
| | 104 | 41-133 | | 60 | 49 | |
| | | | | | 1980-91 | |
| | | | | | 63-91 | |
| | | | | | | |
| | | | | | | |

figures) and the United Nations Statistical Yearbooks (for car figures).
a country reaches a certain level of income. In some cases, the income
the  number of the cars given is the simple average of the numbers for the
threshold  in a certain year but may fall below that level subsequently. In
country  first passes the level and ends in the year after which the
last year for which the data is available). The number of cars in such cases

the data are available.
available, but was less than 10% below that level.

One important, and usually ignored, function of control on luxury consumption is in the realm of politics. By restraining the extent to which the elite could enjoy their wealth for their personal pleasures, luxury-consumption control in the East Asian countries has helped to create the sense that there is a national 'community' with a common project (in this case, economic development), whose burdens and fruits are shared by all the citizens in 'fair' (if not equal) measures. Such a sense of a common project has contributed to the political stability of these countries, which then contributed to investment growth by shoring up investors' confidence. Thus, the political and economic stability of the East Asian countries was as much an outcome of deliberate government policy as of the lack of distributional conflicts due to 'equal income distribution', as is frequently argued in the current literature (for a review of the literature propagating such a view, see Alesina and Perotti, 1994).

### 3.4   Disciplining the recipients of state-created rents

Having ensured that investible surplus is not wasted in luxury consumption, there still remains the problem of ensuring that the investments are made productively, as 'bad' investments will simply waste resources and reduce the amount of surplus available for investment in the next round. Some would argue that market signals will direct the investors into the right areas, but we know that this is simply not true as a general proposition. Especially in the context of late development, industrial development requires the creation of rents by the state to induce investments in 'infant' industries where there are already established producers abroad. However, the statement that the creation of rents by the state is a necessary condition for development does not mean that it is sufficient. This is because, once they are awarded the state-created rents, the investors may have little incentive to raise productivity, as the market discipline has been temporarily weakened (or sometimes eliminated altogether). So it becomes crucial for the state to play the disciplinarian role.

The subject of state discipline has been rather extensively discussed elsewhere (also see Section 5.2), and thus does not require elaboration here, but let us summarise what we regard as the main points that have emerged from the debate up to now (for further discussions, see Toye, 1987; Amsden, 1989; Chang, 1993; and Evans, 1995).

The success of the East Asian states in disciplining the recipients of their rents can be attributed at one level to the famously (or notoriously, depending on one's position) enormous power that they have wielded over corporations through their control over bank credit and other financial sources. However, if it is to be used productively, this power has to be exercised with a commitment to productivity growth. In the East Asian case, such commitment largely stemmed from its brand of developmentalist ideology, which was strengthened by the necessity to compete with Communist neighbours in the case of Korea and Taiwan.

At a more practical level, state discipline in East Asia also owes its success to a number of factors. First of all, the choice of 'strategic' industries was made with a high degree of realism (i.e., a wholesale catch-up across all industries, as in the case of India, was never attempted), although sometimes the choice seemed too risky to many people (e.g., Korea's forays into steel and shipbuilding in the 1970s). Secondly, the emphasis on exports made it possible for the state to judge enterprise performance relatively 'objectively' by watching their performances in the world market, although it was by no means blindly accepting them as the only performance criterion. Thirdly, the state policies were designed on the basis of detailed information on the state of the domestic and the international economies, which was collected from mandatory reporting by the state-supported enterprises and from various public and semi-public agencies (e.g., state trading companies, embassies), thus making them sensitive to the developments in world markets.

## 4.    Trade Policy: Infant-Industry Programmes and Export Promotion

In the early days of international fascination with the East Asian 'miracle', that is, during the 1970s and the early 1980s, the export successes of the East Asian countries were often touted as living proofs of the validity of the doctrine of comparative advantage and free trade to deal with this problem (classic examples include Ranis and Fei,

1975, and Balassa, 1982). When subsequent researches showed that the trade regimes of these countries were full of tariff protections and quantitative restrictions and therefore could not be described as 'free trade' regimes, some orthodox trade economists invented the notion of so-called 'virtual free trade' (Little, 1982; Lal, 1983; World Bank, 1987). It was argued that the anti-export biases of protectionist policies in the East Asian countries were cancelled out by export subsidies, thus resulting in a 'neutral' incentive regime which 'simulated' the free-trade outcome. There are numerous problems with this argument, which we do not have time to go into (for a more detailed criticism, see Chang, 1993; also see Yusuf and Peters, 1985 and Wade, 1990), but there are two main problems. The first is that the relative prices found in the trade regime of protection-cum-export-promotion are not necessarily the same as those under a genuine free-trade regime, and therefore it is not possible to say that the former trade regime 'simulates' the latter.[12] Secondly, the argument ultimately relies on the doctrine of comparative advantage, which had already been rejected in the earlier round of the debate.

Our argument against the doctrine of comparative advantage, which lies behind the neoclassical justification for free trade, is not that it is logically flawed, but that it has very little to say about the relationship between trade, trade policy, and economic development. Let us explain why.

Economic development in a backward country requires importing technologies from more advanced countries and adapting them to local needs and capabilities, unless it is willing to re-invent the wheel, so to speak. And this is the process through which all countries after the first industrial nation, that is, Britain, industrialised – a process known as 'catching up'. This gives the backward countries an opportunity to grow faster than the leader countries, as they can draw on the knowledge stock accumulated by the latter.

---

[12] The point is that it is the variance in the rates of protection across industries that matters rather than the average rate of protection. Following the logic of the 'virtual free trade' argument, we will recommend a Londoner who is moving to New York to bring the same clothes that he used to wear in London, because New York has 'virtually mild weather', because its average temperature is similar to that in London, which has genuinely mild weather.

| Table 1.3: Tariff Rates for Selected Developed Countries in Their Early Stages of Development | | | | |
|---|---|---|---|---|
| (The rates are for manufactured goods except in the case of Japan, which are for all goods) | | | | |
| | **1820** | **1875** | **1913** | **1925** |
| Austria | n.a. | 15-20 | 18 | 16 |
| Belgium | 7 | 9-10 | 9 | 15 |
| France | n.a. | 12-15 | 20 | 21 |
| Italy | n.a. | 8-10 | 18 | 22 |
| Japan | n.a. | 4[a] | 20 | 13 |
| Sweden | n.a. | 3-5 | 20 | 16 |
| United Kingdom | 50 | 0 | n.a. | 5 |
| United States | 40 | 40-50 | 25 | 37 |

a: Before 1911, Japan was made to keep low tariff rates through a series of 'unequal treaties' with the European and North American countries.

**Source**: World Bank, *World Development Report*, 1991, p. 97, Box Table 5.2.

However, being a follower also has its drawbacks. The trouble is that, when a backward country tries to move into a new industry, it finds that its firms have to compete with the already well-established firms from developed countries. In the face of such competition, it is necessary for the follower country to *deliberately* violate the principle of comparative advantage and protect the new, or 'infant', industry from international competition before their national firms can attain internationally competitive levels of productivity. The success of the East Asian countries in effectively promoting the infant industries is too well known to document in any detail (Amsden, 1989; Wade, 1990; Chang, 1993), but at this point it is worth noting that this is how most other now-developed countries developed too – including the US, which was the most protected economy in the world in the late 19th and the early 20th centuries (see Table 1.3; also see Kozul-Wright, 1995).

But then why have many developing countries failed to make their infant-industry programmes work? I argue that this was at least partly because they lacked an export promotion strategy that was well-integrated with the infant-industry programmes, the need for which indeed was emphasised by the early proponents of Latin American import substitution such as Raul Prebisch but was subsequently ignored for various political and economic reasons. The development of infant industries requires the ability to export to earn enough foreign exchange that can be used to acquire new technologies (mainly in the form of buying the machinery that embodies such technology but also of paying for technical licences and technical consultancies).[13] Without a stable supply of foreign exchange and hence of new technologies, a developing country that has no independent research-and-development (R&D) capability is likely to end up reproducing the obsolete technologies that it imported in the past – the most extreme case being North Korea. In other words, export success is a vital element in successful infant-industry promotion, rather than some antithesis of it as depicted in the conventional criticisms of the infant-industry doctrine. Given these considerations, the importance of export in a late-developing context cannot be over-emphasised.

At this point, it is important to point out that, contrary to conventional wisdom, the importance of export success does *not* mean that the country should adopt a 'free trade' policy. As the experience of East Asia shows, achieving export growth in the earlier stage of development can be greatly helped by appropriate government policies.

To begin with, it is widely acknowledged that the export successes of the East Asian countries were greatly helped by policies to keep their currencies slightly undervalued until the 1985 Plaza Accord which drove their currency values up (Dornbusch, 1996)[14] – a contrast to the early Latin American experiences where over-valued exchange rates hindered export growth. As important as the exchange rate policy may be in the short run, however, continued export suc-

---

[13] Needless to say, there are sources other than exporting for foreign exchange, such as foreign aid and foreign direct investments. However, past experience tells us that, except for a small number of exceptionally placed countries, neither of these will be sufficient in the long run.

[14] A departure from such exchange rate policy stance contributed to the outbreak of the recent Korean crisis. See Chang (1998a).

cess in the long run requires the emergence of enough new industries so that the emergence of new, lower-cost competitor countries would not compromise the country's foreign exchange earning capability. Hence the importance of infant-industry promotion for export success, which establishes a two-way interaction loop between the two.

In addition, informational and financial help from the government can be crucial in helping the firms to export. In order to help the exporting firms, the East Asian governments provided export subsidies (which, we should not forget, also violate the principle of comparative advantage, although in the opposite direction from import protection). These subsidies were in the form of subsidised loans for exporters, tariff rebates on export inputs, or generous 'wastage allowances' to the exporters using domestically scarce inputs (so that they can sell some of the 'wastes' in the domestic market at a premium). The East Asian governments also provided information on foreign markets, usually through the government trading agency (such as JETRO in Japan and KOTRA in Korea) but sometimes even through the diplomatic service. There were also efforts to promote the development of private sector organisations which can perform some of such functions (such as exporters' associations, various industry associations, or general trading companies).

So if catching-up by developing countries requires a deliberate violation of comparative advantage (infant-industry programmes *and* export promotion), is there any place for the doctrine of comparative advantage in designing trade policy for developing countries? I think there is.

The doctrine of comparative advantage helps us figure out how much sacrifice a country is making in order to develop the infant industries, and therefore helps us avoid infant-industry promotions of excessive magnitude and duration. However, that is just about it. The doctrine is a static framework which tells us how much we can gain by specialisation, *given* our current factor endowments, but not very much about what we have to do in order to improve our position over time, as even some leading neoclassical trade economists admit (Krueger, 1980). To put it slightly differently, it can help us to know what sacrifices we are making *now* by protecting certain industries, but it does not help us predict what good (or bad) will come out of it *in the long run*. The whole point about infant-industry protection is *not* to ignore the principle of comparative advantage altogether, but to *strategically* violate it, knowing that this will result in a loss in current income but will make it possible, if properly done, to develop new industries which can put the country on a higher growth trajectory in the medium to long run.

To summarise, the secret of East Asian trade policy is in its simultaneous and coordinated pursuit of infant-industry protection and export promotion (sometimes one and the same industry was subject to both at the same time). These two policies are, contrary to conventional wisdom, *not* mutually incompatible. They depend on each other. A successful infant-industry programme needs continued export success if it is to be sustained by a continued inflow of advanced technologies. In turn, continued export success needs successful infant-industry programmes which can sustain the continued upgrading of export industries, as well as other state interventions in areas of exchange rate management, trade credit provision, marketing information service, and product quality control. In designing a successful infant-industry programme, the principle of comparative advantage can help, as it can give the policy-makers some sense of what price their economy is paying in protecting certain new industries. However, the usefulness of the principle of comparative advantage stops just about there, as it does not tell us much about how the economy can maximise its 'returns' from such protection.

## 5.   Industrial Policy

The role of industrial policy – to be more precise, 'selective industrial policy' – has been the most controversial dimension of the debate on the East Asian experience (for an updated review of the debate, see Chang, 1999). Even until the late 1980s, many mainstream economists tried to simply ignore this issue by arguing that there was very little selective industrial policy practised in East Asia. For example, as late as in 1988, one of the leading neoclassical trade economists, Bela Balassa, argued that the Korean state's role, 'apart from the promotion of shipbuilding and steel . . . has been to create a modern infrastructure, to provide a stable incentive system, and to ensure that government bureaucracy will help rather than hinder exports'

(Balassa, 1988: p. S286).

Later, when the weight of the emerging evidence on the width and the depth of selective industrial policy in East Asia was just too much to bear[15], the mainstream economists grudgingly acknowledged its existence, but tried to claim that, perhaps except in Japan, it was at best irrelevant and at worst a failure – the so-called 'East Asian Miracle Report' is the best example (World Bank, 1993). However, the verdict on selective industrial policy in the 'East Asian Miracle Report' has been subject to severe criticisms (e.g., see articles in *World Development Report*, 1994, no. 4; Fishlow *et al.*, 1995; Chang, 1995a: appendix[16]), and now many people accept that selective industrial policy has been on the whole successful in East Asia and may be applicable to other countries. Even the World Bank itself is now willing to acknowledge that selective industrial policy makes theoretical sense and can often be successful, although it still shows great reservation regarding its replicability in other developing countries, on the ground that it is administratively too demanding (World Bank, 1997: Chapter 4; more on this in Section 6).

As the debate on the East Asian selective industrial policy is now fairly well-known, I do not want to summarise the debate here. What I will try to do in the following will be to look at the East Asian experience in industrial policy in three areas which in my opinion need further attention. But before doing that, let me make some remarks on the most controversial theoretical issue in the industrial-policy debate, namely, the relative merits of 'selective' and 'general' industrial policies.

## 5.1   Selective vs. general industrial policies

In various debates on industrial policy, the contrast between 'selective' (or 'targeted') and 'general' (or 'functional') industrial policies has been frequently drawn. Those who are sceptical about state

---

[15]   Details of the East Asian practices can be found from: Magaziner and Hout (1980), Johnson (1982), Dore (1986) and Dosi *et al.* (1989) on Japan; Jones and Sakong (1980), Luedde-Neurath (1986), Amsden (1989), Chang (1993), and Evans (1995) on Korea; Amsden (1985) and Wade (1990) on Taiwan.

[16]   A Spanish translation of Chang (1995a) appears in Chang (1996b).

activism argue that 'selective' industrial policy that targets specific sectors or even firms does not work because it often 'distorts' market signals, is technically difficult to manage, and is liable to interest-group capture and corruption. Therefore, they argue that industrial policy should be of a 'general' kind, providing those 'general' resources that all industries use but are under-provided by the market such as technology, skills, and the infrastructures for transportation and information transmission. Thus recommended are policies like investment in education, support for R&D and infrastructural investment (e.g., Price, 1980; Lindbeck, 1981; World Bank, 1993).

However, in a world of limited financial resources and limited administrative capabilities, there is always going to be some degree of 'selectivity' involved in the conduct of industrial policy. For example, it may be thought that a generalised support for R&D, unlike, say, a subsidised R&D fund for a designated industry, does not involve selectivity. However, unless there are unlimited financial and administrative resources, devoting more resources to support R&D activities means that R&D-intensive industries are now *implicitly* being favoured over other industries. In this way, the so-called 'general' industrial policy may end up targeting certain sectors without acknowledging it, with the consequent risk of policy incoherence.

Moreover, to be successful, many types of 'general' interventions in the end have to entail explicit targeting. Let us take the case of human resource development. While supporting primary education involves relatively little targeting (but even here there could be some targeting in terms of ethnic groups or geographical locations), supporting science and engineering education in universities or even some types of 'technical education' at secondary schools will require explicit targeting of the industries which are going to benefit from such support, given the highly specialised nature of such education – for example, there is no point in producing too many electronics engineers in a country when the industry is still very underdeveloped, unless, that is, there is an explicit policy to develop the industry in the medium term (which is exactly what Korea did during the 1970s).

All in all, what is clear is that selectivity is not something that we can wish away. It has been with us all the time, and it will always be. While there may be a 'public relations' case for not explicitly using terms like 'targeting' or 'selective industrial policy', the practice itself is an issue that has to be, and in fact is being, routinely confronted by the practitioners of industrial policy. Indeed, it may be far better to explicitly acknowledge the inevitability of selectivity and openly discuss which sector to target in which ways, rather than trying to pretend that there is no targeting going on, thereby increasing the danger of incoherence between different targeting exercises. Moreover, in countries with weak administrative capacities, policies that are more precisely targeted may in fact have a better chance of success because it saves on administrative resources. The crucial question, in conclusion, is *not* whether or not industrial policy should be selective, *but* how to be selective in the right areas in the right manner, given the overall industrial policy objectives.

### 5.2    Raising infant industries: Discipline, scale economy, and exports

In the preceding section (Section 4), we pointed out that, like in all the other stories of late development, industrialisation in East Asia required protecting the domestic firms in infant industries from international competition through tariff protection and other non-tariff barriers. However, in many other developing countries, similar exercises have produced unimpressive, and sometimes even very negative, results, and naturally the successes of the East Asian countries in raising infant industries have attracted a lot of attention.

Many commentators, including myself, have attributed the East Asian success in infant-industry promotion to the ability of the state to impose discipline on the recipients of state-created rents, and by now this argument is widely accepted as the most important difference between East Asia and other developing countries (e.g., Toye, 1987; Amsden, 1989; Wade, 1990; and Chang, 1993).[17] However, there is a hitherto neglected element in the logic of infant-industry programmes that needs to be brought out more clearly, if we are to

---

[17] Evans (1995) emphasises that such discipline will be most successfully applied when the autonomy of the state is 'embedded' in the concrete social structure in which it exists.

better understand the difficulties involved in designing the disciplinary measures – that is, the problem of scale economy.

Many modern industries are subject to a significant scale economy, without exploiting which it becomes difficult to achieve international competitiveness. However, the late-developing countries normally have small domestic markets due to low income, a fact that is often exacerbated by small population size, and this puts a serious limit on their firms' ability to exploit scale economy. Moreover, at the earlier stages of development, many of the products from these industries fall into the 'luxury' category, and allowing a rapid expansion of domestic demand for them may hurt capital accumulation, as they are basically consumed by the investing classes (see Section 3.3 for further details). While the control of luxury consumption may be necessary in the earlier stages of development in promoting capital accumulation (as was done in the East Asian countries), such control restricts the domestic market size for many industries even further.

All these mean that infant-industry programmes in the late-developing countries will have to operate under severe constraints on the ability of the domestic firms to exploit scale economy. Faced with this problem, many late-developing-country governments have imposed controls on entry (and exit) and capacity expansion in the industries concerned, and the East Asian countries have not been exceptions in this regard. Their governments have managed extensive regimes of regulation regarding entry and capacity in many industries with scale economy. The problem, however, is that, even with such controls, many domestic markets in many developing countries are still too small to fully realise scale economy. Given this, even when the hoped-for technological learning by the protected firms happens (as in the 'ideal' infant-industry-promotion scenario), it is very difficult for them to achieve internationally competitive levels of productivity, as they operate well below the minimum efficient scale.

As a result, the only way to relax this constraint on productivity set by domestic market size is for the firms in the infant industries to export. However, the problem is that trade protection in these industries was provided in the first place because their firms could not compete with the already established producers from the advanced countries, whether at home or in the export markets. So the developing countries trying to promote infant industries with scale economy are faced with a dilemma. They cannot become competitive in the world market without exporting, which will enable them to exploit scale economy, but they cannot export before they become competitive by raising their productivity.

The typical response by a developing-country government to this dilemma has been to give up the export option but keep the protection. The problem with this solution is that this way the firms never 'grow up' and remain 'infants' for life. Needless to say, this has happened in certain East Asian industries, the Taiwanese passenger-car industry being the best-known example. However, the East Asian policy-makers often took different courses of action. Occasionally, they would 'gamble' by encouraging, or even forcing, the domestic firms to build world-class capacities from the beginning so that they would be able to exploit the scale economy, with the positive side-effect that they will be forced into entering the world market from very early stages for fear of being stuck with an enormous excess capacity (the Korean steel and shipbuilding industries are the best examples). More typically, however, they initially accepted sub-optimal production scales, but used a range of policy measures to bring forward the day when these firms could export and thus produce at more than the minimum efficient scales.

Some of these policies were precisely the export-promoting policies that we discussed earlier (see Section 4), but the others were what are typically known as 'selective' industrial policy measures aimed at raising the productivity of specific industries. They included: (i) organising mergers and negotiated market segmentation in industries with too many producers with sub-optimal scale so that maximum possible scale can be achieved; (ii) subsidising capital equipment upgrading through 'rationalisation' or 'modernisation' programmes aimed at specific industries; (iii) subsidising R&D or training in specific industries directly or indirectly through the operation of public research or training institutes; (iv) spreading information on best-practice technologies in particular industries by various public or semi-public agencies.

The above discussion shows that the ways in which the state in a late-developing context can discipline the recipients of the rents that it has created are significantly affected by the context of late development itself. The need to achieve scale economy compels the government to control entry into many industries, but frequently even this is not sufficient to bring the domestic firms' productivities to the world level. The logical solution to this problem will be either to abandon the industry altogether, as the mainstream economists argue, or to make the firms start exporting as soon as possible, as the East Asian policy-makers attempted (and often succeeded). Needless to say, export success by infant industries cannot be achieved under a 'free trade' policy, and requires policy interventions that will raise the productivity of the firms as well as policies to help them export.

### 5.3  Managing competition:  Allocative efficiency vs. productivity

If scale economy is taken seriously by the policy-makers of a late-developing country with small domestic markets and thus the number of producers in each industry is restricted, an obvious problem that its government faces is the existence of oligopolistic, or even monopolistic, markets. While there is no one-to-one relationship between the number of firms in an industry and the intensity of competition between them (in fact East Asia provides many examples of fierce competition in oligopolistic markets), oligopolistic markets pose a greater challenge to the designers of competition policy. And in countries with serious infant-industry programmes, the resulting absence of competition from imports makes competition policy even more challenging.

In the mainstream competition policy discourse, the allocative inefficiencies that the market power possessed by oligopolistic firms creates are regarded as the most serious problem facing the competition policy-makers, and thus a vigorous Anglo-Saxon (or rather American) style anti-trust policy is recommended to deal with the problem. Thus, even many neoliberal supporters of far-reaching deregulation would concede that anti-trust policy is one area where government activism is legitimate and necessary (Chang, 1997c). Restricting the abuse of power by dominant firms through anti-trust action has certainly been an issue in East Asia, but it was only a minor part of its competition policy, and its focuses were elsewhere.

First of all, as we pointed out earlier, the East Asian governments have deliberately created oligopolistic, or even monopolistic, market structures, in order to exploit scale economy as much as possible, if that was regarded as important in the particular industry concerned. Mainstream economists frequently ignore this point, but many estimates of the allocative inefficiencies arising from 'non-competitive' markets suggest only modest figures (1-2% usually), whereas the cost increase that follows from sub-optimal scale of production is known to be very significant in many industries. To put it differently, scale-economy considerations were given clear priority over market-power considerations in the East Asian competition policy regime.

Secondly, the East Asian governments have been deeply concerned with 'excessive', 'wasteful', or 'destructive' competition. The notion of 'excessive' competition has often been dismissed as a notion based on 'irrational' fears of competition by ignorant bureaucrats, but it makes perfect sense once we acknowledge the importance of dedicated physical and human assets in modern industries (or what Williamson would call 'specific assets'; see Williamson, 1985). Given the existence of such 'specific' assets, any failed project that follows an 'excessive' entry (compared to what is warranted by the demand condition) leads to a 'waste' of resources in the sense that the 'specific' assets employed in the project may not be transferred to other activities without significant losses in their economic values (for further details, see Chang, 1994a: Chapter 3). As a result, the East Asian governments have tried to coordinate investments *ex ante* in order to prevent excess entry, but when excess entry materialised for whatever reason (e.g., erroneous projection, sudden changes in world market conditions, some firms defying the government plan, etc.), they organised (explicit and implicit) recession cartels, negotiated capacity-scrapping arrangements, or even forced merger and market-sharing programmes, to reduce the 'wastes' from excessive competition.

Thirdly, the East Asian governments have willingly suspended anti-trust actions and allowed collusive behaviours by firms, when it was thought that a suspension of competition was necessary for raising productivity (for a more detailed theoretical account, see Chang,

1994a: Chapter 3).[18] For example, the Japanese state has frequently allowed, and often took initiatives in organising, various types of cartels – to weather recession, to coordinate capacity expansion, to encourage joint R&D, to allow collusion in export markets, to promote technological upgrading by small firms, to phase out declining industries, just to name a few (Magaziner and Hout, 1980; Dore, 1986). In Korea, there existed no anti-trust legislation until 1981, and even after that, collusive behaviours were explicitly allowed in 'promising industries' which needed to 'increase R&D, improve quality, and attain efficient production scale', and in 'declining industries' which needed to 'scale down their capacities' (the quotes are from the 6th Five Year Plan (1987-91) document; for further details, see Chang, 1993). In Taiwan, where many large firms have been public enterprises, anti-trust policy has had a different dynamic, but the Taiwanese state did not hesitate to promote mergers if they were deemed necessary for exploiting scale economy (see Wade, 1990: pp. 186-7). The above-mentioned policies frequently ossified the cartels and resulted in industrial stagnation in other countries, but the East Asian countries avoided such danger, because the suspension of competition was regarded as a temporary measure to achieve relatively well-specified goals that were deemed necessary for productivity enhancement (although it could sometimes last quite long), and thus did not result in a general suspension of competition.

Many commentators have criticised the 'lax' attitude by the East Asian governments towards anti-trust policy as evidence of the prevalence of corrupt collusion between the state and big business – or 'crony capitalism', to use the currently popular terminology. However, the above discussion suggests that it resulted more from the (non-neoclassical) view of competition held by the East Asian policy-

---

[18]  The German anti-trust legislation, which has served as a model for the Japanese legislation since the latter's 1953 amendment away from the Anglo-Saxon elements imposed earlier by the American Occupation Authority, also provides many similar 'escape' clauses to cartel and other collusive behaviours, especially by small firms, when they are related to aims like 'rationalisation', 'specialisation' (i.e., negotiated market segmentation), joint export activities, and structural adjustments (Shin, 1994: pp. 343-355).

makers that is very different from the one held by mainstream economists.[19] The emphasis of their (broadly defined) competition policy
was on raising productivity in sunrise industries and managing smooth
resource transfers out of sunset industries without the 'wastes' that
could result from unrestrained competition. And if it was necessary
for those purposes, these governments were quite willing to restrict
entry and capacity expansion (thus creating oligopolistic markets) and
allow collusive behaviours among the firms, although these actions
were taken with clearly defined productivity-related goals and with a
relatively clear time limit.[20]

### 5.4  Technology policy: Controlling the inflows and raising capabilities

The importance of technology in determining the competitiveness of a country needs no further mention. And recent developments in the literature on economics of technology have shown that
policy actions matter greatly for technological development (see essays in Dosi *et al.* (eds.), 1988; Lundvall (ed.), 1992; Nelson (ed.),
1993). For the more advanced countries, the importance of R&D policies has been emphasised (e.g., see Fagerberg, 1996), but for the late-
developing countries, technology policy needs to take a somewhat
different form. Given their need to import and assimilate technologies, policies that regulate the inflows of technology and that enhance
the abilities to absorb the technology, rather than R&D policy, become crucial.

---

[19] Broadly, the view of competition held by the East Asian policy-makers is close to
what I call the 'Continental' (mainly Germanic) view of competition, which is
represented by some politically unlikely bedfellows such as Marx, Schumpeter,
and Hayek, and which contrasts with the Anglo-Saxon view that is epitomised in
neoclassical economics (for some classic works on this contrast, see Hayek, 1949,
and McNulty, 1968; Chang, 1994a: Chapter 3, provides a more updated discussion
on this issue).

[20] An added benefit of such a 'managed competition' regime has been to slow down
the competitive process to a pace that is economically and politically acceptable
to the 'losers' in the process, so that they would not block the necessary structural
changes (Chang, 1994b, whose Spanish translation appears in Chang, 1996b).
For a discussion of this point in the East Asian context, see Chang (1996a).

Unlike some other developing countries which ostensibly pursued 'technological self-sufficiency' only to end up reproducing obsolete technologies imported decades ago in the absence of independent R&D capabilities, the East Asian countries have always been keen to gain access to the most advanced technologies that they can handle. However, they have also been acutely aware of the need to regulate technology inflows in line with the broad industrial strategy and with the specific sectoral needs. So, for example, the government allowed or restricted the import of a certain piece of machinery depending on whether the industry producing that machine was being promoted as a strategic industry, whether the sector using the machine could meet the urgent need for technological upgrading only with imported machines, or whether the machine did not embody overly obsolete technology. Technology licensing was also carefully controlled in order to ensure that the right kinds of technologies were imported on the right terms. Investments by transnational corporations (TNCs) were also heavily regulated, in the belief that accepting a 'package' of finance, technologies, managerial skills, and other capabilities offered by TNCs is not as good for long-term industrial development as encouraging the national firms to construct their own packages, using their own managerial skills – obviously with some necessary outsourcing (on this point, see Helleiner, 1989; Lall (ed.), 1993; and Chudnovsky (ed.), 1993).

East Asian policies towards TNCs deserve a special mention, given the current enthusiasm about globalisation and the role of TNCs in it (for criticisms of the globalisation thesis, see Hirst and Thompson, 1996; Wade, 1996; Chang, 1998c). The restrictive attitude of Japan towards TNCs is well known, but it should be noted that Taiwan and especially Korea also have maintained a rather restrictive regulatory regime *vis-a-vis* TNCs (see Chang, 1998b, for details) – until it had to be abandoned following the IMF bailout programme in the case of Korea. Thus, the East Asian governments imposed restrictions on the areas where TNCs could enter. And even when entry was allowed, they encouraged joint ventures, preferably under local majority ownership, in an attempt to facilitate the transfer of core technologies and managerial skills.[21] Policy measures other than the ones concerning entry and ownership were also used to control the activities of TNCs. For example, the technology that was to be brought in by the investing TNCs was carefully screened and checked as to whether it was not overly obsolete or whether the royalties charged on the local subsidiaries, if any, were not excessive. For another example, in order to maximise technology spillover, those investors which were more willing to transfer technologies were preferred (unless they were technologically too far behind), and local-content requirements were quite strictly imposed.[22]

Policies that regulate the inflows of technology in East Asia would not have been so effective without policies to enhance the capabilities of the domestic firms to absorb the imported technologies. Obviously, these included some policies which do not involve industry-specific measures, such as government funding and management of general education. For the purpose of more specialised skill formation, the East Asian governments also employed a range of mea-

---

[21] For example, in the case of Korea, even in sectors where FDI was allowed, foreign ownership above 50% was prohibited except where FDI was deemed to be of 'strategical' importance, which covered only about 13% of all the manufacturing industries (EPB, 1981: p. 70). These included industries where access to proprietary technology was deemed essential for further development of the industry, and industries where the capital requirement and/or the risks involved in the investment were very large. The ownership ceiling was also relaxed if: (i) the investments were made in the free trade zones; (ii) the investments were made by overseas Koreans; or (iii) the investments would 'diversify' the origins of FDI into the country – namely, investments from countries other than the US and Japan, which had previously dominated the Korean FDI scene. For details, see EPB (1981: pp. 70-1). As a result of such policies, as of the mid-1980s, only 5% of TNC subsidiaries in Korea were wholly owned, whereas the corresponding figures were 50% for Mexico and 60% for Brazil, countries which are often believed to have had much more 'anti-foreign' policy orientations than Korea (Evans, 1987: p. 208). Due to the scarcity of large private sector domestic firms, the Taiwanese government had to be more flexible on the ownership question (33.5% of the TNC subsidiaries were wholly owned as of 1985 (Schive, 1993: p. 319) ), but Taiwan's reliance on FDI on the whole was for most of the time below the developing-country average (see Table 1.1).

[22] One thing to note, however, is that the targets for localisation were set realistically, so that they would not seriously hurt the export competitiveness of the country. It was in fact the case that in some industries they were less strictly applied to the products destined for the export market than those destined for the domestic market.

sures (with certain country variations). They included: (i) deliberate channelling of funding into science and engineering departments in universities, especially those related to 'strategic' industries (e.g., electronics engineering); (ii) public provision of specialised industrial training; (iii) introduction of compulsory training schemes for large industrial firms (which are generally in those industries that were promoted as 'strategic industries'); (iv) introduction of (German-style) skill certification systems that encourage the workers to acquire specialised skills whose possession cannot be easily verified.[23]

Even before a late-developing country reaches the world's technological frontier, there comes a stage when it becomes necessary for it to be engaged in some R&D, because, as the imported technologies become more and more sophisticated, even mere absorption of a technology may require some independent R&D activities. And as is well known, as they reached this stage, the East Asian countries all engaged in highly organised efforts to promote R&D (for the country details, see the country chapters in Nelson (ed.), 1993).[24]  What is notable is that, even when they started spending significant amounts in R&D, the efforts were concentrated in 'applied' areas, often very precisely targeted by the government at particular end products with clear marketability, rather than in 'basic' areas. Although this practice attracted criticisms from certain quarters for not leading to 'genuinely creative' R&D, others argue that such 'goal-oriented' nature is a strength, rather than a weakness, of the East Asian R&D policies, as it means that R&D spending gets directly and quickly translated into advantages in product markets.

The importance of enhancing the level of technology in order to enhance the competitiveness of a country cannot be over-emphasised.

---

[23] Needless to say, many studies have emphasised the role of certain labour institutions, such as lifetime employment and company unionism, in the East Asian countries in encouraging specialised skill formation. However, except for pointing out the fact that the evolution of some of these institutions has been heavily influenced by their governments, the issue need not detain us here. On the role of labour institutions in skill formation in East Asia, see Dore (1987: Chapters 2, 5, 7 and 8) for Japan and You and Chang (1993) for Korea.

[24] Given the absence of large private sector firms, the Taiwanese government has accounted for the bulk of R&D expenditure, whereas in Japan and Korea, R&D spending by the private sector has been larger than that by the public sector except in the earlier stages of their development.

However, the measures that a late-developing country has to take in order to increase its technological level are rather different from what the countries on the frontier have to take. They need to put more effort into monitoring and controlling what kinds of technologies are imported by whom and on what terms, and need to put more emphasis on enhancing skills on the shopfloor. Technology policies in East Asia were neither aimed at achieving some imaginary technological self-sufficiency nor were they blindly following the market forces. They were based on a clear notion of gradual technological upgrading, which involved careful control over the paths of technological evolution through controls over technology inflow and over the formation of the capabilities to absorb imported technologies.

## 6.    The Question of Replicability

The question of replicability has been a persistent theme in the debate on East Asia. In the early days of the debate, when the mainstream economists recommended the supposedly 'free market, free trade' model of East Asia to other developing countries, many dependency theorists pointed out that there were too many historical, geopolitical, and perhaps cultural idiosyncrasies that made the model generally inapplicable, although they did not question the mainstream characterisation of the model itself (on the curious similarities between the early mainstream and the dependency interpretations of the East Asian experience, see Chang, 1990; for criticisms of the 'idiosyncrasy' arguments, see Chang, 1995b, whose Spanish translation appears in Chang, 1996b). Later, when it became clear that the East Asian countries did not succeed on the basis of 'free market, free trade' policy, the mainstream economists adopted the dependency-style argument that they had so vehemently disparaged earlier and argued that the East Asian model could not be replicated, because its success was based on certain unique conditions which other countries did not possess (World Bank, 1993, is the best example).

In the following, we examine two arguments in this vein that have recently become especially popular. The first argument emphasises the importance of a competent bureaucracy in successfully administering the kinds of 'sophisticated' industrial and trade policies that the East Asian countries have used. The second emphasises the difficulty of using the East-Asian-style 'non-market-conforming' trade and industrial policy instruments in the new international trading regime that came out of the Uruguay Round negotiations which established the World Trade Organisation (WTO). How plausible are these arguments?

In response to the first argument, it should be admitted that a competent bureaucracy is certainly needed for an effective administration of East-Asian-style trade and industrial policies. However, it is not clear whether administering such policies necessarily requires more bureaucratic capabilities than other, supposedly 'easier' policies such as macroeconomic policy. This would certainly depend on the extent of intervention and the sophistication of policy tools employed – for example, a deft management of the exchange rate or interest rate may be more difficult than running a few industry-specific technological upgrading schemes.

More importantly, this argument mistakenly believes that the well-developed bureaucracy of the East Asian countries was a part of their historically determined 'initial conditions'. These countries had to spend a lot of time and energy in reforming their bureaucracies and training their bureaucrats before they could establish the kind of bureaucracies that they have now (Cheng *et al.*, 1998). It is instructive to note in this context that Korea had been sending its bureaucrats for training to the Philippines and Pakistan until the late 1960s.

In any case, as many Latin American countries were much more advanced than the East Asian countries until the early 1980s, it will be difficult to argue that they could not adopt at least some 'sophisticated' policies similar to those practised in East Asia because they lacked the (bureaucratic and other) 'capability'. For example, as we can see in Table 1.4, in 1961, even the least developed of the Latin American countries in the sample, namely, Brazil ($129), had a per capita income 1.6 times that of Korea ($82) and manufacturing value added (MVA) 2.3 times that of Korea, and had only a slightly lower ratio of literacy (71% vs. 61%). Even when we compare it with Taiwan, whose per capita income was essentially at the same level ($122 vs. $129), we find that Brazil had a somewhat higher literacy ratio (61% vs. 54%) and 2.3 times MVA. When we compare the East Asian countries with the other Latin American countries in the sample (Ec-

| | 1961 per capita income (current $) | 1961 per capita MVA (1958 $) | Literacy ratio circa 1960 | 1938 per capita MVA (1958 $) | Literacy ratio circa 1945 |
|---|---|---|---|---|---|
| | | | | | |
| Indonesia | 49 | 3 (1958) | 47% | 4 | n.a. |
| Tanzania | 50 | 4 (1958) | 17% | n.a. | n.a. |
| Pakistan | 54 | 9 | 16% | n.a. | 18% (1951) |
| Zaire | 67 | 11 | 31% | n.a. | n.a. |
| India | 69 | 11 | 24% | 6 | 19% (1951) |
| Kenya | 72 | 12 (1958) | 20% | n.a. | n.a. |
| Korea | 82 | 22 | 71% | 9 | 22% (1945) |
| Thailand | 88 | 9 | 68% | 6 | 53% (1947) |
| Sri Lanka | 122 | 18 | 61% | 16 | n.a. |
| Taiwan | 122 | 23 | 54% | 12 | 50% (1950) |
| Brazil | 129 | 50 | 61% | 16 | 43% (1940) |
| Ecuador | 143 | 26 | 67% | 19 | n.a. |
| Ghana | 179 | 8 (1958) | 27% | n.a. | n.a. |
| Philippines | 200 | 16 | 72% | 13 | 52% (1948) |
| Malaysia* | 215 | 27 | 23% | n.a. | 38% (1947) |
| Mexico | 279 | 83 | 62% | 45 | 57% (1950) |
| Chile | 377 | 82 | 84% | 72 | 77% (1940) |
| Argentina | 378 | 114 | 91% | 98 | 86% (1947) |
| South Africa | 396 | 138 | 57% | 62 | n.a. |
| Singapore | n.a. | n.a. | n.a. | n.a. | 46% (1947) |
| Japan | 402 | 227 | 98% | 75 | n.a. |
| USA | 2308 | 926 | 98% | 375 | n.a. |

**Table 1.4: 'Initial Conditions'**

Notes: *Malaya
1. MVA (manufacturing value added) figures are from United Nations, *Growth of World Industry, 1938-61* (1965).
2. Literacy figures circa 1945 are from UNESCO, *Statistical Yearbook*, and UN, *Statistical Yearbook*, various years; McGinn *et al.*, *Education and Development in Korea* (1980), Table 17. Literacy figures circa 1960 are from World Bank, *World Development Report*, various years.
3. Income figures for 1961 are from Kindleberger, *Economic Development* (1965), Table 1.1, except the one for Korea, which is from the Korean *National Account Statistics*.

uador, Mexico, Chile, and Argentina), we find that the latter were all much more advanced than the former. If we accept that the bureaucratic capability of a country would be strongly correlated with the level of its economic development and broad human capital endowment, we find it difficult to agree with the argument that the Latin American countries cannot, or could not, adopt the East-Asian-style-policy because of the lack of 'capability'.

More generally, we should point out that the view that countries need to have some 'special' (bureaucratic and other) capabilities before they can adopt some economic 'model' that is not predominantly 'market-based' (e.g., the East Asian model) is based on the mistaken mainstream belief that while markets, as 'natural' phenomena, can be transplanted anywhere, 'institutions' (including the modern bureaucracy), as man-made things, cannot. Recent developments in institutional economics have persuasively demonstrated, firstly, that the conventional market-institutions dichotomy is misleading, as markets themselves are institutions, and, secondly, that markets are *not* natural phenomena that develop spontaneously, and (like other institutions) have to be deliberately constructed. Indeed, if the market-based Anglo-Saxon model is so easy to replicate, why is it the case that most of the 'success stories', be they German, Japanese, or Scandinavian, were based on some 'deviant' model? The difficulty that many developing and transitional economies are currently experiencing with their neoliberal reforms is just another testimony to how hard it actually is to replicate the predominantly market-based Anglo-Saxon model. In fact, the establishment of market institutions required a lot of government intervention even in the Anglo-Saxon economies in their early days (see Polanyi, 1957, on Britain, and Kozul-Wright, 1995, for the US).

The argument that the East Asian model cannot be replicated elsewhere because of the uniqueness of their institutions sees the institutions as something immutable and thus underestimates the possibility of institutional adaptation and innovation. Like technologies, institutions (and, indeed, 'culture' as a set of informal institutions) are subject to adaptation and innovation, and therefore should not be seen as something immutable that a country inherits from its past. Especially from the point of view of the late-developing countries, adapting imported institutions to the local conditions is as, if not more, important as adapting imported technologies, and the East Asian countries themselves show how important and feasible such institutional adaptation is.[25]

In response to the second argument citing the highly 'liberal' post-Uruguay-Round (henceforth post-UR) world trading regime as a major constraint to adopting some of the East Asian policy tools, three points must be made (the following details are from Akyuz *et al.*, 1998; also see Amsden, 2000).

Firstly, the conventional wisdom overestimates the policy 'freedom' that existed in the pre-WTO international trading system. Even the old General Agreement on Tariffs and Trade (GATT) system imposed many restrictions on the kinds of policy tools which could be employed. As a result, the East Asian countries had to exercise a considerable amount of policy ingenuity and administrative and diplomatic skills to maintain some of their policies even under the pre-WTO system.

Secondly, while the WTO system does put more constraints on the scope of policy tools that can be used, the constraints are not as widespread and binding as they are usually made out to be. For example, the 'balance of payments' clause, which, rather than the 'infant industry' clause, had been the most frequently evoked justification for quantitative restrictions under the pre-WTO regime by the East Asian countries (and other developing countries), still exists under this new regime. Also, subsidies may be more strictly sanctioned against in the WTO system, but there are still 'non-actionable'[26] subsidies such as subsidies for basic research, agriculture, and regional development. And in the case of the poorest countries, some subsidies prohibited in other countries, notably export subsidies, are still allowed. Lastly, the WTO agreements on so-called 'Trade-Related

---

[25] The early Japanese experience is particularly instructive here. When the Japanese first embarked on the industrialisation process, they had to import many foreign institutions, picking what they thought were the most suitable among the 'best practice' ones. So if we look at the early Meiji period, we find an institutional patchwork. The commercial law system was from France, their criminal law from Germany, the Central Bank from Belgium, the Navy from Britain, the Army from Germany, the education system first from America but later from Germany, and so on (for some more details, see Westney, 1987).

[26] This means that retaliatory action cannot be taken against these subsidies.

Aspects of Intellectual Property Rights' (TRIPS) and 'Trade-Related Investment Measures' (TRIMs) do constrain the scope for things like local-content requirements or compulsory technology licensing, but exceptions can be made (although not easily)[27], and a wide range of other measures that can serve similar purposes are not affected by these agreements (e.g., export performance requirements on TNC subsidiaries).

Finally, it needs emphasising that the new trading regime does not prohibit many policy measures that have been used in the East Asian policy regime. Strategic credit rationing by the state, the use of domestic taxes to encourage or discourage particular activities, dissemination of information on export markets and best-practice technology by state agencies, direct and indirect controls on competition in strategic industries, and policies to encourage the formation of specialised skills are only some of the more important examples.

I would agree with those who express skepticism about the replicability of the East Asian model, if all they mean is that countries with different conditions may have to find different solutions to similar problems (for some theoretical discussion, see Chang, 1997a). However, they often have a very exaggerated view about the superiority of the 'initial conditions' of the East Asian countries (Chang, 1998d), and have an unduly pessimistic view about other countries changing their conditions. So they believe that initial institutional (and cultural) conditions are almost perfectly binding and therefore countries which do not start with the East Asian sort of initial conditions cannot emulate them. One curious thing here is that most of these people do not seem to believe that the 'initial conditions' may be equally binding when countries aim to imitate the Anglo-Saxon model that they typically recommend. The same sorts of exaggeration, narrowness of views, and prejudices prevail in the discussions on the effects of the WTO trading regime. The pre-WTO trading regimes are described as somehow very permissive, the constraints imposed by the new regime are highly exaggerated, and the role of policy ingenuity in getting around these constraints is completely ignored.

---

[27]  Local-content requirements can be invoked under the balance-of-payments clause. Compulsory licensing is also allowed under special circumstances.

## 7.    The End of the East Asian Model?

With the 1997 crisis in Korea and the prolonged recession in Japan, there is now widespread talk of the end of the East Asian model. In contrast, the recent strength of the American and the British economies is taken as evidence that the Anglo-Saxon model is finally proving that it is the best economic model there is.

While it is perfectly understandable why there is such a sentiment, we need to put things into perspective. To begin with, not all the East Asian economies are equally in trouble. Korea may have experienced a deep crisis, but Taiwan and Singapore did not have a crisis. Indeed, what is interesting to note is that the Asian countries that have recently experienced problems were either the ones that did not follow the 'East Asian model' (the Southeast Asian countries and Hong Kong) or the ones that moved away from such a model (Japan and Korea).

Moreover, while the Japanese performance may have been inferior to those of the Anglo-Saxon economies during the second half of the 1990s, the performance difference is a lot smaller than what is normally assumed. During the 1990s, the Japanese per capita GDP growth rate, at 1.4%, was only a fraction lower than that of the US at 1.6% and superior to those of Switzerland (-0.4%), Sweden (0.8%), Canada (0.8%), Italy (1.1%), and France (1.3%) (data from the World Bank and the *Financial Times*). Also, according to data from the *Economist* published in April 1999, in terms of the productivity growth rate (that is, the rate of growth of GDP per worker), the US, at 0.9%, was behind Japan, which was at 1.2%, between 1989 and 1998.

Moreover, the recent economic troubles in Japan, and especially Korea, are the result of *departures* from the 'traditional' East Asian model, rather than of *adherence* to it. The 1990s recession in Japan started when the asset bubble that built up following financial liberalisation in the late 1980s finally burst in the early 1990s. The recession that followed owed a lot to the refusal by the Japanese government to intervene quickly and decisively in the financial sector to clean it up in the manner in which the ostensibly less interventionist US government had dealt with a similar problem, namely, the savings-and-loan (S&L) crisis during the 1980s.

The 1997 crisis in Korea was due to the rapid build-up of short-term foreign debts that had fed the investment boom between 1994 and 1996 that was made possible by the abandonment of traditional industrial policy measures (e.g., investment coordination, control on 'excessive competition') by the Kim Young Sam government that took power in 1993 – although the Korean industrial policy had already been weakening from the early 1990s. And what made this debt build-up possible was the ill-designed financial liberalisation programme that was started in 1993 by the same government. The departure from the traditional exchange rate policy also added to the problem (for further details on the Korean crisis, see Chang, 1998a; Chang *et al.*, 1998; and Chang and Yoo, 2000; for details on the Asian crisis in general, see Wade and Veneroso, 1998; Stiglitz, 1998; and Chang, 2000).

With Korea (voluntarily and involuntarily) deregulating its economy at an alarming speed to restore 'international confidence' in its economy and with Japan accelerating its financial deregulation (if not deregulation in other areas) in response to its recent recession, it seems that the East Asian model will be significantly watered down, if not wiped out, in the coming years. However, the evolutionary dynamics of economic institutions are too complex for us to say with full confidence that these economies will become 'Anglo-Saxon' in the near future. After all, it was out of the very American institutional frameworks that had been imposed by the American Occupation Authority after the Second World War that the famous 'idiosyncratic' Japanese and German models emerged. In addition, the changing fortunes of the major OECD economies in the coming years will deflate the over-confident Anglo-Saxon triumphalism and put the whole debate on a more sensible footing. It will be very interesting to watch what happens in Korea and Japan, as well as the US, over the next several years.

## 8.    Summary and Conclusion

During the last 20 years or so, a number of attempts to explain the differential performances across different capitalist countries have generated a belated interest in the institutional diversity of capitalism. Such interest naturally makes us question the wisdom of neoliberal economics, which claims that there is only one efficient way of organising a capitalist economy, namely an idealised version of the Anglo-Saxon economic model based on unconstrained markets with minimal state intervention – a view which is in ascendancy at the moment following the Asian crisis. Among the 'models' that challenge the dominant Anglo-Saxon model is the East Asian model, whose 'economic' (as opposed to 'social') dimension we have examined.

We examined three broad areas of the East Asian model of economic policy – investment policy, trade policy, and industrial policy (including technology policy). We emphasised how the constraints (and opportunities) imposed by the imperatives of late development shaped such policies in these countries, and how they overcame these constraints. In the process, we highlighted some policies which we regard as important but which have received inadequate attention even from those who are sympathetic to the East Asian model. These included, among others: (i) the pro-investment, rather than anti-inflationary, macroeconomic policy; (ii) the control on luxury consumption, which served both economic *and* political functions; (iii) the strict control on FDI, which is contrary to the popular impression that these economies (perhaps except Japan) have had an 'open' FDI policy; (iv) the integrated pursuit of infant-industry protection and export promotion; (v) the use of exports as a tool to exploit scale economy and thus to accelerate the maturation of infant industries; (vi) the productivity-oriented (as opposed to allocation-oriented) view of competition.

Then we discussed whether replicating the East Asian model in other countries is feasible. Noting that a wholesale replication of any socio-economic model, and not just the East Asian model, is impossible, we examined two 'impossibility of learning from East Asia' arguments that are especially popular these days – one related to bureaucratic institutions, and the other related to changes in the international trading regime – and found them wanting. We pointed out that, while both of them have a point, they are misinformed, exaggerated, and biased in their outlook. This discussion was followed by a short commentary on whether the recent economic troubles in some (but not all) East Asian countries signify the end of the East Asian model. We argued that, firstly, the relative performances of the East Asian countries and the Anglo-Saxon economies need to be put into perspective, and, secondly, that the troubles in some East Asian countries are due mainly to their departures from the traditional model, rather than to their adherence to it. We also pointed out that the process of institutional evolution is difficult to predict, and therefore that it is not obvious that countries like Japan, and especially Korea, will emerge as truly Anglo-Saxon economies out of their recent crises that have prompted them to adopt many Anglo-Saxon institutions.

The East Asian model of economic policy may look very different from some other models, especially the Anglo-Saxon one (but perhaps not their earlier reincarnations, e.g., the early US model). However, it also shares many characteristics with other models, especially those of many continental European countries and Latin American countries, not least because they all had to develop their policies under the constraints of late development. The interesting question, however, is not what these similarities are, but what the crucial differences are between the East Asian model of economic policy and those of continental Europe and Latin America.

With a view to drawing lessons for Latin America, I may point out some likely candidates: luxury-consumption control (conspicuously missing in Latin America); an active use of exports as a part of an infant-industry programme (an especially big contrast with Latin America); skilful management of domestic competition, based on a productivity-oriented view of competition; and active policies to promote technology absorption (policies towards TNCs being the biggest difference with Latin America in this area). However, my personal knowledge about most non-East-Asian countries is too inadequate to make much progress here. A series of more systematic comparative studies will be needed before we can distil some useful policy lessons.

# Bibliography

Akyuz, Y., Chang, H-J. & Kozul-Wright, R. (1998). 'New Perspectives on East Asian Development', *Journal of Development Studies*, vol. 34, no. 6.

Albert, M. (1991). *Capitalism vs. Capitalism*. New York: Four Walls Eight Windows.

Alesina, A. & Perotti, R. (1994). 'The Political Economy of Growth: A Critical Survey of the Recent Literature', *The World Bank Economic Review*, vol. 8, no. 3.

Amsden, A. (1985). 'The State and Taiwan's Economic Development', in P. Evans, D. Rueschemeyer & T. Skocpol (eds.), *Bringing the State Back In*. Cambridge: Cambridge University Press.

Amsden, A. (1989). *Asia's Next Giant*. New York: Oxford University Press.

Amsden, A. (2000). 'Industrialisation under New WTO Law', a paper for the UNCTAD X meeting, 12-19 February 2000, Bangkok.

Aoki, M. (1990). 'A New Paradigm of Work Organisation and Coordination? – Lessons from Japanese Experience', in S. Marglin & J. Schor (eds.), *The Rise and Fall of the Golden Age*. Oxford: Oxford University Press.

Aoki, M. & Dore, R. (eds.) (1994). *The Japanese Firm*. Oxford: Oxford University Press.

Aoki, M., Gustafsson, B. & Williamson, O. (eds.) (1990). *The Firm as a Nexus of Treaties*. London: Sage Publications Ltd..

Balassa, B. (1982). 'Development Strategies and Economic Performance', in B. Balassa *et al.*, *Development Strategies in Semi-Industrial Economies*. Baltimore: The Johns Hopkins University Press.

Balassa, B. (1988). 'The Lessons of East Asian Development: An Overview', *Economic Development and Cultural Change*, vol. 36, no. 3, Apr. 1988, Supplement.

Berger, S. & Dore, R. (eds.) (1996). *National Diversity and Global Capitalism*. Ithaca and London: Cornell University Press.

Brittan, S. (1997). 'Asian Model, R.I.P.', *Financial Times*, 4 December 1997.

Bruno, M. & Easterly, W. (1994). 'Inflation Crises and Long-run Growth', mimeo., Policy Research Department, Macroeconomic and Growth Division, World Bank.

Bruno, M. & Sachs, J. (1985). *Economics of Worldwide Stagflation*. Cambridge, Massachusetts: Harvard University Press.

Brusco, M. (1982). 'The Emilian Model: Productive Decentralisation and Social Integration', *Cambridge Journal of Economics*, vol. 6, no. 2.

Cairncross, F. & Cairncross, A. (eds.) (1992). *The Legacy of the Golden Age – The 1960s and Their Economic Consequences*. London: Routledge.

Castells, M., Portes, A. & Benton, L. (eds.) (1989). *The Informal Economy*. Baltimore: The Johns Hopkins University Press.

Chang, H-J. (1990). 'Interpreting the Korean Experience – Heaven or Hell?', Research Paper Series, no. 42, Faculty of Economics and Politics, University of Cambridge.

Chang, H-J. (1993). 'The Political Economy of Industrial Policy in Korea', *Cambridge Journal of Economics*, vol. 17, no. 2.

Chang, H-J. (1994a). *The Political Economy of Industrial Policy*. London and Basingstoke: Macmillan.

Chang, H-J. (1994b). 'State, Institutions, and Structural Change', *Structural Change and Economic Dynamics*, vol. 5, no. 2.

Chang, H-J. (1995a). 'Explaining "Flexible Rigidities" in East Asia', in T. Killick (ed.), *The Flexible Economy*. London: Routledge.

Chang, H-J. (1995b). 'Return to Europe? – Is There Anything That Eastern Europe Can Learn From East Asia?', in H-J. Chang & P. Nolan (eds.), *The Transformation of the Communist Economies – Against the Mainstream*. London and Basingstoke: Macmillan.

Chang, H-J. (1996a). 'Understanding the Recent Regulatory Changes in Japan and Korea', a paper prepared for the project on 'Regulatory Policy and Regulatory Reform for Sustainable Development', Economic Development Institute, World Bank, Washington, D.C.

Chang, H-J. (1996b). *El Papel del Estado en el Cambio Económico*. Mexico City: Editorial Planeta Mexicana.

Chang, H-J. (1997a). 'Markets, Madness, and Many Middle Ways: Some Reflections on the Institutional Diversity of Capitalism', in P. Arestis, G. Palma & M. Sawyer (eds.), *Essays in Honour of Geoff Harcourt – Volume 2: Markets, Unemployment, and Economic Policy*. London: Routledge.

Chang, H-J. (1997b). 'Luxury Consumption Control and Industrialisation in East Asia', mimeo., a background paper prepared for *Trade and Development Report 1997*, UNCTAD, Geneva.

Chang, H-J. (1997c). 'The Economics and Politics of Regulation', *Cambridge Journal of Economics*, vol. 21, no. 6.

Chang, H-J. (1998a). 'Korea: The Misunderstood Crisis', *World Development*, vol. 26, no. 8.

Chang, H-J. (1998b). 'Globalisation, Transnational Corporations, and Economic Development – Can the Developing Countries Pursue Strategic Industrial Policy in a Globalising World Economy?', in D. Baker, G. Epstein & R. Pollin (eds.), *Globalisation and Progressive Economic Policy: What are the Real Constraints and Opportunities?*. New York: Cambridge University Press.

Chang, H-J. (1998c). 'Transnational Corporations and Strategic Industrial Policy', in R. Kozul-Wright & R. Rowthorn (eds.), *Transnational Corporations and the World Economy*. London: Macmillan Press.

Chang, H-J. (1998d). 'Initial Conditions of Development – Comparing the East Asian and the Sub-Saharan African Experiences', a background paper for UNCTAD *Trade and Development Report, 1998*.

Chang, H-J. (1999). 'Industrial Policy and East Asia – the Miracle, the Crisis, and the Future', a paper presented at the World Bank workshop on 'Rethinking the East Asian Miracle', February 1999, San Francisco.

Chang, H-J. (2000). 'The Hazard of Moral Hazard – Untangling the Asian Crisis', *World Development*, vol. 28, no. 4.

Chang, H-J., Park, H-J. & Yoo, C.G. (1998). 'Interpreting the Korean Crisis: Financial Liberalisation, Industrial Policy, and Corporate Governance', *Cambridge Journal of Economics*, vol. 22, no. 6.

Chang, H-J. & Rowthorn, R. (eds.) (1995). *Role of the State in Economic Change*. Oxford: Oxford University Press.

Chang, H-J. & Yoo, C-G. (2000). 'Triumph of the Rentiers?', *Challenge*, January-February 2000.

Cheng, T., Haggard, S. & Kang, D. (1998). 'Institutions and Growth in Korea and Taiwan: The Bureaucracy', *Journal of Development Studies*, vol. 34, no. 6.

Chudnovsky, D. (ed.) (1993). *Transnational Corporations and Industrialisation*. London: Routledge.

Cohen, S. (1977). *Modern Capitalist Planning: The French Model*, 2nd edition. Berkeley: University of California Press.

Cox, A. (ed.) (1986). *State, Finance, and Industry in Comparative Perspective*. Brighton: Wheatsheaf Books.

Dei Ottati, G. (1994). 'Trust, Interlinking Transactions, and Credit in the Industrial District', *Cambridge Journal of Economics*, vol. 18, no. 6.

Dore, R. (1986). *Flexible Rigidities: Industrial Policy and Structural Adjustment in the Japanese Economy 1970-80*. London: The Athlone Press.

Dore, R. (1987). *Taking Japan Seriously – A Confucian Perspective on Leading Economic Issues*. London: The Athlone Press.

Dore, R. (1993). 'What Makes the Japanese Different?', in C. Crouch & D. Marquand (eds.), *Ethics and Markets*. Cambridge: Polity Press.

Dornbusch, R. (1996). 'The Effectiveness of Exchange-Rate Changes', *Oxford Review of Economic Policy*, vol. 12, no. 3.

Dosi, G., Freeman, C., Nelson, R., Silverberg, G. & Soete, L. (eds.) (1988). *Technical Change and Economic Theory*. London: Pinter Publishers.

Dosi, G., Tyson, L. & Zysman, J. (1989). 'Trade, Technologies and Development: A Framework for Discussing Japan', in C. Johnson, L. Tyson & J. Zysman (eds.), *Politics and Productivity*. New York: Harper Business.

EPB (Economic Planning Board) (1981). *Oegoogin Tooja Baeksuh* (White Paper on Foreign Investment) (in Korean). Seoul: The Government of Korea.

Evans, P. (1987). 'Class, State, and Dependence in East Asia: Lessons for Latin Americanists', in F. Deyo (ed.), *The Political Economy of the New Asian Industrialism*. Ithaca: Cornell University Press.

Evans, P. (1995). *Embedded Autonomy – States and Industrial Transformation*. Princeton: Princeton University Press.

Fagerberg, J. (1996). 'Technology and Competitiveness', *Oxford Review of Economic Policy*, vol. 12, no. 3.

Fishlow, A., Gwin, C., Haggard, S., Rodrik, D. & Wade, R. (1994). *Miracle or Design? – Lessons from the East Asian Experience*. Washington, D.C.: Overseas Development Council.

Gerschenkron, A. (1966). *Economic Backwardness in Historical Perspective*. Cambridge, Massachusetts: Belknap Press.

Goldthorpe, J. (ed.) (1984). *Order and Conflict in Contemporary Capitalism*. Oxford: Oxford University Press.

Hall, P. (1987). *Governing the Economy*. Cambridge: Polity Press.

Hayek, F. (1949). 'The Meaning of Competition', in F. Hayek, *Individualism and Economic Order*. London: Routledge & Kegan Paul.

Helleiner, G. (1989). 'Transnational Corporations and Direct Foreign Investment', in H. Chenery & T.N. Srinivasan (eds.), *Handbook of Development Economics*, vol. 2. Amsterdam: Elsevier Science Publishers, B.V..

Hirst, P. & Thompson, G. (1996). *Globalisation in Question*. Cambridge: Polity Press.

Johnson, C. (1982). *MITI and the Japanese Miracle*. Stanford: Stanford University Press.

Johnson, C. (ed.) (1984). *The Industrial Policy Debate*. San Francisco: Institute for Contemporary Studies.

Jones, L. & Sakong, I. (1980). *Government, Business and Entrepreneurship in Economic Development: The Korean Case*. Cambridge, Massachusetts: Harvard University Press.

Koike, K. (1987). 'Human Resource Development and Labour-Management Relations', in K. Yamamura & Y. Yasuba (eds.), *The Political Economy of Japan,* vol. 1. Stanford: Stanford University Press.

Kozul-Wright, R. (1995). 'The Myth of Anglo-Saxon Capitalism: Reconstructing the History of the American State', in H-J. Chang & R. Rowthorn (eds.), *Role of the State in Economic Change*. Oxford: Oxford University Press.

Krueger, A. (1980). 'Trade Policy as an Input to Development', *American Economic Review*, vol. 70, no. 3.

Lal, D. (1983). *The Poverty of Development Economics*. London: The Institute of Economic Affairs.

Lall, S. (ed.) (1993). *Transnational Corporations and Economic Development*. London: Routledge.

Langlois, R. (ed.) (1986). *Economics as a Process*. Cambridge: Cambridge University Press.

Lindbeck, A. (1981). 'Industrial Policy as an Issue in the Economic Environment', *The World Economy*, vol. 4, no. 4.

Little, I. (1982). *Economic Development*. New York: Basic Books.
Luedde-Neurath, R. (1986). *Import Controls and Export-Oriented Development; A Reassessment of the South Korean Case*. Boulder and London: Westview Press.
Lundvall, B-Å. (ed.) (1992). *National Systems of Innovation: Towards a Theory of Innovation and Interactive Learning*. London: Pinter Publishers.
Magaziner, I. & Hout, T. (1980). *Japanese Industrial Policy*. London: Policy Studies Institute.
Marglin, S. & Schor, J. (eds.) (1990). *The Golden Age of Capitalism*. Oxford: Clarendon Press.
McNulty, P. (1968). 'Economic Theory and the Meaning of Competition', *Quarterly Journal of Economics*, vol. 82, no. 4.
Murray, F. (1987). 'Flexible Specialisation in the "Third Italy"', *Capital and Class*, winter, 1987.
Nelson, R. (ed.) (1993). *National Innovation Systems*. New York: Oxford University Press.
Pekkarinen, J., Pohjola, M. & R. Rowthorn (eds.) (1992). *Social Corporatism*. Oxford: Oxford University Press.
Piore, M. & Sabel, C. (1984). *The Second Industrial Divide*. New York: Basic Books.
Polanyi, K. (1957). *The Great Transformation*. Boston: Beacon Press.
Price, V. (1980). 'Alternatives to Delayed Structural Adjustment in "Workshop Europe"', *The World Economy*, vol. 3, no. 2.
Ranis, G. & Fei, J. (1975). 'A Model of Growth and Employment in the Open Dualistic Economy: The Cases of Korea and Taiwan', in F. Stewart (ed.), *Employment, Income Distribution and Development*. London: Frank Cass.
Sachs, J. (1984). 'Comment on C. Diaz-Alejandro, "Latin American Debt: I Don't Think We are in Kansas Anymore"', *Brookings Papers on Economic Activity*, 1984, no.2.
Schive, C. (1993). 'Foreign Investment and Technology Transfer in Taiwan', in S. Lall (ed.), *Transnational Corporations and Economic Development*. London: Routledge.
Schott, K. (1984). *Policy, Power and Order*. New Haven and London: Yale University Press.
Shin, K. (1994). *An International Comparison of Competition Policy: USA, Japan, and Germany* (in Korean). Seoul: Korea Development Institute.
Shonfield, A. (1965). *Modern Capitalism*. Oxford: Oxford University Press.
Singh, A. (1995). 'How Did East Asia Grow So Fast? – Slow Progress Towards An Analytical Consensus', UNCTAD Discussion Paper No. 97, Geneva, United Nations Conference on Trade and Development (UNCTAD).
Stiglitz, J. (1998). 'Sound Finance and Sustainable Development in Asia', keynote address to the Asia Development Forum, jointly organised by

the World Bank and the Asian Development Bank, 9-12 March 1998, Manila.

Studart, R. (1995). 'The Efficiency of Financial Systems, Liberalisation, and Economic Development', *Journal of Post-Keynesian Economics*, vol. 18, no. 2.

Thompson, G. (ed.) (1989). *Industrial Policy: USA and UK Debates*. London: Routledge.

Toye, J. (1987). *Dilemmas of Development*. Oxford: Blackwell.

Vartiainen, J. (1995). 'The State and Structural Change: What can be Learnt from the Successful Late Industrializers?', in H-J. Chang & R. Rowthorn (eds.), *Role of the State in Economic Change*. Oxford: Oxford University Press.

Wade, R. (1990). *Governing the Market*. Princeton: Princeton University Press.

Wade, R. (1996). 'Globalization and Its Limits: Reports on the Death of the National Economy Are Greatly Exaggerated', in S. Berger & R. Dore (eds.), *National Diversity and Global Capitalism*. Ithaca and London: Cornell University Press.

Wade, R. & Veneroso, F. (1998). 'The Asian Crisis: The High Debt Model vs. The Wall Street-Treasury-IMF Complex', *New Left Review*, March-April 1998.

Westney, E. (1987). *Imitation and Innovation: The Transfer of Western Organisational Patterns to Meiji Japan*. Cambridge: Cambridge University Press.

Williamson, O. (1985). *The Economic Institutions of Capitalism*. New York: The Free Press.

World Bank (1987). *World Development Report, 1987*. New York: Oxford University Press.

World Bank (1993). *The East Asian Miracle*. New York: Oxford University Press.

World Bank (1997). *World Development Report, 1997*. New York: Oxford University Press.

You, J. & Chang, H-J. (1993). 'The Myth of Free Labour Market in Korea', *Contributions to Political Economy*, vol. 12.

Yusuf, S. & Peters, R. (1985). 'Capital Accumulation and Economic Growth: The Korean Paradigm', World Bank Staff Working Paper no. 712.

Zysman, J. (1983). *Government, Markets and Growth*. Oxford: Martin Robertson.

# Chapter 2

# THE POLITICAL ECONOMY OF INDUSTRIAL POLICY IN KOREA

## 1.   Introduction

THE rapid growth and structural change of South Korea (henceforth Korea) during the last few decades have spawned a large body of literature which is becoming almost impossible to keep track of.[1] The accumulation of research has revealed that the state played an important role, and the proponents of Korea as a free market have been on the defensive for the last several years. The 'alternative' literature emphasising the role of the state in the Korean developmental experience is still in its infancy, however, despite some important contributions by Jones and Sakong (1980), Luedde-Neurath (1986), and most notably Amsden (1989). This chapter provides some additional empirical support to the alternative literature, and consolidates the theoretical basis for the alternative literature using some recent developments in economic theory like the New Institutionalist Economics.

In Sections 2 and 3 of this chapter we review some mainstream interpretations of the Korean developmental process. It is argued that

---

[1]   Between 1965 and 1986, Korea's annual per capita GNP growth was 6.7%, compared to 2.9% for the developing countries as a whole. Korea's manufacturing growth rate between 1965 and 1980 was 18.7%, compared to 13.2% for Singapore, 9.6% for Brazil, 9.5% for China, 7.4% for Mexico, and 4.3% for India. Between 1980 and 1987, the corresponding figure was 10.6% in Korea, compared to 12.6% in China, 8.3% in India, 3.3% in Singapore, 1.2% in Brazil, and 0.0% in Mexico (World Bank, 1988). The rapid growth was accompanied by major structural change. The production structure in Korea, which had looked more like those of low-income countries like India and Kenya in the 1960s, became more like those of upper-middle-income countries like Argentina, Brazil, and Spain by the mid-1980s.

these explanations, which try to dismiss the role of the state in the Korean developmental process, have a weak theoretical and empirical basis. In Section 4 we examine how state intervention works in Korea. In Section 5 we attempt to explain why state intervention works in Korea. The concluding section draws out some of the implications of our discussion for a new view of the Korean developmental experience and for economic development in general.

## 2.    A Free Market?

Although the formerly common interpretation of the Korean developmental experience as free-market and free-trade economy (e.g., Ranis and Fei, 1975; Balassa, 1982) is rapidly losing its popularity, it is useful to briefly discuss the argument, because the more recent mainstream interpretations examined below can be seen as attempts to rescue the conclusions of the early interpretation.

According to the free-market view, the Korean economy was stagnating in the late 1950s after it had depleted the possibility of 'easy import substitution' in non-durable consumer goods. This 'inward-looking' strategy was inefficient because of the 'distortions' generated by excessive state intervention in various markets. Such 'chaotic' import substitution with multiple exchange rates behind the wall of across-the-board protection, largely using discretionary quantitative restrictions rather than universal tariffs, allowed inefficient firms to survive and discouraged export activities. This, in turn, added to the foreign exchange shortage and hence to the pressure for more import restrictions.

The phenomenal growth of the economy, the argument goes, started with the transition from an inward-looking, or import-substituting industrialisation, strategy to an outward-looking, or export-led growth, strategy. The turning point in this transition was a series of policy reforms around 1965, the most important ingredients of which included: i) the introduction of a unified, realistic exchange rate regime; ii) trade liberalisation involving cuts in tariffs and the abolition of most quantitative restrictions; and iii) a substantial increase in real interest rates. These policies are regarded as having radically improved the performance of the economy for the following reasons. Firstly, realistic exchange rates, by making export activities as profitable as they should be, allowed Korea to follow her comparative advantage in labour-intensive industries, and therefore to reap the gains from foreign trade. Secondly, trade liberalisation improved the efficiency of the economy by exerting competitive pressures on domestic producers. Finally, the rise in interest rates enabled the economy to invest more by mobilising more savings and to use capital more efficiently by restoring the relative price of capital near to its 'realistic' level.

In the words of Ranis and Fei (1975: p. 56), '[s]tabilisation plus dismantling of the various existing direct control measures, on trade, interest rate and foreign exchange . . . created a more market-oriented economy most conducive to access for large numbers of domestic entrepreneurs seeking efficient utilisation of the economy's relatively abundant resources via embodiment in labour-intensive industrial exports.'[2]

There is abundant empirical evidence, however, which runs counter to these explanations. Concerning trade-related reforms, Luedde-Neurath (1986) shows that such reforms were not as thorough as is usually presented and were implemented rather half-heartedly.[3] Firstly, tariffs were still quite high after the 'liberalisation' and the bureaucracy retained the power to impose 'emergency tariffs' (for items with 'excessively' fast import growth) without changing the relevant laws. In the second place, quantitative restrictions, usually under the name of various 'special laws' and import area diversification regulations, were still pervasive after the 'liberalisation'. As late as 1982, 93% of total actual imports (in value terms) were subject to one or more of such restrictions (see Luedde-Neurath, 1986: p. 156, Table 14.4). Thirdly, prohibitive inland taxes were often used virtually to ban importation of luxury consumer items which were subject only to non-prohibitive tariffs.[4] Fourthly, there was extensive

---

[2]   It is interesting to note that one of the authors has, by emphasising the role of 'institutional/organisational changes orchestrated by the governments' of Korea and Taiwan, in effect denied most of what they had said earlier (see Ranis, 1989).

[3]   Although there has been more 'trade liberalisation' since Luedde-Neurath's study, all of the following 'invisible' import restrictions are still in operation.

[4]   For instance, the domestic price of imported scotch whisky, whose tariff was 100%, was over nine times the c.i.f. price after various inland taxes, e.g., liquor tax, luxury consumption tax, and VAT (Luedde-Neurath, 1986: p. 130).

| Table 2.1: Real Interest Rates in Korea, 1960-84 (percent) | | | |
|---|---|---|---|
| Period | Curb Market[a] | Deposits[b] | Export Loans |
| 1960-64 | 31.1 | -6.7 | n.a. |
| 1965-69 | 44.4 | 26.9 | n.a. |
| 1970-74 | 28.2 | -0.2 | -16.3 |
| 1975-79 | 24.0 | -4.5 | -12.5 |
| 1980-84 | 19.7 | 2.4 | 1.3 |

a. Nominal interest rate less consumer price inflation.
b. Nominal interest rate less inflation of the GNP deflator.

Source: Calculated from Dornbusch and Park (1987): p. 419, Table 14.

state support for import substitution, for example, subsidised credits to the import-substitutors and to the purchasers of some domestic products (especially machinery), which in effect acted as import restrictions. Lastly, and most importantly, there was widespread foreign exchange rationing, which meant that often importation of a certain item was impossible not because it was illegal to do so, but because it was impossible to get the foreign exchange to pay for it.

The effect of financial reform has also to be reinterpreted (for a detailed discussion, see Harris, 1987). As may be seen in Table 2.1, the post-reform high interest rates did not last more than a few years, and real interest rates were negative until the 1980s due to inflation. Nevertheless, savings have shown a rising trend, up from less than 10% in the 1950s and the early 1960s to more than 30% in the late 1980s. That is, 'Korea's saving responds little to interest rates. Overall, the Korean experience suggests that there is no need for high positive real interest rates to mobilise saving through the financial system; as long as large negative real interest rates are avoided, the real interest rate is relatively insignificant' (Dornbusch and Park, 1987: pp. 418-9).[5]

---

[5]    In other words, '[b]y paying depositors low real interest rates and by controlling capital outflows, the government implicitly taxed depositors, then channelled the proceeds to favoured sectors for investment' (Dornbusch and Park, 1987: p. 418).

Even if 'liberalisation' in Korea was as comprehensive as the proponents of a free market insist, it is not necessarily true that a 'more market-oriented economy' is more efficient even in the neo-classical sense, as the above quote from Ranis and Fei implies. As the Theory of Second Best tells us, the removal of market distortions in some, but not all, markets does not guarantee that the economy achieves higher allocative efficiency (Lipsey and Lancaster, 1956). Moreover, even if it is true that the move to a 'more market-oriented' economy improved the static allocative efficiency of the economy by moving it closer to its comparative advantage, it does not explain why Korea grew faster (also see Bruton, 1989: p. 1616). There is very little economic theory which supports the view that conforming more closely to comparative advantage leads to higher growth, as even the leading neoclassical trade theorists admit (e.g., see Krueger, 1980). More importantly, when growth involves innovation, there may exist a conflict between the achievement of static allocative efficiency and growth. As Schumpeter (1987: Chapter 8) emphasised, under conditions guaranteeing perfectly free entry and thereby allocative efficiency, there will be no incentive for innovation, because any monopoly rent, or what he calls 'entrepreneurial profits' in his earlier work (Schumpeter, 1961: Chapter 4), will be instantly competed away. As far as innovation is important for growth, this means that growth may be damaged by an improvement in the static allocative efficiency of the economy (also see Subsection 5.1).

## 3.    Market-Preserving State Intervention?

Evidence shows that state intervention has been pervasive in Korea during its rapid industrialisation period. As Bhagwati (1987) correctly argues, '[t]he key question then is not whether there is governmental action in the Far Eastern economies, but rather how have these successful economies managed their intervention and strategic decision making in ways that dominate those of the unsuccessful ones' (p. 285). And, naturally, some neoclassical economists, including Bhagwati himself, have put forward explanations of the Korean experience which try to reconcile the existence of an interventionist state with the rapid growth of the economy.

One such argument is the theory of the virtual free trade regime, which suggests that various measures of state intervention in Korea cancelled each other out to produce a neutral incentive structure (Little, 1982; Lal, 1983; World Bank, 1987). Another is the theory of prescriptive state intervention, which argues that state intervention in Korea does not hinder growth because it leaves room for 'private initiatives' (Bhagwati, 1985, 1987, 1988). In effect, these theories argue that, whatever state intervention there may have been in Korea, it did not affect the workings of the market mechanism, because it was either self-cancelling (virtual free trade) or porous (prescriptive state intervention). Below, we examine these arguments in turn, and argue that they are neither theoretically convincing nor empirically correct.

### 3.1   Self-cancelling state intervention?

According to the proponents of the theory of a virtual free trade regime, in Korea there existed widespread price distortions due to one set of state interventions (e.g., import protection), but they were cancelled out by another set of interventions (e.g., export subsidies), producing a neutral incentive structure between production for export and production for the domestic market. They emphasise the fact that Korean exporters had free access to imported inputs at world market prices, and consequently  bypassed various import restrictions (Lal, 1983). The economic crisis in the early 1980s following the heavy and chemical industrialisation (HCI) drive during the 1970s (in 1980, Korea experienced negative growth for the first time since the industrialisation drive began in the early 1960s) is presented as proof that a departure from incentive neutrality was a disaster (Lal, 1983; for a different interpretation of the early 1980s crisis, see Chang, 1987).

On the theoretical level, it is not clear how meaningful it is to call the import-substitution-cum-export-incentives regime a virtual 'free trade' regime, because there is no reason why the structure of relative prices under this trade regime should be the same as the one under genuine free trade (Yusuf and Peters, 1985: p. 18, no. 49). And, if the relative price structures under the two regimes are different, we cannot say that the incentive structure under the former is 'neutral',

| Table 2.2: Korea's Comparative Industrial Performance, 1979-1988 (Annual real growth rates of production) | | | | | | | |
|---|---|---|---|---|---|---|---|
| | **Brazil** | **Chile** | **Greece** | **Korea** | **Mexico** | **South Africa** | **Spain** |
| Heavy Industries[1] | 0.6 | 1.6 | -0.8 | 17.2 | 2.7 | 0.4 | 2.1 |
| Chemical Industries[2] | 2.6 | 0.6 | 2.2 | 7.5 | 3.4 | 1.3 | 0.8 |
| Light Industries[3] | 1.5 | 2.6 | 0.3 | 7.8 | 1.8 | 2.7 | 1.6 |
| Manufacturing | 1.5 | 2.7 | 0.4 | 11.7 | 2.1 | 1.6 | 1.5 |
| **1986 per capita GNP (dollars)** | 1,810 | 1,320 | 3,680 | 2,370 | 1,860 | 1,830 | 4,860 |

**Source**: UN, *Industrial Statistics Yearbook* (1983, 1984, 1990)

**Notes:**
1. Include the following industries: Iron & Steel, Non-ferrous Metal, Metal Products, Machinery not elsewhere classified, Electrical Machinery, Transport Equipment, and Professional Goods.
2. Include the following industries: Industrial Chemicals, Other Chemicals, Petroleum Refineries, Petroleum & Coal Products, Rubber Products, and Plastic Products not elsewhere classified.
3. Include the following industries: Food Products, Beverages, Tobacco, Textiles, Apparel, Leather & Leather Products, Footwear, Wood Products, Furniture & Fixtures, Paper & Paper Products, Printing & Publishing, Pottery & China, Glass & Glass Products, Non-metal Products, and all other industries.
4. All figures are weighted averages unless otherwise stated. The weights are 1980 (except for South Africa, which is for July 1980-June 1981) output at producers' prices (including indirect taxes and excluding subsidies), except for Greece, South Africa, and Spain, which are at factor values (excluding indirect taxes and including subsidies).

because what matters in determining the relative attractiveness of export and production for the domestic market is the relative price structure, and not the 'average' incentives (for a more detailed discussion, see Wade, 1990: Chapter 5).

Moreover, on the empirical level, it is not true that Korean exporters could freely get inputs (raw material and machinery) at world market prices. Luedde-Neurath (1986: Chapter 4) shows that only raw materials can be described as relatively, but not absolutely, 'freely importable' in the Korean trade regime. The importation of machines was heavily controlled to promote the domestic machinery industry, which was seen as the vital ingredient in building a well-integrated economy (see later). Credits were usually refused to the importers of domestically available machines, and instead, subsidised credits, which often amounted to 90% of the product value, were provided to the purchasers of domestic machinery (KDB, 1981: pp. 473-4).

Moreover, it is quite incorrect to assert that the promotion of the heavy and chemical industries through a departure from the incentive neutrality was a failure. Table 2.2 compares the performance of Korea's three industry groups – that is, light, chemical, and heavy industries – between 1979 and 1988 with those of some countries at comparable levels of development, and, except for Brazil, with similar country size. While the Korean performances in all industry groups have been far better than those in other countries, the difference is especially pronounced in the heavy industries, where the Korean performance was truly spectacular.

The advance of the heavy and chemical industry products was not confined to the domestic market. Table 2.3 shows trade performance for commodities at 1- and 2-digit levels between 1977 and 1987. Almost all the items promoted through HCI – which roughly comprise Standard International Trade Classification (SITC) 5, 67, 68, and 7 – show (often dramatic) improvements in trade balances during this period. The export-import growth differentials (which show the rate at which the sectoral trade deficit [surplus] decreases [increases]) of these items are mostly higher than that between the overall exports and imports, although, again, the performance of chemical products does not particularly stand out. A detailed cost-benefit analysis of the HCI programme is beyond the scope of this chapter, but the above evidence suggests that the HCI programme, far from being a failure, produced impressive growth and trade performance, especially in the heavy industries.

## 3.2  Porous state intervention?

The theory of prescriptive state intervention proposed by Bhagwati (1985, 1987, 1988) tries to resolve the (neoclassical) dilemma of an interventionist state in a rapidly growing economy by characterising the Korean state as a 'prescriptive' state (one which identifies a number of 'dos'), as a contrast to a 'proscriptive' state (one which declares a number of 'don'ts'), such as that of India. According to this theory, state intervention in Korea does not hinder growth because it is less 'stifling'. According to Bhagwati (1988), 'although a prescriptive government may prescribe as badly as a proscriptive government proscribes, a proscriptive government will tend to stifle initiative, whereas a prescriptive government will tend to leave open areas (outside of the prescriptions) where initiative can be exercised' (pp. 98-9). That is, state intervention does not hinder growth because it is porous.

At a superficial level, it is hardly objectionable that an obstructive state will not be very helpful for business, and, by implication, economic growth. However, on closer examination, we find the theory theoretically and empirically unconvincing.

In a world with scarce resources (and therefore with opportunity costs), doing something means not doing something else. In this world, saying 'do' A is equivalent to saying 'don't' do 'not A'. And there can be no presumption that saying 'do' A (= 'don't' do 'not A' ) will allow more initiatives than saying 'don't' do A (= 'do' 'not A'). A prescriptive state can be as 'stifling' as a proscriptive one, since it can make private enterprises do so many things against their will that they are left with little resources to do what they want, even if these activities are not explicitly forbidden. Likewise, a proscriptive state may allow a lot of initiative if it proscribes only a few things. In fact, if we adopt the liberal concept of negative freedom, that is, 'freedom from' (on the different notions of freedom, see Berlin, 1969), we may say that one has less freedom under a prescriptive state than under a proscriptive one, because private enterprises with government prescription are coerced to execute the prescription, whereas the private

## Table 2.3: Trade Performance by Commodity Groups in Korea, 1977-87

| SITC | Commodities | Trade Balance (1977) | Trade Balance (1987) | Export Growth | Import Growth | Differ-ential |
|------|-------------|----------------------|----------------------|---------------|---------------|---------------|
| 0 | Food and Live Animals | 1.1 | 0.5 | 8.2 | 8.5 | -0.3 |
| 1 | Beverages and Tobacco | 0.4 | n.a. | -1.7 | n.a. | n.a. |
| 2 | Crude Materials, excluding Fuels | -7.9 | -6.2 | 4.3 | 11.7 | -7.4 |
| 3 | Mineral Fuels (e.g., petroleum, petroleum products) | -9.9 | -6.0 | 20.4 | 10.7 | 9.7 |
| 4 | Animal, Vegetable Oil and Fat | n.a. | n.a. | n.a. | 5.0 | n.a. |
| 5 | Chemicals and Related Products | -3.7 | -3.7 | 19.6 | 16.6 | 3.0 |
| 6 | Basic Manufactures | 7.2 | 4.5 | 12.9 | 15.2 | -2.3 |
| 61 | Leather, Dressed Fur, etc. | -0.5 | -0.4 | 23.7 | 15.4 | 8.3 |
| 62 | Rubber Manufactures n.e.c. | n.a. | 0.6 | 16.3 | n.a. | n.a. |
| 63 | Wood and Cork Manufacture n.e.c. (e.g., plywood) | n.a. | n.a. | -14.1 | n.a. | n.a. |
| 64 | Paper Products | 0.2 | 0.1 | 16.5 | 19.8 | -3.3 |
| 65 | Textile Yarn, Fabric, etc. | 3.5 | 3.0 | 14.1 | 15.2 | -0.9 |
| 66 | Nonmetal Mineral Manufactures n.e.c. (e.g., cement, glass) | 1.0 | 0.2 | 8.5 | 22.2 | -13.7 |
| 67 | Iron & Steel | -1.1 | 0.5 | 19.6 | 11.7 | 7.9 |
| 68 | Non-ferrous Metals | -0.8 | -0.8 | 27.3 | 18.4 | 8.9 |
| 69 | Metal Manufacture n.e.c. (e.g., tools, cables, cutlery) | 2.1 | 1.2 | 10.7 | 15.5 | -4.8 |
| 7 | Machines & Transport Equipments | -3.6 | 3.2 | 24.7 | 16.9 | 7.8 |

| SITC | Commodities | Trade Balance (1977) | Trade Balance (1987) | Export Growth | Import Growth | Differ-ential |
|------|-------------|----------------------|----------------------|---------------|---------------|---------------|
| 71 | Power Generating Equipments | -1.5 | -0.7 | 31.7 | 12.0 | 19.7 |
| 72 | Machinery for Special Industries (e.g., textile machinery) | -2.0 | -2.1 | 22.6 | 17.0 | 5.6 |
| 73 | Metal Working Machinery | n.a. | n.a. | n.a. | 11.2 | n.a. |
| 74 | General Industrial ` Machinery n.e.c. (e.g., furnaces, pumps) | -2.4 | -1.9 | 35.6 | 15.5 | 20.1 |
| 75 | Office Machinery (e.g., computers) | -0.0 | 0.8 | 39.3 | 28.5 | 10.8 |
| 76 | Telecommunication & Sound Equipment (e.g., TV, phone) | 1.2 | 4.4 | 25.4 | 15.3 | 10.1 |
| 77 | Electric Machinery n.e.c. (e.g., transformers, microchips) | -0.2 | -0.0 | 23.6 | 22.6 | 1.0 |
| 78 | Road Vehicles | -0.4 | 3.1 | 48.2 | 18.5 | 29.7 |
| 79 | Other Transport Equipment (e.g., ships, aircrafts) | 1.2 | 0.4 | 35.3 | 10.3 | 25.0 |
| 8 | Miscellaneous Manufactured Goods | 14.7 | 14.9 | 16.2 | 19.6 | -3.4 |
| 9 | Goods Not Classified by Kinds | n.a. | n.a. | n.a. | n.a. | n.a. |
| | Total | -3.8 | 7.0 | 16.8 | 14.3 | 2.5 |

**Source**: UN, International Trade Statistics (1980 and 1987)

**Notes:**
1. All figures are measured in percent.
2. Data for each commodity group appears only if the value in each year is greater than or equal to 0.3% of the total trade for that year.
3. Trade balance for commodity i is $(X_i - M_i)/\Sigma(X_j + M_j)$, where $X_i$ $(M_i)$ is exports (imports) of commodity i and X (M) is total exports (imports).
4. Export and import growth rates are average annual growth rates between 1977 and 1987 in current value terms.
5. The differentials are the differential between the export and import growth rates.

enterprises with a state proscription are not coerced into any particular action and therefore can choose the best option from whatever is not forbidden by the state (and thereby exercise 'initiatives').

The Korean state's prescriptions were certainly 'stifling' in many ways. The Korean state prescription for private firms to invest in heavy and chemical industries in the 1970s was a proscription against investing in less risky and often more profitable consumer goods industries. The best example in this regard is the shipbuilding industry, which grew literally from scratch to the world's second biggest in less than a decade.[6] The Korean shipbuilding industry was set up in direct response to a personal 'command' from the then president Park Chung Hee, against the will of the Hyundai group, the boldest of Korean business groups, which are famous for their boldness (Jones and Sakong, 1980: pp. 119-20, 357-8). Moreover, if private firms could not be made to do something, the Korean state did not hesitate to set up public enterprises, making the share of public enterprises in GDP almost equal to that of India (Jones and Mason, 1982: pp. 22-3). In a country like Korea where private firms depend heavily on the state-run banking sector for their investment funds, the state's channelling of money into public enterprises can have a very visible impact on 'private initiatives'.

Moreover, the degree of proscriptive intervention by the Korean state has not been so minimal as to warrant the description 'prescriptive' without serious qualifications. In addition to the restrictions on prices of foreign exchange and credit, there was a legally implemented direct price control over all marketed products up to 1973. And even after 1973, the state has reserved the right to impose a price ceiling when necessary. No price change is conceivable without formal and/or informal state permission, except in some unimportant markets.[7] In addition to price controls, most important Ko-

---

[6]   The Korean shipbuilding industry raised its share of world shipbuilding output from nil in 1973 (when the first modern shipyard started production) to 4% in 1980 and then to 21.6% in 1986. Korea now is the second-largest shipbuilding nation in the world (next to Japan), and produces more ships (in gross tonnes) than Western Europe as a whole, whose world production share was 12.2% in 1986 (NRI, 1988: pp. 162-4).

[7]   Reading Korean newspapers, one always finds that 'the government has allowed', and not that 'firm A has decided on', a certain percentage price rise of a product.

rean industries have had restrictions on entry and capacity (see Sub-section 4.2). Frequently, the Korean state 'reorganises' industries which it thinks have 'too many' firms, through state-led mergers and market-sharing arrangements (see Subsection 5.1). It is not clear to us what can be more 'stifling', if so many firms have so little freedom to decide what and how much to produce at what price.

## 4.    How Does State Intervention Work in Korea?

Some mainstream explanations of the Korean developmental experience were discussed above. Their attempts to downplay the role of the state in Korea are clearly unconvincing, on theoretical and empirical grounds. In this section, we present an account of the role of the state in the Korean developmental process. The account tries to draw both from the 'revealed' and the 'stated' policy objectives, which are found in various policy documents, and have hardly been investigated by researchers.[8] The account will be highly stylised, partly due to lack of space, but mainly due to the fact that it aims to raise new issues for future research, rather than to be a comprehensive and conclusive case study.

### 4.1   Themes of Korean state intervention

The basic theme of state intervention in Korea has been the making of an 'independent economy' (*Jarip Gyongjé*) (see various Five Year Plan (FYP) documents and EPB, 1982). The dependence on foreign savings for financing of investments was seen as the major economic problem by Korean policy-makers until recently. Policy-makers regarded the ultimate solution to this problem to be the construction of an economy with the degree of technological capability

---

[8]   The most important policy documents include various Five Year Plan (FYP) documents and the White Paper on the Economy (WP), annually produced by the Economic Planning Board (EPB), the super-ministry with both planning and budgeting authorities. The 1st FYP (1962-66) was issued in 1961, and was revised in 1964. Some of the later FYPs, for example, the 4th and the 6th, were also revised during the plan period, but the changes are mainly in macroeconomic forecasting, rather than in policy themes.

which would permit a reasonable living standard without a chronic balance-of-payments deficit. It was believed that the cause of balance-of-payments problems lay in the underdevelopment of capital and intermediate goods industries, and therefore that 'a shift towards heavy and chemical industries is imperative in order to increase the independence of the Korean economy' (WP, 1970: p. 340) – a principle known in Korea (and Japan) as 'upgrading' of the industrial structure (also see 2nd FYP: pp. 9-10; 3rd FYP: p. 1).

To Korean policy-makers, economic development required giving priority to investment, which was 'essential for growth' (WP, 1968: p. 48). Therefore, macroeconomic policy was geared towards the need to create an expansionary environment – if necessary, through inflationary measures – which was seen as vital for a sustained high level of investment. Until the late 1980s, of course, there existed a persistent savings gap, which had to be filled by foreign savings. Although the filling of the savings gap was believed to depend ultimately on rising income levels (a Keynesian savings assumption), serious attempts were also made to repress consumption demand through policy measures, expressed in unashamedly paternalistic terms like 'the need to establish a sound consumption pattern' (4th FYP: p. 27). The state-owned banks were instructed not to make consumer loans. The heavy reliance on indirect taxes was also justified (against the accusation that it is less equitable than income taxes) in terms of its discouraging effect on consumption (3rd FYP: p. 16). The control was even stricter when it came to consumption which involved foreign exchange expenditure. For example, foreign holidays were banned until the late 1980s, and imports of 'luxury' goods have been either banned or subject to high tariffs and inland taxes (see Section 2). One outcome of such anti-consumption policies is low passenger car ownership, discouraged by high taxation and restrictions on consumer loans until recently. Despite being the citizens of a major exporter of passenger cars, Koreans own far fewer passenger cars than other developing countries at comparable income level. In 1985, there were 73.5 people per passenger car in Korea, whereas the corresponding figures in 1983 were 27.0 in Taiwan, 21.8 in Chile, 16.3 in Malaysia, and 15.2 in Brazil (see NRI, 1988: p. 190, Table 9-8). Given such a clear (stated and revealed) anti-consumption bias, Korean macroeconomic policy may be more appropriately understood as 'investment management' rather than as 'aggregate demand management'.

Maintaining a high investment level through 'investment management' was, however, seen by the Korean policy-makers as necessary but insufficient to upgrade the industrial structure in a short period of time. Macroeconomic policy measures were seen as ineffective to rapidly upgrade the industrial structure, due to their uncertain impact on specific sectors, and were consequently given secondary status to industrial policy. It was explicitly stated that 'the market mechanism cannot be entirely trusted to increase competitive advantage of industries', and therefore sectors with high productivity growth potential had to be identified by the state and designated as 'promising strategic industries' (WP, 1984: p. 123), or 'priority' sectors, and given custom-designed financial, technical, and administrative supports (see later for details). Although macroeconomic constraints often set severe limitations on the conduct of industrial policy, the latter has been actively used whenever deemed necessary and practical. When the aim of macroeconomic stability clashed with the aim of upgrading the industrial structure, the latter was usually allowed to dominate, as testified to by the fact that preferential (subsidised) loans directed to the 'priority' sectors increase faster than general (non-subsidised) loans during recession periods, when the availability of financing can be a matter of life and death for firms (Ito, 1984; Chang, 1987). That is, even when the increase in the overall money supply is contained, the priority sectors are guaranteed financing, at the cost of non-priority sectors. The 'unfair' nature of such policy has been subject to criticisms in and outside Korea, but the dominant attitude in policy-making circles has been that being unfair in the short run is justified in the long run by the greater benefits generated by the priority sectors in the form of faster growth and more efficient structural change.

In moving towards high-productivity sectors, the biggest concern for Korean policy-makers was that these industries are often characterised by large scale economies (e.g., WP, 1968: p. 174).[9] The strong emphasis on scale economies is exemplified by EPB (1982), which diagnoses the cause of the troubles in the heavy and chemical

---

[9]  WP (1968) states that 'it is needless to say that the attainment or otherwise of efficient production scale is the most fundamental determinant of productivity' (p. 174).

industries in the early 1980s – an example which is often thought to be the classic case of overly ambitious investments (e.g., Lal, 1983) – as 'the lack of scale economies due to the participation of too many firms in each industry' (p. 222).

The prevalence of scale economies in many priority sectors posed two challenges to Korean policy-makers. One was that individual firms in these sectors needed to be large, in order to obtain the minimum efficient scale of production. Firms were often instructed by the state to build plants of efficient production scale, which compelled them to start exporting as soon as possible in order not to incur losses due to low capacity utilisation. And whenever firms were thought to be smaller than the minimum efficient scale, state-initiated or state-subsidised mergers were implemented. The most dramatic example of this was the 1980 'industrial reorganisation' (see Subsection 5.1). The mergers of two automobile producers in 1965, of five PVC firms in 1969 (see KDB, 1981) and the mergers within the fertiliser, shipping, and overseas construction industries in the 1980s (see Subsection 5.1; also Leipziger, 1988) are other examples. The other challenge from the presence of large scale economies was the high possibility of 'excessive competition', a term used among Korean (and Japanese) policy-makers to describe the well-known propensity of industries with large sunk costs to engage in price wars. As a result, serious attempts were made to restrict entry and regulate capacity expansion in such industries (see Subsection 4.2).

The apparent anti-trust implication of the above policies (merger, entry restriction, etc.) was regarded as secondary, because the Korean policy-makers thought that 'excessive competition' can result in 'social waste' (e.g., WP, 1968: p. 173). In traditional textbook economics where it is believed that large numbers guarantee competition and small numbers hamper it, the notion that there can be 'excessive competition' and that it can result in 'social waste' may not be readily accommodated.[10] However, as has been suggested by the Austrian/

---

[10] Of course, the mainstream economists have not been unaware of the possibility that competition can be 'wasteful'. The recent growth of the literatures on 'wasteful R&D' (for a survey, see Tirole, 1988: Chapter 10) and 'sunk cost' (for a survey, see Pindyck, 1991) attests to a growing disillusion with the traditional concept of competition even among mainstream economists. However, it seems fair to say that such developments have not been fully incorporated in the mainstream theory of competition in general.

Schumpeterian economics and the New Institutional Economics, competition is not a costless process in the presence of 'specific assets' which may not be redeployed without serious loss in value in cases of investment failures (on the notion of asset specificity, see Williamson, 1985).

Although they were not able to articulate this idea very clearly in theoretical terms, Korean policy-makers have regarded competition as a means to achieve efficiency rather than as an end in itself (on the different notions of competition, see Hayek, 1949; McNulty, 1968; O'Driscoll, 1986). This view is exemplified by the 6th FYP document, which states that collusive behaviour is allowed, and even encouraged, in 'promising industries' which need to 'increase R&D, improve quality [and] attain efficient production scale' and in 'declining industries' which need to 'scale down their capacities' (p. 79). Likewise, the anti-trust law (the Law for the Regulation of Monopoly and for Fair Trade), which came into being in 1981 after four abortive attempts at legislation (in 1964, 1966, 1969, and 1971), emphasised anti-competitive behaviour, rather than market concentration itself, although the growing criticism of the concentration of economic power in the hands of conglomerates brought about an amendment (in 1986) with stronger restrictions on cross-investments between members of the same conglomerates (see Paik et al., 1988: pp. 28-9, 40-2).

Another related theme of Korean state intervention is the policy-makers' attitude towards foreign firms. Korean policy-makers regarded assimilation of advanced technology by domestic firms as a vital condition for an effective industrial upgrading (for the issue of technology assimilation, see Rosenberg, 1982). To them, this meant tight state control over foreign direct investment.[11] Of course, the persistent savings gap had to be filled, but Korean policy-makers preferred (state-guaranteed) foreign loans to foreign direct investment. As a result, the share of foreign direct investment in total foreign

---

[11] Of course, this does not necessarily mean that it is impossible to develop national technological capability by inviting transnationals in. For example, Singapore has developed a sophisticated technological capability with a large multinational presence (see Evans, 1987: pp. 208-9). Likewise, there has been a substantial technological diffusion through subcontracting by transnationals in the Malaysian electronics industry in Penang (see Rasiah, 1990). The important question, then, seems to be what kinds of policies are necessary to promote technological transfer by transnationals.

capital inflow (except foreign aid) between 1962-83 was a mere 5% (see Amsden, 1989: p. 92, Table 5).

Although such restrictions have been weakening recently, even the latest version of the Law for Importation of Foreign Capital (amended 1988), which is regarded as a 'liberal' one by the Korean policy-makers, specifies that foreign direct investment is subject to restrictions in 'priority' industries, infant industries, industries with high imported raw material contents, (especially luxury) consumer goods industries, polluting industries, and agriculture and fishery – which can mean practically all industries, if the state so wishes. Even when foreign direct investment was allowed, foreign majority ownership was practically banned, with some rare exceptions, outside the Free Trade Zones. The fact that only 6% of TNCs in Korea are wholly-owned subsidiaries, compared to 50% in Mexico and 60% in Brazil, suggests a substantial degree of state control over foreign direct investment in relation to ownership (Evans, 1987: p. 208). Even technological licensing, which was preferred to foreign direct investment whenever feasible, was put under heavy restrictions. For example, the latest version of the Law for Importation of Foreign Capital clearly states that technological licensing is banned in industries where local technological capability is deemed to be promising – which, again, can effectively mean any industry.

### 4.2  Industrial policy

As suggested above, the dominance of industrial policy with a view to 'industrial upgrading' has been the most distinctive feature of Korean state intervention (for the seminal work in this line, see Amsden, 1989). The Korean state has chosen several industries at a time as the 'priority' sectors and provided massive support to them. Most of Korea's major industries were designated as priority sectors at some stage and were developed through a combination of massive support and heavy controls from the state. The 'designated' industries had priority in acquiring rationed (and often subsidised) credits and foreign exchange, state investment funds, preferential tax treatments (e.g., tax holidays, accelerated depreciation allowances), and other supportive measures, including import protection and entry restrictions. In return for these supports, they became subject to state controls on technology (e.g., production methods, products), entry, capacity expansion, and prices. The most important tool of such policy was the use of 'policy loans' (i.e., loans with subsidised interest rates and/or priorities in the [ubiquitous] credit rationing), which accounted for 57.9% of total bank loans made between 1962 and 1985 (Y. S. Lee *et al.*, 1987: p. 53, Table III-1).[12]

The practice of giving priority to certain industries identified as important originated in the very early years of Korean development, with the designation of cement, fertiliser, and oil refining in the 1st FYP (1962-66) as 'basic' industries.[13] In the 2nd FYP (1967-71), chemical, steel, and machinery were designated as 'priority' sectors. And during the 3rd and 4th FYP periods (1972-81), especially through the HCI programme (announced in 1973), non-ferrous metals, ship-building, and electronics were added to the list of 'priority' sectors. The practice continued in the 5th and the 6th FYP periods (1982-91), during which machinery, electronics, automobile, chemical, shipbuild-ing, and various high-tech industries (semiconductor, new materials, biotechnology) were designated 'priority' sectors.

Details of such support and control measures can be seen in Table 2.4, which summarises the measures employed in some selected Promotional Laws, enacted in the late 1960s and early 1970s (except for textiles) to provide legal backing for support for and controls over 'priority' sectors. The Korean policy-makers' concern over 'exces-sive competition' and the resulting 'social waste' (see Subsection 4.1) is reflected in the laws in the form of entry restrictions and regula-tions on capacity expansion. Violators of such restrictions could be heavily punished with the revocation of licences, fines, and, in some serious cases, prison sentences. Another interesting feature of these laws is the tight performance monitoring system. The monthly export performance monitoring by the Korean state is already famous (see,

---

[12] Credit availability becomes very important given the high leverage of Korean firms. The average equity participation ratio (as a proportion of total assets) of Korean manufacturing firms was 22.7% during 1971-79 (Cha, 1983: Table V-30). The same figure for 1986 was 22.2%, which is even lower than the Japanese figure for the same year (28.3%). Compare this with 47% for American firms (1986) and 46.8% for Taiwanese firms (1985) (see Paik *et al.*, 1988: p. 43, Table 1-6).

[13] The concept of 'basic' industries was also used in the early French planning prac-tice (Cohen, 1977).

e.g., Jones and Sakong, 1980: p. 97), but all firms in the 'promoted' industries were required to report on not just export performance but also performance in other areas. Failure to report regularly and/or false reporting could be punished with fines and prison sentences. Such a system provided the Korean state with up-to-date and detailed information concerning the state of business in priority sectors, something which is absolutely essential for an effective industrial policy.

More recently, various Promotional Laws were integrated into the Industrial Development Law (enacted in 1986). The novelty of the Industrial Development Law (IDL), compared to the Promotional Laws, is its emphasis on 'rationalisation programmes' with *limited*, albeit extendable, lifetimes (usually 2-3 years). The rationalisation programmes are custom-designed to the needs of individual industries and aim to provide temporary boosts for industries which need import substitution, capacity upgrading, and improvements in international competitiveness on the one hand, and temporary protections to 'declining' industries which need a smooth phasing-out on the other. Rationalisation programmes based on the IDL may be implemented on application from the industry, but it may also be implemented by the government *without any such application*.

The measures employed by the IDL can be divided into three categories (for details, see Kim, 1989: pp. 36, 62; Paik *et al.*, 1988: pp. 46-7; S.H. Lee, 1989: pp. 64-73). In the first place, there are protective measures to ease the adjustment process, which include import restrictions on competing products, reductions in tariffs for raw materials, price controls, and outright subsidies. Second, there are measures related to the attainment of optimal production scale and the prevention of 'excessive' competition. These include restrictions on entry and capacity expansion, state-initiated mergers, coordinated capacity scrapping and/or exit, and market-sharing arrangements (i.e., subdivision of markets into non-overlapping segments). Third, there are measures which aim to raise productivity. These include provision of subsidised credits for such activities as capacity upgrading (or capacity scrapping for 'declining' industries), import substitution of inputs (e.g., machine parts), subsidies for expenditures on R&D and training programmes, and joint research programmes between private firms and government-funded research institutes. As we can see, except for the introduction of limited lifetimes for rationalisation

| Table 2.4: Major Content of Promotional Laws | | | | | | | |
|---|---|---|---|---|---|---|---|
| Major Content<br><br>(Year of enactment) | Machi-nery<br><br>(1967) | Ship-build-ing<br>(1967) | Electro-nics<br><br>(1969) | Petro chemi-cal<br>(1970) | Iron & steel<br><br>(1970) | Non-ferrous metal<br>(1971) | Textile<br><br>(1979) |
| **REGULATIONS** | | | | | | | |
| **Entry Restriction** | x | x | x | x | x | x | x |
| **Capacity Regulations** | | | | | | | |
| Setting Up Facility Standard | x | x | | | | | |
| Capacity Expansion Approval | | | | x | x | | x |
| Incentives to Use Domestically Produced Facilities | x | | x | | | | |
| **Production Regulation** | | | | | | | |
| Regulation of Material Imports | | | | | x | x | |
| Production Standard and its Inspection | x | x | x | | x | x | |
| Restrictions on Technology Imports | x | | x | | | | |
| **Price Control** | | | | x | x | | |
| **Reporting and Inspection** | x | x | x | x | x | x | x |
| | | | | | | | |
| **RATIONALISATION** | | | | | | | |
| Rationalisation Programmes | x | x | x | x | | | x |
| | | | | | | | |
| **R&D SUPPORT** | | | | | | | |
| Subsidies to R&D | x | | x | x | x | | |
| Joint R&D Projects | | | x | | | | |
| | | | | | | | |
| **FINANCIAL SUPPORT** | | | | | | | |
| **Special Purpose Fund** | x | x | x | | x | x | x |
| **Financial Assistance** | x | x | x | | x | x | x |
| **Subsidies** | | | | | | | |
| Direct Subsidy | x | | | | | x | |
| Reduced Public Utility Rates | x | | | | x | | |
| **Tax Preferences** | | | | | | | |
| Special Depreciation | x | | | | | x | |

| Major Content<br><br>(Year of enactment) | Machinery<br><br>(1967) | Shipbuilding<br>(1967) | Electronics<br><br>(1969) | Petro chemical<br><br>(1970) | Iron & steel<br><br>(1970) | Nonferrous metal<br>(1971) | Textile<br><br>(1979) |
|---|---|---|---|---|---|---|---|
| Tax Reduction/<br>  Exemption | x | x | x | x | x | x | |
| SPECIAL INDUSTRIAL<br>COMPLEX | x | | x | x | | | x |
| ADMINISTRATIVE<br>ASSISTANCE<br>Facilitating Overseas<br>  Activities | | | x | | x | | |
| Purchase of Raw<br>  Materials | | | | | x | x | |
| PRODUCERS'<br>ASSOCIATION | x | x | x | | | | x |

**Source**: Kim (1989): p. 34, Table 3.1; S.H. Lee *et al.* (1989): pp. 52-9

programmes, which are absent in the Promotional Laws, the major characteristics of Korean industrial policy have changed very little with the introduction of the IDL. The policy measures used are virtually the same, and the discretion of the bureaucracy remains as great as before (because the eligibility criteria are deliberately made vague enough to cover any industry). The custom-designed nature of individual programmes also remains strong.

Since the enactment of the IDL in 1986, automobiles, coal-mining, dyeing, ferro-alloys, fertilisers, heavy construction machinery, heavy electrical equipment, naval diesel engines, and textile industries have undergone such rationalisation programmes (for details, see S.H. Lee, 1989: pp. 64-72; Kim, 1989). As we have mentioned before, the rationalisation programmes were custom-designed for the different needs of different industries. For industries which needed technology upgrading involving large sunk investments (automobiles, ferro-alloys, heavy construction machinery, heavy electrical machinery, and naval diesel engines industries), emphasis was given to creating a more stable environment for major new investments and R&D

activities, supported by state-led arrangements for market-sharing along product lines (among existing producers), entry restrictions, and subsidies for investment and R&D. For textiles and dyeing industries, which were identified as industries with satisfactory technological capabilities but aging capital stocks, the priority was capacity upgrading, and therefore subsidies were given to producers for scrapping old machines and installing new ones. For the (largely state-owned) fertiliser industry, where the local technological capability was already substantially developed, the programme aimed to introduce more competition in the product market, by granting sales licences to more distributors and by reducing tariffs on fertiliser imports (but at the same time reducing tariffs on raw-material imports). Coal-mining, which was identified as a 'declining' industry, had been under a phasing-out programme, which involved restrictions on entry and capacity expansion, subsidised capacity scrapping, price controls, and import restrictions.

## 5.    Why Does State Intervention Work in Korea?

In the previous section, we gave an account of how state intervention works in Korea. One interesting thing which emerges from our discussion in the previous section is that the policy measures used by the Korean state are not radically different from those often associated with economic failures in developing countries. This is contrary to the widespread belief that the Korean state's role, 'apart from the promotion of shipbuilding and steel . . . has been to create a modern infrastructure, to provide a stable incentive system, and to ensure that government bureaucracy will help rather than hinder exports' (Balassa, 1988: p. S286), while in the Latin American countries, 'there are pervasive controls of investment, prices, and imports and decisions are generally made on a case-by-case basis, thereby creating uncertainty for business decisions' (Balassa, 1988: p. S287). Why does the seemingly disastrous recipe of heavy-handed intervention work in Korea and not in other countries? In this section, we attempt some answers to this difficult question, although a full response to it would require a comparative study of the role of the state in different countries.

## 5.1    State-created rents and industrial development

Schumpeter (1987) emphasised that those who are starting 'new things' (p. 87), or innovating, need to be provided with 'profits far above what is necessary in order to induce the corresponding investment', or what he called entrepreneurial profits, which provide 'the baits that lure capital on to untried trials' (p. 90). According to him, this is because of the riskiness of innovative activity, which is 'like shooting at a target that is not only indistinct but moving – and moving jerkily at that' (p. 88). Schumpeter argued that the entrepreneurial profits, or what modern economics calls '(quasi-)rents', may sometimes be provided by the difficulty of imitating the new technology (or organisation), but sometimes would have to be secured through 'restraints of trade' like cartel arrangements (p. 91). The thrust of Schumpeter's argument is, then, that entry barriers of one form or another are necessary to provide incentives for innovation because it means doing 'new things'.

Establishing an industry in a late-developing country may not involve doing anything 'new' from the global point of view, but poses a similar incentive problem, because it still is a 'new thing' from the national point of view. In order to set up an industry, a late-developing country has to import technology, but making the imported technology work requires a period of 'learning', which is often a costly activity with highly uncertain returns (Rosenberg, 1982; Abramovitz, 1986; Dore, 1989). Such risk means that those who are starting new industries in a late-developing country have to be provided with some form of entry barriers and the resulting rents. Now, in the context of late development, the market mechanism may not provide such rents, if only because the firms who are borrowing technology from someone else cannot, by definition, set up an entry barrier with the help of the technology, as innovators on the frontier are able to do. Therefore, in a late-developing country, the state, as the ultimate guarantor of property rights, has to create some 'restraints of trade' and provide rents to those who are developing new industries (or even set up those industries itself). And this is exactly what the states in many late-developing countries, from Germany and Japan down to Korea and other currently developing countries, have tried to provide through tariff protection and other forms of state-created rents like subsidies and preferential loans.[14]

Of course, as the opponents of industrial policy correctly point out, there are certain dangers associated with industrial promotion through state-created rents. First of all, there is the risk of policy failure due to lack of information, because the state may not have the information necessary to intelligently 'pick the winners' (e.g., Burton, 1983; Grossman, 1988). Second, as the currently popular theory of rent-seeking argues, the existence of state-created rents can lead to 'social waste' by diverting entrepreneurial activities from productive activities into unproductive activities like lobbying (see, e.g., Krueger, 1974; Buchanan et al. (eds.), 1980; Colander (ed.), 1984). Third, state-created rents, once implemented, are not easy to remove, unlike market-created rents. The existence of 'infant' industries which refuse to grow is testimony to such a danger (for some evidence on infant-industry performance, see Bell et al., 1984). Korea, like other countries, had to face all the above problems. Korean policy-makers, naturally, made mistakes. The abuse of bureaucratic power, political favouritism, and corruption are hardly rare in Korea. And the country by no means lacks stories of rent-seeking activity. The puzzle is to explain, then, why in the case of Korea such dangers did not materialise sufficiently to inhibit rapid industrial development.

---

[14] From a purely static point of view, the states in late-developing countries should not deliberately seek to develop new industries, because it means, ceteris paribus, a less efficient use of resources. This was perhaps what was in their minds when various international lenders, including the World Bank and KISA (Korea International Steel Associates) – a consortium formed by steel-makers from the US, West Germany, the UK, and Italy – turned down Korea's three applications for loans to build an integrated steel mill in the 1960s (Amsden, 1989: p. 295; Watanabe, 1987: p. 69) or when the Bank of Japan was fiercely opposing the Ministry of International Trade and Industry's (MITI) effort to develop the automobile industry in the 1960s (Magaziner and Hout, 1980: p. 55). However, in a world where there is learning, the fact that an industry is unprofitable in a developing country at present prices does not mean that it should not be promoted, as the spectacular successes of Korea's (state-owned) steel mill and the Japanese automobile industry testify. After the above-mentioned three unsuccessful attempts to raise money for the steel mill, the Korean state was finally successful in securing funds through the war repatriation from the Japanese government and loans from the Japanese Ex-Im Bank (EPB, 1982: pp. 92-4). Ten years after it started operations, the state-owned steel mill (POSCO) became the fourth-largest and one of the most cost-efficient steel makers in the world (Amsden, 1989: pp. 298-9). The success of the Japanese automobile industry is too obvious to discuss any further.

The informational problem, we agree, is often a very serious one, especially in developing countries where basic statistics and other information which are routinely acquired in developed countries are not available. However, we would argue that the informational problem can be exaggerated and that it is solvable.

First of all, it is simply not true that private firms operate on the basis of perfect knowledge while bureaucrats know nothing about business. Private firms themselves often operate on the basis of 'informed guesses' or 'animal spirits' when they make major investment decisions, especially in new industries. In addition, large private firms, and not just the state, suffer from informational problems in controlling their divisions and subsidiaries. And when the state maintains an efficient information network of its own, as in the case of Korea, the informational gap between the private sector and the state may be virtually non-existent. The Korean state has kept very close track of priority industries through the obligatory reporting system (see Sub-section 4.2). And, in some respects, the state may often be better informed than the private sector, as exemplified by the important role played by the information collected by Korean state agencies, including the diplomatic service, and, more importantly, the Korean Trade Promotion Corporation (KOTRA) in the penetration of new export markets by Korean firms (see Jones and Sakong, 1980: p. 97).

Further, the difficulties of identifying 'sunrise' industries are not as great as often made out by opponents of industrial policy, except perhaps on the very frontier of technological development. There usually exists a widespread consensus as to which industries are 'sunrise' industries. For example, we all know that, say, automobile and microelectronics industries are going to be important in the conceivable future.[15] Especially in 'catching up' situations, it is fairly easy to

---

[15]   The reaction of the Korean conglomerates to the recent move by the Korean state to increase specialisation among them is instructive in this regard. In 1991, the Korean state forced the top 30 conglomerates to choose three 'core' lines of activity, which are to be exempted from the credit restrictions imposed on the member firms of top conglomerates in 1984 (in a move to mitigate the increasing concentration of economic power) in return for higher investments in technological development. Twelve of the top 30 conglomerates, for example, chose petrochemicals as their core business. Cars and electronics were also common choices (*Financial Times*, 23 April 1991). This shows that there exists a common view on which industries are 'sunrise' industries.

identify which sectors to favour and what kinds of support are required for success (Dore, 1986: p. 135). The fact that the Korean economic bureaucracy has been traditionally manned by lawyers (at least until the 1970s) also suggests that 'expert' knowledge in the conventional sense may not be necessary for solving the informational problem.[16]

Recently, the proponents of rent-seeking arguments pointed out that industrial policy may, by opening up opportunities to acquire wealth through unproductive activities such as influence-peddling, divert entrepreneurial efforts away from productive activities. However, if the 'waste' from rent-seeking activities has been an obstacle to growth in Turkey or India (e.g., Krueger, 1974; Mohammad and Whalley, 1984), why has this apparently not been the case in Korea?[17]

Rent-seeking costs are fundamentally 'transaction costs' expended in the process of seeking rents (which will involve activities like information collection, influence-peddling, and bargaining), and have to be strictly differentiated from the rent itself, which is a pure transfer (Chang and Rowthorn, 1990, and Chang, 1991: Chapter 1). Therefore, the mere existence of state-created rents – and therefore the opportunity for rent-seeking – does not mean that resources will actually be spent on rent-seeking. The realised magnitude of rent-seeking costs in a society will depend on how state-created rents can be obtained (Khan, 1989). For example, it has often been suggested that less resources are spent on influencing the state in Korea, because there is not much point in spending resources to influence a

---

[16] In terms of their theoretical foundation, the earlier Korean planning documents do not compare with, say, the Indian ones, which were based on such sophisticated theoretical models as the Mahalanobis model.

[17] Bhagwati (1988) has suggested that 'prescriptive governments provide fewer inducements for such unproductive activities, because the prescriptions leave large areas open for initiatives' (p. 100). Nevertheless, prescriptive policy is no less prone to rent-seeking activities, because the logic of rent-seeking activities is such that, even if there are large areas open for private initiatives, individuals will engage in such activities if their rate of return is higher than in those areas which are 'open for initiatives'. For example, it is well known in Korea that obtaining subsidised credits (by being a producer in a 'priority' sector) is a very profitable business in itself, because one can divert that money into the curb market where real interest rates can be more than 40 percentage points higher than that of the subsidised credit (see Table 2.1).

'hard' state (in the Myrdalian sense) like that of Korea (e.g., Bardhan, 1984). One difficulty with this view is that, as is well known to any-one familiar with Korean politics and business, the country by no means lacks stories of huge corruption scandals, a sign that the Ko-rean state certainly is subject to influence, if less than other, 'softer' states.[18] The explanation thus has to be more sophisticated.

We think one solution to this puzzle lies in the fact that the Ko-rean state is subject to influence, but mainly to influence from a small, exclusive group of agents, that is, the *chaebols*. Although this prac-tice has produced some undesirable distributional consequences, it seems to have reduced rent-seeking costs in Korea in several ways. First, when a small number of people have exclusive access to rents, rent-seeking activities will be less frequent and of smaller magnitude, because others may not join the rent-seeking contests, knowing that they have little chance of success in influencing the state (this is what Bhagwati (1988) calls the 'brother-in-law theorem'). Second, since the *chaebols* as a group have exclusive access, they do not need to spend much resources to find out what kind of agent the present op-ponent is (e.g., his/her strategy and belief), because they are frequently confronted with the same adversaries in different rent-seeking con-tests. Third, the fact that the *chaebols* are conglomerates, with stakes in multiple markets, also reduces rent-seeking costs by the 'bundling of issues'. A bargaining solution can be more easily devised if there are other related bargains which allow more room for arranging side-payments (see Schelling, 1960: pp. 32-3).[19]

Moreover, rent-seeking cost is often of a once-and-for-all na-ture, because once a rent is granted, there will be an 'entry barrier' into the 'rent market' which will discourage the potential entrants from spending resources to dislodge the incumbent. The more seri-

---

[18] The head of one of the country's largest companies is reported to have recently complained that "[t]he government has all the power and you have to purchase approval . . . [and as a result] we pay as much in extortion – legal, semi-legal and illegal extortion – as we do in legitimate taxes" (*FEER*, 30 May 1991: p. 54).

[19] In the 1980 industrial reorganisation, Daewoo, the third largest *chaebol*, remained in the passenger car market as one of the duopolists, but was forced both to exit from the diesel engine industry and to specialise in a cheaper variety of products in the electronic switching system industry; Hyundai, the second largest *chaebol*, remained in the passenger car industry in return for forced specialisations in die-sel engines and in heavy electrical machinery industries.

ous danger associated with the use of state-created rents is that state intervention may protect or even encourage inefficient producers or production methods, with a long-lasting efficiency consequence. This problem is not explicitly discussed in the rent-seeking literature, which normally assumes that all rent-seeking agents are identical and use optimal production methods. However, in the real world, there is no guarantee that someone who is competent (or even lucky) at seeking rents is equally competent as a producer, although this may well be the case, if rent-seeking takes the form of franchise bidding. In Korea, the assumption of 'equal competence' of agents is paradoxically met due to the limitation of access to state-created rents to the *chaebols*, which, as conglomerates, are able to operate in almost any line of business equally well. That is, state-created rents in Korea may generate a certain amount of once-and-for-all 'transaction costs' (rent-seeking costs), which are likely to be small anyway, but generate few long-lasting production inefficiencies (for a seminal argument along this line, see Khan, 1989).

Probably the most serious problem with industrial policy is that, once implemented, state-created rents may be difficult to withdraw due to political pressure from the recipients of such rents. As was powerfully argued by Marx's theory of 'surplus profit' (1981, e.g., pp. 373-4) and Schumpeter's theory of 'entrepreneurial profit' (1961: Chapter 4), the beneficial role of rents, as a means to lure (positive rents) and force (negative rents) firms into more productive activities, hinges on the fact that no rent accruing to 'the innovator' is permanent. In a situation where rents are created by the state, however, these rents may cease to be transitory and become semi-permanent, if the state is unable to withdraw them when necessary.[20]

Indeed, Korea is no different from other countries in that industrial policy has created many inefficient firms. However, what differentiates Korea from other countries is that the Korean state has been willing and able to withdraw supports whenever performance lagged (Khan, 1989; Amsden, 1989; Shapiro and Taylor, 1990). Such state discipline, when combined with the strategy of 'industrial upgrading'

---

[20] The introduction of limited lifetimes for rationalisation programmes due to the implementation of the IDL may be understood as an attempt to increase the 'transitory' nature of rents.

(which involves the creation of new and often bigger rents in more productive industries), has acted as a powerful incentive for the firms to enhance technological capabilities. The imposition of such discipline, of course, has not been a purely technocratic procedure whereby the impartial bureaucrats teach non-performers a lesson, nor has it been a smooth and consensual procedure. It has been, rather, a painful process of continuous bargaining and conflicts between the state and the private sector, which, as we shall see below, sometimes had to be solved by forceful measures which are difficult to imagine in other countries.[21]

In 1969, the proliferation of inefficient firms after a massive investment boom in the late 1960s prompted the Korean state to set up a task force accountable only to the Blue House (the presidential residence) to deal with the problem. Between 1969 and 1972, the task force forced dozens of inefficient firms (exact numbers not released) into mergers, sales, and liquidation (sometimes sweetened by debt roll-overs by the Korea Development Bank). The programme eventually ended with the notorious 8-3 Decree (following the date of its announcement, 3 August 1972), involving a total freeze on all curb market loans which were eating into the profits of many firms under financial distress, with subsequent reduction in their interest rates and/or debt-equity swap (for details, see S.H. Lee, 1985).

After the investment boom of the late 1970s, which led to temporary excess capacity in some major industries, the Korean state stepped in again with the Reorganisation of Heavy and Chemical Industries programme (for more details, see Chang, 1987). Four existing companies in the power-generating equipment industry were merged into Korea Heavy Industries and Construction Co. (KHIC), which was subsequently nationalised, on the ground that the state support needed to make KHIC profitable was too big to be given to a single private firm.[22] In the passenger car industry, one of the three existing producers (Kia) was forced to exit and specialise in trucks

---

[21] For an illuminating discussion of the role of bargaining and conflicts in the process of imposition of state discipline on the private sector, see Khan (1989).

[22] In addition to rolling over KHIC's debt (details not released), the state tried to boost its activities by giving it monopoly rights to produce certain power-generation components and certain heavy construction equipments (*FEER*, 2 June 1983: pp. 67-8).

and buses, with a promise that it would be allowed in again when demand conditions improved (this actually occurred).[23] One of the three companies in the naval diesel engine industry (Daewoo) was forced to exit, and the other two were forced to split the market into two segments and specialise (Hyundai in over-6,000 hp and Ssangyong in under-6,000 hp engines). In the heavy electrical machinery industry, where there existed eight companies, three (Hyosung, Ssangyong, Kolon) were merged into one (Hyosung) and allowed to produce only highly specialised and expensive products. A subsidiary of Hyundai was asked to produce only for its sister companies. Four other minor companies were forced to produce only less sophisticated and cheaper products. Each of the four companies in the electronic switching system industry (Samsung, Gold Star, OPC, and Daewoo) was forced to specialise in a different product. The two companies in the copper smelting industry were merged by forcing one to buy the other's equity, which was supported by equity participation of the Korea Development Bank and a moratorium on bank loans repayment.

---

[23] The history of the passenger car industry characteristically shows how the Korean state shapes up a targeted industry (the following account is based on KDB, 1981: pp. 501-6). The Korean passenger car industry started in 1962 with assemblage of imported semi-knocked-down (SKD) kits. In 1965, there was a state-led merger between the two existing passenger car makers (Senara and Shinjin) into one (Shinjin). In 1968, there were two more entries (Hyundai and Asia), and, thereafter, new entry was banned until 1972, when a lorry producer, Kia, was allowed to enter. In 1974, the government announced the Long-term Plan for Promotion of Automobile Industry to develop local passenger car models (at this point, passenger car producers were still assembling completely-knocked-down (CKD) kits from Toyota, Ford, GM, and Fiat), and forced Asia, which failed to submit a plan for the development of local passenger car models, to exit and its capacities to be bought by Kia. From 1974, local models were developed (Kia's Brisa in 1974, Hyundai's Pony in 1975, GMK's Gemini in 1977). In the meantime, Shinjin withdrew from GMK (its joint venture with GM since 1972) due to a sales crisis of the newly introduced Chevrolet models. Shinjin's stake was bought by the Korea Development Bank (KDB) (hence a KDB-GM joint venture), which ultimately sold it to Daewoo in 1978 (hence a GM-Daewoo joint venture since then). In the 1980 reorganisation of the sector, the original plan was to force Kia to exit and to merge Hyundai and Daewoo, but it was aborted because the policy-makers would not accept Daewoo's plan to abandon local models in favour of GM 'world car' models. The market was maintained as a duopoly between Hyundai and Daewoo until 1987, when Kia was allowed in again.

Another round of state-led mergers and liquidations of inefficient firms occurred between 1984 and 1988 (see S.H. Lee *et al.*,
1989: pp. 60-2). This time, the shipping, overseas construction, and
fertiliser industries, which were identified as declining industries,
formed the focus of the programme. In 1984, three fertiliser producers were liquidated, and 63 shipping companies were merged into 17.
In 1986, a major reorganisation of the overseas construction industry
was implemented. And between 1986 and 1988, 82 inefficient firms
(23 of them in shipping and overseas construction industries) were
forced into liquidation and mergers.

What is notable in the conduct of such 'reorganisation'
programmes is that even the economically and politically powerful
conglomerates, *chaebols*, as individual conglomerates, were not im-
mune to state discipline, although, as a group, they were certainly
privileged in their access to various rents. To the Korean policy-makers, it matters less who runs a business as long as it is run efficiently.
If a particular *chaebol* runs a plant well, fine; otherwise, the ownership has to be transferred to another *chaebol* or even to the public
sector (e.g., nationalisation of KHIC). The fact that the *chaebols* as
conglomerates are potentially able to move into any line of business
(on the basis of their activities in related lines) makes it difficult for a
*chaebol* to keep a particular industry as its fiefdom. Unless it remains
reasonably efficient, other *chaebols* can easily persuade the state that
they can do a better job and get the state support in the next round of
capacity expansion in that industry. Therefore, the *chaebols* had a
powerful incentive to remain efficient, especially when the loss of
state support can mean a sharp downturn in business in a few years'
time, given the state control of credit and the high leverage of Korean
firms. Many *chaebols* which lost state favour (for political and/or
efficiency reasons) went into oblivion or were disbanded and their
carcasses were distributed to other *chaebols*, as exemplified by the
fact that only two of the 10 biggest *chaebols* in 1966 were among the
top 10 in 1974, only five of the 1974 top 10 were in the 1980 top 10,
and only six of the 1980 top 10 were in the 1985 top 10 (Paik *et al.*,
1988: p. 352, Table 35).

## 5.2   The bases of state power: History, politics, and economics

The Korean state played a central role in the country's economic development through its cunning use of state-created rents as an instrument for industrial development. Of course, such a result was only possible because the Korean state was a strong state which could discipline firms whenever necessary.[24] What was the basis for such state power?

It has often been suggested that the Korean state could become strong because the country's historical development left a social structure with no powerful social classes to contest state power (Hamilton, 1983; Lim, 1985; Evans, 1987; Amsden, 1989: Chapter 2). The landed class was eliminated through land reform around the time of the Korean War, and the incipient (largely socialist) political organisations of the working class and the farmers were also crushed during the war and the subsequent domination of Cold War politics. Moreover, it is argued that the country's long history of Confucian tradition produced a society where the state commands the moral high ground and draws in the best talents (e.g., Luedde-Neurath, 1985).[25] The long tradition of centralisation in Korean history seems to have been another factor serving to legitimise the power possessed by the central bureaucracy.[26]

---

[24]   The power of the Korean state has frequently been underrated, especially by some neoclassical economists (e.g., Balassa, 1988), on the ground that the 'size' of the Korean state (defined in terms of public sector expenditure) is relatively small (but see Sachs (1987) for some evidence to the contrary). However, what matters for the effectiveness or otherwise of state intervention is not where the boundary of the state as a legal entity lies, but how far it can exercise its influence. Public sector expenditure as usually defined is a very poor measure of this.

[25]   However, Confucianism in itself is not necessarily beneficial to economic development. Its contempt for commercial and industrial pursuits (the merchant and the craftsman occupied the two lowest castes in the traditional Confucian social hierarchy) could have acted as an obstacle to industrialisation. Actually, Confucianism, often hailed currently as the reason for the Korean success, was often blamed for the relatively poor Korean economic performance in the 1950s.

[26]   Korea has traditionally been even more centralised than other Confucian countries. The Japanese feudal system was fairly decentralised until the Meiji Restoration, and the Chinese system, due to the sheer size of the country, had a strong tendency to dissolve into a decentralised one except in the prime time of a dynasty.

We think that these historical factors are extremely important, and perhaps what differentiate Korea most from, say, India or Latin America (on India, see Datta-Chaudhuri, 1990; on Latin America, see Fishlow, 1990, and Shapiro and Taylor, 1990). The weakness of social classes was certainly important in deciding the balance of power between the state and society in Korea. The Confucian belief in the state as a legitimate social institution (if not necessarily in particular governments and individual political leaders), often lacking in other developing countries, also seems to have been an important factor in making state intervention effective in Korea.

However, we think that such historical factors are, in themselves, not enough to bring about a strong state. For example, if social classes had been weak since the end of the Korean War, why was the Korean state so weak and incompetent in the 1950s? For another example, if Confucianism is conducive to a strong and competent state, why was the Kuomintang government before 1949 so weak and incompetent? Although a full discussion of the subject is beyond the scope of this chapter, we would argue that the strong state should be understood as an outcome of the conscious actions taken by the military regime of General Park Chung Hee, which fundamentally shaped the political economy of the country for decades to come. The strong Korean state was, as we shall soon see, as much, if not more, an outcome of calculated political moves and institutional innovations as of the historical conditions and culture.

The political ideas of the top political decision-makers of the military regime were fundamentally shaped in the shadow of the Japanese variety of corporatism.[27] In terms of their economics, the early Korean top political decision-makers were no fans of the free market,

---

[27] Park was a fierce nationalist strongly influenced by corporatist and communist ideas. His education in the Japanese military academy in Manchuria, which he joined after a brief career as a school teacher, left him deeply influenced by the Japanese variety of corporatism, as is testified by his naming the 'October Restoration' in 1972, his own mid-career political coup to guarantee himself a lifetime presidency, after the Meiji Restoration. He was also strongly influenced by communism, which was a torch-bearer of the Korean nationalist movement under Japanese colonial rule. His brother was an influential local communist leader, and he himself was sentenced to death (but earned an amnesty by publicly denouncing communism) as one of the leaders of a communist mutiny within the Korean army in 1949. His close political aides shared similar ideas.

although they had to pay constant lip service to the 'free enterprise economy', given the critical importance of US support for the political survival of the regime.[28] In addition, whatever little economic knowledge the early Korean economic bureaucracy had was not neoclassical economics but the economic theories of Friedrich List, Joseph Schumpeter, and especially Karl Marx, which dominated Japanese academia and policy-making circles in the first half of the 20th century (see Morris-Suzuki, 1989). The major themes of Korean economic policy-making, for example, the concern with 'social waste' from 'excessive competition', the emphasis on scale economies (and large firms), the obsession with capital accumulation (reflected in the anti-consumption bias), and the desire to develop heavy and chemical industries, make more sense when we understand the intellectual background of the economic bureaucracy. Given such a background, it is more than natural that the political-economic agenda of the Park regime was summarised as 'guided capitalism' (*Gyodo Jabon-Jui*), where the state plays a guardian role.

As soon as it came to power, the Park regime moved swiftly to prepare some institutional ground for its political-economic agenda. One of its first moves was to nationalise all the banks, and therefore to gain control over the financial flows in the economy. Subsequently, new state-owned banks (e.g., the Korean Exchange Bank, the Bank for Medium and Small Firms, the Ex-Im Bank) were set up over a period of time, resulting in full state control over investment loans.[29] At the same time, the Park regime imprisoned many prominent businessmen on the charge of having accumulated wealth through 'illicit' means (e.g., using political connections) and later released them in return for their promises to 'serve the nation through enterprise', which basically meant building new plants in state-designated industries (the so-called 'Illicit Wealth Accumulation' episode; see Jones and Sakong, 1980: pp. 69-70, 281-2). With these two major political blows, the

---

[28] With the growing acceptance of 'private initiative', later policy documents (especially the 5th and the 6th FYP documents) emphasised the government's commitment to the 'private-led economy', but this testifies to the persisting dominance of the state (if the economy was already 'private-led', no comments of this sort would have been necessary).

[29] Short-term working capital, given credit rationing, was mainly provided either by small non-bank financial institutions or by the curb market.

business community suddenly became, morally, criminals on parole on condition that they 'served the nation through enterprise', and, economically, a paper tiger with little power to make investment decisions – the ultimate capitalist prerogative.

Another important institutional innovation made by the Park regime was the centralisation of economic policy-making power in the hands of the super-ministry headed by the deputy prime minister, namely, the Economic Planning Board (EPB) (see Whang, 1991: pp. 86-7). The integration of both planning and budgeting authorities within the EPB eliminated the conflict of interests, if at the cost of concentration of power within the government (which may be objected to on other grounds), between the planning and industrial ministries (which are usually more interested in long-term investments) and the finance ministry (which is usually more interested in short-term stability). Elimination of such conflict made the implementation of industrial policy in Korea more effective than in other 'industrial policy states' like Japan and France where such conflict has been a problem (see Johnson (1982) for Japan; see Hall (1987) for France).

Even the much-vaunted cultural and ideological homogeneity of the Korean society was not purely a historical bounty which the nation accidentally stumbled on. The Park regime mobilised the nation with the ideology of 'Renaissance of the Nation' through the building of *Jarip Gyongjé* (independent economy). Workers were described by the state-controlled media and state-issued school textbooks as 'industrial soldiers' fighting a patriotic war against poverty (although the labour movement was brutally suppressed) and businessmen were given medals for their achievement of export targets as if they were generals who won major battles. Farmers were mobilised into semi-compulsory (unpaid) labour for rural infrastructural development a là Mao Tse Tung, through the 'Sémaul (New Village) Movement' (Michell, 1982: pp. 205-8). Although not all such ideological mobilisations were successful (for example, the Sémaul Movement was much resented) and some may criticise them as 'militarising' the society (e.g., Halliday, 1980), it is undeniable that they were important in promoting the society's ideological homogeneity.

The Korean state has continued to occupy such economic and moral commanding heights throughout the country's developmental period. State control over credit, which has been the most effective means to control the private firms, given their high leverage (see above), continued, although some of the state-owned banks (the so-called 'city banks') were partially 'privatised' in 1982. Despite privatisation, the independence of these banks is almost nil, given their over-exposure to highly-borrowed firms and their consequent dependence on the central bank, which is under the full control of the state.[30] Indeed, following the 'privatisation', the share of 'policy loans' has actually increased, from 56.0% (1962-81) to 67.6% (1982-85), making it very difficult to argue that state control over the banking sector has loosened. In addition to their freedom to make loan decisions, the banks' freedom to set interest rates has also been severely limited. Despite the legal deregulation of rates on loans and long-term deposits in December 1988, it was reported in 1991 that '[i]nterest rates are still strictly controlled by guidance from the Bank of Korea and the Ministry of Finance (*FEER*, 30 May 1991: p. 52).

In addition to its control over the domestic financial flows, the Korean state has maintained tight foreign exchange controls. The buying and selling of foreign exchange has been tightly regulated, and up to a few years ago it was illegal (subject to prison sentence) to possess foreign exchange except for business purposes. The state's control over foreign loans and foreign direct investment has been near-absolute. Although foreign borrowing and, to a lesser degree, foreign direct investment have not been discouraged, the state has had the final say in deciding whether a certain loan or foreign direct investment would be permitted, and on what terms.

Albeit far less important than the control over financial resources, the state's control over material resources through public enterprises should not be ignored. The Korean state has owned various strategic industries, including oil, coal (partly), gas, fertiliser, steel, and electricity. The fact that such crucial intermediate inputs as oil, coal, gas, electricity, steel, and fertiliser (used as a means to control the farmers) are supplied by public enterprises is another important factor contributing to the power of the state.

---

[30] 'The government [as of 1988] appoints senior bank officials and major credit allocation decisions have traditionally been cleared with government authorities' (*FEER*, 21 April 1988: p. 58).

Of course, the regular threat by the Korean state that it is going to use this power to discipline the non-performers (e.g., that it will restrict loans to firms which do not comply with a particular policy) does not always materialise, partly because large business firms have a strong influence on policy formation and implementation. Nevertheless, such a threat is not an idle one and is often realised, as exemplified by the freezing of bank credit (on 8 May 1991) to 14 subsidiaries of eight conglomerates that had not complied with state pressure to sell non-business land (EIU, 1991: p. 20). A still more dramatic example is the Kukje group incident in 1985, when the state deliberately bankrupted the inefficiently run Kukje group, the then-seventh-largest conglomerate in the country, by ordering its major lending bank not to honour its cheques (for details, see *FEER*, 21 April 1988: pp. 58-60). Although it is believed that the decision to let Kukje go under was in part motivated by its lukewarm attitude in meeting the ruling party's financial demands, this is a good example of how far the Korean state can go, if it chooses.

## 6.   Conclusion

To begin with, the Korean experience shows that a development strategy is a complex set of interrelated policies rather than a simple matter of trade regime, as is often implied by debates between the proponents of 'outward-looking' and of 'inward-looking' strategies. Without doubt, trade strategy is a crucial ingredient of a developmental strategy, especially because, as we have seen in the Korean case, the fastest way to build up an advanced industrial base in a developing country is to earn foreign exchange to import advanced technologies and the machines which embody them. Nevertheless, the Korean success was based on a conception of economic development which was far more encompassing than mere trade strategy. Development strategy is a multidimensional problem involving such wide-ranging areas as the establishment of long-term targets for growth and structural change, investments in productive facilities and infrastructure, the supply of an adequate labour force with industrial competence and discipline, and technological catching-up and development. Development strategy should not be discussed in terms of the misconceived dichotomy between export-led (or outward-looking) and import-substituting (or inward-looking) strategies.

Secondly, the Korean experience shows the importance of a long-term dynamic perspective in managing an industrial transition. The industrial transition in Korea was achieved not mainly through the attainment of short-term static efficiency ('getting the prices right'), but mainly through the pursuit of long-term dynamic efficiency through the state's constant creation of rents (or Marxian/Schumpeterian profits). A constant upgrading of industrial structure based on the development of local technological and managerial capabilities was seen by the Korean policy-makers as the surest way to achieve sustained growth and efficient structural change, and hence higher living standards. The state's control over technological transfers and foreign direct investments, and the state's commitment to long-term lending through state-owned banks and various special investment funds have been vital in this respect. Many individual instances of intervention in Korea might have appeared inefficient and sometimes even megalomaniac from a short-term static point of view (e.g., the establishment of steel and shipbuilding industries), but when viewed from a long-term dynamic point of view, most, if not all, make sense.

Thirdly, the Korean experience suggests that a rethinking of the concept of competition is necessary. Until recently, the obsession of Korean (and other, notably Japanese) policy-makers with 'excessive competition' and the resulting 'social waste' had, unfortunately, been regarded as a sign of the stupidity of the bureaucrats who lack a good education in economics. However, as we have pointed out earlier (Subsection 4.1), such concerns are more than legitimate in a world with asset specificity, because, in such a world, competition is not a costless process. Ultimately, competition is a means to achieve efficiency, and not an end in itself. We value competition because it can produce more than what it costs, and not simply because it is categorically good. And, if the technological and institutional conditions are such that there is going to be 'excessive competition', suppressing competition may be efficient. The Korean experience comes as a serious challenge to the mainstream conception of competition, which is unable to explain why the Korean policy-makers could use

all those blatantly 'anti-competitive' (in the neoclassical sense) policies to generate some of the most rapid growth rates and structural
change ever seen in human history.

Last but not least, the Korean experience may be 'unique' in the
sense that it was supported by a set of idiosyncratic institutions, but
this does not mean that it is irrelevant for other countries which share
different histories.[31] Practically all cases of successful industrialisation
after the British one were based on conscious efforts to import and
modify more advanced nations' institutions. Korea, and its predeces-
sor, Japan, are classic examples of such 'institutional learning'. Even
when an institution is not transplantable, it is often possible to create
some, at least partial, functional equivalent for it.[32] And, if all else
fails, there is still the possibility of institutional innovation through
conscious design. For example, the famous Swedish 'consensus' between labour and capital was constructed from the most contested
industrial relations system in Europe of the 1920s (Korpi, 1983: Chapter 3). Moreover, the construction of a new and well-functioning institution need not take a long time. The famous Japanese lifetime
employment is basically a postwar creation (Johnson, 1982: Chapter
4). The French state, once regarded as one of the most 'archaic' states
in Europe, transformed itself into one of the most 'modernising' ones
in the world soon after the Second World War (Cohen, 1977: Chapter
4). And, as we have tried to show, Korea is another example of how
a well-functioning system can be constructed in a reasonably short
period of time through conscious collective actions.

---

[31] For a rare attempt to consider the importance of the idiosyncratic factors in the
developmental experience of East Asian NICs in general (Korea, Taiwan,
Singapore, and Hong Kong), see Nolan (1990).

[32] For example, the Swedish system of state-guaranteed employment and Japanese
lifetime employment are radically different from each other in many respects, but
as far as they create positive attitudes among workers towards the introduction of
more mechanised (and hence generally more productive) technology, they are
functionally equivalent to each other. It is no coincidence that these two countries are the most robotised economies in the world.

# Bibliography

Abramovitz, M. (1986). 'Catching Up, Forging Ahead, and Falling Behind', *Journal of Economic History*, vol.46, no.2.

Amsden, A. (1989). *Asia's Next Giant*. New York: Oxford University Press.

Balassa, B. (1982). 'Development Strategies and Economic Performance', in B. Balassa *et al.*, *Development Strategies in Semi-Industrial Economies*. Baltimore: The Johns Hopkins University Press.

Balassa, B. (1988). 'The Lessons of East Asian Development: An Overview', *Economic Development and Cultural Change*, vol. 36, no. 3, Apr. (1988), Supplement.

Bardhan, P. (1984). *The Political Economy of Development in India*. Oxford: Basil Blackwell.

Bell, M., Ross-Larson, B. & Westphal, L. (1984). 'Assessing the Performance of Infant Industries', *Journal of Development Economics*, (1984), nos. 1/2.

Berlin, I. (1969). 'Two Concepts of Liberty', in I. Berlin, *Four Essays on Liberty*. Oxford: Oxford University Press.

Bhagwati, J. (1985). 'Foreign Trade Regimes', in J. Bhagwati, *Dependence and Interdependence*. Oxford: Basil Blackwell.

Bhagwati, J. (1987). 'Outward Orientation: Trade Issues', in V. Corbo, M. Khan & M. Goldstein (eds.), *Growth-Oriented Structural Adjustment*. Washington, D.C.: IMF & World Bank.

Bhagwati, J. (1988). *Protectionism*. Cambridge, Massachusetts: The MIT Press.

BOK (Bank of Korea) (1987). *National Accounts*. Seoul: BOK.

BOK (Bank of Korea) (1988). *Economic Statistics Yearbook (1988)*. Seoul: BOK.

Bruton, H. (1989). 'Import Substitution', in H. Chenery & T. Srinivasan (eds.), *Handbook of Development Economics*, vol. 2. Amsterdam: Elsevier Science Publishers.

Buchanan, J., Tollison, R. & Tullock, G. (eds.) (1980). *Toward a Theory of the Rent-Seeking Society*. College Station: Texas A&M University Press.

Burton, J. (1983). *Picking Losers . . . ?: The Political Economy of Industrial Policy*. London: Institute of Economic Affairs.

Cha, D.S. (1983). *Öja Do-ip ui Hyokkwa Boonsok* (The Effects of Foreign Capital Inflow). Seoul: Korea Institute for Economics and Technology (KIET).

Chang, H-J. (1987). 'Crisis of Capital Accumulation in South Korea, 1979-82 – An Analysis of Policy Solutions', unpublished M. Phil. thesis, Faculty of Economics and Politics, University of Cambridge.

Chang, H-J. (1991). 'The Political Economy of Industrial Policy – Reflections on the Role of the State Intervention', unpublished Ph.D. dissertation, Faculty of Economics and Politics, University of Cambridge.

Chang, H-J. & Rowthorn, R. (1990). 'Rent-Seeking, Transaction Costs, and State Intervention – Towards a New Institutionalist View of State Intervention', mimeo., Faculty of Economics and Politics, University of Cambridge.

Cohen, S. (1977). *Modern Capitalist Planning: The French Model*, 2nd edition. Berkeley: University of California Press.

Colander, D. (ed.) (1984). *Neoclassical Political Economy*. Cambridge, Massachusetts: Ballinger Publishing Co.

Cumings, B. (1987). 'The Origins and Development of the Northeast Asian Political Economy: Industrial Sectors, Product Cycles, and Political Consequences', in F. Deyo (ed.), *The Political Economy of the New Asian Industrialism*. Ithaca: Cornell University Press.

Datta-Chaudhuri, M. (1990). 'Market Failure and Government Failure', *Journal of Economic Perspectives*, vol. 4, no. 3.

Dore, R. (1986). *Flexible Rigidities: Industrial Policy and Structural Adjustment in the Japanese Economy 1970-80*. London: The Athlone Press.

Dore, R. (1989). 'Latecomers' Problems', *European Journal of Development Research*, vol. 1, no. 1.

Dornbusch, R. & Park, Y. (1987). 'Korean Growth Policy', *Brookings Papers on Economic Activity*, (1987), no. 2.

EIU (Economist Intelligence Unit) (1991). *South Korea – Country Report*, no. 2, 1991.

EPB (Economic Planning Board) (1982). *Gaebal Nyondae ui Gyong-je Jonngchek* (Economic Policy in the Developmental Period). Seoul: EPB.

EPB (Economic Planning Board) (1989). *Major Statistics of Korean Economy (1989)*. Seoul: EPB.

Evans, P. (1987). 'Class, State, and Dependence in East Asia: Lessons for Latin Americanists', in F. Deyo (ed.), *The Political Economy of the New Asian Industrialism*. Ithaca: Cornell University Press.

*FEER (Far Eastern Economic Review)* (various issues).

Fishlow, A. (1990). 'The Latin American State', *Journal of Economic Perspectives*, vol. 4, no. 3.

FYP (Five Year Plan), various years. Seoul: Republic of Korea Government.

Grossman, G. (1988). 'Strategic Export Promotion: A Critique', in P. Krugman (ed.), *Strategic Trade Policy and the New International Economics*. Cambridge, Massachusetts: The MIT Press.

Hall, P. (1987). *Governing the Economy*. Cambridge: Polity Press.

Halliday, J. (1980). 'Capitalism and Socialism in East Asia', *New Left Review*, no. 124.

Hamilton, C. (1983). 'Capitalist Industrialisation in East Asia's Four Little Tigers', *Journal of Contemporary Asia*, (1983), no.1.

Harris, L. (1987). 'Financial Reform and Economic Growth: A New Interpretation of South Korea's Experience', in L. Harris (ed.), *New Perspectives on the Financial System.* London: Croom Helm.

Hayek, F. (1949). 'The Meaning of Competition', in F. Hayek, *Individualism and Economic Order.* London: Routledge & Kegan Paul.

Ito, K. (1984). 'Development Finance and Commercial Banks in Korea', *The Developing Economies,* vol. 22, no. 4.

Johnson, C. (1982). *MITI and the Japanese Miracle.* Stanford: Stanford University Press.

Jones, L. & Mason, E.S. (1982). 'Role of Economic Factors in Determining the Size and Structure of the Public-enterprise Sector in Less-developed Countries with Mixed Economies', in L. Jones (ed.), *Public Enterprise in Less-developed Countries.* Cambridge: Cambridge University Press.

Jones, L. & Sakong, I. (1980). *Government, Business and Entrepreneurship in Economic Development: The Korean Case.* Cambridge, Massachusetts: Harvard University Press.

KDB (Korea Development Bank) (1981). *Palship Nyondae ui Jonryak Sanup* (Strategic Industries of the 1980s). Seoul: KDB.

Khan, M. (1989). 'Clientelism, Corruption, and Capitalist Development: An Analysis of State Intervention with Special Reference to Bangladesh', unpublished Ph.D. thesis, Faculty of Economics and Politics, University of Cambridge.

Kim, J.H. (1989). 'Korean Industrial Policies for Declining Industries', Korea Development Institute (KDI) Working Paper no. 8910, Seoul, KDI.

Korpi, W. (1983). *The Democratic Class Struggle.* London: Routledge & Kegan Paul.

Krueger, A. (1974). 'The Political Economy of the Rent-Seeking Society', *American Economic Review,* vol. 64, June.

Krueger, A. (1980). 'Trade Policy as an Input to Development', *American Economic Review,* (1980), Papers and Proceedings.

Lal, D. (1983). *The Poverty of Development Economics.* London: The Institute of Economic Affairs.

Lee, S.H. (1985). 'Gookka, kyegup mit jabon chookjok' (The State, Classes and Capital Accumulation), in J.J. Choi (ed.), *Hangook jabonjui wa gookka* (Korean Capitalism and the State). Seoul: Hanwool.

Lee, S.H., Kim, S.D. & Hahn, S.H. (1989). *Hangook ui Sanup Jongchek – Sanup Goojo Jongchek Gwanryon Jaryojip* (Korean Industrial Policy – Policies Concerning Industrial Structure). Seoul: Korea Institute for Economics and Technology (KIET).

Lee, Y.S., Lee, J.H. & Kim, D.H. (1987). *Sanup Goomyoong Jongchek ui Hyoyool-hwa Bang-ahn* (A Proposal for Improving the Efficiency of Industrial Financial Policy). Seoul: Korea Institute for Economics and Technology (KIET).

Leipziger, D. (1988). 'Industrial Restructuring in Korea', *World Development,* vol. 16, no. 1.

Lim, H-C. (1985). *Dependent Development in Korea*. Seoul: Seoul National University Press.

Lipsey, R. & Lancaster, K. (1956). 'General Theory of the Second Best', *Review of Economic Studies*, vol. 24, no. 63.

Little, I. (1982). *Economic Development*. New York: Basic Books.

Luedde-Neurath, R. (1985). 'State Intervention and Export-Oriented Development in South Korea', in R. Wade & G. White (eds.), *Development States in East Asia*. Brighton: IDS.

Luedde-Neurath, R. (1986). *Import Controls and Export-Oriented Development; A Reassessment of the South Korean Case*. Boulder and London: Westview Press.

Maddison, A. (1989). *The World Economy in the 20th Century*. Paris: OECD.

Marx, K. (1981). *Capital*, vol. 3. Harmondsworth: Penguin Books.

McNulty, P. (1968). 'Economic Theory and the Meaning of Competition', *Quarterly Journal of Economics*, vol. 82, November.

Michell, T. (1982). 'South Korea: Vision of the Future for Labour Surplus Economies?', in M. Bienefeld & M. Godfrey (eds.), *The Struggle for Development: National Strategies in International Context*. New York: John Wiley & Sons Ltd.

Mohammad, S. & Whalley, J. (1984). 'Rent Seeking in India: Its Costs and Policy Significance', *Kyklos*, vol. 37, no. 3.

Morris-Suzuki, T. (1989). *A History of Japanese Economic Thought*. London and New York: Routledge.

Nolan, P. (1990). 'Assessing Economic Growth in Asian NICs: Some Thoughts on the Conclusions Drawn from Their Experience', *Journal of Contemporary Asia*, (1990), no. 1.

NRI (Nomura Research Institute) (1988). *Sekai ni Hiyakusuru Kankoku Sangyo* (Korean Industries are Joining the World Class). Tokyo: NRI; Korean language edition. Seoul: Panmun Book Company.

O'Driscoll, G. (1986). 'Competition as a Process: a Law and Economics Perspective', in R. Langlois (ed.), *Economics as a Process*. Cambridge: Cambridge University Press.

Paik, N.K., Chang, S.I. & Lee, D.H. (1988). *Hangook ui Sanup Jongcheck – Sanup Jojick Jongchek Gwanryon Jaryojip* (Industrial Organisation Policies of Korea). Seoul: Korea Institute for Economics and Technology (KIET).

Pindyck, R. (1991). 'Irreversibility, Uncertainty, and Investment', *Journal of Economic Lieterature*, vol. 29, no. 3.

Ranis, G. (1989). 'The Role of Institutions in Transition Growth: The East Asian Newly Industrialising Countries', *World Development*, vol. 17, no. 9.

Ranis, G. & Fei, J. (1975). 'A Model of Growth and Employment in the Open Dualistic Economy: The Cases of Korea and Taiwan', in F. Stewart (ed.), *Employment, Income Distribution and Development*. London: Frank Cass.

Rasiah, R. (1990). 'Electronics Industry in Penang', mimeo., Faculty of Economics and Politics, University of Cambridge.

Rosenberg, N. (1982). 'The International Transfer of Technology: Implications for the Industrialised Countries', in N. Rosenberg, *Inside the Black Box: Technology and Economics*. Cambridge: Cambridge University Press.

Sachs, J. (1984). 'Comment on C. Diaz-Alejandro, "Latin American Debt: I Don't Think We Are in Kansas Anymore"', *Brookings Papers on Economic Activity*, 1984, no. 2.

Sachs, J. (1987). 'Trade and Exchange Rate Policies in Growth-Oriented Adjustment Programs', in V. Corbo, M. Khan & M. Goldstein (eds.), *Growth-Oriented Structural Adjustment*. Washington, D.C.: IMF & World Bank.

Schelling, T. (1960). *The Strategy of Conflict*. Cambridge, Massachusetts: Harvard University Press.

Schumpeter, J. (1961). *The Theory of Economic Development*. London: Oxford University Press.

Schumpeter, J. (1987). *Capitalism, Socialism, and Democracy*, 6th edition. London: Unwin Paperbacks.

Shapiro, H. & Taylor, L. (1990). 'The State and Industrial Strategy', *World Development*, vol. 18, no. 6.

Tirole, J. (1988). *The Theory of Industrial Organisation*. Cambridge, Massachusetts: The MIT Press.

UN (United Nations). *Industrial Statistics Yearbook*, various years. New York: UN.

UN (United Nations). *Trade Statistics Yearbook*, various years. New York: UN.

Wade, R. (1990). *Governing the Market*. Princeton: Princeton University Press.

Watanabe, T. (1987). *Venture Capitalism* (translated from Japanese). Seoul: The Korea Economic Daily.

Whang, I.J. (1991). 'Government Direction of the Korean Economy', in G. Caiden & B.W. Kim (eds.), *A Dragon's Progress – Development Administration in Korea*. West Hartford, Connecticut: Kumarian Press.

Williamson, O. (1985). *The Economic Institutions of Capitalism*. New York: The Free Press.

World Bank (1987). *World Development Report 1987*. New York: Oxford University Press.

World Bank (1988). *World Development Report 1988*. New York: Oxford University Press.

WP (White Paper on the Economy), various years. Seoul: Economic Planning Board (EPB).

Yusuf, S. & Peters, R. (1985). 'Capital Accumulation and Economic Growth: The Korean Paradigm', World Bank Staff Working Paper no. 712.

# Chapter 3

# EXPLAINING 'FLEXIBLE RIGIDITIES' IN EAST ASIA

## 1.   Introduction: Flexible Rigidities

THE rise of East Asia, headed by Japan, and followed by the so-called 'Four Little Dragons' (South Korea, Taiwan, Hong Kong and Singapore), and increasingly by the 'Big Dragon' itself (i.e., China), has been the most important  phenomenon in postwar economic history.  Not only have these countries increased the living standards of their people at a rate unprecedented in human history during this period, they have also forced, through their spectacular successes in many export markets, the policy-makers, the managers, and the workers of the older industrial powers of Western Europe and North America to accept that they may have to change at least some of the ways in which they organise their national systems of production and distribution.[1]

The success of the East Asian economies is even more striking when we consider that all of them have a very high population density and relatively poor natural resource endowments, even when we

---

[1]  Between 1950 and 1987, per capita income in Japan grew at 6% per annum, which is 3 percentage points above the average of the 16 largest OECD economies (including Japan).  The next best performers in the OECD were Austria and West Germany, which grew at 3.9% and 3.8% per annum respectively.  During the same period, Taiwan grew at 6.1% per annum, making it the fastest-growing economy in the world, while Korea grew at 5.5% per annum, putting herself in third place in the world growth league, after Taiwan and Japan.  See Maddison (1989) for details.

exclude the city-states of Hong Kong and Singapore (as we will continue to do in the rest of this chapter). Despite these constraints, the East Asian economies, by which we shall mean Japan, Korea, and Taiwan from now on, showed remarkable ability in quickly transforming their production structures and enlarging their shares in world markets.[2] They were especially successful in those industries like electronics and automobile which are subject to rapid shifts in technology and in final demand composition, and therefore required rapid adaptation of production organisations and corporate strategy. They also have shown surprising ability in adjusting to large external macroeconomic shocks like the two oil crises of the 1970s, the large currency appreciations of the late 1980s (in which, for example, Japan experienced almost a doubling of her currency value) and the debt crisis in the case of Korea (the then fourth-largest debtor in the world at the outbreak of the crisis in 1982).[3] In other words, the East Asian economies have shown remarkable flexibilities during the last few decades.

---

[2]  While there are notable differences in various areas between the three countries – for example, state ownership of banks (absent in Japan), the importance of public enterprises (very important in Taiwan, important in Korea, relatively unimportant in Japan), the role of private sector conglomerates (unimportant in Taiwan), the emphasis on heavy and chemical industries (less important in Taiwan), and so on – there are significant commonalities between them to warrant talk of an 'East Asian model'. Such commonalities include: the commanding height occupied by the state in the economy; the importance of an activist elite bureaucracy; the dominance of the executive branch of the state over the legislative; and the prominence given to industrial policy.

[3]  Korea's survival from the debt crisis is due to many factors, the relative importance of which is a matter of debate. Frequently cited reasons include: 'better' use of the borrowed money in the sense that it was largely invested and not consumed, especially in foreign-exchange-generating activities; the continued commitment of the policy-makers to exporting, which gave confidence to the creditors; tight control on capital outflow, which prevented capital flights that magnified the impact of the debt crisis as in other debtor countries; and other more 'historically contingent' factors like the limited exposure to the so-called 'contagion effect' (see Sachs (ed.), 1989, and Hughes and Singh, 1991).

The flexibilities of the East Asian economies are frequently interpreted by those economists who can be broadly defined as 'neoliberal' as a result of their 'free market' policies that allowed economic agents to quickly respond to changing price (and hence profitability) signals (for some recent assessments, see Toye, 1991, and essays in Chang and Rowthorn (eds.), 1995; Colclough, 1991 provides an assessment in the developing-country context). To these economists, the incapacity of some European economies to engineer an efficient structural change in the face of East Asian competition was an outcome of excessive government regulations and interest-group (especially trade union) pressures, which prevented the movement of resources into activities which were rendered more profitable by changing relative prices. This is the so-called 'Eurosclerosis' argument (for a representative sample, see Giersch, 1986; also see Olson, 1982, for a discussion on institutional sclerosis in general). Likewise, the slowdown in the pace of industrialisation from the 1970s and the inability to adjust to various external shocks of the 1980s shown by many developing countries (especially in Africa and Latin America) were interpreted as the results of a set of 'market-unfriendly' government policies which were associated with what is frequently (and somewhat misleadingly) called the import substitution industrialisation (ISI) strategy (the term 'market-friendly' originates from World Bank, 1991; for a critique, see Singh, 1992), hence the pressure for rapid privatisation and liberalisation exerted on borrower countries by the World Bank and the IMF during the last decade or so. The same sort of policy package, if only a more radical version, has been recommended by these institutions and the newly-established European Bank for Reconstruction and Development (EBRD) to the ex-socialist countries currently going through systemic reforms (see, for example, Blanchard *et al.*, 1991; for some critiques, see Bhaduri, 1991; Amsden, 1992; essays in Chang and Nolan (eds.), 1995).

To put it more simply, the neoliberal economists, who obviously have great confidence in the ability of the price mechanism to induce quick (and, by implication, 'desirable') adjustment, regard the 'artificial' restrictions created by the government and 'interest groups' as the major, if not the only, source of economic difficulties in many countries, developed and developing alike.[4] They regard the conditions of free entry and exit as essential for the 'free' exchanges which would allow the movements of resources into more profitable (and, with some qualifications, socially more desirable) activities. To them, all rules, legislations, or other institutions, other than those which are necessary for market exchange to occur at all (e.g., property rights laws, contract laws), are 'rigidities' preventing such movements. They argue that such rigidities not only reduce the ability of an economy to adjust to external shocks but also reduce its ability to generate long-term growth. Their usual recommendation for domestic deregulation and international opening-up naturally follows from such analysis.[5]

Many neoliberal economists supported their arguments by contrasting the 'failures' of the 'sclerotic' economies (of Western Europe, Latin America, Africa, and South Asia) with the 'success' of the 'flexible' ones in East Asia (Japan in the case of OECD countries and South Korea or Taiwan in the case of developing countries). According to them, East Asian economies, being much freer (if not abso-

---

[4]  Of course, describing all government regulations and collective actions as 'artificial' and somehow going against the 'natural' order of the market is one important characteristic of most mainstream economics, and not just neoliberal economics. This belief in the institutional primacy of the market stems from the belief in the market as a self-contained and self-regulating machine (Polanyi, 1957), which is separable from other spheres of our life, especially the political. However, all markets are fundamentally 'political' at least for two reasons. First, the establishment and distribution of property rights and other entitlements is a highly political exercise. Secondly, at least one fundamental set of prices which affect all sectors of the economy, namely, wage rates, are determined by the 'politically' decided restrictions on international migration. Historically also, states created markets, rather than the other way around, as depicted in the Contractarian myth (Chang, 1994a: Chapter 1; also see Coase, 1988). In short, the border between the 'economic' and the 'political' is fuzzy. We were reminded of this clearly in the recent British coal crisis, where the British coal-miners were told to accept the 'world market' prices, which turned out to be determined by the 'political' decisions of the German government to give subsidies to their coal, of the French government to allow the export of their subsidised nuclear electricity, and of the Colombian government to allow child labour in their mines.

[5]  One additional ingredient in the neoliberal agenda is privatisation, which we do not have the space to discuss in this chapter. For some criticisms of the neoliberal arguments for privatisation and some alternative perspectives, see Chang and Singh (1993) and Rowthorn and Chang (1993).

lutely free) from such 'rigidities', are much more responsive to price signals and hence better at adjusting to external shocks and seizing newly emerging profit opportunities.

In the more simplistic (but not necessarily the older) version of the argument, the East Asian successes are attributed to their states which provided an environment for relatively unrestrained individual wealth maximisation, most importantly through their interaction with the world markets.[6] More informed versions accept that there have existed rather widespread state interventions in East Asia, but argue that they were at best irrelevant and at worst harmful but neutralised somehow. One version, namely, the 'virtual free trade' argument (Little, 1982; Lal, 1983, and World Bank, 1987), contends that the 'harmful' interventions (e.g., import substitution) were cancelled out by countervailing ones (e.g., export promotion). Another version, namely, the theory of prescriptive vs. proscriptive state intervention (Bhagwati, 1988), asserts that state intervention in these economies, while being rather extensive, still left a lot of room for private initiatives, unlike, say, in India. The most recent study from the World Bank (World Bank, 1993), while admitting that some interventionist measures like credit rationing worked to a limited extent, comes up with a largely negative verdict on the effectiveness of state intervention in East Asia, especially on the ground that sectoral industrial policy did not work (for a detailed criticism of this argument, see the Appendix of this chapter). All in all, these 'informed' versions acknowledge that there was a lot of state intervention in East Asia but contend that these countries succeeded not because of these interventions, with some minor exceptions, but despite them. Thus, these versions preserve the theoretical thrusts of the neoliberal argument that state-created rigidities are harmful for the economy, while accepting that there was rather widespread state intervention in East Asia.

---

[6]  For example, in as late as 1988, Balassa argued that 'apart from the promotion of shipbuilding and steel', the role of the state in Korea 'has been to create a modern infrastructure, to provide a stable incentive system, and to ensure that government bureaucracy will help rather than hinder exports' (Balassa, 1988: S286).

However, many recent studies have revealed that the East Asian economies, especially the three largest, namely, Japan, South Korea, and Taiwan, did not succeed on the basis of free-market policies, or even 'virtual'-free-market policies.[7] These studies show that, contrary to what we would expect from the neoliberal arguments, these countries were full of the kinds of 'rigidities' which the neoliberal economists usually associate with economic troubles in other countries. What they show is not simply that state interventions (and the associated 'rigidities') existed in these countries but how they played a crucial role in economic development (and not simply being there as at best irrelevant variables) by providing the resources and opportunities for enterprises to upgrade their technologies through learning.

These studies show empirically that the East Asian countries had much wider-ranging and much more forceful state interventions than what is accepted by even the more informed versions of the neoliberal arguments (for more details on this point, see Chang, 1993). Strong sectoral industrial policy in these economies (sometimes directly imposed by the government and sometimes administered by government-supported private sector cartels) meant that the firms in many industries had to face tough restrictions on entry and exit, capacity expansion and reduction, pricing, and the choice (especially importation) of technology. Their financial markets, especially the banking sector, have been very heavily regulated (in Korea and Taiwan, the majority of the banks are still owned by the state), with the overall objective of channelling subsidised loans into certain 'strategic' sectors (Amsden and Euh, 1990; Somel, 1992). Capital outflow was tightly controlled, and all incoming foreign direct investments and foreign borrowings had to be cleared with the government. The labour markets in these economies are often argued to be very flexible, but even here there are quite a few government-imposed practices which belie the simple picture of a 'free labour market' depicted by the neoliberal economists. The East Asian governments frequently

---

[7]    On Japan, see Johnson (1982), Dore (1986 and 1987), Okimoto (1989), and Sheridan (1993). On Korea, see Jones and Sakong (1980), Amsden (1989), and Chang (1993). On Taiwan, see Amsden (1985) and Wade (1990).

use (implicit and explicit) incomes policy, and have enforced certain 'protective' labour legislations which are often associated with labour-market sclerosis in other economies (on the Japanese case, see Koike, 1987; on the Korean case, see You and Chang, 1993).[8]

These studies also show that 'rigidities' in East Asia are created not only by state intervention. Private sector agents in these econo-mies, notably in Japan but also in Korea and Taiwan, have exhibited many 'rigidities' in their behaviours, some of which were deliber-ately created by themselves (sometimes with government encourage-ment, as is the case with Korean subcontracting networks). Let us take some examples from Japan, which is the leader in this respect. Some (but by no means all) of the consumer goods markets are very difficult to penetrate due to the exceptionally high degree of con-sumer loyalties (which, of course, do get eroded over time; on this point, see Dore, 1986). Many industries are organised through a ro-bust network of subcontracting, supported by cross-holding of shares, personnel exchanges, and preferential lending and/or technical assis-tance by the 'mother firms'. Such networking, as it makes changing trading partners almost impossible in the short run, obviously means that the members of the network have to sacrifice profitable trading opportunities outside the network (for a recent study of Japanese sub-contracting networks, see Sako, 1993). Industry associations fre-quently organise cartels during recessions or during major investment booms, often with the help of the state through special legal and ad-ministrative provisions suspending the anti-trust law. As a result, industrial restructuring in Japan often involves complex and highly 'politicised' negotiations concerning capacity, market share, and choice of technology amongst the members of the industry (see Dore, 1986, and Okimoto, 1989). A sizeable section of the workers in large firms and the so-called 'core workforce' in some small firms, which to-gether amount to about one-third of the total workforce in the coun-try, can expect lifetime employment. Wages are frequently deter-

---

[8]  For example, it is interesting to note that one item of labour legislation in (then) West Germany particularly heavily criticised by a leading proponent of the Eurosclerosis argument, namely, the priority of severance pay over other obliga-tions in cases of bankruptcy (Giersch, 1986: p. 16), is practised in such an anti-labour country as Korea (see You and Chang, 1993).

mined to a large extent by seniority and not by effort or the level of qualification, as a freely working labour market would require. These are the kinds of labour-market practices which the proponents of the Eurosclerosis argument would dread to see.[9]

In short, the East Asian economies possess too many characteristics which do not fit into the picture of a 'flexible' market economy depicted by the simpler version of the neoliberal account of the East Asian experience. Moreover, even the more informed versions, which do recognise the existence of state intervention in East Asia, do not provide a satisfactory answer. For one thing, as we pointed out earlier, the range and depth of state intervention in East Asia go much beyond what these versions admit. More importantly, even the theoretically more coherent virtual-free-trade argument and the prescriptive-state argument (not to speak of the recent World Bank report [World Bank, 1993], which lacks a coherent overall theoretical framework) suffer from some major theoretical problems (for details, see Chang, 1993). The theory of virtual free trade ultimately bases its argument on the traditional theory of comparative advantage, which has very little to say on growth issues (as even one of the leading mainstream trade theorists admit; see Krueger, 1980), which really are at the heart of the whole debate on East Asia. The theory of prescriptive state intervention does not recognise the simple fact that, in a world with scarce resources, prescriptions by the state (especially if they are so wide-ranging as in East Asia) inevitably limit the range of initiatives open to the private sector agents.

How then, could the East Asian economies succeed in the face of so many rigidities, which are supposed to prevent efficient economic adjustments? In other words, how can we explain their 'flexible rigidities', as the title of a major book on Japanese industrial policy by Ronald Dore nicely sums up (Dore, 1986)?

In the next section of this chapter, we provide some theoretical discussions which can help us explain this paradox, drawing on the works of Joseph Schumpeter, Herbert Simon, and other more recent

---

[9]    Koike (1987) points out that lifetime employment and the seniority wage system are in fact not unique to Japan, as most white-collar workers in all OECD economies (including Japan) enjoy them. According to him, what is unique in Japan is that a sizeable section of the blue-collar workers also enjoy them.

works on institutional economics. In the subsequent section, we provide an explanation of the 'flexible rigidities' of the East Asian economies. Here, the Japanese economy will be used as the 'archetypical' East Asian economy in our discussion, but examples from Korea and Taiwan will be brought in wherever useful.

## 2.    Some Thoughts on Flexibility

### 2.1   The inevitability of rigidities

All rule-bound behaviours would be 'suboptimal', if we have what Simon (1983) calls Olympian rationality. If agents have boundless abilities to absorb and process information, as assumed in conventional economic theory, then rule-bound behaviours will inevitably limit their abilities to fully exploit profitable opportunities. Nevertheless, as Simon (1975, 1983) argued earlier and Heiner (1983) and Loasby (1991) elaborated more recently, agents with bounded rationality need some behavioural rules which limit the flexibility of their actions, in order to cope with the complexity of the world.[10] In other words, '[a]n omni-flexible world would be so uncertain [to the agents with bounded rationality] as to make action completely impossible' (Nielsen, 1991: p. 8). Hayek's discussion of the role of 'tradition' is also based on the idea that the unquestioned acceptance of certain rules is necessary for the development of reasoned behaviour (Hayek, 1988: pp. 11-28). On a less abstract level, Williamson and others have shown that in a world inhabited by agents with bounded rationality, a hierarchical mode of coordination, which restricts the flexibility of actions of its members, may be more efficient when investments involve asset specificity (Williamson, 1975 and 1985).

Thus seen, contrary to what the neoliberal economists say, 'rigidities' are an essential part of our life, rather than 'artificial' fetters which would not exist except for the government or interest groups, which are often beyond market discipline and only incompletely dis-

---

[10]   And Heiner argues that the rigidity in behavioural rules should be higher for agents with less intelligence.

ciplined by representative democracy (the 'public choice' argument; see Mueller, 1979). Without certain rigidities, no complex system inhabited by agents with bounded rationality can be run efficiently, or run at all. Therefore, a certain degree of rigidity is a prerequisite for the existence of a complex modern economy. The kind of flexibility assumed to be ideal in the neoliberal model may be able to sustain nothing more than an economy made up of, to borrow from Coase's analogy, lone individuals exchanging nuts and berries on the edge of the forest (Coase, 1992: p. 718).

The inevitability of rigidity, however, does not mean that all existing rigidities are 'optimal' in a strong sense and therefore that there is no room for improvement. For one thing, our rationality that designs the rules is imperfect and therefore cannot construct an 'optimal' set (or sets) of rules (and hence rigidities) perhaps except at a very local level.[11] If we were so 'rational' as to be able to find out what is the optimal combination of flexibilities and rigidities for the entire economic system, we probably wouldn't have needed any rule in the first place. Of course, some 'evolutionary' forces may ensure that 'better' rules have higher chances of survival, but at least within the time frame which is relevant for many policy-making situations, such forces are unlikely to have full force. Once established, all rules are difficult to change, and therefore outlive their functions for a considerable time. One reason for such difficulty is that rules which do not claim to be (and, to an extent, are not) beyond the manipulation of calculating individuals will be very ineffective as rules. A rule which is too easily changeable is as good as no rule, and therefore rules have to be difficult to change. Another reason for the difficulty of abolishing obsolete rules is that many rules need to be supported by investments in certain specific physical and human assets, which create incentives for those who made the investments to defend them against

---

[11]    Loasby (1991) sums up the point in a succinct way: 'We try to make sense of the world by imposing patterns on it, and sticking to them as long as they are tolerably successful in allowing us to feel that we understand what we observe and what we experience (p. 6). . . . People prefer not to have to think; but what they like even less is the feeling that they do not understand, and in such a situation they are driven to seek an explanation. A satisfactory explanation is one that will somehow associate the disturbing phenomenon with what is already familiar, and thus restore a pattern of coherence (p. 7).'

attempts to change the rules for the sake of more global interests.

Thus seen, we need to accept that certain rigidities are necessary for the existence and running of a complex system. Of course, this does not mean that all existing rules are optimal, because we cannot 'meta-optimise' by designing 'optimal' rigidities, and because dysfunctional rigidities will not necessarily be instantly 'selected against'. Rules are, due to their very nature, difficult to change, and there may also exist vested interests in sustaining certain dysfunctional rules. This means that there are bound to be many outdated and dysfunctional rules in a society at any point of time.

However, does this mean that therefore there is nothing we can do to improve the world? In fact, according to Hayek (1988), the very belief that we can tinker with the existing 'spontaneous order', which is beyond any human comprehension (what he calls 'rational constructivism'), is the one main source of trouble with modern societies. However, contrary to what Hayek says, the world is full of 'constructed orders', represented by large modern organisations, and not just made up of 'spontaneous orders' emerging out of evolution – this is why Simon (1991) suggests that the modern economy is better described as the 'organisation economy' rather than the 'market economy'. However imperfect they may be, purposeful attempts to design new institutions and improve existing institutions are a defining characteristic of the human race.[12] The fact that such attempts at improvements are likely to be highly imperfect and sometimes even dysfunctional does not mean that there is no point in trying to improve things.

## 2.2   Short-run vs. long-run flexibility

Many modern production technologies involve locking up resources in capital goods which are 'specific' to their current employments. And the same phenomenon of 'specificity' exists for certain human skills, although in this case, the problem is less severe due to

---

[12]   The simple but rarely recognised fact that there is a wide-ranging institutional diversity even amongst the countries which are usually classified as 'capitalist' supports this observation (on the question of the institutional diversity of capitalism, see Chang and Kozul-Wright, 1994).

the higher malleability of human beings compared to physical goods (thanks to their ability to learn new things, although within clear limits). The limited resource mobility arising from asset specificity leads to a certain limit to the flexibility of the owner of that asset in responding to changing profit opportunities.[13] For example, the owner of a steel mill cannot quickly convert his/her factory into a computer factory simply because the profits are higher in the computer industry – although this did happen to a Japanese steel producer, New Nippon Steel, which shifted part of its resources into the computer industry, it was only through purposeful long-range planning.

However, this does not mean that flexibility will be necessarily increased by the use of less 'specific' resources. Whether this is the case will depend on our time frame. Locking up resources in specific capital goods or investing in specific skills definitely reduces the range of action open to an agent. On the other hand, over time, investments in specific assets bring higher incomes (otherwise we would not live in a world full of specific assets), and higher incomes in general (if not necessarily) give one more options and therefore more flexibility. Moreover, higher incomes usually come about through a process of production experience (except in cases of hitting upon mineral or other natural resources), which generates increased 'technological capabilities', which will even further increase an agent's flexibility by allowing him to take courses of action which are not open to less 'capable' agents. An example of this will be the ability of Japan to deal with an oil price hike with the introduction of energy-saving production techniques, an option which is not open to, say, a very poor African country. Thus seen, using less specific assets may increase flexibility in the short run, but may reduce it in the long run. This means that there may be a certain trade-off between short-run flexibility and long-run flexibility in a modern economy which employs specific assets.

---

[13]  With the rise of so-called flexible manufacturing, this characteristic of modern production may have been partly alleviated, as now more machines have become more general, thanks to computer technology (Piore and Sabel, 1984, and Best, 1990), but it is unlikely that flexible manufacturing will become the dominant mode of industrialisation in the foreseeable future, and even less so in the developing countries (Schmitz, 1988).

Schumpeter was a champion of this type of argument (Schumpeter, 1987). According to him, innovation, the activity crucial for productivity growth, requires 'long-range planning' (pp. 102-3), which is possible only in a stable environment provided by what he calls 'monopolistic practices'. Obviously, such practices create rigidities in the firm's short-term response to changes in external conditions. However, according to him, this does not mean that we should get rid of such rigidities, because 'in the spurts and vicissitudes of the process of creative destruction . . . perfect and instantaneous flexibility may even produce functionless catastrophes' (p. 105). Part of the reason is that short-run price wars during recession in industries with large specific assets may result in 'unnecessary' bankruptcies, which are 'wasteful' from the social point of view (for a detailed argument, see Chang, 1994a: Chapter 3), but more importantly it is because an unstable environment inhibits technical progress which often involves a long-term commitment of resources in specific assets, as Schumpeter himself and modern scholars of technology and innovation have argued (see the essays in Dosi et al. (eds.), 1988). Innovative activities also require 'learning' through repeated practice, which requires a stable environment and therefore may have to be supported by 'institutionalised routinised behaviour' (Johnson and Lundvall, 1991: p. 38).

In short, in a world where productivity enhancement requires investments in resources with limited mobility, there exists a certain trade-off between short-run flexibility and long-run flexibility. A good example is the famous Just-In-Time (JIT), or 'lean', production system in the Japanese automobile industry, which operates on the basis of a well-connected and cooperative subcontracting network which can deliver inputs of consistent quality exactly on time (see Best, 1990, and Womack et al., 1991, for details). This system is said to have increased the flexibility of the Japanese producers to cope with rapidly changing demands in the consumer market, but it required building a subcontracting network that can manage timely delivery of inputs with consistent quality. And building this network meant that the short-run profits from being able to switch from one subcontractor to another according to their prices had to be sacrificed. In the short run, such investment certainly reduced flexibility of action, but in the long run the sacrifice of such short-run flexibility paid off in the form of much-increased ability to cope with rapidly changing demands in the world market.[14]

We can extend this argument to the national level. Those who have invested in specific assets have an incentive to restrict the movement of other complementary assets which are more mobile, as they will suffer disproportionately from such movement. They will refuse to accept the 'market' outcome and resort to 'collective action' in order to prevent the cuts in their incomes that follow from restructuring. One obvious way to reduce such resistance is to ban any collective action, as many neoliberal economists argue. However, this may have an adverse consequence on the long-run flexibility of the economy, as it will discourage investments in specific assets, which are often necessary for productivity enhancement, which in turn increases the long-run flexibility of the economy. Therefore, an attempt to increase the short-run flexibility of the economy may result in a reduction in its long-run flexibility, if it reduces the 'safeguard' for investments in specific assets. This is an extension of the familiar old argument for 'socialisation of risk' with a modern twist.

The point then is that, when 'commitment' is necessary for productivity growth, too high a possibility of 'exit' accorded by the lack of 'rigidities' makes commitment too costly and therefore militates against productivity growth (on the concept of exit, see Hirschman, 1970). And if an expansion of wealth, and the increase in technological capabilities generated in the process of wealth expansion, increases an agent's (or a country's) ability to deal with changes in the long run (that is, increases the long-run flexibility of its actions), policies designed to increase short-run flexibility may impair long-run flexibility. If this is the case, limiting the short-run flexibility of certain parts of the national economy may actually have a beneficial effect on its long-run flexibility. In the model of perfect competition which serves as the ideal benchmark for the neoliberal economists, there is no con-

---

[14]   Also, from the point of view of the subcontracting firms or the workers, the involvement in JIT imposed the short-run cost of not being able to reap gains by cleverly using 'exit' options, although again in the long run they benefited from increased flexibility and hence competitive success of their 'mother' firm (in the case of the subcontractors) or their firms (in the case of the workers).

flict between long-run and short-run flexibilities only because perfect resource mobility (together with perfect foresight) is assumed. If this assumption does not hold, long-run flexibility may be obtained only at the cost of short-run rigidities, suggesting some serious flaws in the neoliberal policy prescriptions.

## 2.3    Individual vs. national flexibility

When we talk about the flexibility of the national economy, we need to bear in mind that the national economy is a complex system made up of many agents (individuals and organisations). Neoliberal economists uncritically assume that the maximum flexibility of the national economy is achieved by allowing maximum flexibilities for individual agents. However, flexible behaviours by some agents may result in a reduction in the overall flexibility of the national economy to which the agents belong. A good example of this is the case of capital flight, where the flexible reaction of individuals to 'national' economic trouble can lead to a foreign exchange crisis and eventually to a collapse in investments, which will reduce the flexibility of the national economy both in the short run and in the long run.[15]

The point is that individuals, firms, or sectors in a national economy may react in the most flexible way to the changing environment, but with a disastrous result for the flexibility of the national economy as a whole. It is no coincidence that the only survivor among the largest debtors in the early 1980s from the debt crisis was Korea, which had notoriously harsh control on the movement of foreign exchange out of the country, as we mentioned earlier (see footnote 3). If there is a conflict between the individual and the national flexibilities, it may be desirable from the point of view of the national economy to limit the flexibility of the actions of its constituent parts. But why does this conflict between individual and systemic (in this case, national) economic flexibilities exist?

---

[15]   Needless to say, this statement should not be interpreted as meaning that having capital control on its own will lead to a greater national flexibility.

In the real world, different assets in a national economy have different mobilities partly due to their physical characteristics (e.g., specific capital goods have much lower mobility than financial assets) but also due to the fact that they are subject to different degrees of restrictions on their mobility across national borders. For example, financial assets are subject to much less mobility restrictions than, say, unskilled labour (which, being non-specific, in fact is quite mobile in its purely physical characteristic), partly because of politically determined restrictions on international migration. The trouble is that when the more mobile factors are allowed to freely move out of a national economy in search of better profit opportunities, the less mobile factors left behind may not be able to generate as much output as before. This will lead to a reduction in national income, which will reduce the ability of the national economy to respond flexibly to changes in the environment. Of course, this need not happen if the out-migrating factors may repatriate their incomes, but there is no guarantee that this will happen.

If this is the case, there may be a reason for restricting the freedom of action of those who own resources which are highly mobile across national borders, especially liquid financial assets (for a similar argument, see Amadeo and Banuri, 1991). This certainly restricts the flexibility of the owners of such assets to respond to changing profit opportunities, but it may increase the flexibility of the national economy. Our earlier discussion on capital flight highlights this issue.

Thus, the differential mobility of different assets in a national economy creates a potential for conflict between the national flexibility and the flexibility of its components. In a world with more than one nation, if different assets have different abilities to move across national borders, the flexibility of action by those who own the more mobile factors (e.g., financial capital, professionals with foreign language skills) may, under certain circumstances, result in a reduction in the national income and therefore actually reduce the flexibility of the national economy. If this is the case, there may be a reason to restrict the flexibility of action of some agents for the sake of the flexibility of the national economy.

## 3.    Explaining Flexible Rigidities in East Asia

In the previous section, we argued that a certain degree of rigidity is essential for the existence of all complex systems inhabited by agents with bounded rationality – which, needless to say, will include all real world economies. We also pointed out that the neoliberal argument that allowing freedom for individuals to react to short-run changes in relative prices with maximum flexibility is the best economic policy appears to be inadequate because there may be conflicts between short-run and long-run flexibilities, on the one hand, and between individual and national flexibilities, on the other hand. How do these points help us explain the 'flexible rigidities' of the East Asian economies?

### 3.1    Increasing the capability of the national economy

One distinguishing feature of the East Asian economies was that they did not satisfy themselves with merely reacting to immediate changes in the economic environment (i.e., attaining short-run flexibility) but deliberately went about improving their resource base and technological capabilities, both of which gave them enhanced abilities to deal with changes in the economic environment in the future (i.e., attaining long-run flexibility). To be sure, when they were faced with external shocks, they showed impressive ability to quickly switch the composition of their final demand through devaluation and real wage restraints, but the more important part of the story was that such adjustments were not simply seen as an exercise in getting short-run macroeconomic balances right, but seen as a step within a continuous transformation of their economic structures towards high-technology industries (what is called 'upgrading' by the East Asian bureaucrats). In short, we may describe one purpose of state intervention in East Asia to be that of increasing the long-run flexibility of the national economy (which will help the economy attain high growth, if not anything else) by increasing its capabilities, if necessary at the cost of suppressing short-run flexibility.

As discussed in the first part of this chapter, such policy orientation involved a wide range of forceful state intervention in almost all areas of the economy, most of which, in short, can be described as

attempts to enhance the long-run flexibility of the economy, if necessary by suspending the price-responsiveness of firms in the short run.

One example is provided by the operation of state-supported
cartels in Japan (for more details, see Okimoto, 1989; Singh, 1992;
and Chang, 1994a: Chapter 3). In Japan, the adjustment in the capacity of industries with large sunk costs was not left to the price mechanism, but was carefully controlled through investment cartels (to reduce excessive entry during a boom) and recession cartels (to prevent
price wars and thereby excessive exit during a recession). This was
because of the recognition that 'flexible' actions of the individual firms
in the short run can have potentially harmful effects on the availability of investible resources and the accumulation of technical capabilities through production experiences (learning-by-doing), which affect the long-run flexibility of the economy.

Another example is the policies to promote 'strategic' infant
industries (e.g., steel, shipbuilding, automobile, electronics, etc.)
through import protection and various direct and indirect subsidies
(for details, see Magaziner and Hout, 1980; Amsden, 1989). Such
policies provided the time and resources for the firms in these industries to accumulate technological capabilities through learning, which
proved critical in their later foray into the world markets. This inevitably involved limiting the flexibility of enterprises to operate in
labour-intensive industries which were then more lucrative according to short-run price signals, but by increasing the capabilities of the
national economy it contributed to increasing the long-run flexibility
of the economy.

Of course, as the neoliberal economists will be all too willing to
point out, the suspension of the price mechanism does not necessarily
lead to the enhancement of the long-run flexibility of the economy, as
we have seen in many developing countries. In East Asia, such a
result was achieved because it was made explicit by the state that the
suspensions of the price mechanism which it had initiated or supported were short-term measures intended to increase the long-run
flexibility of the economy. Infant industries which failed to 'grow
up' were wound down, import protections were slowly reduced as the
protected industries acquired technological capabilities, and cartels
were usually disbanded as soon as their aims were achieved.

Many commentators have rightly pointed out in view of such observation that the lesson other countries can draw from the East Asian experience may be limited because the success of this policy regime critically depended on a strong state with a commitment to long-run productivity growth, which is 'unique' to them. Many have also pointed out that there are other conditions which were 'unique' to them – for example, the large inflow of US aid into Korea and Taiwan in the 1950s, the start of their export drives under favourable world demand conditions, and (more controversially) Confucian culture – which make their experience less than relevant to other countries.

It is undeniable that many (but not all) of these conditions are indeed unique. However, the 'uniqueness' of their experiences should not mean that their experiences are irrelevant for other countries (Chang, 1993; Wade, 1995). For one thing, the East Asian countries did not have a strong state committed to productivity growth from the beginning. The incompetence of the Kuomintang government before moving to Taiwan and the incapacity of the Korean state during the 1950s show that the construction of such a state is not something which is beyond human action. Another example is that Confucianism, especially given its disdain for commercial and industrial activities, is not necessarily more conducive to economic development than any other culture (Chang, 1993). More generally, all 'success' stories of industrialisation have their own 'unique' conditions which are difficult to replicate elsewhere – for example, a strong state in Bismarckian Germany, abundant natural resources and massive immigration into the USA in the late 19th century, corporatist class compromise in post-1930s Scandinavia, efficient local states in postwar Northern Italy – but that did not keep the 'follower' countries (including the East Asian ones) from learning from the previous success stories. There is no experience so unique as to keep others from learning something from it, although what exactly is to be learned and to what degree from a particular experience should be different for each country.

## 3.2   Systemic view of flexibility

Another important point in explaining 'flexible rigidities' is that the East Asian countries took a systemic view of flexibility and had no illusion that maximum flexibility for individuals automatically leads to maximum flexibility for the national economy. The East Asian policy-makers acknowledged that certain types of individual flexibilities could be harmful for the national flexibility, and took measures to limit the extent of such flexibilities.

One example of such policy is the restrictions on the outflow of capital (especially important in Korea and Japan in the earlier stages of development). Given the limited international labour mobility, the potentially damaging effect of capital flight was recognised (see above), and therefore state control reduced the ability of the owners of financial assets to maximise their wealth by moving their assets across the national border. And this made their economies less vulnerable to the possibility of macroeconomic shocks turning into crises through the self-reinforcing process of capital flight. This statement, needless to say, should not be interpreted as meaning either that capital control in itself is enough for rapid economic growth (many developing countries provide counter-examples) or that without capital control countries will not grow (a good counter-example is Malaysia). However, it is clear that in East Asia reducing the flexibility of individual actors to use their financial power contributed to national flexibility.

For another example, let us take the case of controls on technology imports. It was recognised by the policy-makers in these countries that, in the face of technological interdependence, allowing individual producers to flexibly choose their technologies according to the changes in returns on different factors may lead to an economic structure which reduces the overall ability of the system to react flexibly to changing world market situations (which in fact was a critical insight behind many early theories of industrialisation like those of Rosenstein-Rodan and Hirschman). This meant that, despite their eagerness to import foreign technologies, the East Asian policy-makers carefully controlled technology imports in accordance with the national development project.

It was accepted that allowing flexible price adjustment for individual producers in industries with large sunk and/or specific assets may sometimes lead to an unnecessary destruction of those industries (see Chang, 1994a: Chapter 3), reducing the national economy's resource base and thereby long-term (if not necessarily short-term) flexibility. Consequently, various restraints on competition were imposed on the terms in which private (and public) enterprises could compete with each other, in such a way as to reduce such potential damage.

Of course, it will be inadequate to suggest that imposing controls on private sector decisions is enough to secure national flexibility. That this is not the case is too well known to discuss further. However, there are clearly cases where individual flexibilities clash with the national flexibility (as we have discussed above), and the willingness and the ability of the East Asian states to impose restrictions on individual behaviours in such cases proved to be beneficial for their national economy's flexibility.

Moreover, we are by no means suggesting that East Asian economies succeeded because each of them operated like a single enterprise in which the interests of the parts are categorically suppressed through a hierarchical decision-making mechanism, as the proponents of the 'Japan Inc.' view would lead us to believe. Although it is absolutely correct to point out that individual flexibilities were often suppressed for the sake of national flexibility, the picture is much more complex.

For one thing, the process involved complex political bargaining, which we will discuss in more detail shortly. Moreover, we have to square the fact of higher incidences of cooperation amongst private sector agents in East Asia with the widely-acknowledged existence of fierce competition among the same set of firms. Of course, these two observations are not necessarily incompatible. Collusive behaviour among East Asian firms is often confined to precisely defined areas with definite purpose (e.g., rationalisation cartels to keep the firms upgrading their equipment from being undercut in the short run by those which exploit the former's teething problems), and therefore does not suppress competition in general. And if one is willing to accept that, in a world where specific investments and 'learning' are necessary for productivity growth, it will be immediately realised that the possibility of socially beneficial cooperation (or collusion, if you will) is much greater than what is usually suggested by conventional Welfare Economics (e.g., infrastructure, education, health).

### 3.3    The politics of flexible rigidities

Another important key to explaining the 'flexible rigidities' of the East Asian economies is the explicit and implicit acceptance by their policy-makers and private sector agents of the fundamentally 'political' nature of the market.   While the East Asian policy-makers would agree with the neoliberals that producer groups may organise to prevent reallocation of resources with undesirable social consequences, they did not share the neoliberal dream of sanitising the resource reallocation process of politics through deregulation (which presumably will make it pointless to put political pressures on the state).   They implicitly recognised that, in a world full of immobile assets, deregulation would not necessarily eliminate incentives to resist structural change through 'political' actions, and therefore accepted that conflicts arising in the process of large-scale structural change are better managed in an explicitly 'political' manner rather than simply left to take care of themselves (on the notion of conflict management, see Amadeo and Banuri, 1991; for its discussion in a 'dynamic' context, see Chang, 1994b, and Chang and Rowthorn, 1995).   Industrial policy in East Asia therefore openly incorporates a 'political' element in its design and implementation.

One good example is the successful scaling down of certain Japanese industries in the 1970s (for details, see Dore, 1986).   When faced with the need to shut down certain labour-intensive and energy-intensive industries, the Japanese government did not allow a wholesale reign of the 'natural' forces of the market.   Instead, it encouraged the producer groups to strike deals which were unashamedly 'political'.   As a result, the final restructuring deals partly reflected considerations of national economic efficiency in the narrow sense – for example, the acceptable (but not necessarily 'optimal') vintage structure of capital stock – but also reflected considerations like the power of status quo (current market shares) and the question of fairness (large firms bearing larger burdens).   For example, in the case of the Japanese shipbuilding industry, '[t]he large companies and efficiency-oriented civil servants wanted to see the big companies cut capacity, and many of the small companies to [sic] close down. The small companies wanted the large ones to take all the cuts. Companies which had newly invested in up-to-date berths . . . wanted special exemptions' (Dore, 1986: p. 145). In this particular case, reflecting the concern for 'fairness' which was essential if the deal was not to be vetoed by smaller producers, exit was ruled out and the cut was graduated to the size of the firm, ranging from 40% for the seven biggest firms to 15% for the 21 smallest (Dore, 1986: p. 145).

Another good example is provided by the so-called Industrial Reorganisation Programme of 1980 in Korea, where the state openly intervened to streamline the troubled heavy industries and forced the private sector firms to strike deals on exits, mergers, market sharing through segmentation, and market swapping in several industries (for details, see Chang, 1993).[16] There was no compelling 'economic' reason why the deals had to be struck in the particular ways they were. In fact, as almost none of the companies involved in the restructuring were making a profit, there was no reason to believe that any of these deals made 'economic' sense. If the only concern was immediate

---

[16]   In this programme, four existing companies in the power-generating equipment industry were merged into Korea Heavy Industries and Construction Co. (KHIC), which was subsequently nationalised on the ground that the state support needed to make KHIC profitable was too substantial to be given a single private firm. In the passenger car industry, one of the three existing producers (Kia) was forced to exit and specialise in trucks and buses with a promise that it would be allowed in again when demand conditions improved – this actually occurred. One of the three companies in the naval diesel engine industry (Daewoo) was forced to exit, and the other two were forced to split the market into two segments and specialise (Hyundai in over-6,000 hp and Ssangyong in under-6,000 hp engines). In the heavy electrical machinery industry, where there existed eight companies, three (Hyosung, Ssangyong, Kolon) were merged into one (Hyosung) and allowed to produce only highly specialised and expensive products. A subsidiary of Hyundai was asked to produce only for its sister companies. Four other minor companies were forced to produce only less sophisticated and cheaper products. Each of the four companies in the electronic switching system industry (Samsung, Gold Star, OPC, and Daewoo) was forced to specialise in a different product. The two companies in the copper smelting industry were merged by forcing one to buy the other's equity, which was supported by equity participation of the state-owned Korea Development Bank (KDB) and a moratorium on bank loan repayment.

profitability, all these enterprises should have been closed down. However, things could have been worse if such deals were not struck at all, and striking openly 'political' deals seemed to have been the only way to do it, as most enterprises involved were members of the powerful conglomerates, which could veto, or at least delay, the whole restructuring process.

Neoliberal economists would argue that such 'political' management of the resource reallocation process is undesirable, because it reduces flexibility of the economy. However, when it comes to a large-scale structural change, 'political' management of the process may in fact increase the flexibility of the economy in the long run, by preventing the industries from being stuck in a costly 'war of attrition'. Our case is further corroborated by the Scandinavian experience, where the most 'rigid' labour markets produce 'flexible' adjustments by providing safeguards to the workers for their investment in skills through a combination of unemployment benefits, relocation assistance, and retraining (Pekkarinen et al. (eds.), 1992). In other words, when specific assets are involved and therefore there are incentives for political renegotiation of current market prices (which, as we argued above, is totally justifiable under certain circumstances), resource reallocation may be facilitated by explicitly facing such pressure, rather than by denying its existence and pretending that the 'market solution' is somehow 'natural'. Although 'excessive' (given the capacity of the state and the balance of power between groups) politicisation of economic policy-making is not desirable, it is equally undesirable to pretend that politics has nothing to do with economics (also see footnote 4).

## 4.    Concluding Remarks

In this chapter, we argued that there are good theoretical reasons to believe that all complex modern economies with specific assets and non-off-the-shelf technology require various institutional 'rigidities' to socialise risk in specific investments and provide a stable environment for learning. In such a world, we argued, there is an inherent conflict between short-run and long-run flexibilities, as short-run flexibilities may discourage productivity-enhancing investments, which are likely to increase long-run flexibility by providing a larger resource base and increased technological capabilities. We also argued that in a world which has more than one national economy and has assets with different mobilities, allowing total flexibility for individuals may lead to a reduction in the flexibility of the national economy, because this may reduce the resource base and hamper productivity growth of the national economy.

The East Asian cases provide ample examples which support our arguments. These economies are full of 'rigidities' of the kinds which the neoliberal economists usually associate with economic failures, but have shown remarkable flexibilities at the national level. The key explanation to these 'flexible rigidities' is found in the ability of their states and private sector agents to develop institutions to enhance long-run, national flexibilities at the cost of short-run, individual flexibilities. It was also argued that, by acknowledging the inherently 'political' nature of the resource reallocation process in a world full of specific assets, these economies could devise policies which facilitated the restructuring process by incorporating political considerations in their implementation.

To conclude, our discussion shows that the neoliberal ideal of a regulation-free and collusion-free economy is, even if it can be obtained, not desirable in a world where the agents have limited capacity to process information and where productivity growth requires specific investments and learning. If the neoliberal programme of deregulation and opening-up is ill-suited for the purpose of constructing flexible national economies, we need to start our search for an alternative programme which is both politically more realistic and institutionally richer. This, in turn, would require some serious rethinking on the costs and benefits of competition and cooperation, the relationship between the economic and the political, and the theory of institutional change, and the role of the state in it. The experience of East Asia may provide some 'spicy' food for that rethinking.

# Appendix

# 'Failures' of East Asian Industrial Policy – A Comment on the World Bank's 'East Asian Miracle' Study

THE World Bank (1993) (henceforth to be called the Report) claims that in East Asia, and especially in Korea (which consistently comes out as supporting the Bank's view on every criterion), 'promoting specific industries generally did not work' (p. 354) on the following grounds. First of all, the changes in the sectoral composition of industries were 'market-conforming'. Secondly, 'activities that were not promoted (for example, textiles) had TFP [total factor productivity] performance as impressive as those that were' (p. 316). Thirdly, there were significant financial costs associated with such policy (for example, Box 6.3 on Korea). All three points look robust at first sight, but once we probe deeper they reveal many factual and methodological problems. Let us take each of these arguments in turn, referring basically to the Korean case (which should be to the Bank's advantage).

In relation to the 'industrial structure' argument, the Report argues that the Korean industrial structure was not that different from what would be expected from factor-endowment-based projection on the grounds that: (i) the Korean textile and clothing industry, which the Report regards as the quintessential labour-intensive sector, is much larger than the international norm (Table 6.15 and pp. 313-4); (ii) there is a negative correlation between the changes in an industry's share in the total manufacturing value added (MVA) and its level of wage or value added per worker (p. 315 and pp. 330-4).

One big problem with this argument is that we cannot equate 'high wage' (used in the Report as a proxy for capital intensity) or 'high value-added' sectors with 'promoted' industries. There were all sorts of reasons other than high value-added component or high capital intensity to promote an industry, including especially its foreign-exchange-earning capability. The prominent case in point is the textile industry, which the Report regards as one of the 'activities that were not promoted' (p. 316) but was, in fact, one of the most heavily promoted industries. Primarily thanks to its foreign-exchange-earning capacity, it was one of the seven industries provided with a special 'promotional law' (for details, see Chang, 1993). And as the major export industry, it received a lot of subsidised 'export loans', which had interest rates well below the official deposit rates (and substantially negative in real terms throughout the 1970s), and other subsidies and tax rebates which were not available to more 'domestic-market-oriented' industries (for details, see Amsden, 1989). Thus seen, the fact that Korea has an 'exceptionally large' textile and clothing industry is proof not that industrial policy did not work but that it worked really well, as this was one of the most heavily promoted sectors. Add to this the fact that Korea has an 'exceptionally large' metal products and machinery industry (Table 6.15), which even according to the Report itself was the result of selective industrial policy, and there is thus very little basis for arguing that 'industrial policy only marginally altered industrial structure' (p. 312). The second component of the industrial structure argument based on correlation analysis also falls, as there is no simple correspondence between the degree of 'promotion' and the levels of an industry's wages or value-added per worker.

More fundamentally, in arguing that the East Asian countries would have developed their current production structure without state intervention, the Report is assuming that such structure would have evolved through market forces. However, this assumption neglects the fact that there are formidable entry barriers for developing countries to move up the ladder of the international division of labour – due to cumulative causations in technical progress (as emphasised even by recent mainstream literature on new growth theory), imperfections in domestic and international financial markets (which the Report itself, in Chapter 5, admits to be substantial), and the lack of marketing skills and infrastructure, and so on. Thus seen, without the full-scale backing of the state, many 'new' industries set up in Korea and other 'industrial policy states' in East Asia would not have been able to organise their finances, not to speak of becoming competitive in the world market by accumulating technological and marketing capabilities. In the absence of an actual example of market-based progress towards an advanced industrial economy during the last century or so (barring the very exceptional case of the colonial city-state, Hong Kong), we are yet to see whether the assumption that the 'advanced' industries would spring up in developing countries on their own is true.

Regarding the TFP argument, we should first of all point out that this argument also suffers from the 'mistaken identity problem' (especially regarding the textile industry) we discussed above. Secondly, the evidence of sectoral TFP growth is ambiguous even from the very studies which the Report uses. For example, one of the TFP studies cited by the Report, namely, Dollar and Sokoloff (1990), shows (Table 4) quite different results from the table in the Report (Table 6.16) in the relative rankings of different industries in terms of TFP. This is obviously because measuring TFP is fraught with all sorts of problems. As Abramovitz (1989) points out, the result will critically depend on all sorts of underlying assumptions about the shape of production functions, the adjustment made for the improving 'quality' of inputs (especially the supply of a more educated labour force), and the assumptions regarding the 'interaction' between technology, physical capital, and human capital. When it comes to a country like Korea, which experienced very rapid structural change, the result will also critically depend on the period covered. For example, the Report uses the data for 1966-85, but in at least the first half of this period, many 'promoted' industries did not get promoted, and worse still, many of them did not even exist in their present modern forms (e.g., iron and steel, shipbuilding, semiconductor). For some industries which started in the late 1970s (e.g., heavy machinery, automobile), the period covered is almost irrelevant, once we allow a period of 'maturation' of several years.

A still more fundamental question is whether TFP growth is the single best indicator of the 'success' or otherwise of an industry. For one thing, Chang (1993) shows the impressive balance-of-payments contributions made in the late 1980s by those Korean industries 'promoted' through the Heavy and Chemical Industrialisation (HCI) programme in the 1970s. For another, the 'promoted' industries could generate spillovers which are not captured by sectoral TFP growth figures. The Report uses TFP growth at two-digit level on the ground that 'spillover' exists only within the boundary of two-digit sectors (p. 326), stating that a recent study 'on the pattern of spillovers of R&D in industrial economies demonstrates that the major beneficiaries are closely related sectors, often sectors that would be identified with a two-digit classification' (p. 326). However, this study, being on R&D spillovers in industrial economies, is of only limited relevance for developing economies, where more important forms of spillovers may be things like the formation of a skilled labour force and the increase in generalised engineering capability.

The Report's third line of argument against industrial policy is that it incurs costs in the form of: (i) direct fiscal/financial cost in the form of subsidies through policy loans and tax exemptions; (ii) costs from 'writing off' the principals of non-performing loans; (iii) the issuance of subsidised funds to 'rationalised' firms and preferential access to Central Bank discounts. This argument also has problems. First of all, the fact that HCI had certain 'costs' is beside the point. The whole point of the exercise was to gain long-run benefits at the expense of some short-run costs. What is important is what the net benefit was. Secondly, it has to be also pointed out that how high one believes these 'costs' to have been depends on the counterfactual one employs, as even the Report itself admits in its sober moments. Even if we accept the counterfactuals assumed in the Report, the cost is highly overestimated, because the non-performing loans were largely accounted for by the construction and the shipping industries, which had very little to do with HCI – according to Amsden (1994), the construction industry alone accounted for 60% of the non-performing loans.

## Bibliography

Abramovitz, M. (1989). 'Thinking about Growth', in *Thinking about Growth*. Cambridge: Cambridge University Press.

Amadeo, E. & Banuri, T. (1991). 'Policy, Governance, and the Management of Conflict', in T. Banuri (ed.), *Economic Liberalisation: No Panacea*. Oxford: Clarendon Press.

Amsden, A. (1985). 'The State and Taiwan's Economic Development', in P. Evans, D. Rueschemeyer & T. Skocpol (eds.), *Bringing the State Back In*. Cambridge: Cambridge University Press.

Amsden, A. (1989). *Asia's Next Giant*. New York: Oxford University Press.

Amsden, A. (1992). 'Can Eastern Europe Compete by "Getting the Prices Right"?', Political Economy Working Paper, no. 37, New School for Social Research.

Amsden, A. (1994). 'Why isn't the Whole World Using the East Asian Model to Develop?: Review of the World Bank's *East Asian Miracle Report*', *World Development*, vol. 22. no. 4.

Amsden, A. & Euh, Y-D. (1990). 'Republic of Korea's Financial Reform: What are the Lessons?', UNCTAD Discussion Paper, no. 30. Geneva, UNCTAD.

Balassa, B. (1988). 'The Lessons of East Asian Development: An Overview', *Economic Development and Cultural Change*, vol. 36, no. 3, supplement.

Best, M. (1990). *The New Competition*. Cambridge: Polity Press.

Bhaduri, A. (1991). 'Conventional Stabilisation and the East European Transition', mimeo., The Vienna Institute for Comparative Economic Studies.

Bhagwati, J. (1988). *Protectionism*. Cambridge, Massachusetts: The MIT Press.

Blanchard, O., Dornbusch, R., Krugman, P., Layard, R. & Summers, L. (1991). *Reform in Eastern Europe*. Cambridge, Massachusetts: The MIT Press.

Chang, H-J. (1993). 'The Political Economy of Industrial Policy in Korea', *Cambridge Journal of Economics*, vol. 17, no. 2.

Chang, H-J. (1994a). *The Political Economy of Industrial Policy*. London and Basingstoke: Macmillan.

Chang, H-J. (1994b). 'State, Institutions, and Structural Change', *Structural Change and Economic Dynamics*, vol. 5, no. 2.

Chang, H-J. & Kozul-Wright, R. (1994). 'Organising Development: Comparing the National Systems of Entrepreneurship in Sweden and South Korea', *Journal of Development Studies*, vol. 30, no. 4.

Chang, H-J. & Nolan, P. (eds.) (1995). *The Transformation of the Communist Economies – Against the Mainstream*. London and Basingstoke: Macmillan.

Chang, H-J. & Rowthorn, R. (eds.) (1995). *Role of the State in Economic Change*. Oxford: Oxford University Press.

Chang, H-J. & Rowthorn, R. (1995). 'Role of the State in Economic Change – Entrepreneurship and Conflict Management', in H-J. Chang & R. Rowthorn (eds.), *Role of the State in Economic Change*. Oxford: Oxford University Press.

Chang, H-J. & Singh, A. (1993). 'Public Enterprises in Developing Countries and Economic Efficiency – A Critical Examination of Analytical, Empirical, and Policy Issues', *UNCTAD Review*, no. 4.

Coase, R. (1988). 'The Firm, the Market, and the Law', in *The Firm, the Market, and the Law*. Chicago: The University of Chicago Press.

Coase, R. (1992). 'The Institutional Structure of Production', *American Economic Review*, vol. 82, no. 4.

Colclough, C. (1991). 'Structuralism versus Neo-liberalism: An Introduction', in C. Colclough & J. Manor (eds.), *States or Markets?: Neo-liberalism and the Development of Policy Debate*. Oxford: Clarendon Press.

Dollar, D. & Sokoloff, K. (1990). 'Patterns of Productivity Growth in South Korean Manufacturing Industries, 1963-79', *Journal of Development Economics*, vol. 33, no. 2.

Dore, R. (1986). *Flexible Rigidities: Industrial Policy and Structural Adjustment in the Japanese Economy 1970-80*. London: The Athlone Press.

Dore, R. (1987). *Taking Japan Seriously – A Confucian Perspective on Leading Economic Issues*. London: The Athlone Press.

Dosi, G., Freeman, C., Nelson, R., Silverberg, G. & Soete, L. (eds.) (1988). *Technical Change and Economic Theory*. London: Pinter Publishers.

Giersch, H. (1986). 'Liberalisation for Faster Economic Growth', Occasional Paper no. 74. London: Institute of Economic Affairs.

Hayek, F. (1988). *The Fatal Conceit – The Errors of Socialism*. London: Routledge.

Heiner, R. (1983). 'The Origin of Predictable Behaviour', *American Economic Review*, vol. 73, no. 4.

Hirschman, A. (1970). *Exit, Voice, and Loyalty*. Cambridge, Massachusetts: Harvard University Press.

Hughes, A. & Singh, A. (1991). 'The World Economic Slowdown and the Asian and Latin American Economies: A Comparative Analysis of Economic Structure, Policy, and Performance', in T. Banuri (ed.), *Economic Liberalisation: No Panacea*. Oxford: Clarendon Press.

Johnson, B. & Lundvall, B. (1991). 'Flexibility and Institutional Learning', in B. Jessop, H. Kaastendiek, K. Nielsen & O. Pedersen (eds.), *The Politics of Flexibility – Restructuring State and Industry in Britain, Germany, and Scandinavia*. Aldershot: Edward Elgar.

Johnson, C. (1982). *MITI and the Japanese Miracle*. Stanford: Stanford University Press.

Jones, L. & Sakong, I. (1980). *Government, Business and Entrepreneurship in Economic Development: The Korean Case.* Cambridge, Massachusetts: Harvard University Press.

Koike, K. (1987). 'Human Resource Development and Labour-Management Relations', in K. Yamamura & Y. Yasuba (eds.), *The Political Economy of Japan, vol. 1.* Stanford: Stanford University Press.

Krueger, A. (1980). 'Trade Policy as an Input to Development', *American Economic Review*, vol. 64, no. 3.

Lal, D. (1983). *The Poverty of Development Economics.* London: Institute of Economic Affairs.

Lipsey, R. & Lancaster, K. (1956). 'General Theory of the Second Best', *Review of Economic Studies*, vol. 24, no. 63.

Little, I. (1982). *Economic Development.* New York: Basic Books.

Loasby, B. (1991). *Equilibrium and Evolution.* Manchester: Manchester University Press.

Maddison, A. (1989). *The World Economy in the 20th Century.* Paris: OECD.

Magaziner, I. & Hout, T. (1980). *Japanese Industrial Policy.* London: Policy Studies Institute.

Mueller, D. (1979). *Public Choice.* Cambridge: Cambridge University Press.

Nielsen, K. (1991). 'Towards a Flexible Future – Theories and Politics', in B. Jessop, H. Kaastendiek, K. Nielsen & O. Pedersen (eds.), *The Politics of Flexibility – Restructuring State and Industry in Britain, Germany, and Scandinavia.* Aldershot: Edward Elgar.

Okimoto, D. (1989). *Between MITI and the Market: Japanese Industrial Policy for High Technology.* Stanford: Stanford University Press.

Olson, M. (1982). *The Rise and Decline of Nations.* New Haven: Yale University Press.

Pekkarinen, J., Pohjola, M. & Rowthorn, R. (eds.) (1992). *Social Corporatism.* Oxford: Clarendon Press.

Piore, M. and Sabel, C. (1984). *The Second Industrial Divide.* New York: Basic Books.

Polanyi, K. (1957). *The Great Transformation.* Boston: Beacon Press.

Rowthorn, R. & Chang, H-J. (1993). 'Public Ownership and the Theory of the State', in T. Clarke & C. Pitelis (eds.), *The Political Economy of Privatisation.* London: Routledge.

Sachs, J. (ed.) (1989). *Developing Country Debt and the World Economy.* Chicago and London: University of Chicago Press.

Sako, M. (1993). *Prices, Quality and Trust.* Cambridge: Cambridge University Press.

Schmitz, H. (1988). 'Flexible Specialisation – A New Paradigm of Small-scale Industrialisation?', IDS Discussion Paper, no. 261.

Schumpeter, J. (1987). *Capitalism, Socialism and Democracy*, 6th edition. London: Unwin Paperbacks.

Sheridan, K. (1993). *Governing the Japanese Economy.* Cambridge: Polity Press.

Simon, H. (1975). *Administrative Behaviour*, 3rd ed. New York: The Free Press.

Simon, H. (1983). *Reason in Human Affairs.* Oxford: Basil Blackwell.

Simon, H. (1991). 'Organisations and Markets', *Journal of Economic Perspectives*, vol. 5, no. 2.

Singh, A. (1992). '"Close" vs. "Strategic" Integration with the World Economy and the "Market-Friendly Approach to Development" vs. an "Industrial Policy": A Critique of the World Development Report (1991) and an Alternative Policy Perspective', mimeo., Faculty of Economics and Politics, University of Cambridge.

Somel, C. (1992). 'Finance for Growth: Lessons from Japan', UNCTAD Discussion Paper, no. 44, Geneva, UNCTAD.

Toye, J. (1991). 'Is There a Neo Political Economy of Development?', in C. Colclough & J. Manor (eds.), *States or Markets?: Neo-liberalism and the Development of Policy Debate.* Oxford: Clarendon Press.

Wade, R. (1990). *Governing the Market.* Princeton: Princeton University Press.

Wade, R. (1995). 'The Role of the State in East Asia', in H-J. Chang & R. Rowthorn (eds.), *Role of the State in Economic Change.* Oxford: Oxford University Press.

Williamson, O. (1975). *Markets and Hierarchies; Analysis and Antitrust Implications.* New York: The Free Press.

Williamson, O. (1985). *The Economic Institutions of Capitalism.* New York: The Free Press.

Womack, J., Jones, D. & Roos, D. (1991). *The Machine that Changed the World: The Story of Lean Production.* New York: Harper Perennial.

World Bank (1987). *World Development Report 1987.* New York: Oxford University Press.

World Bank (1991). *World Development Report 1991.* New York: Oxford University Press.

World Bank (1993). *The East Asian Miracle – Economic Growth and Public Policy.* New York: Oxford University Press.

You, J. & Chang, H-J. (1993). 'The Myth of Free Labour Market in Korea', *Contributions to Political Economy*, vol. 12.

# Chapter 4

# HOW IMPORTANT WERE THE 'INITIAL CONDITIONS' FOR ECONOMIC DEVELOPMENT?: EAST ASIA VS. SUB-SAHARAN AFRICA[1]

## 1.    Introduction: Origins of the Debate on Initial Conditions

FOLLOWING the economic successes of the four East Asian newly industrialising countries (NICs) – namely, the Republic of Korea, Taiwan (China), Hong Kong, and Singapore – during the last few decades, there has been a widespread, if poorly conducted, debate on how much of their successes had been due to the beneficial 'initial conditions' they had historically inherited, rather than the policies and the institutions they had consciously adopted.

The earliest, now largely forgotten, incarnation of this debate was initiated by the then popular dependency theorists during the 1970s and the early 1980s. The East Asian success was an apparent refutation of the thesis of the dependency theory that industrialisation was impossible in the so-called 'periphery' countries due to the exploitative international economic system. Some dependency theorists tried to explain away the East Asian case by arguing that economic development in the region was superficial and unsustainable, but this soon proved untenable, given the continued success of the region. Other dependency theorists tried to deal with the East Asian NICs by pointing out that their success is largely explained by a number of unique historically and/or externally determined conditions that cannot be replicated in other periphery countries.

That the city-states of Hong Kong and Singapore were 'special' could hardly be disputed, but even in the cases of Korea and Taiwan,

[1]    I thank John Sender for his discussion and Marco Schejtman for his research assistance.

it was argued, there were many special conditions such as: the buoyant world market demand of the 1950s and the 1960s when these countries started their export drive; the legacy of Japanese colonialism that left behind an exceptionally good manufacturing base and a highly educated labour force; and the high level of US aid due to their strategic importance in the Cold War.

At the time, this argument was very heavily criticised by the mainstream economists (e.g., Bhagwati, 1977).[2] The mainstream economists argued that the East Asian NICs succeeded because they had pursued 'good' (that is, free-market, free-trade) economic policies, and not because they had been blessed with some special conditions. They argued that good policies should work regardless of the particular natural or socio-political conditions of individual countries. The implication was that the countries that did not pursue such policies had only themselves to blame.

The irony is that, more recently, the mainstream economists have completely changed their position on this issue. The heated debate on the cause of the East Asian miracle in the 1980s and the early 1990s has conclusively shown that the East Asian countries succeeded not through free-market and free-trade but through carefully designed interventionist policies. When they had to admit this, the mainstream economists suddenly started emphasising how the 'heterodox' policies used by the East Asian countries cannot be emulated by other countries because those policies worked only thanks to the unique initial conditions that the former countries possessed. For the most important example, the famous *East Asian Miracle* report by the World Bank (1993) emphasised that the (partial, it hastened to add) success of the unique interventionist models of the Northeast Asian economies (or the World Bank's terminology for Japan and the four East Asian NICs) owed a great deal to unique initial conditions such as a

---

[2]  It is interesting to note that the orthodox Marxists were also very critical of the dependency theorists regarding the explanation of the East Asian industrialisation. The orthodox Marxist argued that capitalism has an inherent tendency to penetrate and destroy the pre-capitalist modes of production, however brutal the process may be, and therefore that there is nothing exceptional in the industrialisation of the East Asian NICs (e.g., Warren, 1973, and 1980).

high-quality bureaucracy and exceptional human resource endowments.[3]

This chapter seeks to contribute to the debate on 'initial conditions' by showing that the advantages enjoyed by the East Asian countries in terms of initial conditions are nowhere as great as they are commonly assumed to be. For this purpose, the chapter takes a close look at the differences in initial conditions between East Asia and Sub-Saharan Africa (henceforth SSA), a region which is supposed to have been most disadvantaged in terms of initial conditions. When relevant, we will also look at other country groups such as Latin America, Southeast Asia (Malaysia, Thailand, and Indonesia), and the advanced countries. The initial conditions we examine in the chapter are human resource endowments (Section 2), natural resource endowments (Section 3), physical and social infrastructure (Section 4), previous industrial experiences (Section 5), and foreign aid (Section 6).

One 'innovation' of the chapter is that the data coverage is extended, wherever possible and relevant, back to before 1960, the year that is most frequently used as 'year zero' in other studies on initial conditions (perhaps because the World Bank data set starts only from 1960?). This extension of the time horizon, sometimes back to the late-1930s, shows that the gap between East Asia and SSA was even smaller in the earlier periods, suggesting that not all initial conditions were 'initial', in the sense that they are historically inherited and immutable.

---

[3]    This intellectual U-turn is not simply a sign of intellectual dishonesty and opportunism. At the deeper level, it reveals an important limitation in the mainstream thinking on the nature of the market and other economic institutions. In the mainstream view, the market is assumed to be a 'natural' institution, while other institutions are seen as (poor) man-made substitutes (see Chang, 2002 for a theoretical criticism of this view). Consequently, the mainstream economists tend to believe that market-oriented economic systems are easily transplantable, while many 'special' conditions are required if economic systems that depend on non-market institutions (e.g., the state, strong unions, producer cooperatives) are to function well (Chang, 1997). This view is behind the widespread adoption of the Big-Bang reform models in the former Communist countries during their transition period, and led to systemic collapses and massive falls in living standards in most of these countries (see essays in Chang and Nolan (eds.), 1995).

## 2.    Human Resource Endowments

Early records of literacy, especially in SSA, are difficult to come by. Table 4.1 shows the literacy ratios in all SSA countries and selected Asian and Latin American countries in 1950 and 1960.

What is interesting to note is that around 1950, the human resource endowments of the Asian countries measured in terms of literacy were rather good, but nothing exceptional. It is not surprising that they did not have as good human resource bases as those of the Latin American countries, given their generally lower levels of development at that point, but it is notable that, around 1950, Korea had a literacy ratio (22% in 1945) which was lower than those in five out of 16 SSA countries around the time for which the data are available (Mauritius, 51.8%; Zimbabwe, 36.5%; Lesotho, 34.9%; Madagascar, 33.5%; South Africa, 27.5%) and only marginally higher than those in three more (Cape Verde, 20.8%; Botswana, 20.5%; Uganda, 19.5%).

The data for the majority of the SSA countries became available only in the 1960s, by which time Korea had already raised its literacy ratio up to 70.6%, which is higher than the literacy level reached by any of the 37 SSA countries for which the data were available. However, we can at least say that the Korea of 1945 would not have looked out of place in SSA in the early 1960s in terms of literacy record. The 22% literacy ratio that it had in 1945 was lower than that in 10 out of the 37 SSA countries in 1960 (Mauritius, 60.8%; South Africa, 57%; Zambia, 41.4%; Zimbabwe, 39.4%; Namibia, 38.4%; Uganda, 34.9%; Botswana, 32.7%; Democratic Republic of Congo, 31.3%; Cape Verde, 27.2%; Ghana, 23%).

One interesting thing to note here is that the two economies that have been regarded as respective examples of developmental 'failures' in East Asia and Latin America, namely, the Philippines and Argentina, had the best literacy records in their respective regions in the early postwar days (60% and 87% circa 1950; 74% and 91% circa 1960), suggesting that a good human resource endowment alone does not lead to economic development.

Table 4.2 provides the data on the number of scientists and technicians per 100,000 people for selected developing countries in SSA, Asia, and Latin America since the 1960s. Obviously, this table has to be taken with more than a grain of salt. To begin with, there is a big

**Table 4.1:    Literacy Ratios in Sub-Saharan Africa (SSA), Asia, and Latin America** (for population aged 15 and above in 1950 and 1960 unless stated otherwise)

| | 1950 | 1960 | | 1950 | 1960 |
|---|---|---|---|---|---|
| **SSA** | | | Reunion | - | - |
| Angola | 3.0%[1] | - | Rwanda | - | 16.7%* |
| Benin | - | 8% | Senegal | - | 5.6% ('61) |
| Botswana | 20.5% ('46) | 32.7% ('64) | Seychelles | - | - |
| Burkina Faso | - | 1.5%* | Sierra Leone | - | 6.7% ('63) |
| Burundi | - | 13.9%* | Somalia | - | 1.5%* |
| Cameroon | - | 18.9%* | South Africa | 27.5%[2] ('46) | 57% |
| Cape Verde | 20.8%[1] | 27.2%[2] | Sudan | 12% ('56) | 14.7% ('66) |
| CAR | - | 7.8%* | Swaziland | 4.9%[1] | - |
| Chad | - | 5.6% ('63) | Tanzania | - | 10% |
| Comoros | - | - | Togo | - | 10% |
| Congo | - | 15.6% ('61) | Uganda | 19.5% ('59) | 34.9%* |
| DRC (ex-Zaire) | 15.4% ('55) | 31.3%* | Zambia | - | 41.4% ('63) |
| Equatorial Guinea | - | - | Zimbabwe | 36.5% ('45) | 39.4%* |
| Ethiopia | - | 6% ('65) | **ASIA** | | |
| Gabon | - | 12.4% | China | - | - |
| Gambia | - | 6%* | Hong Kong | - | 71.4% ('61) |
| Ghana | - | 23% | Indonesia | - | 53% |
| Guinea | - | 8.6% ('65) | Korea | 22% ('45) | 70.6% |
| Guinea-Bissau | 1.0% | 4.9%* | Malaysia | 38.2% ('47) | 53% |
| Ivory Coast | - | 5%* | Philippines | 60% ('48) | 74.2% |
| Kenya | - | 19.5%* | Singapore | 46.5% ('47) | - |
| Lesotho | 34.9%[1] ('46) | - | Taiwan | 50.1%[4] | - |

| | 1950 | 1960 | | 1950 | 1960 |
|---|---|---|---|---|---|
| Liberia | | 8.9%* | Thailand | 52% ('47) | 67.7% |
| Madagascar | 33.5% ('53) | - | **LATIN AMERICA** | | |
| Malawi | 6.5% ('45) | - | Argentina | 86.4% ('47) | 91% |
| Mali | - | 2.5%* | Brazil | 49.4% | 61% |
| Mauritania | - | 5% | Chile | 80.2% ('52) | 84% |
| Mauritius | 51.8% ('52) | 60.8%³* | Ecuador | 55.7% | 68% |
| Mozambique | 2.0% | 11.4%* | Mexico | 56.8% | 65% |
| Namibia | - | 38.4% | Peru | 43.4% ('40) | 60.6%⁵ ('61) |
| Niger | - | 1.4%* | Venezuela | 52.2% | 63% |
| Nigeria | 11.5% ('52) | 15.4%* | | | |

**Source**: UNESCO, *Statistical Yearbook*, various years; World Bank, *World Development Report*, various years.

CAR = Central African Republic; DRC= Democratic Republic of Congo.
* = 1962
1 = all ages; 2 = population over the age of 10; 3 = population over the age of 13;
4 = population over the age of 6; 5 = population over the age of 17.

problem of data comparability across countries due to definitional problems: who passes as a 'technician'?; are the Korean scientists of comparable quality with the Chilean scientists? Secondly, the data unfortunately do not start until the mid-1960s, which obscures the fact that the gap between East Asia and SSA would have been smaller in the earlier periods. This is not an insignificant problem, given that it was, as we shall see below, in terms of increasing post-primary education, rather than primary education, that the East Asian countries truly outperformed the SSA countries in the 1950s. Despite these qualifications, the table gives us some useful insights into the 'high-end' human resource endowments (compared to the 'low-end' human resource endowments measured in Table 4.1) of different countries.

The table shows that at least since the mid-1960s, the East Asian

## Table 4.2: The Stocks of Scientific and Technical Manpower in Selected SSA, Asian, and Latin American Countries in the 1960s and the 1970s (per 100,000 population)

|  | 1960s | | | 1970s | | |
|---|---|---|---|---|---|---|
|  | Year | Scientists | Technicians | Year | Scientists | Technicians |
| **SSA** | | | | | | |
| Botswana | 1967 | 33 | 111 | 1972 | 125 | 117 |
| Burkina Faso | 1967 | 3 | 2 | - | - | - |
| Cameroon | 1967 | 12 | 47 | 1976 | 152 | - |
| Congo | 1966 | 21 | 38 | - | - | - |
| Gambia | - | - | - | 1973 | 90 | - |
| Ghana | 1966 | 64 | 345 | 1970 | 80* | 17* |
| Kenya | 1964 | 28 | 75 | 1975 | 38* | 44* |
| Liberia | 1962 | 193 | 100 | - | - | - |
| Malawi | 1967 | 20 | 79 | 1977 | 72 | - |
| Mauritius | - | - | - | 1972 | 736 | - |
| Nigeria | 1969 | 7 | 13 | 1970 | 35 | 27 |
| Rwanda | 1967 | 6 | 13 | 1978 | 37 | |
| Somalia | 1965 | 7 | 38 | - | - | - |
| Sudan | 1965 | 13 | 27 | 1971 | 67* | 11* |
| Swaziland | - | - | - | 1977 | 317* | - |
| Togo | 1967 | 12 | 21 | 1971 | 23* | 10* |
| Zambia | - | - | - | 1973 | 235 | 556 |
| **Asia** | | | | | | |
| Hong Kong | 1965 | 56 | - | 1971 | 1.023* | 967* |
| Korea | 1969 | 71 | 165 | 1976 | 1,397 | 3,200 |
| Malaysia | 1966 | 122 | 182 | - | - | - |
| Philippines | 1965 | 257 | 382 | - | - | - |
| Singapore | 1966 | 104 | 705 | 1975 | 481 | - |
| Taiwan | 1964 | 505 | 2,613 | - | - | - |
| Thailand | 1969 | 16 | - | 1975 | 48* | 113* |
| **Latin America** | | | | | | |
| Argentina | 1965 | 703 | - | 1976 | 1,622 | 8,779 |
| Brazil | - | - | - | 1970 | 585 | 1,273 |
| Chile | 1969 | 152 | 85 | 1970 | 747 | - |
| Ecuador | 1962 | 254 | 410 | 1974 | 486 | 496 |
| Peru | 1964 | 32 | - | 1974 | 144* | 102* |
| Venezuela | 1964 | 165 | - | - | - | - |

**Source**: UNESCO, *Statistical Yearbook*, various years.

*= economically active manpower only

## Table 4.3: Primary and Secondary School Enrolment Ratios in Sub-Saharan Africa (SSA), Asia, and Latin America
(% of the relevant age cohorts)

| | 1950 | | 1960 | | | 1950 | | 1960 | |
|---|---|---|---|---|---|---|---|---|---|
| | P | S | P | S | | P | S | P | S |
| **SSA** | | | | | Reunion | 70% | 4% | 128% | 20% |
| Angola[1] | 15% | 0.9% | 21% | 2% | Rwanda | 11% | 0.4% | 46% | 2% |
| Benin | 9% | 0.7% | 26% | 2% | Senegal | 7% | 1% | 27% | 3% |
| Botswana | 22% | 0.6% | 42% | 1% | Seychelles | 50% | 12% | - | - |
| Burkina Faso | 2% | 0.1% | 8% | 0.5% | Sierra Leone | 7% | 1% | 23% | 3% |
| Burundi | - | - | 18% | 1% | Somalia | 1% | 0.2% | 9% | 1% |
| Cameroon | 25% | 0.7% | 65% | 2% | South Africa | 39%[4] | | 89% | 15% |
| Cape Verde[1] | 20% | 6% | - | - | Sudan | 6% | 0.5% | 25% | 3% |
| CAR | 7% | 0.8% | 32% | 1% | Swaziland | 29% | 2% | 58% | 5% |
| Chad | 1% | 0.1% | 16% | 0.4% | Tanzania | 10% | 1% | 28% | 2% |
| Comoros | 6% | 0.2% | 14% | 1% | Togo | 17% | 1% | 44% | 2% |
| Congo | 24% | 3% | 78% | 4% | Uganda | 18% | 2% | 49% | 3% |
| DRC (ex-Zaire) | 33% | 1% | - | - | Zambia | 35% | 0.6% | 48% | 1% |
| Equatorial Guinea | 29% | 1% | - | - | Zimbabwe | 44% | 1% | 96% | 6% |
| Ethiopia[2] | 3% | 0.2% | 5% | 1% | **ASIA** | | | | |
| Gabon | 21% | 1% | 100% | 5% | China | 21% | 3% | - | - |
| Gambia[1] | 5% | 2% | 12% | 3% | Hong Kong | 26% | 16% | 82% | 24% |
| Ghana | 15% | 1% | 59% | 3% | Indonesia | 29% | 3% | 67% | 6% |
| Guinea | 3% | 0.3% | 30% | 2% | Korea | 53% | 20% | 94% | 27% |
| Guinea-Bissau[3] | 4% | 0.9% | 25% | 3% | Malaysia | 45% | 7% | 96% | 19% |
| Ivory Coast | 6% | 0.7% | 46% | 2% | Philippines | 74% | 22% | 95% | 26% |
| Kenya[3] | 26% | 2% | 47% | 2% | Singapore[1] | 51% | 11% | 111% | 32% |
| Lesotho | 59% | 2% | 83% | 3% | Taiwan | 48% | 15% | 67% | 35% |
| Liberia | 11% | 0.7% | 31% | 2% | Thailand | 52% | 7% | 83% | 12% |

|            | 1950 |      | 1960 |      |             | 1950 |      | 1960 |      |
|------------|------|------|------|------|-------------|------|------|------|------|
|            | P    | S    | P    | S    |             | P    | S    | P    | S    |
| Madagascar | 22%  | 3%   | 52%  | 4%   | **LATIN AMERICA** |      |      |      |      |
| Malawi     | 39%  | 0.4% | 63%  | 1%   | Argentina   | 66%  | 21%  | 98%  | 32%  |
| Mali       | 3%   | 0.4% | 10%  | 1%   | Brazil      | 28%  | 10%  | 95%  | 11%  |
| Mauritania | 2%   | 0.3% | 8%   | 0.4% | Chile       | 66%  | 18%  | 109% | 24%  |
| Mauritius  | 51%  | 8%   | 98%  | 24%  | Ecuador     | 41%  | 9%   | 83%  | 12%  |
| Mozambique | 12%  | 2%   | 48%  | 2%   | Mexico      | 39%  | 4%   | 80%  | 11%  |
| Namibia    | -    | -    | -    | -    | Peru[1]     | 43%  | 9%   | 83%  | 15%  |
| Niger      | 1%   | 0.1% | 5%   | 0.3% | Venezuela   | 40%  | 6%   | 100% | 21%  |
| Nigeria    | 16%  | 1%   | 36%  | 3%   |             |      |      |      |      |

**Source**: UNESCO, *Statistical Yearbook*, various years.

CAR= Central African Republic; DRC= Democratic Republic of Congo.
P= Primary Schools; S= Secondary Schools.
1= 1950 figures are for 1951; 2= 1950 figures are for 1955;
3= 1950 figures are for 1952; 4= combined figure for primary and secondary levels.

countries had more scientific and technical manpower than did most of the SSA countries for which the data are available, although they were generally behind the Latin American countries. However, the table also shows that there were some SSA countries that outperformed the East Asian countries. For example, Ghana in 1966 had 64 scientists per 100,000 people, which was more than what Hong Kong had (56). For another example, Liberia in 1962 (193) had 2.5 times more scientists than what Korea had in 1969 (71) or twice what Singapore had in 1966 (104). Ghana in 1966 (345) had more technicians than what Korea had in 1969 (165).

By the mid-1970s, the East Asian countries had widened the gap significantly – in the 1960s, Korea had only 10% more scientists per capita than what Ghana had (71 vs. 64 per 100,000 population), but it now had 17 times more (1,397 vs. 80 per 100,000 population).

To sum up, already in the 1960s, the East Asian countries were on the whole better endowed with human resources at the higher end of the skills spectrum than were the SSA countries. However, the gap between the two groups of countries was not overwhelming and quite a few SSA countries were in better positions than at least some of the East Asian countries. The gap seems to have become truly wide only in the 1970s.

A similar picture emerges when we examine school enrolment ratios shown in Table 4.3, which allow us to predict the future profile of a country's human resource endowments.

In the 1950s, primary school enrolment ratios in the East Asian NICs were quite impressive, but were not out of the ordinary. In particular, Hong Kong, with a 26% primary school enrolment ratio in 1950, fared worse than 11 out of the 43 SSA countries for which the data are available, as well as all the Latin American countries in the sample. Korea (53%), Singapore (51%), and Taiwan (48%) did much better than Hong Kong, But even so there were a few SSA countries (Lesotho, 59%; Mauritius, 51%; Reunion, 70%; Seychelles, 50%) that were doing better.

By 1960, the primary school enrolment ratio had risen to 82% in Hong Kong, 94% in Korea, and 111% in Singapore, although Taiwan still lagged behind at 67%. This rapid increase in East Asia, however, was at least partially matched by those in some SSA countries, with Reunion (128%) beating even Singapore (111%) to claim the world's highest primary school enrolment ratio, while countries like Gabon (100%), Mauritius (98%), and Zimbabwe (96%) surpassed the very impressive Korean performance (94%) and countries like Congo (78%), Lesotho (83%), and South Africa (89%) beat Taiwan (67%).

The East Asian performance looks much better, however, when it comes to enrolment at the secondary level. Already with respectively 15%, 16%, and 20% secondary school enrolment ratios in 1950, Taiwan, Hong Kong, and Korea outperformed all the SSA countries for which the data are available. Even the performance of Singapore (11%), the regional laggard in this respect, was better than that of all SSA countries for which the data were available except for Seychelles (12%). The performance gap between East Asia and SSA in this regard increased even further by 1960, following the East Asian countries' educational drives in the 1950s, but even here there is an SSA country like Mauritius (24%) that matched the performance of some East Asian countries (Hong Kong, 24%).

The school enrolment data that we examined in Table 4.3 suggests that it was at the secondary level, rather than at the primary level, where there was a real difference between the East Asian countries and the SSA countries. This suggests that we need to reconsider the current orthodoxy that developing countries should concentrate on primary education.

All in all, we can conclude that the East Asian countries did have better human resource endowments than those of the SSA countries but that the difference was not large until the 1950s. Korea in 1945 would not have looked out of place in early post-independence SSA in terms of human resource endowments. And more than a handful of SSA countries did better in terms of primary school enrolments than did the East Asian countries even until the early 1960s. When it comes to secondary education enrolment, the gap between East Asia and SSA becomes much larger, but even here the difference did not clearly get translated into an exceptional 'stock' advantage in terms of skilled manpower for the East Asian countries until as late as the mid-1960s, as shown in Table 4.2.

## 3.    Natural Resource Endowments

After the spectacular success of the resource-poor East Asian countries, it has recently become fashionable to argue that rich natural resource endowments hamper, rather than help, economic growth – the so-called 'resource curse' thesis (e.g., Sachs and Warner, 1997 and 2001). In particular, the growth failure in SSA is often 'explained' by their rich natural resource endowments.

The first question we need to ask in this regard is whether the SSA countries are really 'resource-rich'. One important reason why these countries are classified as being 'resource-rich' is because a country's resource richness is often 'measured' in terms of 'apparent' indicators, such as the share of natural resources in total exports. However, when a country is poor, it is inevitable that the share of natural resources in its exports is high – even famously resource-poor countries like Korea or Taiwan used to be primary commodity exporters before the 1960s. Therefore, we need to look at 'underlying' (rather than 'apparent') measures of resource endowment, such as

## Table 4.4: Total, Productive, and Arable Land Endowments in the SSA, East Asian, Latin American, and the Advanced Countries (hectares per capita)

| | Year | T | P | A | | Year | T | P | A |
|---|---|---|---|---|---|---|---|---|---|
| **SSA** | | | | | Sierra Leone | 1964 | 3.0 | 2.7 | 1.6 |
| Angola | 1953 | 28.9 | 16.9 | 0.2 | Somalia | 1960 | 28.2 | 23.4 | 0.4 |
| Benin | 1963 | 5.0 | 1.8 | 0.7 | South Africa | 1960 | 7.1 | 6.1 | 0.7 |
| Botswana | 1961 | 109.6 | 105.7 | 0.3 | Sudan | 1954 | 23.7 | 14.9 | 0.7 |
| Burkina Faso | 1962 | 6.0 | 2.8 | 1.1 | Swaziland | 1964 | 4.6 | 4.3 | 0.7 |
| Burundi | 1960 | 0.9 | - | - | Tanzania | 1963 | 8.2 | 7.1 | 1.1 |
| Cameroon[1] | 1954 | 9.0 | 8.8 | 1.3 | Togo | 1960 | 3.8 | 2.7 | 1.5 |
| Cape Verde | - | - | - | - | Uganda | 1964 | 2.5 | 1.2 | 0.5 |
| CAR | 1970 | 34.0 | 24.4 | 1.0 | Zambia | 1959 | 23.7 | 21.5 | 1.1 |
| Chad | 1962 | 40.4 | 21.2 | 2.2 | Zimbabwe | 1956 | 11.4 | 8.4 | 0.5 |
| Comoros | - | - | - | - | **ASIA** | | | | |
| Congo | 1963 | 33.5 | 0.9 | 0.6 | China | 1954 | 1.5 | 0.5 | 0.2 |
| DRC (ex-Zaire) | 1959 | 16.5 | 10.5 | 3.6 | Hong Kong | 1964 | 0.015 | 0.009 | 0.002 |
| Equatorial Guinea | 1963 | 10.9 | 10.1 | 0.9 | Indonesia | 1954 | 2.2 | 1.7 | 0.2 |
| Ethiopia | 1964 | 4.9 | 3.6 | 0.6 | Korea | 1964 | 0.3 | 0.3 | 0.1 |
| Gabon | 1962 | 54.1 | 40.3 | 0.3 | Malaysia | 1963 | 4.4 | 4.1 | 0.7 |
| Gambia | 1964 | 2.7 | 1.3 | 0.5 | Philippines | 1964 | 0.9 | 0.7 | 0.4 |
| Ghana | 1964 | 3.0 | 2.4 | 0.7 | Singapore | - | - | - | - |
| Guinea | 1960 | 7.7 | 0.3 | - | Taiwan | 1960 | 0.3 | 0.3 | 0.1 |
| Guinea-Bissau | 1970 | 5.7 | 5.4 | 0.6 | Thailand | 1963 | 1.8 | 1.3 | 0.4 |
| Ivory Coast | 1964 | 60.6 | 44.9 | - | **LA** | | | | |
| Kenya | 1961 | 6.9 | 0.7 | 0.2 | Argentina | 1960 | 13.3 | 11.6 | 0.9 |
| Lesotho | 1954 | 3.8 | 3.1 | 0.5 | Brazil | 1957 | 13.0 | 10.4 | 0.3 |
| Liberia | 1964 | 8.7 | 5.6 | 3.7 | Chile | 1955 | 11.1 | 4.6 | 0.8 |
| Madagascar | 1962 | 10.2 | 9.4 | 0.5 | Ecuador | 1961 | 6.4 | 4.8 | 0.7 |
| Malawi | 1955 | 3.1 | 1.7 | 1.0 | Mexico | 1960 | 5.5 | 4.4 | 0.7 |
| Mali | 1960 | 30.1 | 29.0 | - | Peru | 1962 | 12.5 | 8.8 | 0.2 |
| Mauritania | 1964 | 96.4 | 45.9 | 0.2 | Venezuela | 1961 | 12.0 | 4.8 | 0.3 |

|  | Year | T | P | A |  | Year | T | P | A |
|---|---|---|---|---|---|---|---|---|---|
| Mauritius | 1964 | 0.2 | 0.2 | 0.1 | **ADVANCED** |  |  |  |  |
| Mozambique | 1970 | 9.6 | 7.8 | 0.4 | Australia | 1963 | 69.9 | 46.2 | 3.0 |
| Namibia | 1954 | 171.9 | 138.1 | 0.1 | Canada | 1961 | 51.2 | 23.9 | 2.3 |
| Niger | 1963 | 39.0 | 10.3 | 4.6 | Finland | 1964 | 6.7 | 4.7 | 0.6 |
| Nigeria | 1961 | 2.1 | 1.2 | 0.5 | New Zealand | 1964 | 10.3 | 8.0 | 0.3 |
| Reunion | 1964 | 0.6 | 0.6 | 0.2 | Norway | 1964 | 8.3 | 1.7 | 0.2 |
| Rwanda | 1962 | 0.9 | 0.7 | 0.4 | Sweden | 1964 | 5.4 | 2.9 | 0.4 |
| Senegal | 1960 | 6.2 | 5.6 | 1.8 | USA | 1959 | 5.1 | 4.2 | 1.0 |
| Seychelles | - | - | - | - |  |  |  |  |  |

**Source**: The data on land are from FAO (Food and Agriculture Organisation), *Production Yearbook*, various years. The data on population are from Mitchell (1992, 1993, and 1995).

CAR= Central African Republic; DRC= Democratic Republic of Congo.
T= total land; P= productive land (non-arable but currently or potentially productive land such as forest, pastures, and meadows); A= arable land.
1= French Cameroon only.

mineral deposits. And if we look at these indicators, the SSA countries do not look particularly resource-rich.

Table 4.4 shows the per capita endowments (hectares per capita) of total land, 'productive' land (non-arable but currently or potentially productive land such as forests, pastures, and meadows), and arable land across the SSA, East Asian, Latin American, and the more resource-rich advanced countries for various years between 1953 and 1970, although mostly during the 1960s. The spread of the dates can be justified on the ground that these numbers do not change radically over a decade.

From the table, we can see that, while it is true that the East Asian countries are very poorly endowed with land, it is not obvious that the SSA countries were particularly 'disadvantaged' in this regard (that is, well-endowed with land, according to the 'resource curse' thesis). The table shows that, while many (but by no means all) SSA countries may have had a large amount of productive land, the gap between them and the East Asian countries becomes much smaller when it comes to arable land. For an example, in per capita terms, Namibia (138.1 ha/pc) may have 460 times the productive land of

Korea (0.3 ha/pc), but its per capita arable land, at 0.1 ha/pc, is the same as that of Korea. For a less extreme example, Angola, at 16.9 ha/pc, may have over 56 times the productive land of Taiwan (0.3 ha/pc), but its arable land is only twice as much (0.2 ha/pc vs. 0.1 ha/pc).

How about mineral resources then? Table 4.5a lists the shares of a country's reserves in world total reserves of 18 major minerals as of 1990 for the SSA, Latin American, and the mineral-rich advanced countries that appeared in previous tables (we exclude the East Asian NICs because none of them have any meaningful reserves of the listed minerals). Since we record the country only if the share is 'significant', that is, greater than 0.1% of world reserves, most of the SSA countries do not appear in this table because of the insignificance of their reserves – of the 46 SSA countries that we have examined so far, only eight make it into Table 4.5a.

Table 4.5b presents the 'relative reserve indexes' for the minerals listed in Table 4.5a, which are the shares in world reserves divided by the country's share in world population, in order to eliminate the bias from different country sizes – so the index becomes 1 if the country's share in a particular mineral's world reserves is equal to its share in world population, and it becomes bigger (or smaller) than 1 if its mineral reserve share is bigger (or smaller) than its population share. Ideally, both mineral reserve figures and population figures should have been for the earlier periods, but as the mineral reserve data were available only for 1990, we used the 1990 reserve figure and 1960 population figure (on the reasonable ground that mineral reserve figures usually do not change dramatically over time).

Both tables show that very few SSA countries are actually exceptionally well endowed with mineral resources. South Africa is an obvious exception, as it has 'significant' (more than 0.1% of world total) reserves in eight out of 18 minerals, and has far more than its 'fair share' (that is, the relative reserve index is larger than 1) in 7 out of 17 minerals, excluding diamond, for which reserve estimates are not very meaningful as it occurs as a tiny concentration in the ore (one part in 20 million). For chromium, it has more than 100 times its 'fair share'.

Impressive as this may sound, however, it is easily matched by the New World advanced economies. The USA, Canada, and Australia record, respectively, 11, 12, and 15 'significant' reserves out of 18 minerals, and have more than their 'fair shares' in 7, 12, and 12 minerals out of the 17 for which reserve figures are meaningful (that is, excluding diamond).

Of the seven SSA countries other than South Africa that are in the table, only the Democratic Republic of Congo (copper and diamond), and Nigeria (oil and natural gas) have significant reserves in more than one mineral, and all the others (Angola, Botswana, Guinea, Zaire, and Zimbabwe) have significant reserves only in one mineral each, although they all have more than their 'fair share' in that mineral.

So the data presented in Tables 4.4, 4.5a, and 4.5b show that the SSA countries in general are not exceptionally well endowed with natural resources. There are certainly several SSA countries that deserve such a description, but the vast majority of the SSA countries do not.

Interestingly, according to our indicators, quite a few advanced countries, especially from the New World but also from Scandinavia, are actually more resource-rich than are most SSA economies, suggesting that resource richness alone cannot prevent economic development (see Wright and Czulesta, 2004, for further criticisms of the 'resource curse' thesis using these and other examples). Indeed, during the first half of the 20th century, the resource-rich countries of Scandinavia and the New World, both advanced and developing, were in fact doing much better than the resource-poor East Asian countries. Between 1900 and 1950, the annual average growth rates of GDP per capita were 2.1% in Norway (the highest growth rate in the world), 2.0% in Sweden and Canada, 1.9% in Finland, 1.8% in Chile and Brazil, 1.7% in the USA, 1.6% in Peru, 1.2% in Argentina and Mexico, and 0.8% in Australia, while they were 0.1% for Korea and 0.4% for Taiwan (Maddison, 1989: p. 15, Table 1.2).

## 4. Physical and Social Infrastructures

It is frequently believed that the East Asian NICs benefited from the superior physical and social infrastructures that they had inherited from their colonial masters, especially Japan. Is this true?

Table 4.6 shows the number of telephones in use per 1,000 in-

## Table 4.5a: Reserves of Key Minerals in SSA, Latin American, and

| | HC | SC | O | NG | CP | L | N | T |
|---|---|---|---|---|---|---|---|---|
| **SSA** | | | | | | | | |
| Angola | | | | | | | | |
| Botswana | | | | | | | | |
| DRC | | | | | 8 | | | |
| Guinea | | | | | | | | |
| Nigeria | | | 1.8 | 2.4 | | | | |
| S. Africa | 10.6 | | | | | | | 5 |
| Zambia | | | | | 4 | | | |
| Zimbabwe | | | | | | | | |
| **LA** | | | | | | | | |
| Brazil | | | 0.3 | | | | 1 | 20 |
| Chile | | | | | 26 | | | |
| Mexico | | | 5.1 | 1.6 | | 4 | 4 | |
| Peru | | | | | | | | |
| Venezuela | | 0.2 | 5.9 | 2.5 | | | | |
| **Advanced** | | | | | | | | |
| Australia | 8.6 | 8.8 | 0.2 | 0.3 | | 20 | 5 | 3 |
| Canada | 0.8 | 0.8 | 0.8 | 2.2 | 4 | 10 | 13 | |
| Norway | | | 0.8 | 1.4 | | | | |
| USA | 21.6 | 24.5 | 3.4 | 3.9 | 17 | 15 | | |

**Source**: Hargreaves *et al.* (1994).

DRC = Democratic Republic of Congo; S. Africa = South Africa.
HC = hard coal; SC = soft coal; O = crude oil; NG = natural gas; CP = copper; L = lead;
CH = chromium; MGS = magnesium; G = gold; S = silver; D = diamond; P = platinum.
* = Reserve estimates are not meaningful for diamonds, as diamond occurs as a tiny
diamond reserves.

| Z | I | MGA | B | CH | MGS | G | S | D | P |
|---|---|-----|---|----|----|---|---|---|---|
|  |  |  |  |  |  |  |  | * |  |
|  |  |  |  |  |  |  |  | * |  |
|  |  |  |  |  |  |  |  | * |  |
|  |  |  | 26 |  |  |  |  |  |  |
|  | 4 | 47 |  | 70 |  | 47 |  | * | 80 |
|  |  |  |  | 10 |  |  |  |  |  |
|  |  | 3 | 13 |  |  | 2 |  |  |  |
|  |  |  |  |  |  |  | 13 |  |  |
| 5 |  |  |  |  |  |  | 9 |  |  |
| 12 | 16 | 3 | 20 |  | 6 | 3 | 9 | * |  |
| 15 | 7 |  |  |  |  | 4 | 13 |  | 2 |
| 13 | 6 |  |  |  |  | 11 | 11 |  | 1 |

N = nickel; T = tin; Z = zinc; I = iron ore; MGA = manganese; B = bauxite;

concentration in the ore (one part in 20 million), but these countries have major

| Table 4.5b: 'Relative Reserve Indexes' of Key Minerals in | | | | | | | |
|---|---|---|---|---|---|---|---|
| | HC | SC | O | NG | CP | L | N | T |
| **SSA** | | | | | | | | |
| Angola | | | | | | | | |
| Botswana | | | | | | | | |
| DRC | | | | | 17 | | | |
| Guinea | | | | | | | | |
| Nigeria | | | 1.3 | 1.7 | | | | |
| S. Africa | 18.5 | | | | | | | 8.7 |
| Zambia | | | | | 24 | | | |
| Zimbabwe | | | | | | | | |
| **LA** | | | | | | | | |
| Brazil | | | 0.1 | | | | 0.4 | 8.5 |
| Chile | | | | | 102 | | | |
| Mexico | | | 4.3 | 1.4 | | 3.4 | 3.4 | |
| Peru | | | | | | | | |
| Venezuela | | 0.8 | 24 | 10 | | | | |
| **Advanced** | | | | | | | | |
| Australia | 25 | 26 | 0.6 | 0.9 | | 58 | 14 | 8.7 |
| Canada | 1.3 | 1.3 | 1.3 | 3.7 | 6.7 | 17 | 22 | |
| Norway | | | 6.7 | 12 | | | | |
| USA | 3.6 | 4.0 | 0.6 | 0.6 | 2.8 | 2.5 | | |

*Source*: Hargreaves *et al.* (1994).

DRC = Democratic Republic of Congo; S; Africa = South Africa.
HC = hard coal; SC = soft coal; O = crude oil; NG = natural gas; CP = copper; L = lead;
MGS = magnesium; G = gold; S = silver; D = diamond; P = platinum.
* = Reserve estimates are not meaningful for diamonds, as diamond occurs as a tiny reserves.

| | | | | | | | | | |
|---|---|---|---|---|---|---|---|---|---|
| **SSA, Latin American, and Selected Advanced Countries** | | | | | | | | | |
| **Z** | **I** | **MGA** | **B** | **CH** | **MGS** | **G** | **S** | **D** | **P** |
| | | | | | | | | * | |
| | | | | | | | | * | |
| | | | | | | | | * | |
| | | | 243 | | | | | | |
| | 7 | 82 | | 122 | | 82 | | * | 80 |
| | | | | 78 | | | | | |
| | | 1.3 | 5.5 | | | 0.9 | | | |
| | | | | | | | 11 | | |
| 15 | | | | | | | 27 | | |
| 35 | 46 | 8.7 | 58 | | 17 | 8.7 | 26 | * | |
| 25 | 12 | | | | | 6.7 | 22 | | 3.3 |
| 2.2 | 1 | | | | | 1.8 | 1.8 | | 0.2 |

N = nickel; T = tin; Z = zinc; I = iron ore; MGA = manganese; B = bauxite; CH = chromium;

concentration in the ore (one part in 20 million), but these countries have major diamond

habitants as an indicator of the quality of a country's physical infrastructure. In 1950, Hong Kong, with 18.36 telephones per 1,000 people, was leading Asia in this respect, but even it was behind some Latin American countries (Argentina, 46.53 and Chile, 22.66) and, interestingly, also some SSA countries, such as South Africa (28.93) and the Gambia (26.02). Taiwan, with 5.37 telephones per 1,000 people as late as in 1956, was behind Zimbabwe (11.06) and Namibia (11.90), and Korea, with 0.84, was behind 17 out of the 30 SSA countries for which the data are available.

The relative standing of East Asia was somewhat higher on this account around 1960, but not by much. Hong Kong (35.57) was still leading the Asian group, but was still behind Argentina (62.88), Gambia (73.39), and South Africa (49.99). Taiwan, with 8.60 phones per 1,000 people, was still behind a number of SSA countries such as Namibia (30.69) and Zimbabwe (20.83), while Korea, whose number of phones increased by more than five times from 0.84 in 1952 to 4.36 in 1960, was still behind 11 out of the 37 SSA countries for whom the data were available.

Table 4.7 shows what we call the 'railway density index', another indicator of the quality of physical infrastructure. The index is calculated as the length of railways (in km) divided by the population (in 1,000) and by the total area of the country (in 1,000 hectares), and multiplied by one million to produce a 'familiar-looking' figure. The reason why the total length of railways is divided by population is obvious, but it is also divided by the area of the country in order to account for the fact that countries with large areas will need longer railways simply to provide the same level of rail services.

What is notable about our railways index is that it decreases for most countries over time, most likely reflecting the increasing importance of motor cars in 20th century industrialisation, compared to the 19th century, and possibly also because of rapid population growth in most countries during the period we cover in the table. It is also notable that, unlike in the cases of other indicators explored in this chapter, the relative standing of the East Asian countries does not radically improve over time, although we have to remember that the improvements in rail service quality that the East Asian countries have achieved (faster and/or more comfortable trains, increased punctuality, less cancellations, etc.) cannot be captured by our simple index.

| Table 4.6: Telephones in Use (per 1,000 inhabitants) | | | | | |
|---|---|---|---|---|---|
| | **1950** | **1960** | | **1950** | **1960** |
| **SSA** | | | Reunion | 20.49[4] | 17.75 |
| Angola | 0.48 | 0.83 | Rwanda | - | 0.38[5] |
| Benin | 0.87* | 0.98 | Senegal | - | 6.75 |
| Botswana | - | 1.91[5] | Seychelles | - | - |
| Burkina Faso | 0.87* | 0.23 | Sierra Leone | - | 2.31[5] |
| Burundi | - | 0.70[5] | Somalia | - | - |
| Cameroon | 0.20 | 1.06 | South Africa | 28.93 | 49.99 |
| Cape Verde | - | - | Sudan | 1.07[1] | 2.13 |
| CAR | 0.40** | 0.84 | Swaziland | - | 8.70[5] |
| Chad | 0.40** | 0.66 | Tanzania | 0.80[3] | 1.50 |
| Comoros | - | - | Togo | 0.83 | 1.39 |
| Congo | 0.40** | 5.16 | Uganda | 0.96[2] | 2.06 |
| DRC (ex-Zaire) | 0.45 | 1.98 | Zambia | 2.05[1] | 7.17 |
| Equatorial Guinea | - | - | Zimbabwe | 11.06 | 20.83 |
| Ethiopia | 0.12[1] | 0.58 | **ASIA** | | |
| Gabon | 0.40** | 4.24 | China | 0.41 | 2.38 |
| Gambia | 26.02[1] | 73.39 | Hong Kong | 18.36[2] | 35.57 |
| Ghana | 1.60[1] | 3.54 | Indonesia | 0.57 | 1.32 |
| Guinea | 0.87* | 0.94 | Korea | 0.84[2] | 4.36 |
| Guinea-Bissau | - | - | Malaysia | 4.62 | 11.0 |
| Ivory Coast | 0.87* | 2.12 | Philippines | 0.99 | 4.13 |
| Kenya | 3.32[2] | 5.11 | Singapore | - | - |
| Lesotho | - | - | Taiwan | 5.37[4] | 8.60 |
| Liberia | - | - | Thailand | 0.31 | 1.61 |
| Madagascar | 1.32 | 2.56 | **LATIN AMERICA** | | |
| Malawi | 0.37[2] | 1.46 | Argentina | 46.53 | 62.88 |
| Mali | 0.87* | 0.74 | Brazil | 10.59 | 14.56 |
| Mauritania | - | - | Chile | 22.66[1] | 25.44 |
| Mauritius | 10.44[1] | 13.55 | Ecuador | 2.79[1] | 6.71 |
| Mozambique | 0.70 | 1.82 | Mexico | 10.88 | 14.95 |
| Namibia | 11.90 | 30.69 | Peru | 5.90 | 10.88 |
| Niger | - | 0.35 | Venezuela | 14.91[1] | 27.49 |
| Nigeria | 0.36[1] | 0.99 | | | |

**Source**: Mitchell (1993 and 1995).

CAR= Central African Republic; DRC= Democratic Republic of Congo.
*= corresponds to French West Africa (Benin, Burkina Faso, Guinea, Ivory Coast, Mali)
**= corresponds to all French Equatorial Africa (Central African Republic, Chad, Congo, and Gabon) in 1951.
1= 1951; 2= 1952; 3= 1953; 4= 1956; 5= 1963.

## Table 4.7: Railway Density Index
(railways in km, divided by area in 1,000 ha and by population in 1,000, and then multiplied by 1 million)

| | 1940 | 1950 | 1960 | | 1940 | 1950 | 1960 |
|---|---|---|---|---|---|---|---|
| SSA | | | | Reunion | 2,083 | 2,066 | 1,491 |
| Angola | 4.77 | 4.68 | 2.31 | Rwanda | - | - | - |
| Benin | 42.91 | 31.76 | 25.53 | Senegal | 2.42[6] | 2.05[6] | 16.36 |
| Botswana | 36.59 | 24.45 | 20.67 | Seychelles | - | - | - |
| Burkina Faso | 2.57 | 2.23 | 2.55 | Sierra Leone | - | 38.59 | 32.25 |
| Burundi | - | - | - | Somalia | 1.16 | 0.99 | - |
| Cameroon | 2.86[1] | 2.17[1] | 1.94 | South Africa | 15.55 | 12.41[7] | 9.83 |
| Cape Verde | - | - | - | Sudan | - | 1.47 | 1.58 |
| CAR | - | - | - | Swaziland | - | - | - |
| Chad | - | - | - | Tanzania | 4.51 | 1.54[2] | 1.60[2] |
| Comoros | - | - | - | Togo | 89.32 | 67.51 | 56.66 |
| Congo | 23.54 | 18.00 | 15.43 | Uganda | 6.76 | 1.54[2] | 1.60[2] |
| DRC (ex-Zaire) | - | - | 1.58 | Zambia | 8.56 | 5.72 | 5.47[8] |
| Eq. Guinea | - | - | - | Zimbabwe | 32.78 | 24.50 | 5.47[8] |
| Ethiopia | 0.59 | 0.4 | 0.34 | ASIA | | | |
| Gabon | - | - | - | China | 0.03[9] | 0.04 | 0.06 |
| Gambia | - | - | - | Hong Kong | - | - | - |
| Ghana | 8.85 | 8.58 | 6.10 | Indonesia | - | 0.48[10] | 0.40 |
| Guinea | - | 10.02 | 8.46 | Korea | 13.45[11] | 13.83 | 12.12 |
| Guinea-Bissau | - | - | - | Malaysia[12] | - | 11.63 | 10.08 |
| Ivory Coast | - | - | - | Philippines | 2.51 | 1.89[13] | 1.25 |
| Kenya | 9.05 | 1.54[2] | 1.60[2] | Singapore[12] | - | 11.63 | 10.08 |
| Lesotho | - | - | - | Taiwan | 40.77[14] | 32.81 | 23.55 |
| Liberia | - | - | - | Thailand | 3.63. | 1.79 | 15.48 |
| Madagascar | 3.44 | 3.24 | 2.70 | LA | | | |
| Malawi | 26.39 | 20.03 | 15.82 | Argentina | 9.70 | 9.13 | 7.78 |
| Mali | 2.42[6] | 2.05[6] | 1.31 | Brazil | 0.88 | 0.84 | 0.64 |
| Mauritania | - | - | 6.50[3] | Chile | 20.75 | 18.64 | 14.82 |
| Mauritius | 2,120 | 1,817 | 1,074[4] | Ecuador | 13.77 | 12.59 | 9.62 |
| Mozambique | 4.99[5] | 5.98 | 6.11 | Mexico | 5.29 | 4.62 | 3.47 |
| Namibia | - | - | - | Peru | 3.11 | 3.04 | 1.99 |
| Niger | - | - | - | Venezuela | 2.79 | 2.28 | 0.73 |
| Nigeria | | 1.01 | 0.74 | | | | |

Source: Mitchell (1993 and 1995).

CAR= Central African Republic; DRC= Democratic Republic of Congo.
1= French Cameroon only; 2= East African Rails, which includes Uganda and Tanzania; 3= 1963; 4= 1959; 5= on operations only; 6= Senegal plus Mali; 7= standard gauge only; 8= Zambia and Zimbabwe; 9= 1930; 10= 1951; 11= 1945; 12= Malaysia and Singapore; 13= 1952; 14= 1938.

Even with these qualifications, it is clear from the table that the East Asian countries did not start their industrialisation with much better railway systems than those of the SSA countries. For example, between 1940 and 1960, in terms of our index, Korea was behind such SSA countries as Benin, Botswana, Congo, Malawi, Senegal (in 1960), Sierra Leone, Togo, and Zimbabwe (in 1940 and 1950) – not to speak of the exceptional island countries of Mauritius and Reunion. Even Taiwan, which was about 2-3 times better endowed with rail infrastructure than Korea was in those days, was behind such SSA countries as Sierra Leone and Togo.

Tables 4.8 and 4.9, which provide the data for infant mortality and life expectancy, try to capture the quality of what is normally known as 'social infrastructure', which, in relation to these two particular indicators, includes, among other things, the public administrative system, health care institutions, the institutions to take care of the aged and the very young, and female educational system (which is supposed to affect infant mortality through its effects on household budget management and nutritional care).

Infant mortality data, shown in Table 4.8, are scant for 1940 and 1950, especially for the SSA countries. What little data that exist are mostly for the whites only. The data became extensively available only from 1960. In that year, with 36 and 37 infant deaths per 1,000 live births, Singapore and Hong Kong were in a different league from all the other countries in the table, possibly reflecting their unique advantages as city-states. However, even Korea, with a per capita income ($82 in current dollars) less than half that of Ghana ($179) and on a par with that of Kenya ($72), had an infant mortality rate lower than any SSA country in the sample. Even more impressively, Korea's infant mortality rate was lower than that of all the Latin American countries except Argentina, whose per capita income then ($378) was five times that of Korea (all the income figures are for 1961; Korea's income figure is from the Korean national account statistics and the income figures for the other countries are from Kindleberger, 1965: Table 1.1).

The same picture can be found in life expectancy figures shown in Table 4.9. In 1960, Korea, with 53 years of life expectancy at birth, was the worst performer among the four East Asian NICs (Singapore, 69; Hong Kong, 63; Taiwan, 64), but even it outperformed all the

## Table 4.8: Infant Mortality Rate (per 1,000 live births)

| | 1940 | 1950 | 1960 | | 1940 | 1950 | 1960 |
|---|---|---|---|---|---|---|---|
| **SSA** | | | | | | | |
| | | | | Reunion | - | - | - |
| Angola | - | - | 208 | Rwanda | - | - | 147 |
| Benin | - | - | 206 | Senegal | - | - | 182 |
| Botswana | - | - | - | Seychelles | - | - | - |
| Burkina Faso | - | - | 252 | Sierra Leone | - | - | 234 |
| Burundi | - | - | 150 | Somalia | - | - | 152 |
| Cameroon | - | - | 162 | South Africa | 50* | 36* | 135 |
| Cape Verde | - | - | - | Sudan | - | - | 168 |
| CAR | - | - | 195 | Swaziland | - | - | - |
| Chad | - | - | 195 | Tanzania | - | - | 152 |
| Comoros | - | - | - | Togo | - | - | 182 |
| Congo | - | 75* | 171 | Uganda | - | - | 139 |
| DRC (ex-Zaire) | - | - | 150 | Zambia | - | - | 151 |
| Eq. Guinea | - | - | - | Zimbabwe | 41* | 35* | 118 |
| Ethiopia | - | - | 175 | **ASIA** | | | |
| Gabon | - | - | - | China | - | - | 165 |
| Gambia | - | 130[1] | - | Hong Kong | - | 100 | 37 |
| Ghana | - | 120[1] | 143 | Indonesia | 40* | 29* | 150 |
| Guinea | - | - | 208 | Korea | 107 | - | 78 |
| Guinea-Bissau | - | - | - | Malaysia | 139 | 102 | 72 |
| Ivory Coast | - | - | 173 | Philippines | - | - | 106 |
| Kenya | - | - | 138 | Singapore | - | 81[1] | 36 |
| Lesotho | - | - | 144 | Taiwan | 136 | - | 147 |
| Liberia | - | - | 194 | Thailand | 104 | 68[3] | 103 |
| Madagascar | - | - | 109 | **LA** | | | |
| Malawi | - | - | 207 | Argentina | 90 | 76[4] | 61 |
| Mali | - | - | 195 | Brazil | - | - | 118 |
| Mauritania | - | - | 185 | Chile | 217 | 153 | 114 |
| Mauritius | - | - | - | Ecuador | 159 | 115[1] | 140 |
| Mozambique | 54*,[2] | 49*,[1] | 160 | Mexico | 126 | 82[3] | 91 |
| Namibia | - | - | - | Peru | 128 | 94 | 163 |
| Niger | - | - | 191 | Venezuela | 122 | 91[3] | 85 |
| Nigeria | | - | 183 | | | | |

**Source**: UN, *Statistical Yearbook,* various years.

CAR= Central African Republic; DRC= Democratic Republic of Congo.
1= 1948; 2= 1942; 3= 1949; 4= 1946.
*whites only.

| Table 4.9: Life Expectancy at Birth | | | | | |
|---|---|---|---|---|---|
| | **1960** | **1975** | | **1960** | **1975** |
| **SSA** | | | Reunion | - | - |
| Angola | 32 | 39 | Rwanda | 36 | 41 |
| Benin | 34 | 41 | Senegal | 36 | 40 |
| Botswana | - | - | Seychelles | - | - |
| Burkina Faso | 32 | 38 | Sierra Leone | 36 | 44 |
| Burundi | 34 | 39 | Somalia | 35 | 41 |
| Cameroon | 36 | 41 | South Africa | 47 | 52 |
| Cape Verde | - | - | Sudan | 41 | 49 |
| CAR | 35 | 41 | Swaziland | - | - |
| Chad | 34 | 39 | Tanzania | 37 | 45 |
| Comoros | - | - | Togo | 34 | 41 |
| Congo | 36 | 44 | Uganda | 43 | 50 |
| DRC (ex-Zaire) | 40 | 44 | Zambia | 39 | 45 |
| Equatorial Guinea | - | - | Zimbabwe | 44 | 52 |
| Ethiopia | 34 | 44 | **ASIA** | | |
| Gabon | - | - | China | 51 | 62 |
| Gambia | - | - | Hong Kong | 63 | 70 |
| Ghana | 37 | 44 | Indonesia | 40 | 48 |
| Guinea | 34 | 41 | Korea | 53 | 61 |
| Guinea-Bissau | - | - | Malaysia | 52 | 59 |
| Ivory Coast | 36 | 44 | Philippines | 49 | 58 |
| Kenya | 43 | 50 | Singapore | 69 | 70 |
| Lesotho | 38 | 46 | Taiwan | 64 | 71 |
| Liberia | 37 | 44 | Thailand | 49 | 58 |
| Madagascar | 36 | 44 | **LATIN** | | |
| Malawi | 35 | 41 | **AMERICA** | | |
| Mali | 35 | 38 | Argentina | 65 | 68 |
| Mauritania | 36 | 39 | Brazil | 56 | 61 |
| Mauritius | - | - | Chile | 56 | 63 |
| Mozambique | 36 | 44 | Ecuador | 51 | 60 |
| Namibia | - | - | Mexico | 56 | 63 |
| Niger | 36 | 39 | Peru | 49 | 56 |
| Nigeria | 34 | 41 | Venezuela | 57 | 65 |

**Source**: World Bank, *World Development Report*, various years.

CAR= Central African Republic; DRC= Democratic Republic of Congo.

SSA countries for which the data were available, although its record fell short of those of most Latin American countries in the sample, except for Ecuador (51) and Peru (49).

Thus, it emerges from Tables 4.8 and 4.9 that, unlike in relation to other 'initial conditions', where they did not have an unambiguous headstart (Korea, especially, would not have looked out of place in SSA until the 1950s on most indicators), the East Asian countries did have a clear headstart around the 1950s in terms of social infrastructure.

## 5.    Previous Industrial Experiences

Reviving an old dependency argument, some recent studies have emphasised that Japanese colonialism was different from its European counterparts in that it developed manufacturing industries in its main colonies, namely, Korea and Taiwan (e.g., Kohli, 1994). According to this story, the large industrial base that Korea and Taiwan inherited from their colonial past gave them headstarts in their subsequent industrialisation. Is this true?

The data on manufacturing and/or industrial (manufacturing plus mining, electricity, and gas) activities in the 1940s and the 1950s are scant, but Table 4.10 provides us with some useful information.

In 1938, Korea's per capita manufacturing value-added (MVA) was $9 (in 1958 dollars) while Taiwan's was $12. These figures, however, probably over-estimate the manufacturing capabilities in these countries. In 1938, Japan was a war economy – it was in a war with China and preparing for a possible clash with the Western powers. As is well known, war economies run well beyond their underlying capacities, and thus the 1938 MVA figures for Korea and Taiwan, Japan's main colonies, would over-estimate the manufacturing capabilities of these countries.

Per capita MVAs in Korea and Taiwan were basically halved to $5 and $6 respectively by 1948, reflecting the end of the war economy and the post-colonial disruption in production (as the Japanese who held most managerial and skilled positions departed and as political situations became turbulent). Therefore, these figures certainly under-estimate these countries' manufacturing capabilities.

**Table 4.10:  Per Capita Value Added in Industry (IVA) and in Manufacturing (MVA) in 1958 US dollars**
(IVA figures are in brackets)

|  | 1938 | 1948 | 1958 |
|---|---|---|---|
| **SSA** | | | |
| Democratic Republic of Congo | | | |
| (ex-Zaire) | - | 6 (17) | 14 (30) |
| Ghana | - | - | 8 (26) |
| Kenya | - | - | 12 (14) |
| Mozambique | - | 4 (5) | 10 (11) |
| South Africa | 62 (130) | 84 (146) | 133 (217) |
| Tanzania | - | 3 (4)[3] | 3 (7) |
| Uganda | - | - | 6 (8) |
| Zimbabwe* | | - | 36 (66) |
| **Asia** | | | |
| Indonesia | 4 (7) | 3(5) | 3 (7) |
| Korea | 9 | 5 (6) | 20 (24) |
| Malaysia | - | 20 (45) | 27 (40) |
| Philippines | 13 (16) | 9 (10) | 15 (17) |
| Taiwan | 12 (15) | 6 (8) | 18 (21) |
| Thailand | 6 (9)[1] | 9 (9) | 8 (9) |
| **Latin America** | | | |
| Argentina | 98 (104)[1] | 137 (143) | 124 (133) |
| Brazil | 16 (18)[1] | 22 (24) | 41 (44) |
| Chile | 72 (94) | 77 (102) | 75 (99) |
| Ecuador | 19 (21) | 21 (23) | 27 (30) |
| Mexico | 45 (61)[1] | 55 (68) | 72 (84) |
| Peru | 14 (30) | 17 (28) | 25 (45) |
| Venezuela | - | 39 (212) | 115 (378) |

**Source**: United Nations, *The Growth of the World Industry, 1938-1961*, 1965.

*= Zimbabwe and Malawi.
1= 1939; 2= 1949;  3= 1953.

Given the above considerations, it may be reasonable to say that the 'real' per capita MVA in these countries around 1950 was somewhere in between the figures for 1938 and the figures for 1948. Taking the average of the two, we get $7 for Korea and $9 for Taiwan. How do these compare to those of other countries?

To begin with, these figures compare very poorly with the Latin American figures of the same period. In 1948, even the least industrialised Latin American country in the sample, Peru ($17), had a per capita MVA about twice the 'adjusted' Taiwanese figure ($9) and 2.5 times the 'adjusted' Korean figure ($7). The more advanced Latin American countries were in a totally different league. In the same year Argentina ($137) produced more than 15 times per capita MVA than our 'adjusted' Taiwanese figure ($9), while Chile ($77) produced 11 times and Mexico ($55) eight times that of the 'adjusted' Korean figure ($7).

There is a real poverty of data for the SSA countries on this front in 1948. This must partly reflect the fact that there were few manufacturing or industrial activities to report, but only partly – for example, we do not have the 1948 figure for Zimbabwe, which was one of the most industrially advanced developing countries at the time. Even if we discount South Africa, which, with $84 per capita MVA, was in a totally different league from the East Asian countries then, we find from the table that those few SSA countries for which the data were available were not far behind the East Asian countries.

The Democratic Republic of Congo (former Zaire, then Leopoldville Congo) recorded $6 per capita MVA, which was higher than the 'apparent' per capita MVA of Korea that year ($5), and only slightly lower than its 'adjusted' figure ($7). Mozambique ($4) and Tanzania ($3) were certainly behind Korea and well behind Taiwan, but the gap between even the more-developed Taiwan and these two SSA economies was inconsequential compared to the gaps between Taiwan itself and South Africa or the more advanced Latin American countries.

By 1958, the manufacturing sectors in Taiwan and Korea had advanced rather dramatically, with Korea recording $20 and Taiwan $18, which substantially narrowed the gaps separating them from the more advanced developing countries of the time. So, for example, while Argentina ($124) and South Africa ($133) were still well ahead, their per capita MVAs were now only 6-7 times larger, instead of 10-15 times (of the 'adjusted' figures) as in 1948.

Despite these advances, however, both Korea and Taiwan were still well behind Zimbabwe (plus Malawi in this particular statistic), at $36 per capita MVA in 1958. Other SSA countries were still behind the East Asian countries, but not by a huge margin. The Democratic Republic of Congo, at $14, comes close to these countries, and the more industrialised of the SSA countries like Kenya ($12) and Mozambique ($10) were still producing more than half the East Asian per capita MVA – a gap that is smaller than what existed between the East Asian countries and Peru in 1948 that we talked about above.

The less industrialised of the SSA countries in the table (Ghana, $8; Uganda, $6; Tanzania, $3) were by this time well behind the East Asian countries, but they were still producing MVAs which were basically in the same league as the figures that Korea and Taiwan had recorded in 1948 – 'apparently' $5 and $6 respectively, or $7 and $9 respectively when 'adjusted'.

The gaps between the East Asian and the SSA countries become even smaller in some cases when we look at the industrial-value-added (IVA) figures, which include not just the MVA but also the value-added from non-manufacturing industrial activities, such as mining, electricity, and gas. In 1958, the Democratic Republic of Congo, at $30, was producing 25% more IVA than Korea ($24) and about 40% more IVA than Taiwan ($21), while Ghana, at $26, was also producing more IVA than both countries. Thus seen, it may be reasonable to say that the Democratic Republic of Congo and Ghana, which had a smaller manufacturing sector but a bigger industrial sector than did Korea and Taiwan, were basically at the same level of industrial development as the two East Asian economies even in 1958.

To sum up, in terms of the development of the manufacturing sector, we may say that in the 1940s and the 1950s, the East Asian countries did have some (but not a big) advantage over many SSA countries, but that they were still way behind South Africa and Zimbabwe, as well as the Latin American countries. However, when we broaden our horizon to include the whole industrial sector, there are a couple more SSA countries (Democratic Republic of Congo and Ghana) that were ahead of East Asia even until the late 1950s. Even the gap that existed between the East Asian countries and the less-industrialised SSA countries was rather insignificant until the 1940s. And even after the gap had widened during the 1950s, their figures were still within the same league, rather than in totally different leagues (as was the case with the gaps between countries like Argentina, South Africa, Venezuela, and Chile, on the one hand, and Korea and Taiwan, on the other hand).

Thus, the picture that emerges in relation to previous industrial experiences is similar to those in relation to other indicators of 'initial conditions' that we have examined so far. Overall, the East Asian NICs did have some advantage over many SSA countries, but there were some SSA countries that were better placed than the East Asian countries at least on some measures. And up to the 1950s, whatever gap that existed between the East Asian countries and the less advanced SSA countries was rather small.

## 6.    Foreign Aid

The East Asian countries, especially Korea and Taiwan, are supposed to have received exceptionally large amounts of foreign aid in the earlier stages of their development because of their strategic positions in the Cold War. The extra resources that had come in as foreign aid are supposed to have given these countries a headstart in the pursuit of economic development over other countries that were not as lucky.

Internationally comparable data on foreign aid  before the 1960s is surprisingly difficult to find. This is a problem for our discussion, because foreign (mostly American) aid to Korea and Taiwan was particularly high in the 1950s, when the Cold War was at its height. However, Table 4.11, which shows per capita net receipts of official assistance (foreign aid) in current dollars during the first and the second half of the 1960s, provides some useful information.

In the table, we can see that, of the four East Asian NICs, the 'foreign aid' story does not apply to Hong Kong and Singapore (Hong Kong got very little, while Singapore's receipt was nothing exceptional), but that Korea and Taiwan were indeed getting rather large amounts of foreign aid during the 1960s. For example, during 1960-64, Korea and Taiwan received more foreign aid than did any other

**Table 4.11: Per Capita Net Receipt of Official Assistance (Foreign Aid) from the DAC Countries*** (yearly average over the specified periods in current US dollars)

| | 1960-64 | 1965-68 | | 1960-64 | 1965-68 |
|---|---|---|---|---|---|
| **SSA** | | | Reunion | - | - |
| Angola | 3.28[1] | 2.34[1] | Rwanda | - | 3.62 |
| Benin | 9.84[2] | 7.14 | Senegal | 9.84[2] | 12.68 |
| Botswana | - | 26.91 | Seychelles | - | 35.20 |
| Burkina Faso | 9.84[2] | 3.83 | Sierra Leone | 3.46 | 5.01 |
| Burundi | - | 2.77 | Somalia | 9.23 | 0.50 |
| Cameroon | 9.84[2] | 6.85 | South Africa | - | - |
| Cape Verde | - | - | Sudan | 1.85 | 1.64 |
| CAR | 9.84[2] | 12.35 | Swaziland | - | 28.65 |
| Chad | 9.84[2] | 5.74 | Tanzania | 3.53 | 2.98 |
| Comoros | - | - | Togo | 9.84[2] | 7.16 |
| Congo | - | 25.34 | Uganda | 3.16 | 2.77 |
| DRC (ex-Zaire) | 6.60 | 6.24 | Zambia | - | 9.13 |
| Equatorial | | | Zimbabwe | - | 0.35 |
| Guinea | - | - | | | |
| Ethiopia | 1.06 | 1.52 | **ASIA** | | |
| Gabon | 9.84[2] | 28.73 | China | - | - |
| Gambia | - | 9.18 | Hong Kong | - | 0.63 |
| Ghana | 1.82 | 8.44 | Indonesia | 1.03 | 1.50 |
| Guinea | 9.84[2] | 3.73 | Korea | 8.10 | 8.21 |
| Guinea-Bissau | 3.28[1] | 2.34[1] | Malaysia | 2.63 | 4.52 |
| Ivory Coast | 9.84[2] | 9.74 | Philippines | 1.36 | 2.85 |
| Kenya | 5.21 | 6.15 | Singapore | - | 3.96 |
| Lesotho | - | 14.16 | Taiwan | 6.85 | 5.32 |
| Liberia | 30.00 | 31.89 | Thailand | 1.47 | 1.77 |
| Madagascar | 9.84[2] | 7.07 | **LATIN AMERICA** | | |
| Malawi | 3.75 | 7.26 | Argentina | 2.23 | 1.99 |
| Mali | 9.84[2] | 4.16 | Brazil | 2.29 | 2.44 |
| Mauritania | 9.84[2] | 7.46 | Chile | 13.02 | 15.56 |
| Mauritius | - | 7.01 | Ecuador | 3.14 | 4.64 |
| Mozambique | 3.28[1] | 2.34[1] | Mexico | 1.30 | 2.28 |
| Namibia | - | - | Peru | 0.94 | 4.79 |
| Niger | 9.84[2] | 6.18 | Venezuela | 2.18 | 7.08 |
| Nigeria | 8.27 | 2.25 | | | |

Source: OECD (1967 and 1970).

CAR= Central African Republic. DRC= Democratic Republic of Congo.

*DAC (Development Assistance Committee) countries include, in alphabetical order, Australia, Austria, Belgium, Canada, Denmark, France, Germany, Italy, Japan, the Netherlands, Norway, Portugal, Sweden, Switzerland, the UK, and the USA.

1= The figure is for Angola, Guinea-Bissau, and Mozambique, which were at the time collectively known as 'Portuguese Overseas Provinces'.

2= The figure is for the whole of Francophone Africa, which includes Benin, Burkina Faso, Cameroon, Central African Republic, Chad, Gabon, Guinea, Ivory Coast, Madagascar, Mali, Mauritania, Niger, Senegal, and Togo.

Asian or Latin American country in the table, except Chile, which got the highest per capita foreign aid among the countries in the table during this period. Between 1965-68, the same picture is repeated, except that Taiwan's receipt was now lower than that of Venezuela as well.

However, when we compare Korea or Taiwan with the SSA countries, it is not possible to say that they were in better positions in terms of foreign aid. Between 1960 and 1964, assuming (rather implausibly but for the lack of a better alternative) that all the Francophone African countries, for which individual country breakdown is not available, got identical per capita foreign aid, there were 17 out of the 29 SSA countries for which the data were available that received more foreign aid per capita than either Korea or Taiwan did (the latter was about 20% lower than the former). Between 1965 and 1968, of the 40 SSA countries for which the data were available, 13 got more foreign aid per capita than did Korea, while 24 got more than did Taiwan.

Thus, the foreign aid data for the 1960s shows that, while Korea and Taiwan did get relatively large amounts of aid, especially when compared to other Asian or Latin American countries, their receipts were at about the 'average' level when compared to those of the SSA countries. Moreover, it is also very important to note that the Cold War did not just bring benefits (in the form of foreign aid) to the East Asian countries. Korea had to spend an enormous amount of resources on reconstruction after the Korean War (1950-53), a 'hot' manifestation of the Cold War. The Korean War destroyed more than 50% of the country's manufacturing base and more than 75% of the country's railways (Chang & Grabel, 2004: p. 42). Both Korea and Taiwan spent 5-6% of GDP on defence expenditure, when other countries could get away with 2-3%.[4] Given all these, it is difficult to say whether their strategic positions in the Cold War gave Korea and Taiwan any large net advantage over other developing countries.

---

[4]    The average defence spending for the IMF's 130 member countries was 3.6% of GDP in 1990 and 2.4% of GDP in 1995. See Chang and Grabel (2004: p. 45, note 1).

## 7.    Conclusion

Our examination of the evidence from the 1940s to the early 1960s suggests that, except in the area of social infrastructure (measured, very partially, in terms of infant mortality and life expectancy), there is no evidence that the East Asian NICs, especially Korea, were exceptionally well placed to achieve successful economic development in the following decades.

On most indicators of initial conditions, they were well behind the Latin American countries, partly for the obvious reason that they were then much less developed than the latter. The comparison with the SSA countries is much more difficult, because of the paucity of data for the SSA countries during this period. However, from the data we can collect, it seems fair to say that on most indicators the East Asian NICs were better placed than were many of the SSA countries, but by no means all of them. Moreover, even when they were ahead, the gaps were often modest.

Especially in the case of Korea, which was (and still is) the least developed of the East Asian NICs, its position on most indicators of initial conditions during the period under our investigation was indistinguishable from that of an 'above-average' SSA country (say, those belonging to the second quintile of the SSA distribution). The other East Asian countries, namely, Taiwan, Hong Kong, and Singapore, on most indicators, were similar to, or slightly better placed than, the 'top' SSA countries (excluding South Africa, which was well ahead of them). However, it will be difficult to say that even they were in a different league from the SSA countries, as indeed were many Latin American countries.

To conclude, our investigation in this chapter shows that East Asia was not exceptionally placed in terms of the initial conditions of economic development, as is widely believed now, even when compared to the SSA economies. East Asian exceptionalism based on the initial-conditions argument has too long been abused as a way to get rid of 'inconvenient' cases for particular theories of economic development – first by the dependency theorists and now by the mainstream economists. It is time that scholars of economic development stop taking an easy route out of their theoretical impasse through the initial-conditions argument.

# Bibliography

Bhagwati, J. (1977). 'Introduction', in J. Bhagwati (ed.), *The New International Economic Order: The North-South Debate*. Cambridge, Massachusetts: MIT Press.

Chang, H-J. (1997). 'Markets, Madness, and Many Middle Ways: Some Reflections on the Institutional Diversity of Capitalism', in P. Arestis, G. Palma & M. Sawyer (eds.), *Essays in Honour of Geoff Harcourt – Volume 2: Markets, Unemployment, and Economic Policy*. London: Routledge.

Chang, H-J. (2002). 'Breaking the Mould – An Institutionalist Political Economy Alternative to the Neo-Liberal Theory of the Market and the State', *Cambridge Journal of Economics*, vol. 26, no. 5.

Chang, H-J. & Grabel, I. (2004). *Reclaiming Development – An Alternative Economic Policy Manual*. London: Zed Press.

Chang, H-J. & Nolan, P. (eds.) (1995). *The Transformation of the Communist Economies – Against the Mainstream*. London and Basingstoke: Macmillan.

Hargreaves, D., Devaney, J. & Eden-Green, M. (1994). *World Index of Resources and Population*. Aldershot: Dartmouth.

Kindleberger, C. (1965). *Economic Development*. New York: McGraw-Hill.

Kohli, A. (1994). 'Where Do High Growth Political Economies Come From?: The Japanese Lineage of Korea's "Developmental State"', *World Development*, vol. 22, no. 9.

Maddison, A. (1989). *The World Economy in the 20th Century*. Paris: OECD.

Mitchell, B. (1992). *International Historical Statistics: Europe, 1750-1988*, 2nd edition. London: Macmillan.

Mitchell, B. (1993). *International Historical Statistics: The Americas, 1750-1988*, 3rd edition. London: Macmillan.

Mitchell, B. (1995). *International Historical Statistics: Africa, Asia and Oceania, 1750-1988*, 2nd edition. London: Macmillan.

OECD (Organisation for Economic Cooperation and Development) (1967). *Flow of Financial Resources to Countries in Course of Economic Development, 1961-5*. Paris: OECD.

OECD (Organisation for Economic Cooperation and Development) (1970). *Flow of Financial Resources to Countries in Course of Economic Development, 1965-8*. Paris: OECD.

Sachs, J. & Warner, A. (1997). 'Sources of Slow Growth in African Economies', *Journal of African Economies*, vol. 6, no. 3.

Sachs, J. & Warner, A. (2001). 'The Curse of Natural Resources', *European Economic Review*, vol. 45, no. 4.

UNESCO (various years). *Statistical Yearbook*. New York: United Nations.

United Nations. (various years). *Statistical Yearbook*. New York: United Nations.

Warren, B. (1973). 'Imperialism and Capitalist Industrialisation', *New Left Review*, no. 81, September/October 1973.

Warren, B. (1980). *Imperialism: Pioneer of Capitalism.* London: Verso.

World Bank (1993). *The East Asian Miracle.* New York: Oxford University Press.

World Bank (various years). *World Development Report.* New York: Oxford University Press.

Wright, G. & Czulesta, J. (2004). 'The Myth of the Resource Curse', *Challenge*, vol. 47, no. 2.

# Chapter 5

# THE HAZARD OF MORAL HAZARD
# – UNTANGLING THE ASIAN CRISIS

## 1. Introduction

IT has been widely argued that the 1997 Asian crisis was not the result of simple macroeconomic mismanagement but the result of certain deep-rooted institutional deficiencies that created moral hazard among its industrial and financial enterprises, leading to inefficient investments and/or excessive risk-taking.[1] While the IMF bailout has also been identified as a potential source of moral hazard for the international lenders (e.g., McKinnon and Pill, 1998; Frankel, 1998), most accounts argue that the national institutions of the Asian countries were the main sources of moral hazard behind the crisis.

The first and perhaps most popular variant of the moral-hazard argument is that of 'crony capitalism', where personal connections and political patronage, rather than entrepreneurial abilities, determine who gets access to credit and other resources and on what terms (e.g., Krugman, 1998b; Frankel, 1998). Others emphasise the role of industrial policy in providing (at least implicit) guarantees to investment projects in government-favoured industries, thus encouraging their managers to take excessive risk (e.g., *The Economist,* 15 November 1997; Brittan, 1997). McKinnon and Pill (1998) and Krugman (1998a) identify deposit insurance and other implicit guarantees for banks as the major source of moral hazard. Still others argue that the large firms in the crisis-stricken countries, especially Korea, had taken

---

[1] Frankel (1998) sums this position up: 'The main problem in East Asia was not macroeconomics, but structural'.

excessive risks because they knew that the governments would be unwilling and/or unable to let them go bankrupt for fear of knock-on effects on the rest of the economy – the logic of so-called 'too big to fail' (e.g., Yoo, 1997; Pyo, 1998; Burton, 1998).

These arguments have profoundly influenced the currently dominant prescription for policy changes and institutional reforms issued by the IMF and many leaders in Asian and international policy-making circles. According to this prescription, the Asian countries should radically liberalise their economies, as this will not only abolish market-defying industrial policy but also reduce the scope for cronyism. Greater transparency in the conduct of business and politics is also demanded as a measure to expose cronyistic transactions. Those who support the 'too big to fail' (henceforth TBTF) story argue for measures that will lead to the weakening and hopefully the dismemberment of large business groups, such as restrictions on cross-subsidies and mutual loan guarantees, greater reliance on the stock market, and the strengthening of minority shareholder rights. Put together, these policy recommendations amount to the dissolution of what have been regarded as the main ingredients of the so-called 'East Asian' economic model – close government-business relationship (now re-branded cronyism), bank-based financial system, industrial policy, large (and diversified) business groups, and relational (as opposed to arm's-length) contracting.[2]

While the dominance of the moral-hazard argument continues, there have been, fortunately in my view, a sizeable number of studies – very interestingly cutting across the traditional orthodox-unorthodox divide – which take a dim view of this argument and instead argue that the Asian crisis was mainly caused by the 'manias, panics, and crashes' mechanism (the term is due to Charles Kindleberger)

---

[2]    The Southeast Asian economies of Thailand, Indonesia, and Malaysia were once praised by the World Bank (1993) and by others for their allegedly greater market orientation than that of the East Asian countries (Japan, Korea, Taiwan, and Singapore). However, after the 1997 crisis, they have been lumped together by many commentators with the East Asian countries as practitioners of 'Asian capitalism'.

inherent in unregulated financial markets.[3] Unfortunately, however, the existing criticisms of the moral-hazard argument have been rather fragmented and brief, so there seems to be value in providing a comprehensive criticism of this dominant view – the task that the present chapter sets out to take up.

This chapter is organised in the following way. The next section (Section 2) puts the problem of moral hazard into historical perspective by pointing out that, contrary to the popular perception, moral hazard has been an integral part of the development of modern capitalism. The subsequent section (Section 3) analyses the five main variants of the moral-hazard argument that we identified above – industrial policy, cronyism, deposit insurance, the logic of TBTF, and IMF bailouts – to see whether they are theoretically coherent and how important (or not) they were in generating the Asian crisis. The last section (Section 4) sums up our discussion and draws policy conclusions.

## 2.    Moral Hazard and the Development of Capitalism

It is by definition true that, whenever they do not need to bear the full consequences of their actions, economic agents will behave 'irresponsibly' in the sense that they take more risk than they would do otherwise. Although the actual extent of such 'irresponsible' behaviour is often much less than what is assumed in the standard theory (as the assumption of total selfishness of individuals that the latter is based on does not hold in reality), this problem has been a long-running concern.

Throughout the history of capitalism, a range of institutions that protect individuals from bearing the full consequences of their actions have been developed – limited liability, central banking (and other lender-of-last-resort facilities), insurance, and the underwriting

---

[3]    The argument emphasising the inherently unstable and irrational nature of unregulated financial markets has been endorsed both by a number of orthodox economists (e.g., Corden, 1998; Furman and Stiglitz, 1998; Radelet and Sachs, 1998; Stiglitz, 1998) and by many unorthodox economists (e.g., Kregel, 1998; Singh, 1999; Taylor, 1998; Chang *et al.* [eds.], 2001).

of risky ventures by the government (especially, but not only, in late-developing countries). Predictably, these institutions have been accused of encouraging 'irresponsible' behaviour by severing the link between economic agents' actions and their responsibilities.

Especially to the observers of early capitalism, who regarded greed and fear as the two main forces that drive and restrain the capitalist system, the emergence of the above-mentioned risk-sharing institutions amounted to eliminating fear, thus unbinding greed and thereby pushing the system off the even keel. This sentiment is best summed up in the remark by Herbert Spencer when he voiced his opposition to the development of lender-of-last-resort facilities – he argued that '[t]he ultimate result of shielding man from the effects of folly is to people the world with fools' (quoted in Kindleberger, 1996: p. 146).[4] Modern discourses on these institutions may have taken more technically sophisticated forms, particularly with the help of the new techniques of information economics, but the underlying view is essentially the same – when risk is not fully borne by the actor, there will be 'excessive' risk-taking. But is it necessarily bad to allow people to off-load risk to some other people (or rather the society at large)? This depends on which particular institutional arrangement we are talking about in which particular context, as there are many respectable reasons for the 'socialisation of risk' that the above-mentioned institutions provide.

For example, take limited liability – one institution that probably had generated the most heated debate for its potential to create moral hazard. Although most of us take it for granted these days, limited liability aroused great suspicion in its early days. Commenting on late-19th-century Britain, Rosenberg and Birdzell (1986) document how even decades after the full-scale introduction of the principle of limited liability (although limited liability had been occasionally granted by royal charters, it was generalised only in 1855), small businessmen 'who, being actively in charge of a business as well as its owner, sought to limit responsibility for its debts by the device of incorporation' were still frowned upon (p. 200).

---

4   The original source is H. Spencer, 'State Tampering with Money and Banks', in *Essays: Scientific, Political, and Speculative* (London: Williams and Northgate, 1891), vol. 3, p. 354.

However, capitalism would not have developed in the way it did without the institution of limited liability, because, without it, it would have been impossible to make the risky large-scale investments that have characterised the modern industrial economy. As Richardson (1960) argues, '[i]f ... uncertainty [involved in investment decisions] is very great, it may be that the decisions could not be taken unless liability for their consequences were generalised as widely as possible' (p. 221). In the words of Rosenberg (1994), '[t]he willingness to undertake experiments in both the social and technological spheres depends upon some sort of limitation upon the negative consequences for the individual if the risky enterprise should fail, as it frequently did' (p. 97), and therefore '[t]he emergence of business firms with limited liability ... was central from the point of view of facilitating investment in risky undertakings' (p. 96).

For another example, the introduction of lender-of-last-resort facilities, and more specifically central banking (central banks are not the only possible lenders of last resort)[5], aroused the same concern as what the introduction of limited liability did (see the above quote from Spencer). However, the classic works by Kindleberger (1984 and 1996) show how the development of various lender-of-last-resort facilities, including modern central banking (and explicit deposit insurance schemes in some countries), had been critical in the development of banking and thus of the ability to finance industry in Europe and the US.[6]

---

[5]  Before the emergence of central banking, the leading banks – the top London banks in the UK and the top New York banks in the US – were willing and forced to take this role, although their effectiveness in this regard was limited for obvious reasons. See Kindleberger (1996: Chapter 10) for further details.

[6]  On the provision of lender-of-last-resort facilities before the start of modern central banking, Kindleberger (1996) says: 'Intuitive politicians in the British government and the intuitive merchant-bankers who ran the Bank of England thought it best to give power to grant relief neither wholly to the Bank nor wholly to the government, but to leave it uncertain. If the giving of relief were formally within the power of either the Bank or the government, pressure from the public would be difficult to resist' (pp. 155-6). And then he goes on: 'Within too large a group, responsibility inheres in no one. With a single entity responsible, pressure for action may build up irresistibly. The optimum may be a small number of actors, closely attuned to one another in an oligarchic relation, like-minded, applying strong pressure to keep down the chisellers and free-riders, prepared ultimately to accept responsibility' (p. 156).

The point that we are trying to make here is not that limited liability, central banking, or any other institution that socialises risk does not create any moral hazard, although, as we argued earlier, they may not create as much moral hazard as they are often believed to. The point is that the social benefits of these institutions (investments of larger scale and of longer gestation, more innovation, the prevention of systemic financial collapses, etc.) are on the whole greater than the social costs arising from the moral hazard they create.

According to Rosenberg, '[t]he history of capitalism involved the progressive introduction of a number of institutional devices that facilitated the commitment of resources to the innovation process by reducing or placing limitations upon risk while, at the same time, holding out the prospect of large financial rewards to the successful innovator' (Rosenberg, 1994: p. 96). North (1981) also emphasises that 'economic organisation that induces economic growth may well do so by internalising the benefits and externalising the costs and hence raising the private rate of return to "productive" economic activity at the expense of costs imposed on other groups in society' (p. 62).

Thus seen, it may be said that moral hazard has been an essential element in the development of capitalism – or to put it more provocatively, capitalism has developed on the basis of moral hazard. The exact institutional form taken was different (limited liability, lender-of-last-resort facility, industrial policy, etc.), but the principle was the same – socialisation of risk. It is therefore misleading to look at only the cost side of those institutions that socialise risk while ignoring their benefits, and to condemn them. Once we recognise this, it becomes easier to see how misleading the present discourse on moral hazard as applied to the Asian crisis is.


## 3.    Moral Hazard in the Asian Crisis

In the prevailing discourse on the recent Asian crisis, the notion of moral hazard has occupied the central place. However, as we mentioned at the beginning (Section 1), in this discourse, different sources of (alleged) moral hazard in the afflicted countries are lumped together under the banner of 'Asian capitalism' and do not get their respective logic explored to the full. In this section, we separate out different sources of moral hazard from one another so that we can better analyse how well each of them is conceptualised, on the one hand, and how important they were respectively in the making of the Asian crisis, on the other hand.

## 3.1  Industrial policy

Those who emphasise the 'state capitalism' aspect of the Asian countries argue that industrial policy was the major source of moral hazard in these countries (e.g., *The Economist*, 15 November 1997; Brittan, 1997). The argument is that the Asian governments, in their attempts to promote their favoured industries, had explicitly and implicitly underwritten the investments in them, which naturally encouraged lax management and excessive risk-taking. This argument is best summed up in the following passage from *The Economist*: 'Most of the financial mess is of Asia's own making, and nowhere is this clearer than in South Korea. For years, the government has treated the banks as tools of state industrial policy, ordering them to make loans to uncreditworthy companies and industries' (15 November 1997).[7]

In discussing this view, we first need to point out that, contrary to the widespread assumption, state guarantee through industrial policy need not be bad. There are all kinds of 'market failures' that justify socialisation of risk through industrial policy as revealed in the recent debates: the presence of 'specific' assets that make free entry and exit socially costly; complementarity between investments across industries (the 'Big Push' consideration); externalities present in R&D efforts and other knowledge-generating investments; infant-industry considerations arising from the cost of learning; and the capital market failure that makes long-term financing more expensive than what

---

[7]    Although it is often mixed up with the 'crony capitalism' argument that we discuss in Subsection 3.2, the industrial-policy argument can be, and should be, analytically separated from the former, as it does not necessarily assume nepotism or corruption in the choice of favoured industries and companies.

is socially desirable (Chang, 1994: Chapter 3; Stiglitz, 1996; Lall, 1998; Chang, 1999).[8] Once again, the point is not that such socialisation of risk does not generate any moral hazard, but that the benefits that it brings about (e.g., higher productivity, better-coordinated investments, prevention of the 'wastes' from duplicative investments) can more than offset the costs from the moral hazard that it may generate. The success of industrial policy in various East Asian countries in the past is good proof of this.

Of course, as we are all familiar with, there are many examples of failed industrial-policy attempts all over the world (including in the successful East Asian countries). However, these failures have occurred because of poor policy design and implementation (owing sometimes to political reasons and sometimes to the inevitable imperfection of human foresight), and not because the principle of socialisation of risk itself is inherently wrong. Recent debates have shown that the net benefit from industrial policy critically depends on how exactly it is designed and implemented: how realistically the 'target' industries are selected in light of the country's technological capabilities and world market conditions; how closely the policy is integrated with an export strategy so that there is some 'objective' criterion to judge enterprise performance; how politically willing and able the state is to discipline the recipients of the rents that it creates; how competent and politically insulated the bureaucracy that implements the policy is; how closely the state interacts with the private sector while not becoming its hostage; and so on (Amsden, 1989; World Bank, 1993; Chang, 1994; Evans, 1995; Akyuz et al., 1998).

---

[8]　It was not just in East Asia but also in a number of European countries (e.g., France, Austria, Finland, and Norway) that industrial policy played an important role, at least until the 1970s. However, the industrial-policy debate since the 1980s concentrated on the East Asian experience. Reviews of the earlier phase of this debate, which focused on Japan, can be found in Johnson (ed.) (1984: Introduction) and Chang (1994: Chapter 3). The more recent phase of the debate revolved around the 'East Asian Miracle Report' by the World Bank (1993). Critical assessments of this report's position on industrial policy can be found in Lall (1994), Fishlow et al. (1994), Chang (1995), and Chang (1999).

Moreover, whether or not we believe in particular justifications for industrial policy, it is empirically difficult to sustain that industrial policy was responsible for the Asian crisis.[9]

First of all, while we should not ignore the role that it played in developing some natural-resource-related industries, the extent of industrial policy in Southeast Asia has been rather limited (for country details, see Jomo and Rock, 1998). Thailand has had very little in the way of systematic industrial policy except in the agricultural processing industry. Indonesia may have had a little more recourse to industrial policy, but many of its industrial-policy programmes (such as support for the aircraft industry) were haphazard and poorly conceived, especially when compared to the programmes in the East Asian countries. Malaysia has had a more systematic industrial policy, but it can hardly be described as the dominant factor in the country's policy regime in the way that it was in the East Asian countries.

In fact, before the crisis, the World Bank (1993) was making a big deal out of the fact that the Southeast Asian countries had grown fast without the East-Asian-style industrial policy, while some of the Bank's critics also argued that the absence of such policy was precisely the reason why these economies failed to achieve an effective industrial upgrading.[10] In short, industrial policy could not have been a major factor in causing crises in the Southeast Asian economies, because there was, simply, little of it around.

---

[9] Here, we are ignoring some essentially 'cronyistic' policies that were dressed up as industrial policy, notably in Indonesia (more on this in Subsection 3.2).

[10] The difficulties that the Southeast Asian economies were having in upgrading their industrial structure were best manifested in their high and premature reliance on imported labour during the last several years. On the eve of the crisis, Malaysia, a country with a 9-million-strong labour force, had up to 3 million legal and illegal immigrant workers, while Thailand, with a 34-million-strong labour force, is believed to have had around 2 million foreign workers. The comparable figure in Japan, a country with a 66-million-strong workforce and per capita income nearly 10 times higher, is about 3 million. The importance of real-estate-related investments in the Southeast Asian countries before the crisis also seems to suggest that there were not enough new investment opportunities opening up in the manufacturing sector because of the absence of a forward-looking industrial policy combined with effective investments in infrastructure and skills (Henderson, 1998).

Then how about Korea? Isn't it one of the archetypal 'industrial policy states' and therefore isn't it natural that industrial policy was the main factor behind its crisis, as the above quote from *The Economist* sums up? Such conjecture sounds even more plausible when we recall that the over-investment that caused the Korean crisis was mostly in industries, rather than in real estate development as in the case of Southeast Asia (see Henderson, 1998 on the role of real estate investments in Southeast Asia). However, this story does not sit well with the facts.

Contrary to the popular perception, industrial policy was largely absent in Korea in the build-up to the current crisis. It is true that up to the mid-1980s the country practised one of the most comprehensive and systemic industrial policies in the world. However, slowly from the late 1980s, and very rapidly from 1993 with the inauguration of the Kim Young Sam administration, the Korean government had dismantled industrial policy, except for R&D support in some high-technology industries (see Chang, 1998 for further details). If industrial policy was largely absent, it seems rather difficult to blame the Korean crisis on it.

Anyway, in the Korean case, it is not even the case that moral hazard was widespread under its traditional industrial policy regime. First of all, its government was willing and able to withdraw its support even from firms investing in its favoured sectors, if the performance lagged (Amsden, 1989; Chang, 1993; Evans, 1995). For this purpose, it closely monitored the performance of the enterprises receiving its support, and routinely intervened to encourage (and sometimes force) mergers and takeovers of inefficient enterprises. And even the largest conglomerates were not free from such disciplining by the state (see Subsection 3.4 for further details). Moreover, given the highly export-oriented nature of the Korean firms, it was very difficult for an inefficient firm to hide its problems for long. In other words, there was actually little room for moral hazard for the government-supported firms in the traditional Korean system, as continued government support was contingent on their performance and was not guaranteed by their just being in the 'right' industries.

In fact, we can go even further and argue that it was actually the demise of industrial policy, rather than its continuation, which was mainly responsible for the 1997 crisis in Korea. It was, for example, the end to the policy of investment coordination that allowed the pro-liferation of duplicative investments in the key industries that fuelled the massive foreign borrowing between 1993 and 1997 (for more details, see Chang *et al.*, 1998). In addition, the demise of industrial policy, as well as the official end in 1993 of the three-decade-old five-year-planning practice, led to the disappearance of the 'rational' criteria according to which government support had been previously allocated and therefore made it easier to gain access to credit for risky ventures through 'cronyistic' connections or clever political manoeuvring (see Subsection 3.2 for further details).[11]

Let us summarise our argument in this section. The state's un-derwriting of risky investments through industrial policy may create some room for moral hazard and consequently certain social costs, but these costs have to be set against the gains that it may bring. Moreover, whether and how much moral hazard is created by indus-trial policy depends on how it is designed and implemented. Empiri-cally, there is little evidence that industrial policy was an important factor behind the Asian crisis. It is rather well known that industrial policy has always been sparse, if not absent, in Southeast Asian coun-tries, but even in Korea, industrial policy was largely dismantled by 1993. In the Korean case, it can even be said that the demise of indus-trial policy critically contributed to the crisis, by removing the re-straints on duplicative investments and possibly creating more room for cronyism.

---

[11]  The best example of the former – cronyism – was the case of Hanbo, whose collapse in January 1997 revealed a web of high-level corruption involving the then President's closest political aides regarding bank-lending decisions. The best example of the latter – clever political manoeuvring – was the use of regionalist sentiment by Samsung in securing the government's approval for its new auto venture. One of the ways in which Samsung diffused the government's opposi-tion to its entry into the already-crowded automobile industry (an opposition which was already feeble anyway, given the government's commitment to a 'free mar-ket' policy and hence the abandonment of the traditional policy of investment coordination) was to decide to locate its factory in Pusan, the then President's hometown and power base. See Chang (1998) for further details.

## 3.2    Cronyism

If analytically less well-defined, the notion of cronyism has certainly attracted more attention than industrial policy as the main culprit of the Asian crisis. The cronyism story is often mixed up with the industrial-policy story, partly because sometimes cronyistic support was provided under the guise of industrial policy, especially in some Southeast Asian countries. However, analytically, government support based on cronyism and that based on industrial policy concerns need to be clearly distinguished from one another.

If the industrial-policy story argues that the Asian governments have provided guarantees to industrial and financial enterprises in their desire to develop certain industries against the market logic, the cronyism story sees them as providing such guarantees in order to promote the interests of their political allies. The root of such political alliance, it is argued, can be nepotism (or what Krugman, 1998b, calls 'minister's nephew' syndrome) but it can also be the exchange of economic favours for political funding. Lenders, the story goes, naturally regarded enterprises with cronyistic connections as having no downside risk (as the government would rescue them if they got into trouble), and were willing to lend them as much as they wanted, thus inflating asset bubbles that led to the crisis (Krugman, 1998b).

One obvious problem with this story is that cronyism, in various forms and degrees, has been a feature in all the crisis-stricken Asian countries throughout their high-growth periods, and therefore it cannot explain why it did not cause similar crises before.

One possible explanation is that the nature of cronyism prevailing in these societies had changed shortly before the current crisis. For example, in the Korean case, the weakening of 'developmentalism' (and the consequent dismantling of industrial policy, financial regulation, and five-year planning) since the late 1980s significantly reduced the scope for state influence in resource allocation, but it at the same time made it easier to abuse whatever residual influence that the state still had through bribery or nepotism (see Chang, 1998). The result was a spilling-over of political corruption from the traditionally corrupt areas (such as urban planning and defence contracts) into the main manufacturing industries, which were previously insulated from corruption to a high degree (for further details, see Chang *et al.*,

1998). In the Thai case, some commentators point out that the increasing dominance of redistribution-oriented provincial politicians during the last decade or so seems to have increased the importance of pork-barrel politics (Pasuk and Baker, 2001).

However, neither of the above accounts suggests that the changes in the form and the extent of corruption in Korea or Thailand were so significant as to turn cronyism into the major problem that it was not before. In Indonesia and Malaysia as well, it is difficult to detect signs that cronyism got much worse in the build-up to the crisis. In fact, for whatever it's worth, the 'corruption perception index' compiled by Transparency International showed that corruption was perceived to be diminishing in all the crisis-stricken countries on the eve of the crisis, in spite of the well-established historical regularity that during financial euphoria the incidence of corrupt behaviour tends to increase both in the private sector and in the public sector (Kindleberger, 1996, Chapter 5).[12]

Anyway, whatever its true extent was, it is not clear whether cronyism can ever be a major explanation of the Asian crisis, because cronyism by definition has to be selective and therefore it does not make sense to argue that all (or even the bulk of) those Indonesian firms which had foreign loans, those Korean merchant banks that led the foreign lending boom, or those Thai financial companies which were speculating in real estate had such good political connections that they could expect bailouts in times of trouble. If some foreign creditors thought this was the case, they should have practised themselves those 'advanced' credit risk assessment techniques that they are now so eager to preach to the Asian financial institutions.

---

[12] On a scale of 0 (very corrupt) to 10 (very clean), Korea's score went down from 3.93 during 1980-85 to 3.50 during 1988-92, but significantly went up to 5.32 in 1996. Thailand showed the same pattern – that is, the corruption problem was perceived as having become worse in the late 1980s and the early 1990s but as much improved on the eve of the crisis compared to the early 1980s. The figures were 2.42 (1980-85), 1.85 (1988-92), and 3.33 (1996). In the Malaysian case, corruption was also perceived to have become worse and then better, although the perception of corruption in 1996 was worse than that of the early 1980s – its figures were 6.29 (1980-85), 5.10 (1988-92), and 5.32 (1996). Indonesia, starting from a very low base, showed a continuous and marked improvement right up to the crisis – its figures were 0.20 (1980-85), 0.57 (1988-92), and 2.65 (1996).

To conclude, cronyism did play a role in the generation of the crisis in the Asian countries, but it is unlikely to have been more than a minor factor. Cronyism has been a permanent feature of these countries at least in certain sectors during the last few decades, and there is little evidence that the changes in its form and extent that did occur in some of these countries (notably Korea and Thailand) were so significant as to create a crisis. In fact, in all the crisis-stricken countries, corruption was perceived to have been diminishing in the build-up to the crisis. By definition, cronyism has to be selective, and therefore it cannot have affected more than a small portion of the borrowings. If some international lenders thought otherwise, it seems to be good proof that irrational euphoria can grip people's minds during a financial mania.

### 3.3  Deposit insurance

Deposit insurance was singled out by, for example, McKinnon and Pill (1998) as the main source of moral hazard in the Asian economies, or for that matter, any economy experiencing over-borrowing (also see Krugman, 1998a). According to this argument, bank deposits are (at least implicitly) guaranteed by all governments because of the importance of the bank liabilities in the domestic payments system, and such guarantee creates moral hazard on the side of the banks which then lend to misconceived or speculative projects.

One point to note immediately is that even many of those who advance the deposit-insurance story accept that there is a clear benefit from such insurance, which is to preserve the stability of the domestic payments system (at least McKinnon and Pill, 1998, do that unequivocally). As we pointed out earlier (Section 2), the real question here is then whether the costs from moral hazard that deposit insurance creates are greater than the gains from the stability of the domestic payments system that it also provides. And, as we have seen in Section 2, economic historians suggest that the gains have been generally far greater.

More importantly, even ignoring the fact that deposit insurance may have more benefits than costs, the problem with this story is that deposit insurance does not necessarily create moral hazard for the bank managers who make the lending decisions. By definition, it is the depositors who are protected from this arrangement, and not the bank managers. Therefore, whether deposit insurance gives the bank manager the incentive to make imprudent lending decisions will be critically determined by the degree to which his/her job security and remuneration depend on the quality of his/her decisions, and not merely by the existence of deposit insurance. In this sense, the widely-used analogy between deposit insurance and fire insurance is fundamentally misleading, because in the latter case the insured has (some) control over the likelihood of the insurance money being paid out, while in the former case the insured (the depositor) does not have much meaningful control over the likelihood.[13]

Kindleberger's (1996) observation on the 1982 debt crisis supports our view that deposit insurance in itself need not create moral hazard on the part of the bank managers:

'Have the money-centre banks loaned rather recklessly to Third World countries during the 1970s, secure in the knowledge that they would not be allowed to fail? There have been appearances of that sort. But the penalties for bank mismanagement requiring rescue operations are still substantial. Depositors may not lose, but stockholders suffer and risk-prone banks may have trouble raising capital. In addition, officers of failed banks tend to be fired. Sometimes this is not financially embarrassing because of golden handshakes or parachutes, clauses in contracts of hire that provide for substantial severance pay over an extended period. Few of these appear to provide for cancellation in the case of blatant mismanagement, as perhaps, in equity, they ought to do. Reputations generally suffer. Not always, however.' (p. 196)

The point is that, if the bank managers know that they will lose their jobs and suffer in reputation when their banks fail, the knowledge that their banks will be bailed out by the government does not give them much comfort. In this case, deposit insurance will not create moral hazard on the part of the bank managers. Of course, as Kindleberger points out in the above quote, in practice the bank man-

---

[13] In theory, it will be possible that deposit insurance makes the depositors lax in playing their role in disciplining the bank managers by shopping around for better-managed banks. The question, of course, is how important such a mechanism is in practice in disciplining the bank managers, especially in the short run.

agers do not necessarily get fully punished for their poor decisions, but this is the result of a poorly designed incentive system for the bank managers, and not the result of deposit insurance *per se.*

The empirical limitation of the deposit-insurance story as applied to the Asian crisis is that it cannot really explain why, if deposit insurance was what was driving the over-lending, it was the non-bank financial institutions (e.g., the Korean merchant banks, the Thai finance companies) or the non-financial corporations (e.g., Indonesian corporations), rather than the banks, that led the over-lending process. Neither the non-bank financial institutions nor non-financial corporations had the same extent of government guarantees as the banks, as proven by the fact that many of these institutions were promptly closed down after the outbreak of the crisis (in contrast to the banks, most of which were bailed out). When combined with the fact that there was also an enormous surge of portfolio investment inflows before the crisis (which obviously has no guarantee whatsoever), the above facts suggest that it was not mainly because of perceived guarantees that so much foreign capital flowed into the crisis-stricken economies (Corden, 1998).

In conclusion, it is not very clear how deposit insurance in itself could have generated over-borrowing and over-lending in the crisis-stricken Asian countries. If government guarantee were to play an important role in encouraging moral hazard on the part of those who make lending decisions, there should have been (at least the perception of) a guarantee that their job and reputation will be safe whatever happens to the institutions they manage, and not just a guarantee for the depositors. There is no evidence that such guarantee existed in the countries concerned. Moreover, when a high proportion of foreign capital inflows to these countries were either in the form of loans to the non-bank financial institutions and the non-financial corporate sector, which by no means had similar (even implicit) guarantee as the banking sector, or in the form of portfolio investment, it is difficult to believe that it was the perception of government guarantee that was driving the surge in capital inflows.

## 3.4   The logic of 'too big to fail'

This argument has been quite popular among those who write on the Korean crisis. Many of these commentators have argued that the reckless, unfocused diversification of the big conglomerates (known as the *chaebols*) is to blame for the country's crisis. These large conglomerates, they argue, took excessive risk because they knew that they were 'too big to fail' in the sense that the government cannot afford to sit and watch them go bankrupt for fear of large-scale 'ripple effects' such as large-scale unemployment and bankruptcy of subcontracting firms (e.g., Yoo, 1997; Pyo, 1998; Burton, 1998). They point to the government rescue of some large firms in the past as evidence that the logic of TBTF has been in operation in the country – the most frequently cited example being the nationalisation of the bankrupt third-largest car manufacturer Kia in the build-up to the crisis (for the details on the fate of Kia, see Chang, 1998).[14]

The logic of TBTF seems difficult to dismiss, especially given that it is indeed practised by all governments in all capitalist countries, including the ones that claim to be the most market-oriented. The rescue of the US hedge fund, Long Term Capital Management (LTCM), is one prominent recent example, but the late 1970s rescue of the bankrupt Swedish shipbuilding industry through nationalisation by the country's first right-wing government for over 50 years or the early 1980s rescue of the carmaker Chrysler by the avowedly free-market Reagan administration also seem to demonstrate the power of the logic of TBTF.

However, there is confusion in the TBTF story between the rescue of a firm and the rescue of its owners or managers who are responsible for creating the situation where the rescue is needed. To the manager, it is not much of a consolation that his/her firm is saved by the government due to its large size, if the rescue operation involves the termination of his/her contract. So if a manager knows that his/her job would be in jeopardy if the firm performs badly, there is little moral hazard on his/her part. The same goes for the owners. If the

---

[14]   Kia was subsequently sold to the largest Korean car manufacturer Hyundai in the autumn of 1998 through an open international bidding process.

owners know that the rescue operation will require ceding of their corporate control (as has almost always been the case in Korea – see below), they cannot afford to be lax in management (in cases where they are owner-managers) or in supervising the hired managers.

In this sense, the rescue of LTCM, which did not involve the removal of the incumbent management (although its control was weakened due to debt-equity swaps), has definitely given a very bad signal to the rest of the financial industry and will probably encourage moral hazard in the future. On the other hand, the rescue of Kia, which involved a change in the top management, could not have sent such a signal to the managers of other large enterprises. In other words, whether government bailout of some large firms encourages moral hazard by the managers of other large firms depends on whether it is accompanied by punishments for bad management.

The evidence from Korea is not on the side of the TBTF story. Especially in the 1960s and the 1970s, when the country was going through rapid structural changes, it was not infrequent to see even some of the largest *chaebols* going bankrupt and their carcasses being divided up through state-mediated takeovers. The second largest *chaebol* during the 1960s, Samho, had all but disappeared by the late 1970s after a series of bankruptcies of its core firms. The Gaepoong *chaebol*, which ranked between third and fourth during the 1960s, virtually disappeared by the mid-1970s following a series of business failures. The Donglip *chaebol*, which ranked ninth in the early 1960s, went bankrupt by the end of the decade. The owner of what was once the largest car manufacturer in the country, Shinjin, was forced to sell it off to the state-owned Korea Development Bank (which then sold it to Daewoo) in the late 1970s, when it got into trouble. Dongmyung, the *chaebol* built around what was the world's largest producer of plywood around the early 1970s, went bankrupt in 1980.

These are striking statistics. For example, the collapse of three of the top 10 *chaebols* of the 1960s (namely, Samho, Gaepoong, and Donglip) is equivalent in American terms to the disappearance by the early 1980s of Standard Oil (New Jersey), Ford Motor, and IBM, which ranked second, third and ninth respectively in the *Fortune* US enterprise ranking in 1964. As a result, until the mid-1980s, there was a very high turnover even in the ranks of the top 10 *chaebols*. Only three of the top 10 *chaebols* in 1966 were among the 1974 top 10 and only five of the 1974 top 10 were in the 1980 top 10 (Chang, 1994, p. 123).

After the mid-1980s, and especially in the 1990s, the ranking of the top 10 *chaebols* remained highly, if not completely, stable, but among the lesser *chaebols* there was still a high turnover. Between 1986 and 1996, among the 20 *chaebols* that ranked between 11th and 30th, there were on average 14 changes in the rankings and 2.2 new entries into the group every year (Park, 1998, Table 9). Between 1990 and 1996 alone, three of the top 30 *chaebols* (Hanyang, Yoowon, and Woosung) went bankrupt, showing that there is no substance to claims such as: 'In Korea, none of the *chaebols* had been allowed to fail for a decade before Hanbo steel collapsed in early 1997' (Radelet and Sachs, 1998: p. 42). In 1997, in the build-up to and at the beginning of the crisis, six of the top 30 *chaebols* (Kia, Halla, Jinro, Hanbo, Sammi, and Haitai) went bankrupt, again debunking the TBTF story (Chang *et al.*, 1998).

Of course, all these are not to deny that the Korean government not infrequently injected money into ailing large enterprises through the state-owned banks (especially the development bank, Korea Development Bank). However, these financial injections were conditional, with very few exceptions, on the change of ownership and top management, and were always accompanied by tough terms of financial restructuring. In other words, the rescue of large enterprises by the Korean government should be seen as government-mediated take-over or restructuring rather than as bailout in the strict sense (*à la* LTCM).[15]

Let us summarise this section. The logic of TBTF seems compelling, given that all governments, and not just the Asian ones, have rescued some technically bankrupt large enterprises. However, whether such rescue will lead to moral hazard on the part of the managers of other large firms depends on the terms of the rescue, especially whether

---

[15] When the amount of money involved in the rescue operation (e.g., debt write-offs, tax exemption, and other direct and indirect subsidies) was considered too large, the government went for direct nationalisation. The merger and subsequent nationalisation of the four companies in the power-generating equipment industry in the early 1980s is the best example (see Chang, 1993: pp. 148-9, for further details).

and how much the existing managers are made to pay for their mistakes (recall our distinction between the Kia and the LTCM types of government rescue). It is only when the managers are not properly punished that the logic of TBTF works. Looking at the Korean case, to which the logic of TBTF has been most widely applied, we find no evidence that this logic was in operation in any meaningful degree. Even the largest firms routinely went bankrupt, and state rescue programmes almost always involved the ousting of the existing owners and managers, while always imposing tough terms of financial restructuring. What these programmes did was to enable the firm to continue as a going concern, but not to let the incumbent managers get away with their mistakes and thus create moral hazard for the managers of other large firms.

## 3.5  IMF bailouts

Some commentators suggest that the IMF bailouts during various postwar debt crises have created moral hazard on the part of international lenders (e.g., McKinnon and Pill, 1998; Frankel, 1998). According to this argument, the history of IMF bailouts, and especially the Mexican bailout of 1995, has convinced the international lenders to Asia that they will be able to get their money back whatever happens in the borrowing country, encouraging them to make excessively risky lending. Some right-wing politicians and journalists (but none of the academics cited above) have even used this as an argument for abolishing, or at least severely weakening, the IMF.

While it is undeniable that the history of IMF bailouts has created moral hazard on the part of the international lenders, there are two qualifications to be made with respect to this argument.

First of all, as we pointed out earlier, all lender-of-last-resort facilities, of which the IMF bailout is one, provide the benefits of maintaining the integrity of the financial system and of encouraging socially useful risk-taking through socialisation of risk. These benefits need to be set against the costs from the inefficiency resulting from the moral hazard it creates. As we had discussed this point in more detail in the earlier parts of the chapter, we need not dwell on it any further here (see Sections 2 and 3.3).

Secondly, the IMF bailouts have not always been fully effective in protecting the international lenders/investors. Most international lenders/investors probably got away unscathed through the IMF bailout in the 1995 Mexican crisis or indeed in the current Asian crisis (Palma, 1998), but many of them have taken a good beating due to various unilateral and negotiated debt moratoria during the 1982 debt crisis (recall the quote from Kindleberger, 1996, cited in Subsection 3.3) and the 1998 Russian crisis. And these losses have forced some, although by no means all, top bank managers out of their jobs (for example, the chief of the Union Bank of Switzerland resigned in the aftermath of the Russian crisis). In other words, the effectiveness of IMF bailouts in saving the international lenders is not fully predictable, and therefore the extent of moral hazard created by them may not have been as large as what some authors suggest.

Moving more specifically to the role of IMF bailouts in the creation of the Asian crisis, I wish to argue that, although previous IMF bailouts must have created some moral hazard for the international lenders, it is doubtful whether this played an important role in the making of the Asian case.

It is very unlikely that those who were lending to the region would have seriously thought that they were taking more risk than they should only, or even mainly, because the IMF would save them if anything went wrong. It is not that the international lenders would have doubted the high likelihood (if not certainty) of IMF rescue in an international debt crisis, whether in Asia or elsewhere. The point is that, given the record of very high growth and the absence of serious economic crises in the region during the last few decades, it seems unlikely that the possibility of IMF rescue was an important variable in the decisions behind the loans to the crisis-stricken Asian economies.[16]

In the case of Korea, it is even more doubtful whether IMF rescue even figured in international lending decisions at all. During the period between 1993, when the country's debt build-up started, and

---

[16]   In contrast, lending decisions to Russia and Brazil during the last couple of years seem to have critically depended on the likelihood of IMF rescue, given the obvious unsustainability of the macroeconomic policy, especially the high interest rate policy, in these countries.

the eve of the crisis in 1997, the country officially 'graduated' from World Bank tutelage, joined the Organisation for Economic Cooperation and Development (OECD), experienced a significant rise in sovereign credit rating, and saw an increasing number of its firms gaining enough international creditworthiness to be able to float corporate bonds in advanced country markets. Given these developments, it seems highly unlikely that IMF bailouts had figured in international lending decisions to Korea in any meaningful degree, if at all.

The credit ratings for all the would-be crisis economies were actually improving from 1995 until the eve of the crisis (Radelet and Sachs, 1998: pp. 41-2). If the international lenders believed that the Asian economies were heading for major trouble and would need an IMF bailout soon, they would have started demanding extra risk premium on their lending to Asia, given that there is always the possibility that the IMF package may not be of sufficient size, may not arrive on time, and may involve some forced debt work-out arrangements. Indeed, the speed of exit by foreign lenders to Asia just before the signing of the IMF agreements in the crisis-stricken countries suggests that they were not sure at all that the 'cavalry' would arrive on time (and in sufficient numbers).[17]

So to conclude this section, it is fair to say that the IMF bailouts have created moral hazard on the part of the international lenders, although these bailouts may be necessary evils and although they did not always fully save all the international lenders. Empirically, it seems unlikely that the moral hazard created by the history of IMF bailouts of international lenders was a major factor behind the over-lending to the Asian countries. During the last few decades, the countries in the region had almost unbroken records of growth and very few episodes of crises, and therefore it is implausible that the international lenders were lending excessively to these countries in the belief that the IMF would come to their rescue if something went wrong. Not that the IMF would not have (and it indeed did). The point we are trying to

---

[17]    Radelet and Sachs (1998) argue that the fact that foreign lenders kept lending to the Asian economies despite their long-voiced worries about the weak bankruptcy provisions (which make the collection of collateral difficult) is another piece of evidence that they perceived the possibility of the loans to the Asian economies going wrong to be very low (p. 42).

make is that, given the extremely low (perceived) possibility that these countries, especially the soon-to-be-OECD-member Korea, would need an IMF rescue (as suggested by the improving credit ratings of these countries), the moral hazard created by IMF bailouts could not have been a major factor behind the decisions by the international lenders.

## 4.    Summary and Conclusion

The present chapter has tried to untangle the current debate on the Asian crisis by examining the theoretical and empirical foundations of some of the currently most popular arguments which are based on the notion of moral hazard.

At the beginning of the chapter, we pointed out that, contrary to popular belief, moral hazard is not some abnormality that exists only in Asia, but has been an integral part of the development of capitalism. Capitalism has developed on the basis of moral hazard in the sense that institutions that socialise risk, such as limited liability and lender-of-last-resort facilities, were essential in encouraging socially desirable but privately risky investment and innovation activities. We argued that these institutions do generate moral hazard, but the inefficiencies arising from such moral hazard may be more than offset by the gains from the greater investments and innovation that they allow.

With the above as the general historical backdrop, we identified five types of explanation of the Asian crisis built around the notion of moral hazard – industrial policy, cronyism, deposit insurance, the logic of 'too big to fail', and the IMF bailouts – and critically examined them one by one. The following problems with these explanations were identified.

First of all, some of the arguments are simply too ill-defined and thereby lead to conceptual confusion. Cronyism is the best example of this. Cronyism, by definition, has to be selective, but many of those who use this concept do not even seem to understand this, and keep implying that this relationship applies to more or less all major business transactions (including foreign borrowings) in Asian countries.

Secondly, some of the arguments patently mis-specify the problem. For example, in the deposit-insurance argument and the IMF-bailout argument, lender-of-last-resort facilities are identified as the source of moral hazard when it is really the deficiency of the incentive mechanism for the (national and international, respectively) bank managers that is at the heart of the problem. In the case of the TBTF argument or the industrial-policy argument, it is not recognised that the heart of the problem is whether the government punishes industrial managers for their mistakes, and not the mere existence of government intervention itself.

Last but not least, these arguments simply do not sit well with the facts. Industrial policy is blamed for the crisis when it was largely absent in the build-up to the crisis in all the countries concerned. Cronyism is assumed to have gone out of control despite the fact that it was, if anything, actually perceived to be diminishing on the eve of the crisis in all crisis-stricken economies. Likewise, deposit insurance is criticised for encouraging over-borrowing, when it was often non-bank financial institutions and industrial enterprises that did not have similar (explicit or implicit) insurance which led the borrowing boom. The TBTF argument fails to recognise that large firms in Korea have not been routinely bailed out by the government, and that, even when they were, the incumbent managers were forced out. It is also highly doubtful, given their excellent past economic record, whether the possibility that the Asian 'miracle' economies (and especially the soon-to-be-OECD-member Korea) may need IMF bailouts had figured in any meaningful degree, if at all, in the decisions by the international lenders.

To conclude, while the explanations built around the notion of moral hazard contain some germs of truth (some more than others), they are conceptually ill-defined, mis-specify the problems, and are empirically unconvincing. The policy conclusions from these flawed analyses, consequently, remain partial and often misleading. Indeed, the concept of moral hazard has been so much abused in the recent debate on the cause of the Asian crisis to the point of it becoming an intellectual hazard itself. By pointing out the fundamental weaknesses in the moral-hazard arguments, it is hoped that the present chapter has strengthened the case for the newly-emerging consensus across the intellectual spectrum that we will not be able to prevent similar crises in the future without fundamental rethinking on the mode of domestic financial regulation and the international financial architecture.

## Bibliography

Akyuz, Y., Chang, H-J. & Kozul-Wright, R. (1998). 'New Perspectives on East Asian Development', *Journal of Development Studies*, vol. 34, no.6.

Amsden, A. (1989). *Asia's Next Giant*. New York: Oxford University Press.

Brittan, S. (1997). 'Asian Model R.I.P.', *Financial Times*, 4 December 1997.

Burton, J. (1998). 'Boxed into a Corner', *Financial Times*, 23 November 1998.

Chang, H-J. (1993). 'The Political Economy of Industrial Policy in Korea', *Cambridge Journal of Economics*, vol. 17, no. 2.

Chang, H-J. (1994). *The Political Economy of Industrial Policy*. London and Basingstoke: Macmillan.

Chang, H-J. (1995). 'Explaining "Flexible Rigidities" in East Asia', in T. Killick (ed.), *The Flexible Economy*. London: Routledge.

Chang, H-J. (1998). 'Korea: The Misunderstood Crisis', *World Development*, vol. 26. no. 8.

Chang, H-J. (1999). 'Industrial Policy and East Asia – The Miracle, the Crisis, and the Future', a paper presented at the World Bank workshop on 'Rethinking East Asian Miracle', 16-7 February 1999, San Francisco, USA.

Chang, H-J., Palma, G. & Whittaker, D.H. (eds.) (2001). *Financial Liberalization and the Asian Crisis*. Basingstoke and New York: Palgrave.

Chang, H-J., Park, H-J. & Yoo, C.G. (1998). 'Interpreting the Korean Crisis: Financial Liberalisation, Industrial Policy, and Corporate Governance', *Cambridge Journal of Economics*, vol. 22, no. 6.

Corden, M. (1998). 'Sense and Nonsense on the Asian Crisis', The Sturc Lecture, delivered on 8 November 1998, at the Paul H. Nitze School of Advanced International Studies, Johns Hopkins University.

Evans, P. (1995). *Embedded Autonomy – States and Industrial Transformation*. Princeton: Princeton University Press.

Fishlow, A., Gwin, C., Haggard, S., Rodrik, D. & Wade, R. (1994). *Miracle or Design? – Lessons from the East Asian Experience*. Washington, D.C.: Overseas Development Council.

Frankel, J. (1998). 'The Asian Model, the Miracle, the Crisis and the Fund', a speech delivered at the US International Trade Commission, 16 April 1998.

Furman, J. & Stiglitz, J. (1998). 'Economic Crises: Evidence and Insights from East Asia', *Brookings Papers on Economic Activity*, 1998, no. 2.

Henderson, J. (1998). 'Uneven Crises: Institutional Foundations of East Asian Economic Turmoil, Transitional Communities', Working Paper, WPTC-98-13, Faculty of Anthropology and Geography, University of Oxford.

Johnson, C. (ed.) (1984). *The Industrial Policy Debate*. San Francisco: Institute for Contemporary Studies.

Jomo, K.S. & Rock, M. (1998). 'Economic Diversification and Primary Commodity Processing in the Second-tier South-East Asian Newly

Industrialising Countries', UNCTAD Discussion Paper, no. 136. Geneva: United Nations Conference on Trade and Development (UNCTAD).

Kindleberger, C. (1984). *A Financial History of Western Europe.* London: George Allen and Unwin.

Kindleberger, C. (1996). *Manias, Panics, and Crashes*, 3rd edition. London and Basingstoke: Macmillan.

Kregel, J. (1998). 'Yes, "It" Did Happen Again – the Minsky Crisis in Asia', a paper presented at the conference on 'The Legacy of Hyman Minsky', December 1998, Bergamo.

Krugman, P. (1998a). 'What Happened to Asia?', mimeo., Department of Economics, Massachusetts Institute of Technology.

Krugman, P. (1998b). 'Fire-sale FDI', a paper presented at the NBER Conference on 'Capital Flows to Emerging Markets', 20-21 February 1998.

Lall, S. (1994). 'Does the Bell Toll for Industrial Policy?', *World Development*, vol. 22, no. 4.

Lall, S. (1998). 'Selective Industrial and Trade Policies in Developing Countries: Theoretical and Empirical Issues', a paper prepared for project on 'Economic Policymaking and Implementation in Africa: A Case for Strategic Trade and Selective Industrial Policies', organised by the IDRC (International Development Research Centre), Nairobi Office.

McKinnon, R. & Pill, H. (1998). 'International Overborrowing – A Decomposition of Credit and Currency Risk', *World Development*, vol. 26., no. 7.

North, D. (1981). *Structure and Change in Economic History.* New York: W.W. Norton.

Palma. G. (1998). 'Three and a Half Cycles of "Mania, Panic and [asymmetric] Crash": East Asia and Latin America Compared', *Cambridge Journal of Economics*, vol. 22, no. 6.

Park, H-J. (1998). 'Strategy, Competition, and Organisational Structure of the *Chaebol*', mimeo., School of Oriental and African Studies, University of London.

Pasuk, P. & Baker, C. (2001). 'Thailand's Crisis: Neo-Liberal Agenda and Local Reaction', in H-J. Chang, G. Palma & D.H. Whittaker (eds.), *Financial Liberalization and the Asian Crisis*. Basingstoke and New York: Palgrave.

Pyo, H.K. (1998). 'Excess Competition, Moral Hazard, and Industrial Trauma in Korea (1997-1998)', a paper presented at the conference on 'The Aftermath of the Asian Crisis', 13-4 May 1998, Washington, D.C..

Radelet, S. & Sachs, J. (1998). 'The East Asian Financial Crisis: Diagnosis, Remedies and Prospects', *Brookings Paper on Economic Activity*, 1998, no. 1.

Richardson, G. (1960). *Information and Investment.* Oxford: Oxford University Press.

Rosenberg, N. (1994). *Exploring the Black Box.* Cambridge: Cambridge University Press.

Rosenberg, N. & Birdzell, L. (1986). *How the West Grew Rich*. London: I.B. Tauris & Co. Ltd.

Singh, A. (1999). '"Asian Capitalism" and the Financial Crisis', in J. Michie & J. Grieve Smith (eds.), *Global Instability – The Political Economy of World Economic Governance*. London: Routledge.

Stiglitz, J. (1996). 'Some Lessons from the East Asian Miracle', *The World Bank Research Observer*, vol. 11, no. 2.

Stiglitz, J. (1998). 'Sound Finance and Sustainable Development in Asia', a speech delivered at the Asian Development Forum, 12 March 1998, Manila, the Philippines.

Taylor, L. (1998). 'Capital Market Crises: Liberalization, Fixed Exchange Rates and Market-driven Destablization', *Cambridge Journal of Economics*, vol. 22, no. 6.

World Bank (1993). *The East Asian Miracle*. New York: Oxford University Press.

Yoo, S.M. (1997). 'Evolution of Government-Business Interface in Korea: Progress to Date and Reform Agenda Ahead', Working Paper, no. 9711, Korea Development Institute, Seoul.

# Chapter 6

# INTERPRETING THE KOREAN CRISIS –
# FINANCIAL LIBERALISATION,
# INDUSTRIAL POLICY AND
# CORPORATE GOVERNANCE

## 1. Introduction

AS the interpretation of its economic 'miracle' has been, so the interpretation of the 1997 crisis in Korea remains highly controversial.[1] Although there are many important issues which have been raised by the Korean crisis, such as exchange rate policy, labour market policy, and the architecture of the international financial system (Chang, 1998a), three issues have been especially controversial in the debate: financial liberalisation, industrial policy, and corporate governance.

In this chapter, we examine these three issues and argue that the recent crisis in Korea is not the result of excessive government intervention that encouraged 'moral hazard', as is often believed. We show that the crisis resulted from uncoordinated and excessive investments by the private sector, financed by imprudent amounts of short-term foreign debt, which in turn had been made possible by rapid and ill-designed financial liberalisation (especially capital account liberalisation) and a serious weakening of industrial policy. We also point out that, while it has some important shortcomings, Korea's supposedly pathological corporate governance system was neither the main source of the current crisis nor something that has to be radically restructured if Korea is to regain its growth momentum, as many observers outside and inside Korea currently believe.

---

[1] See Chang (1993) for a review of the earlier phases of the debate on the Korean experience. The most recent phase of the debate has been prompted by World Bank (1993). See Fishlow *et al.* (1994) and Akyuz *et al.* (1998) for criticisms of the World Bank view.

## 2.    Financial Liberalisation: Capital Account Liberalisation and the Debt Crisis

While there are those who believe that the recent crises in Korea and other Asian countries are mainly the results of some systematic malaise, even comparable to that found in the former communist countries before the fall of the Berlin Wall (Brittan, 1997; Krugman, 1998), many commentators agree that they were largely the products of mismanaged financial liberalisation and financial market panic (Stiglitz, 1998; Radelet and Sachs, 1998; Wade, 1998; Chang, 1998a).

In the 'traditional' system, the Korean government controlled all the internal and especially cross-border financial flows very tightly (Chang, 1993).[2] Although there was a series of financial liberalisations during the 1980s, these were 'cautious and slow in terms of ... order and speed' (Park, 1996: p. 252), and the system remained a tightly controlled one until the early 1990s (Amsden and Euh, 1990). However, from the early 1990s, the Korean government started relaxing its control over the financial sector significantly and, under the Kim Young Sam government, which came to power in 1993, the liberalisation process was greatly accelerated (see Table 6.1).

The five-year financial liberalisation plan announced by the Kim government in 1993 was regarded as the first such plan to have a relatively well-defined (although not precise) timetable and unambiguous policy contents. It aimed at, among other things, interest rate deregulation, abolition of 'policy loans', granting of more managerial autonomy to the banks, reduction of entry barriers to financial activities and, most importantly, capital account liberalisation, something that Korea's previous plans of financial liberalisation had characteristically failed to include (Choi, 1993).

---

[2]    In fact, Korea experimented briefly with (domestic but not international) financial liberalisation in the late 1960s. This exercise was once hailed as a model for financial liberalisation in developing countries, but later researches revealed that it was not as extensive as had been supposed, and it was subsequently abandoned following the little-known (outside Korea) financial crisis of the early 1970s that had to be resolved by a state-imposed moratorium on all 'curb market' loan servicing in 1972 through the infamous '3 August Decree' (see Harris, 1987, and Chang, 1993, for further details).

**Table 6.1: Major Financial Liberalisation Measures in Korea During the 1990s**

1) **Interest rate deregulation (in four stages: 1991 to July 1997)**
   - By 1997, all lending and borrowing rates, except demand deposit rates, were liberalised

2) **More managerial autonomy for the banks and lower entry barriers to financial activities**
   - Freedom for banks to increase capital, to establish branches, and to determine dividend payments (1994)
   - Enlargement of business scope for financial institutions (1993)
     - : continuous expansion of the securities business of deposit money banks (1990, 1993, 1994, 1995)
     - : freedom for banks and life insurance companies to sell government and public bonds over-the-counter (1995)
     - : permission for securities companies to handle foreign exchange business (1995)
   - Abolition of the limits on maximum maturities for loans and deposits of banks (1996)

3) **Foreign exchange liberalisation**
   - Adoption of the Market-Average Foreign Exchange Rate System (1990)
   - Easing of the requirement for documentation proving 'real' (i.e., non-financial) demand in foreign exchange transactions (1991)
   - Setting up of foreign currency call markets
   - Revision of the Foreign Exchange Management Act (1991)
     - : changing the basis for regulation from a positive system to a negative system
   - Introduction of 'free won' accounts for non-residents (1993)
   - Allowance of partial won settlements for the export or import of visible items (1993)
   - Foreign Exchange Reform Plan (1994)
     - : a detailed schedule for the reform of the foreign exchange market structure
   - A very significant relaxation of the Foreign Exchange Concentration System (1995)

---

**4) Capital market opening**
- Foreign investors are allowed to invest directly in Korean stock markets with ownership ceilings (1992)
- Foreigners are allowed to purchase government and public bonds issued at international interest rates (1994), equity-linked bonds issued by small and medium-sized firms (1994), non-guaranteed long-term bonds issued by small and medium-sized firms (Jan. 1997), and non-guaranteed convertible bonds issued by large companies (Jan. 1997)
- Residents are allowed to invest in overseas securities via beneficiary certificates (1993)
- Abolition of the ceiling on the domestic institutional investors' overseas portfolio investment (1995)
- Foreign commercial loans are allowed without government approval in so far as they meet the guideline established in May 1995
- Private companies engaged in major infrastructure projects are allowed to borrow overseas to pay for domestic construction cost (Jan. 1997)
- Liberalisation of borrowings related to foreign direct investments (Jan. 1997)

**5) Policy loans and credit control**
- A planned termination of all policy loans by 1997 is announced (1993)
  : a step-wise reduction in policy loans to specific sectors (e.g., export industries and small and medium-sized firms)
- Simplifying and slimming down the controls on the share of bank's loans to major conglomerates in its total loans

---

The decision to liberalise the capital account substantially was in a sense a consequence of Korea's economic success. Until 1986, Korea had suffered from chronic current account deficits, which motivated and enabled its government to have strict foreign exchange controls, the two pillars of which were the so-called Foreign Exchange Concentration System, under which all foreign exchange had to be surrendered to the central bank, and the Foreign Exchange Management Act, which put severe restrictions on the use of foreign exchange (e.g., limits on overseas remittances, on overseas real estate acquisition, or even on expenditure on foreign tourism, which was severely restricted until the late 1980s).

However, given the Foreign Exchange Concentration System, the large trade surpluses between 1986 and 1989 generated excess liquidity in the system, prompting the government to scale it down. Although the trade surpluses disappeared subsequently, the surge of capital inflow in the 1990s that made up for it provided the justification for the continued raising of the ceiling on foreign exchange holdings until the system was finally reduced to near-insignificance in 1995. At the same time, the increased credit ratings of Korean corporations and banks in the international financial markets meant that the private sector started regarding government involvement in their foreign exchange transactions as a burden rather than a necessity (previously they simply had not had the creditworthiness to borrow in the international capital market without government guarantees).

Adding to these 'structural' pressures was the continued pressure from the US government to open up the financial market. The March 1992 bilateral talks were its culmination, and it was the agreement arising from these talks that formed the basis for the 1993 financial liberalisation programme. The decision of the Kim government made in 1993 to apply for membership of the OECD also subjected Korea to further external demands for financial market liberalisation.

By 1995, government regulations on foreign borrowing had been significantly reduced, and the result was a mushrooming of foreign debt, which nearly trebled from $44 billion in 1993 to $120 billion in September 1997 (it fell slightly to $116 billion by November 1997).[3] This debt build-up was almost twice as fast as that of 1979-85, the period of the country's earlier (near) debt crisis – Korea's foreign

---

[3] The definition of foreign debt here follows the World Bank definition, and therefore is different from the concept of 'external liabilities', which include the offshore borrowings of Korean banks and overseas borrowings of the overseas branches and subsidiaries of Korean banks. The IMF and the Korean government started using this definition following their accord on 28 December 1997. At the end of November 1997, Korea's external liabilities amounted to $157 billion, of which $92 billion was of less than a year's maturity.

debt grew at 17.8% per annum during 1979-85, while it grew at 33.6% per annum during 1994-96.[4]

What has to be noted here, however, is that, although Korea's foreign debt was large and fast-growing, it was not at an obviously unsustainable level. The World Bank considers countries with debt/ GNP ratios under 48% as low-risk cases, and Korea's debt/GNP ratio was only 22% in 1996, and was still around 25% on the eve of the crisis.[5] The corresponding figures at the end of 1995 were 70% for Mexico, 57% for Indonesia, 35% for Thailand, 33% for Argentina, and 24% for Brazil (World Bank, 1997). Also, in terms of another common indicator of debt burden, i.e., debt service ratio (total debt service to exports of goods and services), Korea was well below the World Bank 'warning' threshold (18%) at 5.4% in 1995 and 5.8% in 1996. These compare very favourably with those of countries like Mexico (24.2%), Brazil (37.9%), Indonesia (30.9%) and Thailand (10.2%) in 1995 (World Bank, 1997).

However, the overall debt figures mask one critical problem with Korea's foreign debt, namely, its maturity structure. The share of short-term debt (which is defined as debt with less than a year's maturity) in total debt rose from an already high 43.7% in 1993 to an astonishing 58.3% at the end of 1996 (BAI, 1998). The magnitude of these figures can be put into perspective if we recall that, on the eve of the 1980s debt crisis (between 1980 and 1982), the average ratio of short-term to overall debt for the non-OPEC developing countries was only 20% (Koener *et al.*, 1986: p. 8, Table 1.1).

Leading this rapid build-up of short-term foreign debts were the inexperienced merchant banks (officially called 'merchant banking corporations') newly licensed by the Kim government in the name of financial liberalisation – nine of them in 1994, and 15 in July 1996, in

---

[4]   By 1997, as shown by Bank for International Settlements (BIS) data, which is also frequently used, Korea's foreign debt was already slowing down. Its foreign debt increased from $105 billion at the end of 1996 to $120 billion in September 1997 – an annualised growth rate of 19% – and, as we have already seen, actually decreased to $116 billion by the end of November 1997.

[5]   In the World Bank classification, a country is 'less indebted' when the debt/GNP ratio is less than 48%, 'moderately indebted' when this ratio is between 48% and 80%, and 'severely indebted' when it is over 80%. For the exact definitions, see World Bank (1997, vol. 1: pp. 49-50).

addition to the total of six that existed before the 1993 financial liberalisation programme. The total foreign debt stock of the merchant banks rose by around 60.1% per annum during 1994-96, from $7.27 billion to $18.62 billion (BAI, 1998), vastly outpacing the growth of total foreign debt at 33.6% per annum that we already referred to as unprecedented. Moreover, supervision of the merchant banks, unlike that of the deposit banks, was virtually non-existent, to the extent that the Kim government was apparently not even aware of the huge mismatch in the maturity structures between their borrowings (64% of their $20 billion total foreign borrowings were short-term) and lendings (85% of them long-term) that existed on the eve of the crisis.

The rapid debt build-up itself can be explained by the investment boom among Korean corporations, which benefited from the demise of the country's famous industrial policy that had put a break on excessive competition (see Section 3 for further details) and from the relaxation of financial policies that traditionally controlled the amount and term structure of foreign borrowing. However, the large share of short-term debt needs more explanation.

Firstly, liberalisation was much more extensive in relation to short-term foreign borrowing than to long-term foreign borrowing. For example, while those who were contracting long-term loans were required to provide detailed information and obtain permission from the Ministry of Finance and Economy (MOFE), as the combined finance and planning ministries was called in President Kim Young Sam's days, short-term borrowers were not required to do this. Combined with the stricter information requirements for long-term loan applications that foreign lenders typically impose, this gave the borrowers the incentive to go for short-term loans in order to cut the 'overhead' costs of borrowing.

Secondly, given the Kim government's commitment to financial liberalisation, there was an expectation that Korea's credit rating in the international financial market would keep on improving and therefore that international lending rates for Korean banks and companies would fall. And given the uncertainty over the exact dates of various liberalisation measures announced in 1993 (only the year, but not the month, in which these steps were to be taken had been announced), many Korean borrowers seem to have taken a 'wait and see' approach by continuously rolling over short-term loans rather than taking out long-term ones, an approach supported by the international lenders, who were perfectly willing to roll over Korean loans until the eve of the crisis.

To summarise, the post-1993 financial liberalisation in Korea was critical in generating the 1997 crisis, as, for the first time in the country's history, it instituted a very substantial, if not full-scale, capital account liberalisation. It was not simply the extent of the liberalisation but also its design that contributed to the crisis, as it gave the incentive to borrowers to contract short-term loans and allowed poor asset-liability management to go unchecked. However, this cannot be the whole story, as we need to explain why the investment boom that demanded all this borrowing was so strong. This is where we turn to the issue of industrial policy.

## 3. Industrial Policy: Over-investment and 'Crony Capitalism'

It has now almost become conventional wisdom that the Korean government was encouraging, and sometimes even forcing, corporations into unprofitable business through its industrial policy. However, we shall argue here that it was the demise of industrial policy, rather than its perpetuation, which drove the Korean economy into crisis.

On its assumption of power in 1993, the Kim Young Sam government abolished the practice of five-year planning, which had provided an overarching policy coordination framework since its introduction in 1962, in favour of the poorly constructed '100-day Plan for the New Economy', which is now regarded by many people as little more than a publicity stunt. At the same time, in the name of government administrative 'rationalisation', the planning ministry, Economic Planning Board (EPB), was merged with the Ministry of Finance (MOF), forming the super-ministry, Ministry of Finance and Economy (MOFE), which symbolised the demise of (indicative) 'planning' in Korea.

Most critically, the Kim Young Sam government accelerated the dismantling of selective industrial policy that had started in the late 1980s. The rising domestic and international criticism of selective industrial policy since the late 1970s culminated in the introduction of the Industrial Development Law (IDL) in 1986 by the then government of Mr Chun Doo Hwan. Although the IDL emphasised the 'functional' rather than sectoral approach to industrial policy, it had provisions for sectoral rationalisation programmes (with a limited time duration), and thus allowed for a selective industrial policy, had the government had the will. And indeed in the early days of the IDL, this was the case – several major rationalisation programmes were implemented throughout the late 1980s and the early 1990s, covering, among others, industries such as automobiles, heavy construction machinery, heavy electrical machinery, ferro-alloys, naval diesel engines, dyeing, textile, and coal mining (for more details, see Chang, 1993: pp. 142-4).

However, the will to conduct selective industrial policy started to wane from the late 1980s with the rise of the neoliberal ideology and the growing power of the *chaebols* (conglomerates), which now hankered for greater freedom in their investment decision-making (Chang, 1998b). We see the first sign of such a change in 1989, when the then government of Mr Roh Tae Woo for the first time openly refused to coordinate investments in the petrochemical industry despite the looming threat of massive over-capacity, although it later had to make a U-turn and intervene when the industry got into serious trouble owing to over-capacity (e.g., by imposing a compulsory export quota).

The ambiguity that the Roh government showed over industrial policy was replaced by the unambiguous aversion to it held by the Kim Young Sam government, which seriously weakened, if not totally negated, most industrial policy measures (the notable exception being the promotion of R&D in some high-technology industries). Given that the 'traditional' Korean, and other East Asian, industrial policy provided an investment coordination mechanism that checked 'excessive competition' (for further theoretical discussion, see Chang, 1994: Chapter 3), this led to over-investment, which resulted in falling profitability due to low capacity utilisation and/or falling export prices (many Korean exporters account for large shares in the world markets and therefore are not price-takers), and eventually in major corporate failures in a number of leading industries, including electronics (more specifically semiconductors), automobiles, steel, petrochemicals, and shipbuilding. Let us consider a couple of prominent examples in order to illustrate how the demise of industrial policy affected Korean industry.

In the steel industry, the Kim government supported what many, if not all, people regarded as an over-ambitious steel venture by Hanbo, a medium-sized *chaebol* with a dubious track record in manufacturing. The decision was emphatically not taken as a part of any coherent industrial policy, and looked particularly strange when the government had already refused to endorse the largest conglomerate Hyundai's entry into the steel industry. As it turned out, Hanbo collapsed in early 1997, and it was subsequently revealed that behind the government support for Hanbo lay corruption involving the then president's closest aides and probably his son, thus delivering the first blow to foreign confidence in the Korean economy.

The Kim government also licensed Samsung to enter the already-overcrowded car industry in 1993. What is fascinating about this entry is that it destabilised the industry before it produced a single car – Samsung's cars did not come on the market until 1998. Relatively lacking in strength in machine-related industries and having deliberately located the factory in the president's hometown, Pusan, despite the fact that the (reclaimed) site needed massive fortification, Samsung's venture looked questionable from the beginning. In the event, it saw a solution in the acquisition of the then third (but previously second) largest manufacturer, Kia, whose manufacturing capability was highly regarded but whose financial strength was in doubt. Kia, a unique *chaebol* in that it was not family-owned and did not have a very diversified industrial portfolio despite its size (it was the eighth largest), tried to defend itself from the threat of takeover by Samsung in two ways, both of which proved unsuccessful. Firstly, it tried to stabilise its cash flows by further diversifying its portfolio. In this context, the expansion of its specialised steel business proved particularly disastrous. Secondly, it made further pre-emptive investments in the car industry, which did not prove very successful. What followed is well known. The Kim government dithered over the fate of Kia over an extended period of time, until it finally nationalised it, thus seriously weakening foreign confidence in Korea (for further details, see Chang, 1998a).

The stories of Hanbo's steel venture and Samsung's car venture not only illustrate the perils of dismantling the investment coordination mechanism in a high-investment-high-growth regime, but also suggest that the relationship between the state and business in Korea had undergone an important change under the Kim government.

The corruption surrounding the Hanbo case was, despite current perceptions, not typical of what was going on in the country under its state-led model of development. It goes without saying that, in the traditional model, large sums of money flowed from big business to politicians and top bureaucrats. These flows were often tied to particular projects in areas like urban planning and government procurements, but they were rarely directly related to particular projects in the main manufacturing sectors, such as we see in the Hanbo case.

Moreover, under the Kim government, for the first time in post-1960s Korean history, we heard the names of particular *chaebols*, such as Samsung, talked about as being 'close to the regime'. In the old regime, the *chaebols* as a group were preferentially treated, but rarely was any of them regarded as being closer to the government than others. Under the Kim government, there was a fundamental transformation in the state-business relationship in Korea, which meant that the major manufacturing sectors were now not as insulated from corrupt political exchanges as they had been.

The abolition of five-year planning and the serious weakening of sectoral industrial policy played a very important part in this process. With the well-publicised 'rational' criteria for intervention previously provided by the five-year plans and sectoral policies gone, it was now much easier to 'bend the rules' for political reasons. This meant the end of the 'generalistic' state-business relationship that characterised the Korean model and the rapid rise of a 'particularistic' (or 'cronyistic', to use the currently popular expression) relationship, and more importantly, as we have seen, its spread into the major manufacturing industries which were previously largely insulated from corruption. In this sense, it may be said that, contrary to common perception, it was only under the Kim Young Sam government that genuine 'crony capitalism' was born in Korea.

The above discussion suggests that industrial policy in Korea was not responsible for the over-investments that were behind the

1997 crisis. It was rather its abolition by the Kim Young Sam government that made such investments easier. In addition, our discussion suggests that the abolition of industrial policy also made it easier to 'bend the rules', facilitating the rise of 'particularistic' (or 'cronyistic') state-business links in relation to the critical manufacturing sectors.

## 4.    Corporate Governance: Moral Hazard and High Debt

One currently popular account, advocated by, among others, Krugman (1998), acknowledges that the 1997 crisis in Korea and other Asian countries is the direct result of private corporate sector profligacy, but argues that this would not have been possible without the implicit guarantee provided by the government for the banks and industrial corporations. It is argued that this system has led to 'moral hazards' among the Korean corporations that result in reckless investments and low efficiency, as reflected in low corporate profitability.

This view is also reflected in the IMF programme for Korea, which demands that the country should take measures that will weaken, and hopefully eventually dismantle, the large, diversified, family-owned *chaebols*. The proposed measures for this purpose include the banning of mutual payment guarantees among the member firms of the same *chaebol*, the demand for the publication of consolidated balance sheets for the whole *chaebol* (rather than for individual firms), the strengthening of minority shareholder rights through stricter disclosure requirements, and in general, measures that are supposed to make high corporate gearing difficult, if not impossible.

The first obvious problem with Krugman's account is that the ostensibly low corporate profitability in Korea is mainly due to high interest payments, rather than to inefficiency. Table 6.2 shows that Korea's post-interest-payments profitability (the ratio of 'ordinary income' to sales) was low owing to high corporate gearing – 2.8% as opposed to 7.9% in the USA (1995), 5.1% in Taiwan (1995), 4.3% for early Japan (1955-73) and 2.9% for 1995 Japan. However, this should not be interpreted as showing Korean corporate inefficiency, as Korea's corporate profitability before interest payments (measured by the ratio of 'operating income' to sales) has not been low by international

|  | Table 6.2: An International Comparison of Corporate Profitability (%) | | | | | |
|---|---|---|---|---|---|---|
|  | Korea (1973-1996) | Korea (1996) | Japan (1955-1973) | Japan (1995) | Taiwan (1995) | USA (1995) |
| Operating Income/Sales | 7.4 | 6.5 | 7.2* | 3.3 | 7.3 | 7.7 |
| Financial Expenses/Sales | 5.5 | 5.8 | 3.4 | 1.3 | 2.2 | n.a. |
| Ordinary Income/Sales | 2.8 | 1.0 | 4.3 | 2.9 | 5.1 | 7.9 |
| Total Borrowing/Total Assets | n.a. | 47.7 | n.a. | 34.8 | 26.2 | 26.4 |
| Debt/Equity | 338.4 | n.a. | 320.7 | n.a. | n.a. | n.a. |

**Source**: Bank of Korea (various years) and *Japan Statistical Yearbook* (various years).

Definitions:

Operating Income = Gross Profit – Selling and General Administrative Expenses.

Ordinary Income = Operating Income + Net Non-Operating Income.

Note: * 1961-73

standards. Over the 1973-96 period, this figure for Korea averaged 7.4%, which was similar to that for the USA (7.7%) and Taiwan (7.3%) recorded in 1995. Moreover, low post-interest profitability did not harm investment momentum in Korea, since the government used a range of methods to ensure that the income appropriated by the financial sector was recycled to the manufacturing corporate sector (see Akyuz *et al.*, 1998).

Now, at this point it may be argued that, whatever the 'real' efficiency of the Korean corporations, they were very prone to failure because of their high debt burden, and that therefore the government had to bail them out routinely, thus creating the incentive for moral hazard.

However, firstly, there is no instance, at least in the last two decades, where the Korean government has bailed out a failing *chaebol*. Between 1990 and 1996 alone, as many as three of the 30 biggest *chaebols* went bankrupt (Hanyang, Yoowon, and Woosung), not to speak of the six that went bankrupt in 1997 (Kia, Hanbo, Sammi, Haitai, Jinro, and Halla). Certainly, there were occasions where individual firms belonging to a *chaebol* got assisted, but this invariably involved a government-mediated takeover of the firm (by another *chaebol* or by the government-owned banks) or the imposition of terms of enterprise restructuring that severely restricted managerial autonomy (e.g., Daewoo shipbuilding in the late 1980s). In this set-up, there is little room for moral hazard, as the managers know that they will lose control over the enterprise if they fail to perform. The important thing in relation to the moral hazard story is not whether some struggling enterprises have been helped out by the government (they have) but whether bad management gets punished or not.[6] Especially during the 1990s, notwithstanding the rise of 'cronyistic' relationships with a few particular *chaebols*, the overall government-*chaebol* relationship has been strained as never before, and therefore whatever little prospect of government bailout that might have previously existed is likely to have diminished even further.[7]

Secondly, if the *chaebols* were counting on government bailout, they would not have increased their exposure to the non-bank financial institutions (NBFIs), such as the merchant banks, as they did, since it was generally accepted that, given their greater freedom from government regulation and their small size, the NBFIs were themselves highly unlikely to be bailed out in cases of failure. The share of the top 30 *chaebols* in total bank loans fell from 19.5% in 1991 to 13.9% in 1995, despite the fact that from 1994 there was some relaxation of restrictions on bank lending to *chaebols*. In the case of the six *chaebols* that went bankrupt in 1997 in particular, reliance on the NBFIs, especially the merchant banks, was very heavy. For example, the Halla group borrowed 50% of its 6.5 trillion won debts from the merchant banks (*Maeil Business News*, 8 December 1997).

And thirdly, the investments that the *chaebols* had made in the

---

[6]  There was little room for moral hazard on the part of lenders either. Defaulted loans have remained as 'non-performing loans' on their balance sheets, damaging their profitability.

[7]  Since the 1980s, successive Korean governments have introduced a series of 'anti-*chaebol*' policies, including ceilings on the share of the top 30 *chaebols* in total bank loans, restrictions on mutual payment guarantees among member firms of the same *chaebols*, and pressures on the *chaebols* to sell 'non-business' property. The *chaebols* for their part have stepped up their publicity campaign against government regulation since the early 1990s.

build-up to the crisis were mainly in industries with stable returns, rather than 'high risk, high return' industries, which those investors operating under moral hazard will be inclined to choose. Table 6.3 shows how, during the few years leading up to the crisis, investment in the six 'stable' leading export industries where the *chaebols* were particularly heavily represented – namely, petrochemicals, petroleum refining, iron and steel, automobiles, electrical and electronics, and shipbuilding – grew much faster than investment in manufacturing in general as well as overall investment.[8] Of course, these industries did not remain 'stable', since, in the absence of investment coordination, over-capacity and falling profitability resulted. It is instructive that of the six *chaebols* which failed in 1997, five failed in one of these six industries. For example, Hanbo, Kia, and Sammi failed mainly owing to their failures in steel, Halla failed in shipbuilding, while Haitai, a food-processing conglomerate, stalled owing to its ill-fated foray into the electronics industry.

In addition to the 'moral hazard' argument, the currently popular view of Korea's 'pathological corporate governance' sees high corporate gearing as another major problem. The most obvious problem with this view is that Korea's corporate financing system had obviously served the country well until the crisis. While the argument by Wade and Veneroso (1998) that high corporate gearing is an inevitable consequence of high household savings may be debatable (after all, as seen in Table 6.2, despite its high household savings ratio, Taiwan has a corporate gearing ratio as low as that of the USA), their argument that the high-corporate-debt system has been an effective way of generating 'patient' long-term investments deserves to be emphatically repeated (also see Dertouzos *et al.*, 1989; Albert, 1991; Hutton, 1995).

It may be reasonably argued, of course, that, despite its desirable features, the high-corporate-debt system is still a very risky one, as is proved by recent events in Korea. At one level, this is obviously true, but the fact that Japan had nothing remotely approaching the current Korean crisis (or, for that matter, Korea's early 70s or early

---

[8]   In these six industries, investment by the top 30 *chaebols* accounted for 82.3% of total investment on average between 1994 and 1996. See Choi (1995, 1996, and 1997).

### Table 6.3: Trends in Facility Investment in Korea
(growth rates, %)

|  | 1972-9 | 1980-2 | 1983-91 | 1992-3 | 1994 | 1995 | 1996 |
|---|---|---|---|---|---|---|---|
| All industries | 43.3 | 1.3 | 20.0 | -1.0 | 36.7 | 37.9 | 17.3 |
| Manufacturing | 43.6 | -11.3 | 29.6 | -8.9 | 56.2 | 43.5 | 17.1 |
| The 'six' industries | n.a. | n.a. | 20.3* | -6.8 | 68.2 | 48.7 | 25.1 |
| Non-manufacturing | 49.9 | 21.8 | 10.1 | 15.5 | 9.5 | 26.9 | 17.7 |

Source: KDB (various years).

Note: The 'six' are petroleum refining, petrochemicals, iron and steel, electrical and electronics, automobile, and shipbuilding.
*1987-91

80s crises), despite a corporate gearing ratio that was as high as that in Korea, shows that high corporate debt per se cannot be the cause of the current crisis. During its 'high growth' period, that is, between 1955 and 1973, the debt-equity ratio of Japanese manufacturing corporations was 320%, which was at an equivalent level to the Korean figure of 338% between 1973 and 1996 (JBS, various years; BOK, various years). The Japanese debt-equity ratio peaked at around 500% in the mid-1970s, and was still as high as 385% in 1980 (JBS, various years). This comparison suggests that, had it not been for the ill-designed financial liberalisation policy and the demise of industrial policy that led to over-investment, high corporate debt in Korea would not have produced a crisis.

Our questioning of the currently popular view of the Korean corporate governance system does not mean that there was nothing wrong with that system. Features like continued family control (which runs counter to meritocracy) and the poor quality of financial reporting should certainly be rectified. However, our view is that most of these can be eliminated without changing the fundamental nature of the system – such as portfolio diversification (as far as it is not excessive) and the flowing-back of the profits transferred to the financial sector. Trying to Americanise the corporate governance system may only adversely affect the Korean corporations' ability to invest and upgrade, the features that made them so formidable in international markets.

## 5.   Conclusion

In this chapter, we have examined some common views on the current Korean crisis, focusing on issues relating to financial liberalisation, industrial policy, and corporate governance. We have presented evidence that shows how these views lack a solid empirical basis, and have argued that it was the dismantling of the traditional mechanisms of generating and coordinating long-term investment, rather than the perpetuation of the traditional regime, that made Korea's corporate debt and foreign borrowing situations difficult. We have also argued that, although things were difficult, they were not obviously near to crisis point, and therefore what actually happened cannot be explained without reference to the panic that gripped the financial markets following the Southeast Asian crises and the high-profile corporate bankruptcies (Hanbo and Kia). We have examined the forces behind the policy changes that led to the crisis and concluded that, while there were certain structural and external forces that were difficult to resist (e.g., the growing power of the conglomerates, growing US pressures for market opening, etc.), policy failures certainly have to take a large portion of the blame.

When what remains of the 'traditional' Korean economic system after the Kim Young Sam government's liberalisation drive is now being dismantled by the IMF programme, it may seem pointless to talk about the merits of the old system, whatever they were. However, changes in formal institutions, which can never specify the full universe of individual and institutional interactions, cannot fully determine the future, and in that sense, it may be too early to predict what will happen to the Korean economic system in the long run. After all, was it not out of the very American system that the American Occupation Authority imposed on Germany and Japan that the famous German and Japanese economic systems emerged?

## Bibliography

Akyuz, Y., Chang, H-J. & Kozul-Wright, R. (1998). 'New perspectives on East Asian Development', *Journal of Development Studies*, vol. 34, no. 6.

Albert, M. (1991). *Capitalism vs. Capitalism.* New York: Four Walls and Eight Windows.

Amsden, A. & Euh, Y. (1990). 'Republic of Korea's Financial Reform: What are the Lessons?', Discussion Paper, no. 30. Geneva: United Nations Conference on Trade and Development (UNCTAD).

BAI (Board of Audit and Inspection) (1998). *The Analysis and Evaluation of the (1997) Foreign Exchange Crisis* (in Korean). Seoul: Board of Audit and Inspection, The Government of Korea.

BOK (Bank of Korea) (various years). *Financial Statement Analysis.* Seoul: Bank of Korea.

Brittan, S. (1997). 'Asian Model R.I.P.', *Financial Times*, 4 December 1997.

Chang, H-J. (1993). 'The Political Economy of Industrial Policy in Korea', *Cambridge Journal of Economics*, vol. 17, no. 2.

Chang, H-J. (1994). *The Political Economy of Industrial Policy.* London and Basingstoke: Macmillan.

Chang, H-J. (1998a). 'Korea: The Misunderstood Crisis', *World Development*, vol. 26, no. 8.

Chang, H-J. (1998b). 'An Alternative View on Regulatory Reform in Korea', a paper presented at the conference on 'Korea's Transition to a High-Productivity Economy', 6-7 February 1998, held at the Centre for Korean Studies, University of Hawaii at Manoa, Honolulu.

Chang, H-J. & Nolan, P. (1995). *The Transformation of the Communist Economies – Against the Mainstream.* London and Basingstoke: Macmillan Press.

Choi, B. (1993). 'Financial Policy and Big Business in Korea: The Perils of Financial Regulation', in S. Haggard, C. Lee & S. Maxfield (eds.), *The Politics of Finance in Developing Countries.* Ithaca, New York: Cornell University Press.

Choi, S-N. (1995 and 1996). *Analysis of the 30 Korean Big Business Group.* Seoul: Economic Research Institute.

Choi, S-N. (1997). *The Korean Big Business Group for 1997.* Seoul: Centre for Free Enterprise.

Dertouzos, M., Lester, R. & Solow, R. (1989). *Made in America.* Cambridge, Massachusetts: The MIT Press.

Fishlow, A., Gwin, C., Haggard, S., Rodrik, D. & Wade, R. (1994). *Miracle or Design? – Lessons from the East Asian Experience.* Washington, D.C.: Overseas Development Council.

Harris, L. (1987). 'Financial Reform and Economic Growth: A New Interpretation of South Korea's Experience', in L. Harris *et al.* (eds.), *New Perspectives on the Financial System.* London: Croom Helm.

Hutton, W. (1995). *The State We're In*. London: Jonathan Cape.

JBS (Japanese Bureau of Statistics) (various years). *Japan Statistical Year-book*. Tokyo: Japan Bureau of Statistics.

KDB (Korea Development Bank) (various years). *Survey of Facility Investment*. Seoul: Korea Development Bank.

Koener, P., Maass, G., Siebold, T. & Tetzlaff, R. (1986). *The IMF and the Debt Crisis*. London: Zed Books.

Krugman, P. (1998). 'What happened to Asia?', mimeo., Department of Economics, Massachusetts Institute of Technology.

Park, W-A. (1996). 'Financial Liberalisation: The Korean Experience', in T. Ito & A. Krueger (eds.), *Financial Deregulation and Integration in East Asia*. Chicago: The University of Chicago Press.

Radelet, S. & Sachs, J. (1998). 'The Onset of the East Asian Financial Crisis', *Brookings Papers on Economic Activity*, 1998, no. 1.

Singh, A. (1975). 'Takeovers, Economic Natural Selection and the Theory of the Firm: Evidence from the Post-war U.K. Experience', *Economic Journal*, vol. 85, no. 3.

Stiglitz, J. (1998). 'Sound Finance and Sustainable Development in Asia', a paper delivered at the Asia Development Forum, 10-13 March, Manila.

Taylor, L. (1987). *Varieties of Stabilisation Experience*. Oxford: Oxford University Press.

Wade, R. (1998). 'The Asian Debt-and-Development Crisis of 1997-?: Causes and Consequences', *World Development*, vol. 26, no. 8.

Wade, R. & Veneroso, F. (1998). 'The Asian Crisis: The High Debt Model vs. The Wall Street-Treasury-IMF Complex', *New Left Review*, March-April 1998.

World Bank (1993). *The East Asian Miracle*. New York: Oxford University Press.

World Bank (1997). *Global Development Finance*. Washington, D.C.: World Bank.

# Chapter 7

# INDUSTRIAL POLICY AND EAST ASIA – THE MIRACLE, THE CRISIS AND THE FUTURE

## 1. Introduction

THE issue of industrial policy has been arguably at the heart of the debate on the East Asian developmental experience during the last two decades or so. In the late 1970s and the early 1980s, there was an intense international debate on the issue, largely prompted by the Japanese industrial success during the first three decades of the postwar period.[1] In the late 1980s, similar policies in the next tier of East Asian success stories such as South Korea (henceforth Korea) and Taiwan stirred up the second phase of the debate.

Unlike in the case of Japan, the interventionist nature of whose industrial policy was widely (if not universally) acknowledged, the orthodoxy regarding Korea and Taiwan until the early 1980s was that they were free-market, free-trade economies with little industrial policy (e.g., Ranis and Fei, 1975; Balassa *et al.*, 1982). From the early 1980s, however, there emerged a number of researches that questioned this orthodoxy and emphasised the role of industrial policy in the economic success of these countries (Jones and Sakong, 1980; Evans and Alizadeh, 1984; Amsden, 1985; Luedde-Neurath, 1986). Partly as a consequence of these, some mainstream commentators started to acknowledge the existence of industrial policy in these countries, al-

---

[1] Important works that emphasised the positive contribution of Japanese industrial policy include Magaziner and Hout (1980), Johnson (1982), and Reich (1982). In the opposite camp, Schultze (1983) and Badaracco and Yoffie (1983) were influential. Reviews of this first phase of the industrial-policy debate can be found in: Johnson (ed.) (1984: Introduction); Thompson (ed.) (1989); and Chang (1994: Chapter 3).

though they denied that it made much impact – either on the ground that industrial policy measures in these countries were self-cancelling (e.g., the 'virtual free trade' position of Little, 1982, and World Bank, 1987) or on the ground that they were porous (e.g., the theory of 'proscriptive vs. prescriptive' intervention proposed by Bhagwati, 1988). The publication of the works by Amsden (1989) on Korea and Wade (1990) on Taiwan was the culmination of the so-called 'revisionist' offensive that started in the early 1980s, to which the World Bank's *East Asian Miracle* report (World Bank, 1993) was the mainstream answer.[2]

Contrary to the expectation of its authors, the *East Asian Miracle* report (henceforth EAM) failed to put an end to the debate. First of all, important methodological and empirical criticisms of the report were made (see the special symposium in *World Development*, 1994, no. 4; Fishlow *et al.*, 1994; Singh, 1994), but its authors have not provided convincing answers to them. Moreover, there were issues that were, at least in my view, inadequately addressed, both by the authors of the report and its critics, in the earlier debate surrounding the report. A more balanced assessment of the role of industrial policy in East Asia requires examination of these issues. Thirdly, the recession in Japan and the financial crises in a number of other East Asian economies, which occurred since the publication of the EAM, have made popular the view that industrial policy created economic problems, rather than 'miracles', in the region. Given that one main conclusion of the EAM was that industrial policy has had few positive impacts, rather than that it was harmful, these recent events call for a re-examination of the role of industrial policy in the region.

This chapter is organised in the following manner. First of all, we will present a critical review of the EAM (Section 2). Here, we will devote more efforts to raising issues that were neglected in the earlier debate, rather than to going over the issues that were already debated. Next, we assess the currently popular view that industrial policy was behind the 'downfall' of the East Asian model (Section 3).

---

[2]   For a more detailed review of the evolution of the debate on industrial policy leading up to the publication of the *East Asian Miracle* report, see Chang (1993). For the political background to the publication of the report, see Wade (1996).

Then we discuss whether the more recent economic, political, and institutional changes (both at the national and international levels) have made the use of industrial policy in East Asia less feasible in the future (Section 4). This is followed by concluding remarks (Section 5).

## 2.    The *East Asian Miracle* Report on Industrial Policy: Contributions and Limitations

The *East Asian Miracle* report distinguished itself from the previous publications by the World Bank and most mainstream economists on the role of industrial policy in East Asia at least in two respects.

First of all, it acknowledged the existence of industrial policy in the non-Japanese East Asian countries. As we mentioned earlier, in the case of Japan, the existence of interventionist industrial and trade policies was widely acknowledged from the early days, while the very existence of industrial policy was a matter of intense debate in the case of Korea and Taiwan even until the late 1980s.[3] The EAM accepted the contention of the 'revisionists' that the extent and the degree of industrial policy in these countries were much larger than what the mainstream economists cared to admit before, and started the discussion from there.

Secondly, the EAM clearly accepted a number of important theoretical justifications for industrial policy – such as the so-called 'Big Push' argument and the existence of learning externalities (see below). This was a big contrast to many earlier mainstream works, which argued that market failures were limited to areas like infrastructure, education, and health, and therefore that there was no reason for governments to intervene in industry, especially at the sectoral level.

---

[3]  For example, as late as 1988, the famous mainstream trade economist Bela Balassa was arguing that 'apart from the promotion of shipbuilding and steel, [the role of the state in Korea] has been to create a modern infrastructure, to provide a stable incentive system, and to ensure that government bureaucracy will help rather than hinder exports' (Balassa, 1988: S.286).

Having abandoned the early mainstream practice of dismissing the issue of industrial policy as theoretically unjustifiable and/or largely absent in the East Asian countries, the EAM resorted to two arguments of a more practical bent in order to come up with a negative verdict on industrial policy.

First of all, it tried to show empirically that industrial policy, despite its widespread existence, did not make much difference either to the production structure or to the productivity performance of the East Asian countries. Secondly, it argued that, whatever its contribution to the development of some East Asian countries may have been, industrial policy cannot be adopted by the developing countries of today because they face different domestic and international conditions. It was argued, firstly, that the latter countries lack the domestic institutions needed for the effective implementation of East-Asian-style industrial policy (especially a competent bureaucracy), and, secondly, that the kind of 'permissive' international trading environment that the East Asian countries enjoyed during the time when they actively used such policy (that is, between the 1950s and the 1970s) has ceased to exist, especially following the recent conclusion of the Uruguay Round of the GATT talks.

In the rest of this section, we critically examine the three aspects of the EAM's verdict on industrial policy that we mentioned above – its (partial) theoretical acceptance of industrial policy (Section 2.1), its empirical refutation of the success of the policy in East Asia (Section 2.2), and the practical objections that it raises to the transferability of the policy to other countries (Section 2.3) – and bring out some issues that we think were inadequately dealt with in the earlier debate.

## 2.1    Theoretical justifications for industrial policy

As we have repeatedly mentioned, the EAM acknowledged some important justifications for industrial policy, unlike the previous orthodox publications on the subject. First of all, the need to coordinate complementary investments, in the presence of significant scale economies and capital market imperfections, was acknowledged – this is the well-known 'Big Push' argument. Secondly, the role that the state can play as the organiser of domestic firms into implicit cartels in their negotiations with foreign firms or foreign governments was recognised. Thirdly, the importance of learning externalities was emphasised.

However, in the same breath, the EAM dismissed another important theoretical justification for industrial policy, namely, infant industry promotion, on the ground that its success is not guaranteed. I find this refutation rather peculiar, since all the other theoretical justifications for industrial policy that the EAM accepted do not guarantee success of the policies based on them either. But apart from this rather obvious point, I do not think there is much added value in my elaborating on the theoretical arguments that have already been accepted by the EAM. Therefore, I wish to discuss a few other theoretical justifications for industrial policy which were more or less ignored by the EAM (and in fact by many of its critics) and discuss their implications.

### 2.1.1 Coordination of competing investments

The first of the under-explored justifications for industrial policy is the issue of coordinating investments not simply between complementary investment projects but between competing projects – what is known as 'managed competition'. This issue was actually the central point of contention in the industrial policy debate of the early 1980s surrounding the Japanese experience, but was curiously ignored by the EAM.

The logic here is that the oligopolistic competition that characterises many modern industries with significant scale economy often leads to excess capacity, unless there is a coordination of investment activities across competing firms. Excess capacity leads to price war, which damages the profits of the firms concerned and may force them to scrap some of their assets. It can also lead to bankruptcy.

Needless to say, asset scrapping and bankruptcy are useful and costless ways of rearranging property rights in a world without transaction costs and 'specific assets' (the term is due to Williamson, 1985), but we do *not* live in such a world. This means that the specific assets involved in this process have to be scrapped or reallocated to alternative uses that can create much less value out of the assets concerned, thus incurring a social cost. If the emergence of excess capacity can be prevented through the *ex ante* coordination of competing investments, such social cost may be reduced (for more detailed arguments, see Chang, 1994: Chapter 3; also see Telser, 1987, and Amsden and Singh, 1994).

Many mainstream economists have argued that excess capacity is a non-issue, especially for small economies that are price-takers, because what cannot be consumed in the domestic market can always be exported. However, this is often not a viable option, at least in the short run (and it is the short run that counts here). First of all, at least since the late 1970s, many industries have been suffering from chronic over-capacity on the world scale.[4] Moreover, real-world markets are often segmented along the lines of quality, design, and geography, and therefore the 'world market' may not be as big as it seems, given that it takes time and resources to break into new market segments. In addition, some small economies have deliberately built capacities which are far beyond their domestic markets and have become price-makers, rather than price-takers, even on the world scale. For example, Korea, despite being a relatively small economy, is the world's first or second largest producer of ships (depending on the year) and the third largest producer of microchips (the largest, if we take memory chips only), and therefore what the country produces does have an important impact on world prices. Indeed, this is why the end to the practice of coordination among competing investments became such a problem in Korea recently (see Section 3 for more details).

Given these considerations, there is a clear theoretical justification for coordinating competing investments. And, indeed, such coordination has been one of the most important components in the industrial policy regimes of the East Asian countries – as manifested in their continuous concern over 'excessive competition' or 'wasteful competition' and the attempts to minimise duplicative investments through mechanisms such as industrial licensing and investment car-

---

[4]  Of course, this does not mean that new entries cannot or do not happen. The East Asian producers have been quite good at gaining market shares in some industries with a chronic over-capacity problem. However, successful entry into these industries will be much more difficult than that into other industries.

tels (see Chang, 1993, for further details).[5] By ignoring this important issue, the EAM ended up neglecting a huge chunk of industrial policy in East Asia.

### 2.1.2 Further implications from scale economy

The EAM certainly gave a clear recognition to the importance of scale economy in modern industrial development, when it talked about coordination of complementary investments. However, this is not the only way scale economy matters.

First of all, scale economy has an important implication for the cost competitiveness of a country's industry. Economists may have traditionally debated whether the social cost from monopoly is 1% or 2% of total output, but in industries with significant scale economy, choosing a sub-optimal scale of capacity can often mean 30-50% differences in unit costs. For this reason, the East Asian governments have used measures such as industrial licensing, government procurement, export requirements, and subsidies in order to ensure that factories would be built at scales which are not too much below (and hopefully above) the minimum efficient scale. Of course, this invited criticisms on anti-trust grounds, but their attitude has been that monopolistic firms producing at optimal scale are much less of a drag to the economy than 'competitive' firms all producing at sub-optimal scales.

---

[5]  When duplicative investments emerged for whatever reason (e.g., government's failure to take timely action, non-compliance by the firms), the East Asian governments tried to minimise excess capacity by encouraging, and sometimes forcing, mergers or recession cartels. There were of course national differences. The Japanese government preferred to use recession cartels, while the Korean government periodically resorted to forced mergers. Examples of the latter include the so-called 'industrial restructuring programme' of the early 1980s (which affected industries such as automobile, naval diesel engine, copper smelting, power-generating equipment, heavy electrical machinery, and electronic switching system) and the so-called 'Big Deal' programme following the 1997 crisis (which affected industries such as semiconductor, automobile, power-generating equipment, naval diesel engine, aircraft, petrochemical, petroleum refining, and railway carriage).

Secondly, scale economy also has a hitherto-ignored link with luxury consumption control (for a more detailed discussion, see Chang, 1997a). The well-known practice of luxury consumption control in East Asian countries – most notoriously, but by no means exclusively or even mainly, through import control – has often been interpreted as no more than a thinly disguised protectionist ploy or as a manifestation of the paternalistic desire to impose what the government sees as a 'sound consumption pattern' (the phrase was explicitly used in, for example, the 4th Five Year Plan document of Korea, p. 27). However, there was much more to these controls. First of all, it was thought important to restrict conspicuous consumption for the purpose of reducing class conflicts, especially given the (real and imagined) presence of the Communist threat. Secondly, there was the desire to maximise the investible surplus by repressing luxury consumption out of profit. Thirdly, and most relevantly to our discussion here, restrictions on the consumption of luxury varieties in industries like the passenger car industry, where consumer demand for variety is important, were regarded as important in enabling the producers to attain the maximum possible scale in production.[6]

To sum up, while the EAM acknowledged the crucial role of scale economy in necessitating the coordination of complementary investments, it did not explore its role beyond this. However, while it may sound less fancy than coordinating complementary investments and giving industrial development a 'big push', ensuring the achievement of scale economy in key industries was in practice probably a much more important aspect of East Asian industrial policy than the former.

### 2.1.3 'Protective' industrial policy, social insurance, and structural change

Another aspect of industrial policy that has received little recognition in the East Asian context is its 'protective' role. It is widely

---

[6]    The cost inefficiency that results from the presence of excessive product variety is widely recognised in, for example, the South African car industry, and for that matter in the same industry of one East Asian country, namely, Taiwan (where about 10 producers each produces several thousand cars in an industry where the minimum efficient scale is believed to be around 300,000 units per year).

believed that what distinguishes industrial policy in East Asia is that it concentrated on 'picking winners', rather than 'protecting losers' as was often the case in other countries. There is certainly a large element of truth in such view. However, protective industrial policies were also widespread in East Asia, if less so than in other countries. Therefore, we need to go deeper if we are to understand why protective industrial policy in East Asia did not end up blocking structural change as in other countries.

We argue that there were two functions that the protective industrial policies in East Asia served. The first function was the more short-term-oriented one of providing 'social insurance' to firms which are in temporary difficulty but cannot borrow their way out of it due to capital market imperfections.[7] Like the policy of coordinating competing investments, the practice can be justified in terms of asset specificity, in that it will be socially inefficient to scrap specific assets in the face of a temporary setback, if the net present values of their future income streams are larger than the costs of supports needed to keep them employed in their current uses (assuming full asset specificity – namely, their value in alternative uses is zero). The best example of such policy is the famous Japanese practice of sanctioning (but closely supervising and disciplining) 'recession cartels' in industries deemed to be in temporary difficulty (see Dore, 1986, and Chang, 1994: Chapter 3, for more details).

The second, and probably more important, function was the more long-term-oriented one of promoting structural change. When an industry is in need of a large-scale adjustment, those who had made specific (human and physical, or even relational) investments in the industry face a situation where their next best option is a total scrapping of their assets and therefore a drastic reduction in their income. Unless there is a mechanism that allows them an acceptable level of income during the transition period when they run down their existing assets and re-tool themselves (e.g., purchasing new equipment, retraining of workers), they will have an incentive to resist the change by political means. In such a situation, measures to reduce the impacts of adjustment on the owners of specific assets can accelerate,

---

[7] I thank Joe Stiglitz for highlighting this dimension of protective industrial policy, which was only implicit in the earlier version of this chapter.

rather than slow down, structural change by reducing political resistance to the change, if they also provide incentives for (physical and mental) re-tooling (for a more detailed argument, see Chang and Rowthorn, 1995).[8]

In Japan, 'cartels for structurally-depressed industries' (or SDI cartels) were granted to declining industries in return for their efforts to phase out obsolete capacities and upgrade their technologies (Dore, 1986, provides a fascinating study of this experience; also see Renshaw, 1986). During the late 1980s, some of the declining industries in Korea, such as textile, received temporary supports (e.g., subsidies for equipment upgrading, exemption from anti-trust law), through the rationalisation programmes sanctioned by the Industrial Development Law, on the condition that they achieve certain targets in relation to technology upgrading (see Chang, 1993, for details).

What distinguishes these policies from similar policies in other countries is that they were 'forward-looking' in the sense that they made it explicit that the aim of the protection was not to preserve the industries concerned but to phase them out 'in an orderly manner' or to technologically upgrade them. Perhaps more importantly, they also had well-specified performance targets for the beneficiaries, thus preventing the policies from turning into 'nursing homes' for declining industries. In other words, because of the way they were designed and implemented, protective industrial policies in East Asia seem to have promoted, rather than hindered, structural change.

To summarise, the EAM, by concentrating on 'developmental' industrial policy, ignored 'protective' industrial policy. Such industrial policy is often regarded as blocking structural change and therefore not justifiable, but it has played a positive role in East Asia in two ways. Firstly, it provided social insurance to producers who are experiencing temporary difficulty but cannot borrow their way out

---

[8]    Different countries have dealt with this problem in different ways. Many European economies have used unemployment insurance to soften the blow of structural change on the owners of specific human skills and *ad hoc* subsidies to do the same for the owners of specific physical equipment. More proactively, the Scandinavian countries combined such a system with an 'active labour market policy', which provided retraining and relocation subsidies to the workers. As we shall see, the East Asian countries used protective industrial policy in order to deal with this problem.

of it due to capital market imperfections. Secondly, and more importantly, it promoted structural change by easing the difficulties involved in moving 'specific' resources out of the declining sectors or in upgrading them. Such policy was perhaps not the most important aspect of East Asian industrial policy, but was by no means an unimportant aspect, especially for the more advanced ones like Japan and Korea.

## 2.2   Empirical refutation

The essence of the EAM's empirical verdict on the role of industrial policy in East Asia can be summarised, at the risk of some simplification, as follows: there is no evidence that the industries promoted by industrial policy had higher output growth or more rapid productivity growth than the other industries.

The detailed methodologies and the data used in this study have already been subject to a range of well-known criticisms, including the problems inherent in the definition and the measurement of total factor productivity (see Lall, 1994; Kwon, 1994; Rodrik, 1994; and Singh, 1994, among others; also see Chang, 1995: Appendix). As they are mostly of a technical (which of course does not mean 'trivial') nature, the summary of which may take up quite considerable space, in this section I want to do no more than raise a couple of methodological points that had not been adequately addressed in the earlier debate surrounding the EAM.

One major problem in testing the effects of industrial policy in the way that the EAM attempted – namely, trying to correlate the extent of government support for an industry (however measured) and the industry's performance – is that, as far as one major justification for industrial policy lies in the existence of externalities, it is by definition very difficult (if not entirely impossible) to measure its effects at the sectoral level (the two-digit level in this case), as its effects will spill over into other sectors. If we can measure the effects of such policy, we probably did not need it in the first place.

The EAM does acknowledge this problem but justifies its sectoral approach on the ground that spillover effects are mostly confined to 'closely related sectors, often sectors that would be identified with a two-digit classification' (p. 326). The problem with this conclusion is that it is based on one study on the pattern of spillovers of R&D in industrial economies. Apart from the fact that it is dangerous to draw such a strong conclusion from a single study, it is not clear how relevant such a study is to understanding the role of industrial policy in developing economies. For developing economies, where R&D plays at best a minor role, more important forms of spillover effects may be such things as the formation of a skilled labour force and the increase in generalised engineering capability, and therefore the result of the study on R&D spillover that the EAM cites has only limited relevance, even if it were true (for more details, see Chang, 1995: Appendix).

Another problem with the empirical study presented in the EAM is that it suffers from a serious 'identification problem'. It has been already pointed out by Lall (1994) that the EAM classifies the industries at the two-digit level, which is too coarse a classification to identify the activities that were promoted – typically, industrial promotion was targeted at a much lower level, sometimes even involving supports defined at the firm level. We can also say that such classification is at the same time too fine, because some major components of industrial policy, such as export promotion, were conducted at a much broader and cross-sectoral level.[9] However, there is a more fundamental dimension to this 'identification problem', which is that the EAM did not bother to find out which industries, at whatever levels of classification, were *actually* promoted.

The statistical work conducted in the EAM is based on the notion that the East Asian governments promoted industries that had higher value-added or higher capital intensity. However, the problem is that the choice of industries to be promoted in these countries was never made on simple criteria like 'capital intensity' or 'value-added component'. Rather, the choice reflected a whole set of considerations, including, to name just a few, international market conditions, the

---

[9]  The EAM distinguishes industrial policy as a separate category from export promotion policy. However, this is not right because export promotion policy was a key element in the industrial policy regimes of the East Asian countries. New industries that the government wanted to promote almost invariably needed to have access to foreign exchange in order to buy the new technologies and the equipments that embody them, and knowing this, the government saw export success as a prerequisite of industrial upgrading. Also see Rodrik (1994).

availability of relevant domestic technological capabilities, and the net foreign exchange implication of promoting the industry concerned.

For example, the Korean textile industry, which the EAM regards as the quintessential 'non-promoted' industry (p. 316), in fact received a lot of promotional supports even *after* the government launched its (in)famous Heavy and Chemical Industrialisation programme in 1973 – it even had a special promotional law made for it in 1979. This was because of the industry's critical role as the main supplier of foreign exchange (it was the largest export industry until well into the 1980s), which was necessary for the country to import capital equipment and buy technology licences that were needed for the 'infant' industries. Given this, the fact that the Korean textile industry was, according to the EAM, unusually large by international standards is proof *not* of the failure of Korean industrial policy, as the EAM argues, but of its success (for more details, see Chang, 1995: Appendix).

In other words, the EAM has classified industries into promoted ones and ones that were not, according to what it *thought* was the industrial policy practice in the East Asian countries, rather than according to what actually *was* the practice in these countries. Such disregard as to what was actually going on in the countries concerned is quite similar to its failure in the theoretical section to consider (if only to disapprove) the justifications behind some central components of industrial policy in these countries, such as coordination of competing investments, policy measures to attain scale economy, and the use of 'protective' industrial policy.[10]

---

[10]    Paying attention to these hitherto-ignored aspects of industrial policy makes our empirical tests more difficult. Traditionally, many studies have used indicators such as subsidies and tariffs in order to measure the extent of industrial policy in an industry. However, recognising these additional aspects means that we also need to take into account less quantifiable things like the costs saved from coordination of competing investments and from measures to achieve scale economy, or the benefits from the acceleration of structural change that protective industrial policy may accord (which will be even more difficult to measure, as they are likely to spill over into the rest of the economy).

## 2.3   The replicability problem

One important line of argument employed by the EAM against industrial policy was that the policy requires certain conditions in order to be successful and therefore that other countries which do not meet these conditions cannot use such policy.

Two kinds of arguments were made in this regard. First of all, it was argued that, in order to make industrial policy work even to the (allegedly) limited extent that it worked in East Asia, a country needs certain institutions, especially a highly capable bureaucracy like the ones we can only find in the Northeast Asian countries (Japan, Korea, Taiwan, Hong Kong, and Singapore). Secondly, it was pointed out that industrial policy is not feasible anymore, because the new international trading regime that emerged out of the Uruguay Round of the GATT talks has made the tools of industrial policy that the Northeast Asian countries had used 'illegal'. How persuasive are these arguments?

### 2.3.1  Institutional capability

The EAM argues that successful management of industrial policy, as one of those 'selective' policies that go beyond the 'fundamentals', requires certain unusual institutional capabilities that can rarely be found outside Northeast Asia. The report argues that effective implementation of 'contests' among the recipients of state supports, which is necessary for a successful industrial policy, requires 'the competence, insulation, and relative lack of corruptibility of the public administrations in Japan and Korea' (p. 102).[11] From this, the report concludes that the more market-oriented economies of Southeast Asia provide a better role model for other developing countries, for their success proves that there is a lot of mileage that countries with poor administrative and other institutional capabilities can derive from concentrating on achieving the 'fundamentals', which does

---

[11]   The EAM also cites 'the pragmatism and flexibility of governments' as another condition, but this subsequently plays a much less important role in the argument.

not require advanced institutional capabilities (macroeconomic stability, human resource development, agricultural development, among others).[12]

The problem with this argument is not so much that anyone seriously doubts whether an effective conduct of selective industrial policy (or for that matter, any policy) requires a bureaucracy that has the competence and the political influence to impose 'hard budget constraints' on the recipients of state support according to relatively transparent rules. This proposition is in fact what many 'revisionists' have repeatedly emphasised. So at that level there is really no dispute.

The problem is that the EAM is implicitly assuming that the more 'selective' a policy is, the more difficult it is to administer and thus the more institutional 'props' (such as a good bureaucracy) it needs – or, to put it differently, the closer an economic system is to the *laissez-faire* ideal, the easier it becomes to run it. Is this true?

First of all, well-functioning markets require institutional prerequisites as much as well-functioning policies require them, although of somewhat different kinds – developed contract law, an efficient capital market, and an effective dispute settlement mechanism, to name just a few – because, without these institutions, market exchange becomes very costly (Chang, 1997b). A successful modern free-market economy will also require highly capable *private sector bureaucracies* that can successfully manage large and complex firms. The enormous difficulties that many developing and transition economies are having in constructing the basic institutions of the market economy and the private sector bureaucratic capabilities are clear testimonies to the fact that more market-oriented economic systems are *not necessarily* easier to construct and run than more interventionist systems.

Secondly, in the same vein, it is not clear to me at all whether industrial policy necessarily requires a more capable bureaucracy than the 'fundamental' policies. This will, for one thing, depend on the

---

[12] The list of 'fundamentals' in the EAM keeps changing, because it does not really have a good theory of which area of policy is more important and why. However, these three items are almost always included in the list.

nature and the scale of the policies concerned. For example, is promoting a small number of relatively unsophisticated industries necessarily more difficult than, say, administering a large-scale primary educational programme? For another example, running a good macroeconomic policy in the face of a large (positive or negative) external shock is often a lot more difficult than running selective industrial policy (as the East Asian economies are finding to their chagrin these days). The point is *not* that industrial policy is necessarily more (or less) difficult to run than other policies, but that we cannot make a categorical statement about the ease or the difficulty of a particular type of policy without looking at the particular case at hand.

Thirdly, it is not clear whether the capable bureaucracies in Northeast Asia were the products of 'highly unusual historical and institutional circumstances' (p. 366). At first sight, this seems more than reasonable. We all know that the Northeast Asian countries have behind them at least a thousand (and more, in the case of Chinese-speaking countries) years of history of meritocratic bureaucracy, and this surely must prove that these countries are highly unusual – or does it?

Let us start answering this question by first thinking about Singapore. Is it really the Confucian tradition that has made its bureaucracy what it is? At least to me, the principles that lie behind the Singaporean bureaucracy seem more British than Confucian. Take the case of Taiwan. When its bureaucracy was running mainland China before 1949, it already had the longest tradition of meritocracy and competitive recruitment in the world, but that did not prevent it from being one of the least competent and the most corrupt bureaucracies of the time. Did Korea always have an exceptionally competent bureaucracy? The Korean bureaucracy was also notorious for its incompetence and nepotism in the 1950s (Cheng *et al.*, 1998), and it was sending its bureaucrats for training to countries like Pakistan and the Philippines even until the late 1960s. It was only through continuous efforts at civil service reform, and *not* as a result of history and tradition, that Korea managed to create a competent and relatively clean bureaucracy – this is a point to which even the EAM gave a side glance (Box 4.4).

The point is *not* that history and tradition do not matter, but that capabilities (and the institutions that embody them) can be built and destroyed a lot more easily than is assumed in the EAM (and by many other people). It is true that the process of capability-building often takes time, but this is not the same as saying that countries which do not have high capability should never try 'difficult' policies (such as industrial policy). Such capability can be, and has often been, built rather quickly, not least because there is also 'learning-by-doing' in administration as in production. Institutions are, in other words, subject to imitation and innovation, as are technologies (Westney, 1987). Indeed, the World Bank itself has later come around to accepting, although still not wholeheartedly, the line of criticism that we deployed above, as we can see from its 1997 annual report that emphasised the need for state capability-building (World Bank, 1997).

### 2.3.2   Changing international trading environment

The EAM cites the birth of the new international trading regime, following the conclusion of the Uruguay Round of the GATT talks and the birth of the World Trade Organisation (WTO), as a severe constraint on the use of the kinds of interventionist trade and industrial policy measures employed by the Northeast Asian countries (p. 25, p. 365). While it accepts that there is some room for manoeuvre[13], its verdict on the effect of the WTO regime on developing-country policy autonomy seems overly pessimistic.

To begin with, we should not exaggerate the additional constraints on trade and industrial policies that the WTO regime has brought about by talking as if everything was allowed under the pre-Uruguay-Round regime. The old regime also had a large number of restrictions on the range of acceptable policy instruments, and therefore the Northeast Asian countries had to exercise a lot of ingenuity in choosing the means of industrial policy and diplomatic skills to iron out problems with their trading partners.

---

[13]  For example, the EAM does recognise that there is a time provision of up to eight years for the developing countries to bring their trade policies in line with those practised in advanced countries (p. 365). It also acknowledges that there are other means than subsidies or export-directed credit programmes that may be used in order to promote exports (p. 25).

Secondly, it should not be forgotten that the WTO regime is still an evolving system. We still do not fully know, a good few years after the launch of the WTO, how the abstract principles stated in its charter are going to be translated into practice. Its exact characteristics will be determined only with the accumulation of precedents over time, because, as with any other legal system, its principles are stated in fairly general terms and therefore need to be actively 'interpreted'.

Thirdly, we need to point out that the restrictions on the use of subsidies in the WTO regime are not as binding as they are portrayed to be in the EAM and elsewhere. For one thing, there are subsidies which are perfectly legal (the so-called 'non-actionable' subsidies) – these include 'non-specific' subsidies and certain types of 'specific' subsidies (those for basic R&D, agriculture, disadvantaged regions, and equipment upgrading to meet higher environmental standards). There are also subsidies which are 'actionable' (e.g., the trading partner can impose countervailing duties) although not prohibited. However, in this case, the complaining country has to prove that the subsidy concerned has caused a 'material damage', which is not easy especially when it concerns developing countries with tiny market shares. The only subsidies which are prohibited outright are subsidies that require their recipients to meet certain export targets or to use domestic goods instead of imported goods. However, the poorest countries (defined roughly as countries with less than $1,000 per capita income) are in fact exempt from even this.

Fourthly, as in the pre-WTO regime, countries are allowed under the WTO regime to raise tariffs or introduce quantitative restrictions when they have balance-of-payments problems. Given that practically almost all of them are in a permanent balance-of-payments crisis, this provides significant room for manoeuvre for the developing countries. Indeed, it was actually almost invariably on this ground, rather than under the infant industry provision of the GATT, that the East Asian countries imposed tariffs and quantitative restrictions that they used for infant industry promotion (Akyuz *et al.*, 1998: p. 31). Of course, these measures are supposed to be commensurate to the scale of the balance-of-payments problem, which means that there is a clear restriction on the total magnitude of measures that can be used. However, the WTO expressly allows the individual countries to choose *where* to impose these measures (i.e., how they define 'non-essential imports'), so there is actually significant room for selectivity in the use of these measures, which is after all what the debate is about.

To summarise, it is true that the WTO regime has put greater restrictions than before on the range of trade and industrial policy tools that are acceptable. However, the restrictions are by no means as wide-ranging and severe as the EAM suggests, and there is more room for manoeuvre for developing countries, especially the poorest ones which are given some special exemptions. Given that the pre-WTO world trading regime was by no means permissive, it seems doubtful whether the birth of the new international trading regime makes the past industrial policy practices in East Asia as irrelevant for other developing countries as they are argued to be.

## 3.    The East Asian Crisis (and the Japanese Stagnation) and Industrial Policy

The debate on East Asian industrial policy recently took a new turn following the continued stagnation in Japan and the economic crises in a number of other countries in the region.[14]

As we already pointed out in a number of places, many mainstream economists have until recently tried hard to deny the very existence of industrial policy in East Asia. Even many of those mainstream economists who acknowledged its existence (including the authors of the EAM) were basically arguing that it made little, if any, difference to the economies concerned. With the recent economic troubles in the region, however, many of those who denied the existence or the effectiveness of industrial policy in East Asia have made an intellectual U-turn, and argued that industrial policy was widespread and 'effective' in the region – although effective in the negative sense of creating inefficiencies and encouraging excessive risk-taking (for a more comprehensive critique of this argument, see Chang, 2000).

---

[14]    For some comprehensive discussions of the East Asian crisis, see Radelet and Sachs (1998), Stiglitz (1998), Singh (1998), Furman and Stiglitz (1998), and Chang (1999).

Before we discuss the role of industrial policy in the East Asian crisis, we need to put this crisis into perspective. The point is that, while the scale of crisis in many countries in the region is truly mind-boggling, it is by no means the case that the whole region is falling apart. Taiwan is still going strong and Singapore has managed to keep its head above water. As for Japan, the problem seems more to be in perception than in reality (although this is not to say that therefore the stagnation can be ignored). True, during the 1990s, the country has been in the longest stagnation in its postwar history, but even then its relative performance *vis-a-vis* the US, which is supposed to have entered a new 'Golden Age', seems quite respectable. For example, if we use the most updated World Bank data set, its average per capita GDP growth rate between 1990 and 1997 has been 1.0%, a rate which is not much below the 2.0% attained by the US economy. According to *The Economist*, between 1989 and 1998, the average per capita GDP growth rates in Japan and the US were in fact *identical* at 1.6%, and the labour productivity growth rate was actually *higher* in Japan at 1.2%, compared to 0.9% of the US (*The Economist*, 10 April 1999, p. 67). These figures suggest that the current stagnation of the Japanese economy by no means signifies the demise of an economic system.

The main difficulty with the argument that industrial policy was behind the Asian crisis is that it is in fact mostly the more market-oriented Southeast Asian countries and Hong Kong, rather than the industrial-policy states of Northeast Asia, that are in crisis. In the Japanese case, there is widespread agreement that the recent economic problem was caused by poor macroeconomic policy, rather than industrial policy. Despite their industrial policy practices, Taiwan and Singapore are not experiencing crises. Of course, the inclusion of Korea, a well-known practitioner of industrial policy, in the list of crisis countries complicates things, but we begin to see a consistent pattern when we note that the Korean industrial policy was actually largely dismantled by the mid-1990s. Let us elaborate on this line of argument.

To begin with, let us look at the Southeast Asian countries. While the EAM certainly underestimated the role that industrial policy played in these countries – it played an important role in developing some natural-resource-related industries (e.g., see Jomo and Rock, 1998) –

it is undeniable that industrial policy was not a major element in the policy regimes of the Southeast Asian countries. Thailand and Indonesia have had little industrial policy, except in agricultural processing industries in the case of Thailand and in a few 'prestige' projects (e.g., aircraft) in the case of Indonesia. Malaysia has had a more systematic industrial policy, but it can hardly be described as the dominant factor in the country's policy regime in the way that it was in the Northeast Asian countries. Indeed, during the last decade or so, many observers of the Southeast Asian countries have argued that the absence of industrial policy is precisely why they were finding it increasingly difficult to upgrade their industry and export structures. In short, industrial policy could not have been a major factor behind the crises in the Southeast Asian economies, because there was, simply, little of it around. Indeed, it was the real estate investments that had nothing to do with industrial policy, rather than industrial investments, that led to the Southeast Asian bubbles (see Henderson, 1998, for more details).

Then how about Korea? Isn't it one of the archetypal industrial-policy states and therefore a case proving the defects of industrial policy? The fact that the over-investments that caused the country's crisis were mostly in industries, rather than in real estate development as in the case of Southeast Asia, also seems to corroborate this argument.

However, contrary to the popular perception, industrial policy was largely absent in Korea in the build-up to the current crisis. Slowly from the late 1980s, but very rapidly from 1993 with the inauguration of the Kim Young Sam administration, the Korean government dismantled industrial policy, except for R&D supports in some high-technology industries (see Chang, 1998b, for further details). Therefore, it is difficult to blame the Korean crisis on industrial policy as it was not around anymore in any meaningful way.

In fact, we can go even further and argue that it was actually the *demise* of industrial policy, rather than its continuation, that was one major factor behind the current crisis in Korea (see Chang *et al.*, 1998, and Chang, 2000 for further details). Most importantly, the end to the policy of investment coordination among competing firms (see Subsection 2.1.1) allowed the proliferation of duplicative investments in the key industries that constituted one major cause of the crisis and are now the subjects of the so-called 'Big Deal' industrial restructuring (see footnote 5 for some more details).

To summarise, contrary to the popular perception, the recent economic problems in East Asia do *not* show us that industrial policy was a major drag on the economies of the region. Above all, given the fact that there was little industrial policy around in the crisis countries (including Korea, which had largely dismantled such policy by the mid-1990s), it seems highly implausible to argue that such policy was responsible for the crisis. On the contrary, it can even be argued that it was the absence of such policy that contributed to the crisis, at least in some of the countries concerned.

## 4.    Some Thoughts on the Future of Industrial Policy in East Asia

So what is the future for industrial policy in East Asia? To some, this question may sound pointless, given the wide-ranging liberalisation measures that have been instituted following the IMF packages implemented in the region, and also given, at least for the moment, the conversion of most governments in the region to the liberal cause.

However, formal laws and rules cannot fully determine the workings of an economic system – after all, it was out of the very American formal institutional structures that the Occupation Authorities imposed after the Second World War that the 'idiosyncratic' Japanese and German economic systems had developed. Moreover, policy needs and fashions change, and therefore it is not certain whether the governments in the region will maintain their current policy stances in the future. Therefore, I think it is still useful to explore the more structural economic and political trends to reflect on whether the governments in the region can use an activist industrial policy in the future, should their political commitments and vision change.

### 4.1   Economic maturity

It has been popular during the last decade or so among the researchers of the more advanced East Asian economies (Japan, Korea, and Taiwan) to argue that the attainment of economic maturity in these economies has made industrial policy almost impossible to implement. There are two variants to this argument – one based on the problem of complexity, and the other based on the problem of uncertainty.

The complexity argument is that, with economic development, economies become more complex, and therefore it becomes more difficult to administer centrally. This argument is accepted as a truism by almost everyone, but I am not so sure whether I agree with it.

It is true that, other things being equal, a more complex problem increases the informational requirements of its successful policy solution, and therefore is more difficult to manage centrally. But the problem is that other things are *not* equal.

First of all, a more mature economy is likely to have a better administrative capability, if only because its bureaucracy will have had more opportunity to engage in 'learning-by-doing'. As we pointed out in Section 2.3.1, it is not only in production activities that learning-by-doing exists. The implication is that even a relatively 'simple' policy will be difficult to administer for developing-country bureaucracies with low capability, while more advanced economies have bureaucracies which can deal with quite complex policies with ease.

Secondly, a more developed economy is typically better organised into larger and better-managed units (e.g., large modern corporations, producer associations, community organisations). This means that it is easier to implement a given policy in a more mature economy, as the latter is likely to have more effective 'intermediate' enforcement mechanisms. Indeed, this was precisely one of the factors that Marx and his followers (including the anti-socialist Schumpeter) thought would make socialism increasingly feasible with economic development. The point can also be made from the opposite end. It is well known that industrial policies are typically very difficult to implement in industries where firms are very small and are not organised into industry or regional associations.

In short, a more mature economy typically (if not always) has more complex tasks at hand, but at the same time it typically has better capabilities (both at the governmental level and at the social level) to manage those tasks. Therefore, it is not clear whether centralised coordination through industrial policy becomes necessarily more difficult with economic development and maturity.

A related, but slightly different, line of argument is based on the problem of uncertainty, rather than complexity. The argument is that, when a country reaches the frontier of technological development, it becomes much more uncertain what the government should be doing to help the industry. I find this argument more compelling than the one based on complexity that we have just examined.

However, it is one thing to say that industrial policy becomes more difficult in 'frontier' industries, and it is another to say that this makes industrial policy impossible in a mature economy. For one thing, most of the justifications of industrial policy that we reviewed above should hold for frontier industries too. Indeed, some of these justifications may become even stronger with economic maturity (e.g., learning externalities). Moreover, even in a frontier industry with genuine uncertainty about its future, there is no reason why an intelligent bureaucracy in close consultation with the private sector should not be able to identify the broad trends and provide support for certain types of productivity-enhancing activities. The best example of the successful use of industrial policy in the frontier industries is provided by the experience of Japan during the 1980s and the early 1990s (e.g., see Okimoto, 1989, Fransman, 1990, and Weiss, 1995, for some examples).

Now, I must point out that this argument, which is very sensible in the context of some frontier industries in the most advanced economies, has been, unfortunately, liberally applied to situations which do not deserve it. Even in the most advanced countries like Japan, there are many industries that are still in a catch-up position. When it comes to economies like Korea and Taiwan, the argument is unconvincing. Despite what the locals, especially the Koreans, like to think, these economies are still a good 2-3 decades behind Japan in almost all industries. Therefore, if industrial policy worked well in Japan as late as the late 1980s and the early 1990s, it should work for Korea and Taiwan in the early decades of the new millennium, if not necessarily beyond. It is needless to say that the argument is basically irrelevant when it comes to the Southeast Asian economies.

To sum up, the first variant of the 'maturity' argument – namely, the complexity argument – does not seem compelling to me. As economies mature, policy implementation capability increases both at the governmental and at the 'intermediate' levels, and therefore it is not clear whether they necessarily become more difficult to manage centrally. The second variant – namely, the uncertainty argument – is more convincing, but its applicability is pretty limited – it applies basically only to Japan among the East Asian countries. Moreover, even with an overall economic maturity, a country will still have many industries where the technological capability has not reached the world's frontier. And even in those industries at the frontier, the more sensible solution is often not the abandonment of industrial policy but a modification in its form, as the Japanese experience since the 1980s shows.

## 4.2   Democratisation

It has long been argued that interventionist industrial policy requires strong states which can override sectional interests. Therefore, it is argued, increasing democratisation of the East Asian countries during the last decade or so should make such policy politically less acceptable and therefore less feasible. This argument is used especially in relation to countries like Korea and Taiwan, which have recently gone through a substantial degree of democratisation.

However, it is not clear to me whether industrial policy is incompatible with a democratic polity. Countries like France, Japan, Austria, Norway, and Finland, whose democratic credentials and consensus orientation in politics during the postwar period no one will dispute, have all successfully used industrial policy in one way or another. In fact, one can go one step further and even argue that, if there is a democratic consensus on it (as there had been in the above-mentioned countries), industrial policy can be even more effectively implemented, given that every policy requires for its long-term success some degree of consent by those who are going to be affected by it (see Weiss, 1995: Chapter 2, for a similar argument).

In my view, what seems to be creating the impression that democracy and industrial policy are mutually incompatible is the fact that industrial policy in Taiwan, and especially Korea, has lost its political legitimacy in the eyes of the population because of its past association with dictatorship. However, there is no inherent reason why industrial policy cannot regain its legitimacy even in these countries, if a democratic political consensus can be built around it. While it may be argued that at least in Korea there is no chance of that happening in the near future, this is an argument which is based on an assessment of the present political situation in the country, and therefore has to be distinguished from the argument that industrial policy is inherently incompatible with democracy.

To summarise, the association between industrial policy and authoritarianism in the minds of the observers of certain East Asian countries is understandable, but this association is a product of history, rather than a manifestation of some underlying law. If we applied the same logic to the experience of 19th-century Britain, USA, or some European countries, we would have probably concluded that a free-market policy was incompatible with democracy, which is indeed what most Liberals of the time thought to be the case (on the earlier view on the relationship between democracy and liberalism, see Bobbio, 1990; also see Polanyi, 1957).

## 4.3 Changing balance of power between the government and the private sector

Throughout their economic development, but especially more recently, the East Asian countries have witnessed the rise of large private sector industrial and financial corporations, and their increasing internationalisation. This has prompted many people to argue that industrial policy that restricts private sector interests will not be possible anymore, as the private sector firms now have enormous political influence, given the weight that they have in the economy and also given their ability to veto government policy by 'exiting' from the domestic economy.

The argument obviously makes a lot of sense. Corporations which have become economically and politically more powerful and have more freedom to move around the world certainly would be, other things being equal, better able to resist government policies that sacrifice their individual interests for the sake of national goals. And indeed in Korea, the giant conglomerates (the *chaebols*) have aggressively campaigned during the 1990s to convince the population that the government should abandon its industrial policy and financial regulations.[15]

However, we need to be careful in jumping from such an observation to the conclusion that economic development means the rise of the private sector, which, when combined with globalisation, makes industrial policy impossible.[16]

The problem here is that it is not clear whether there is an inevitable association between economic development, the rise of the private sector, and the demise of industrial policy. For one thing, the experience of Taiwan shows that economic development need not lead to the emergence of a powerful private sector, as the process of corporate development is as much a political process as an economic process (Fields, 1995). The Japanese experience is also consistent with such an observation. The Japanese corporations had already become very powerful and internationally mobile during the 1970s and the 1980s, but Japan had great success with industrial policy during that period, because these firms accepted the legitimacy of industrial policy and cooperated with the government for its success.

Moreover, it needs to be pointed out that the extent of internationalisation of even the largest corporations in East Asia is still limited. Judging from the experiences of other countries with a longer history of internationalised business, the chance that they will turn into truly 'transnational' corporations without a 'home base' in the foreseeable future is low. When we also note that globalisation is

---

[15] In 1996, the Korea Federation of Industries, the association of the *chaebols*, prepared a report arguing for the abolition of all government ministries except the ministries of defence and foreign affairs and for the consequent reduction of government staff by 90%. The report had to be officially withdrawn because it was unfortunately leaked in advance by a careless reporter and created a popular uproar. While the chance of such a proposal being taken seriously was non-existent even in Korea that was then (and still is to a large extent) in the grip of an anti-statist reaction, the incident is illustrative of the aggressiveness that the *chaebols* were showing in pushing for greater business freedom in the recent period.

[16] For a comprehensive critique of the argument that globalisation makes industrial policy impossible, see Weiss (1998). Chang (1998a) makes a similar argument more specifically in relation to the rise of transnational corporations.

a trend that can be, and has been (in the aftermath of the Great Depression), reversed, it is not clear whether the current process of globalisation will continue until it makes industrial policy impossible.[17]

So, in the end the argument that industrial policy has become less feasible in East Asian countries because their economic development has led to growth in the power of the private sector, which naturally resists industrial policy, is problematic. It may fit the Korean example rather well, but as a general proposition, it is rather suspect. This is because there is no direct causal link between economic development and the rise of the private sector (recall the Taiwanese counter-example), on the one hand, and between the rise of the private sector (including its internationalisation) and the demise of industrial policy (recall the Japanese counter-example), on the other hand.

## 5.    Concluding Remarks

So what are the main conclusions that we can draw from our 'rethinking' on the issue of industrial policy in East Asia?

First of all, there are more theoretical justifications for industrial policy than acknowledged by the EAM, and we need to explore these issues deeper. This is important, especially given that those justifications (e.g., coordination of competing investments, scale economy) were probably more important in the actual formation of industrial policy in the East Asian countries than the ones acknowledged by the EAM (e.g., 'Big Push', formation of implicit cartels in international negotiations).

Secondly, we need to think much harder to find the ways to test the true effects of industrial policy. Apart from the detailed method-

---

[17]    The world economy was almost as globalised in the late 19th and the early 20th centuries as it is now on many indicators, and on some indicators even more. For example, international labour mobility was much higher then and international policy uniformity was much greater then – especially given the Gold Standard and the lack of tariff autonomy in all countries except the strongest (even Japan did not have tariff autonomy until 1899). See Bairoch and Kozul-Wright (1996) for the historical evidence.

ological criticisms that have already been made of the tests conducted on the issue in the EAM, which we did not have the space to summarise, there remain some issues that we need to resolve in future research. For example, how should we deal with the problem of externalities? Should we, and how do we, for another example, quantify the effects of policies such as the achievement of scale economy through licensing policy, the prevention of a price war through the encouragement of a recession cartel, or the reduction in the resistance to technological change in the long run through the use of 'protective' industrial policy? These are only some of the questions that we need to explore and debate further before we can be confident about our empirical studies, if we ever can be.

Thirdly, the capability argument used by the EAM against other countries wanting to adopt East-Asian-style industrial policy is not without its merits, but it has important limitations. First of all, it is not clear why industrial policy regardless of its scale and sophistication requires an exceptionally competent bureaucracy. And, secondly, bureaucratic capability is something that can be accumulated through deliberate efforts and learning-by-doing. It should also be added that it is not as if more market-oriented systems do not require high institutional capabilities, as we can see in the difficulties that many transitional and developing economies are currently experiencing in establishing a 'free market system'.

Fourthly, the WTO argument against the feasibility of industrial policy in the present era, which was also emphasised by the EAM, draws an overly pessimistic conclusion without looking at the full array of possibilities that exist for policy manoeuvre.

Fifthly, as for the argument that the recent stagnation in Japan and crises in other East Asian countries prove that industrial policy has been in the end detrimental for these economies, it should be pointed out that it is actually the countries which did not have or which ditched industrial policy that are in crisis.

Lastly, as for things like economic maturity, democratisation, and the rise of the private sector's power, which are frequently cited as reasons why industrial policy will not be feasible anymore even in the countries that have successfully used it, we argue that they presuppose causal links which are not robust and are not really backed by empirical evidence.

While I confess to being an unreconstructed interventionist (but *not* of a naïve kind, I believe), I do respect other people who believe that things like industrial policy are politically objectionable and economically unfeasible. In this chapter, I have tried to make these people 'rethink' their positions by showing some theoretical and empirical problems with the prevailing view on East Asian industrial policy. I do not have the illusion that many of these people will convert to a new cause because of this chapter, but it will have been worth my effort if it has made some of them realise that there are still many issues that need to be settled in the area and we need further research on them.

# Bibliography

Akyuz, Y., Chang, H-J. & Kozul-Wright, R. (1998). 'New Perspectives on East Asian Development', *Journal of Development Studies*, vol. 34, no. 6.

Amsden, A. (1985). 'The State and Taiwan's Economic Development', in P. Evans, D. Rueschemeyer & T. Skocpol (eds.), *Bringing the State Back In.* Cambridge: Cambridge University Press.

Amsden, A. (1989). *Asia's Next Giant.* New York: Oxford University Press.

Amsden, A. & Singh, A. (1994). 'The Optimal Degree of Competition and Dynamic Efficiency in Japan and Korea', *European Economic Review*, vol. 38, nos. 3/4.

Badaracco, J. & Yoffie, D. (1983). '"Industrial Policy": It Can't Happen Here', *Harvard Business Review*, November/December.

Bairoch, P. & Kozul-Wright, R. (1996). 'Globalisation Myths: Some Historical Reflections on Integration, Industrialisation and Growth in the World Economy', UNCTAD Discussion Paper, no. 113. Geneva: United Nations Conference on Trade and Development (UNCTAD).

Balassa, B. (1982). 'Development Strategies and Economic Performance', in B. Balassa *et al.*, *Development Strategies in Semi-Industrial Economies.* Baltimore: The Johns Hopkins University Press.

Balassa, B. (1988). 'The Lessons of East Asian Development: An Overview', *Economic Development and Cultural Change*, vol. 36, no. 3, Apr. 1988, Supplement.

Bhagwati, J. (1988). *Protectionism.* Cambridge, Mass.: The MIT Press.

Bobbio, N. (1990). *Liberalism and Democracy.* London: Verso.

Chang, H-J. (1993). 'The Political Economy of Industrial Policy in Korea', *Cambridge Journal of Economics*, vol. 17, no. 2.

Chang, H-J. (1994). *The Political Economy of Industrial Policy.* London and Basingstoke: Macmillan.

Chang, H-J. (1995). 'Explaining "Flexible Rigidities" in East Asia', in T. Killick (ed.), *The Flexible Economy.* London: Routledge.

Chang, H-J. (1997a). 'Luxury Consumption Control and Industrialisation in East Asia', mimeo., a background paper prepared for *Trade and Development Report 1997.* Geneva: UNCTAD.

Chang, H-J. (1997b). 'The Economics and Politics of Regulation', *Cambridge Journal of Economics*, vol. 21, no. 6.

Chang, H-J. (1998a). 'Transnational Corporations and Strategic Industrial Policy', in R. Kozul-Wright & R.E. Rowthorn (eds.), *Transnational Corporations and the World Economy.* London and Basingstoke: Macmillan Press.

Chang, H-J. (1998b). 'Korea: The Misunderstood Crisis', *World Development*, vol. 26, no. 8.

Chang, H-J. (2000). 'The Hazard of Moral Hazard – Untangling the Asian Crisis', *World Development*, vol. 28, no. 4.

Chang, H-J., Park, H-J. & Yoo, C.G. (1998). 'Interpreting the Korean Crisis: Financial Liberalisation, Industrial Policy, and Corporate Governance', *Cambridge Journal of Economics*, vol. 22, no. 6.

Chang, H-J. & Rowthorn, R. (1995). 'Role of the State in Economic Change: Entrepreneurship and Conflict Management', in H-J. Chang & R. Rowthorn (eds.), *Role of the State in Economic Change*. Oxford: Oxford University Press.

Cheng, T., Haggard, S. & Kang, D. (1998). 'Institutions, Economic Policy, and Growth in the Republic of Korea and Taiwan Province of China', *Journal of Development Studies*, vol. 34, no. 6.

Dore, R. (1986). *Flexible Rigidities: Industrial Policy and Structural Adjustment in the Japanese Economy, 1970-80*. London: The Athlone Press.

Evans, D. & Alizadeh, P. (1984). 'Trade, Industrialisation, and the Visible Hand', *Journal of Development Studies*, vol. 21, no. 1.

Evans, P. (1995). *Embedded Autonomy – States and Industrial Transformation*. Princeton: Princeton University Press.

Fields, K. (1995). *Enterprise and State in Taiwan and Korea*. Ithaca, New York: Cornell University Press.

Fishlow, A., Gwin, C., Haggard, S., Rodrik, D. & Wade, R. (1994). *Miracle or Design? – Lessons from the East Asian Experience*. Washington, D.C.: Overseas Development Council.

Fransman, M. (1990). *The Market and Beyond: Information Technology in Japan*. Cambridge: Cambridge University Press.

Furman, J. & Stiglitz, J. (1998). 'Economic Crises: Evidence and Insights from East Asia', *Brookings Papers on Economic Activity*, 1998, no. 2.

Henderson, J. (1998). 'Uneven Crises: Institutional Foundations of East Asian Economic Turmoil', Transational Communities Working Paper, WPTC-98-13, Faculty of Anthropology and Geography, University of Oxford.

Johnson, C. (1982). *MITI and the Japanese Miracle*. Stanford: Stanford University Press.

Johnson, C. (ed.) (1984). *The Industrial Policy Debate*. San Francisco: Institute for Contemporary Studies.

Jomo, K.S. & Rock, M. (1998). 'Economic Diversification and Primary Commodity Processing in the Second-tier South-East Asian Newly Industrialising Countries', UNCTAD Discussion Paper, no. 136. Geneva: United Nations Conference on Trade and Development (UNCTAD).

Jones, L. & Sakong, I. (1980). *Government, Business and Entrepreneurship in Economic Development: The Korean Case*. Cambridge, Massachusetts: Harvard University Press.

Kwon, J. (1994). 'The East Asia Challenge to Neoclassical Orthodoxy', *World Development*, vol. 22, no. 4.

Lall, S. (1994). 'Does the Bell Toll for Industrial Policy?', *World Development*, vol. 22, no. 4.

Little, I. (1982). *Economic Development.* New York: Basic Books.

Luedde-Neurath, R. (1986). *Import Controls and Export-Oriented Development; A Reassessment of the South Korean Case.* Boulder and London: Westview Press.

Magaziner, I. & Hout, T. (1980). *Japanese Industrial Policy.* London: Policy Studies Institute.

Okimoto, D. (1989). *Between MITI and the Market: Japanese Industrial Policy for High Technology.* Stanford: Stanford University.

Polanyi, K. (1957). *The Great Transformation.* Boston: Beacon Press.

Radelet, S. & Sachs, J. (1998). 'The East Asian Financial Crisis: Diagnosis, Remedies and Prospects', *Brookings Paper on Economic Activity*, 1998, no. 1.

Ranis, G. & Fei, J. (1975). 'A Model of Growth and Employment in the Open Dualistic Economy: The Cases of Korea and Taiwan', in F. Stewart (ed.), *Employment, Income Distribution, and Development.* London: Frank Cass.

Reich, R. (1982). 'Why the US Needs an Industrial Policy', *Harvard Business Review*, January/February.

Renshaw, G. (1986). *Adjustment and Economic Performance in Industrialised Countries: A Synthesis.* Geneva: International Labour Office (ILO).

Rodrik, D. (1994). 'King Kong Meets Godzilla', in A. Fishlow *et al.*, *Miracle or Design? – Lessons from the East Asian Experience.* Washington, D.C.: Overseas Development Council.

Schultze, C. (1983). 'Industrial Policy: A Dissent', *The Brookings Review*, Fall.

Singh, A. (1994). '"Openness" and the "Market-friendly" Approach to Development: Learning the Right Lessons from Development Experience', *World Development*, vol. 22, no. 12.

Singh, A. (1998). 'Financial Crisis in East Asia: "The End of the Asian Model?"', Issues in Development Discussion Paper, no. 24. Geneva: International Labour Office.

Stiglitz, J. (1998). 'Sound Finance and Sustainable Development in Asia', keynote address to the Asia Development Forum, jointly organised by the World Bank and the Asian Development Bank, 9-12 March 1998, Manila, the Philippines.

Telser, L. (1987). *A Theory of Efficient Cooperation and Competition.* Cambridge: Cambridge University Press.

Thompson, G. (ed.) (1989). *Industrial Policy: US and UK Debates.* London: Routledge.

Wade, R. (1990). *Governing the Market.* Princeton: Princeton University Press.

Wade, R. (1996). 'Japan, the World Bank, and the Art of Paradigm Maintenance: The East Asian Miracle in Political Perspective', *New Left Review*, 1996, May/June.

Weiss, L. (1998). *The Myth of the Powerless State*. Cambridge: Polity Press.

Westney, E. (1987). *Imitation and Innovation: The Transfer of Western Organisational Patterns to Meiji Japan*. Cambridge: Cambridge University Press.

Williamson, O. (1985). *The Economic Institutions of Capitalism*. New York: The Free Press.

World Bank (1987). *World Development Report 1987*. Oxford: Oxford University Press.

World Bank (1993). *The East Asian Miracle*. New York: Oxford University Press.

World Bank (1997). *World Development Report 1997*. Oxford: Oxford University Press.

# Chapter 8

# THE TRIUMPH OF THE RENTIERS?

## 1. Introduction

THE causes of the 1997 Korean crisis, together with those of the crises in other Asian countries, have been hotly debated. Especially in the early days of the crisis, many commentators argued that the crisis was caused by some fundamental institutional deficiencies of the Korean economy that encouraged inefficiencies and excesses by protecting investors from the adverse consequences of their decisions.[1] However, others, including surprisingly many mainstream economists, have argued that the crisis was largely the result of a mixture between premature and ill-managed financial liberalisation (and the dismantling of other interventionist policies) and instability in the international financial market.[2] This chapter sheds some new light on this debate from a historical perspective by analysing the 1997 Korean crisis in comparison with the country's two earlier episodes of financial crisis (1970-72 and 1980).

We argue that the 1997 crisis signifies an important watershed in modern Korean economic history. It was, first of all, the result of the growing disintegration of the traditional economic system, where industrial interests were put before financial rentier interests. More

---

[1]  Examples include Brittan (1997), Krugman (1998a, 1998b), Frankel (1998), and McKinnon and Pill (1998).

[2]  The mainstream works that argue along this line include Corden (1998), Furman and Stiglitz (1998), Radelet and Sachs (1998), and Stiglitz (1998). Non-mainstream works along this line include Kregel (1998), Singh (1998), Taylor (1998), Chang (1998 and 2000), and the articles published in the November 1998 special issue on the Asian crisis of the *Cambridge Journal of Economics*.

importantly, the management of the crisis has been in the interests of the rentiers and is transforming the economic system in a way that is likely to end the traditional dominance of industry over finance. Full-scale financial liberalisation, the re-moulding of the corporate governance system in the Anglo-American image, and complete capital account opening are among the main changes that will push the country in such a direction. We contrast this with the 1970-72 crisis, which was resolved through a most dramatic expropriation of the rentier class through a government-imposed moratorium on informal financial market loans, and the 1980 crisis, whose resolution involved only relatively mild and mostly formalistic financial liberalisation measures. We conclude the chapter by discussing why we think that the transition to the new pro-finance economic system is likely to dampen the country's growth dynamics in the long run.

## 2.    The Korean Financial System During the High-Growth Period

If we are to fully understand the nature of the 1997 crisis, we need to understand the nature of the country's traditional financial system, whose disintegration lay behind it. The main elements of the financial system that lasted until the early 1990s were the following.

First of all, financial policy was run as an accessory to industrial policy. Although the Korean government had a great aversion to running public debt, it ran a relatively loose monetary policy in order to maintain a generally expansionary macroeconomic environment. An expansionary macroeconomic environment was regarded as crucial in sustaining the 'investors' confidence' necessary for continued high investments, which in turn were regarded as crucial for industrial upgrading (Chang, 1993). In this process, the financial rentier class was 'repressed', as reflected in the low profitability of financial institutions and as most dramatically exemplified by the government-declared moratorium on the 'curb market', or informal market, loans in 1972 (see Section 3.1).

Underlying such a regime of 'financial repression' was the view of the then ruling elite that the financial rentier class was at best a 'necessary evil' and at worst a parasitic group damaging the industrial enterprises necessary for national development.[3] Although such a view softened over time and eventually gave way to the monetarist thinking (which essentially puts the interest of the financial sector before that of the industrial sector), it will be difficult to make sense of Korea's financial system before the mid-1990s without recognising that the government basically saw finance as a servant to industry.

Secondly, the country's financial system was a 'bank-based' one, and a government-dominated variety of it at that. In the 1962 revision of the central bank act, the Minister of Finance was made the head of the Monetary Board (later renamed the Monetary Policy Committee) of the Bank of Korea, thus depriving the central bank of its independence.

Moreover, the banks were, regardless of their ownership status, practically run as public enterprises. A substantial proportion of the banks were 'special purpose banks' that were 100% owned by the government – such as Korea Development Bank, Korea Exchange Bank, Korea Housing Bank, and the Bank for Small and Medium-Sized Firms. Even in the case of the other banks, where the government did not have the majority stake, the government maintained its absolute control through the 'temporary' law introduced in 1961, which limited private shareholders' voting rights, and subsequently through the 1981 provision in the Banking Act that replaced the 'temporary' law, which set an 8% ceiling on bank share ownership for any individual or group of related shareholders.

Thirdly, through its control of the banking system, the government implemented various directed (and usually subsidised) credit

---

[3]   Such a view is well reflected in the following commentary on the pre-1961 financial system made by the official Summary of the First Five Year Plan (published in 1962): '[O]nly the privileged few who had access to bank credits were able to enjoy profit from production activities .... Instead of making creative and honest efforts to improve management and techniques of production, many entrepreneurs went into unsavoury league with politicians and bureaucrats seeking to amass easy fortunes .... Industries were compelled to resort to high interest private loans, and, consequently, usurious lending activities flourished .... The degradation of banking not only discouraged development but also distorted or corrupted the ideals underlying national institutions and distorted the sense of social justice' (pp. 11-2; translation by Kim, 1995).

programmes, known as 'policy loans'. As is well known, these loans were the key instrument in the industrial policy regime of Korea.[4]

The regime of policy loans was perfected when the Korean equivalent of the Japanese 'main bank' system was introduced in May 1974, following the 1970-72 debt crisis (see Section 3.1), on the recognition that tight monitoring is necessary in order to ensure efficient use of policy loans (and of foreign debts that usually accompanied policy loans). By appointing one of the largest lending banks to each *chaebol* (the main beneficiaries from policy loans) as its 'main bank', the government made sure that there was someone who took an active interest in supervising the use of policy loans. If the main bank was not satisfied with the performance of the recipients of its policy loans, it had to report it to the government, which then would decide on the punishment for the lax performance (e.g., refusal to extend new loans).

Fourthly, and probably most importantly for the purpose of this chapter, tight capital control existed – on both inflows and outflows. Unlike Japan or Taiwan, which have had 'structural trade surpluses' since the 1960s, Korea suffered from a chronic foreign exchange shortage.[5] And when combined with the structural political uncertainty due to the presence of North Korea, extremely tight control on capital outflow was seen as absolutely necessary – those who engaged in capital flight could be sentenced to death in extreme cases. Central to this regime of control were the so-called Foreign Exchange Concentration System, under which all foreign exchange had to be surrendered to the central bank, and the Foreign Exchange Management Act, which put severe restrictions on the use of foreign exchange (e.g., limits on overseas remittances, on overseas real estate acquisition, or even on expenditure on foreign tourism, which was severely restricted until the late 1980s).[6]

---

[4]  The importance that was attached to policy loans is testified by the fact that, even in times of macroeconomic stabilisation, the amount of policy loans was actually increased at the expense of other loans (see Itoh, 1982).

[5]  The country recorded a trade surplus only for three years, 1986-88, during the entire postwar period before the 1997 crisis, after which a massive collapse of imports resulted in trade surplus.

[6]  As we shall see later, this system of foreign exchange control began to be relaxed from the late 1980s (see Section 4).

At the same time, the Korean government almost fully controlled foreign borrowing and the use of the borrowed capital with a view to minimising what it considered 'unnecessary' or 'wasteful' use of scarce foreign exchange. Government control of foreign borrowing meant that it could not only control the overall level of capital inflows but also affect investment decisions at the micro level, given the critical importance of imported capital goods for investment in a late-developing country like Korea.[7]

## 3.   The Historical Precedents

Since the early 1960s, the Korean economy has experienced three episodes of a big surge in foreign borrowing, all of which eventually ended up in a debt crisis. The first debt crisis, which happened during 1970-72, was the result of the introduction of McKinnon-Shaw-style financial reform in 1965. The second episode, which occurred during 1980-82, was the outcome of the Heavy and Chemical Industrialisation (HCI) programme launched in 1973, which was financed by cheap oil money following the First Oil Shock and abruptly ended by the world recession following the Second Oil Shock. The third is, of course, the 1997 crisis. In this section, we put the current crisis in historical perspective by briefly discussing the causes and the resolution of the two earlier episodes of debt crisis.

---

[7]   The Korean government's provision of payment guarantees to all foreign borrowings during this period has been criticised for creating 'moral hazard' on the part of the borrowers. However, especially for a developing country, whether or not foreign borrowings have been formally guaranteed by the government, a foreign debt crisis will compel the government to provide *ex post* payment guarantees to foreign lenders. The best example that illustrates this point in the Korean context is the 1997 crisis, where the government was forced to provide such *ex post* guarantee despite the fact that, in the debt build-up during the 1990s, it did not provide any *ex ante* payment guarantees. If the government has to provide *ex post* payment guarantees once a debt crisis breaks out, it may be better for it to provide *ex ante* guarantee while trying to minimise moral hazard in the system by tightening the loan approval and monitoring procedure than to delude itself into believing that it can completely disengage itself from cross-border financial transactions.

## 3.1    The unknown crisis: the late 1960s to the early 1970s

Korea introduced McKinnon-Shaw-style financial reform in 1965, which raised the real interest rate to an unprecedented level (27%). This naturally created a huge interest rate gap between domestic loans and foreign loans, generating a very strong incentive to contract foreign loans. The result was a rapid accumulation of foreign debt. Korea's total foreign debt rose 3.7-fold between 1964 and 1967, and nearly doubled between 1967 and 1968. Thanks to a government clampdown in 1969, its growth slowed down considerably (between 1969 and 1971, it grew by 62.3%), but domestic financial problems accumulated in the meantime. High economic growth from the mid-1960s had enhanced business optimism, leading to an investment boom, but the high interest rates that prevailed after 1965 badly squeezed corporate profitability, prompting many firms to borrow even more, often in the 'curb market', where interest rates were above 40%.

The investment boom also created a massive balance-of-payments problem (the current account deficit was equivalent to 26% of GDP in 1969), prompting an IMF intervention in 1970. The combination of devalued currency, high interest rates, and tight money supply that followed the IMF programme resulted in a sharp fall in the profitability of non-financial firms and a rapid piling-up of non-performing assets in the banking sector. In 1969, things were bad enough for the government to launch a forceful programme of corporate mergers and acquisitions, but by 1972, the country was on the brink of a full-blown debt crisis.

In response, the Korean government implemented a series of extraordinary measures, the most important of which was the President's Emergency Decree on Economic Stability and Growth announced on 3 August 1972 (the so-called 'August 3 Decree'). The essence of this Decree was the bailing out of debt-ridden manufacturing firms by imposing a moratorium on the payment of all corporate debts to the curb market lenders for three years, after which all the loans were to be converted into five-year loans at about one-third the interest rate prevailing in the curb market. At the same time, an extensive rescheduling of bank loans was implemented and the corporate governance system was improved by strengthening the banks' monitoring and sanction functions over the conglomerates, or *chaebols*.

## 3.2   The notorious crisis: the late 1970s to the early 1980s

With corporate profitability restored through the August 3 Decree and associated measures, the Korean economy started to accelerate once again. In 1973, the government announced the famous (or
notorious, depending on one's viewpoint) Heavy and Chemical
Industrialisation (HCI) programme, with an emphasis on six strategic
industries – steel, non-ferrous metal, shipbuilding, chemical, electronics, and machinery. The government provided support to the designated industries through preferential bank loans, public investment
and loan programmes, tax exemptions, accelerated depreciation allowances, cuts in import tariffs for capital and intermediate goods,
and so on.

After experiencing a minor decline in the growth rate during
1974-75 in the aftermath of the First Oil Shock, the economy started
a major investment and growth spurt, which was to transform its structure for good (see Chang, 1993, for details). However, before the
massive investments in the new industries could pay back, the Second Oil Shock in 1979 and the subsequent introduction of monetarist
policies in the US and other industrial economies pushed the economy
into an unprecedented crisis. The import bill skyrocketed with the
quadrupling of oil prices, the major export markets were in serious
recession, and above all, the hike in interest rates resulted in a crush-
ing foreign debt repayment burden.

In the face of the macroeconomic instability and corporate distress, the Korean government announced a stabilisation programme
with IMF support in January 1980. However, the tight monetary policy
wreaked havoc on the corporate sector, and by June 1980, it moved
away to an expansionary policy stance. In addition, it launched an
'industrial restructuring' programme, which forced mergers and market segmentations on six industries suffering from over-capacity, such
as passenger car and heavy electrical machinery. Some financial
liberalisation measures and partial bank privatisation were implemented, but the government maintained its strong grip on the financial sector. Strong capital control was maintained[8] and the regulations

---

[8]   It was no coincidence that there was virtually no capital flight from Korea during
     the early 1980s – a major contrast with some Latin American debtor countries
     during the time (Sachs, 1984).

on foreign debt contracts were strengthened (Amsden and Euh, 1990).

By 1985, the crisis was largely resolved and the Korean economy entered a new economic boom accompanied by unprecedented trade surplus between 1986 and 1988. The resolution of the 1980 crisis did not involve direct attacks on financial rentier interests as in the early-1970s crisis, but still bore the hallmark of the pre-1990s Korean economic system. Despite the initial credit squeeze, the pro-investment stance of macroeconomic policy was restored and sustained, and the state control over finance (especially capital control) was largely maintained. The state-mediated corporate governance system was also very much in evidence, as seen in the industrial restructuring exercise. This recurrent pattern, however, breaks down in the management of the 1997 crisis, to which we now turn.

## 4.     The Misunderstood Crisis: 1993 to 1997

As we mentioned above, in the immediate aftermath of the 1980 crisis, some financial liberalisation measures were taken, but they did not change the basic nature of the Korean financial system. However, from the late 1980s, there happened a number of structural changes that created pressures for more fundamental changes in the financial system.

First of all, the importance of non-bank financial institutions (NBFIs) started to increase rapidly from the mid-1980s, and by the late 1980s, their importance in the financial system started to outweigh that of the banks.[9] Given that these institutions were subject to much less strict governmental regulations, the government's grip on the financial system increasingly weakened. The *chaebols* were especially keen to acquire NBFIs, as their ownership of banks was strictly regulated.

---

[9]     The share of commercial bank assets in total assets of financial institutions fell from 80% in the first half of the 1970s (the 1971-76 average) to 73% by the early 1980s (the 1979-81 average). By 1985, this ratio fell to 59% and then finally below 50% in 1988 (48%). The fall slowed down since then, and the ratio stayed at 42% during the mid-1990s (the 1993-96 average).

Secondly, the large trade surplus generated between 1986 and 1989 made the existing mechanisms of capital account control problematic. Given the Foreign Exchange Concentration System, under which all foreign exchange had to be surrendered to the central bank, the large trade surplus generated excess liquidity in the system, prompting the government to relax restrictions on foreign exchange use. Although the trade surplus disappeared subsequently, the surge of capital inflows in the 1990s provided the justification for the continued relaxation of regulations on foreign exchange holding and use, until the system was finally reduced to near-insignificance in 1995.

Thirdly, from about the late 1980s, Korean corporations and banks started enjoying sufficient creditworthiness in the international financial markets such that they did not need government guarantees anymore. This made them start regarding government involvement in their foreign exchange transactions as a burden rather than a necessity as before, weakening the government's hold over the financial sector even more.

By the early 1990s, the above-mentioned 'structural' changes were building up into very strong pressure towards full-blown financial liberalisation. Meanwhile, since the late 1980s, the US government started to put enormous pressure on the Korean government to open up the financial market. The agreement from the March 1992 bilateral talks with the US subsequently formed the basis for the radical 1993 financial liberalisation programme. The decision of the Kim Young Sam government made in 1993 to apply for membership of the OECD also subjected Korea to further external demands for financial market liberalisation and opening-up.

A series of liberalisation and opening-up measures taken in the early 1990s finally resulted in a fundamental change in the Korean financial system. The changes included, among other things, interest rate deregulation, abolition of 'policy loans', granting of more managerial autonomy to the banks, reduction of entry barriers to financial activities and, most importantly, capital account liberalisation, something that Korea's previous plans of financial liberalisation had characteristically failed to include.

As is well known, the result of this financial liberalisation was the accumulation of a huge short-term foreign debt, which led to the 1997 financial crisis. Foreign debt nearly trebled between 1993 and

1997 (from $44 billion to $120 billion). This debt build-up was almost twice as fast as that of 1979-85, the period of the country's second financial crisis – Korea's foreign debt grew at 17.8% per annum during 1979-85, while it grew at 33.6% per annum during 1994-96. While Korea's overall foreign debt was not at an obviously unsustainable level[10], its maturity structure posed a serious problem. The share of short-term debt in total debt rose from an already high 43.7% in 1993 to an astonishing 58.3% by the end of 1996. The magnitude of this problem can be seen by recalling the fact that during the times of the first and the second crises, this figure never rose above 20% and 35% respectively.

While the downfall (and the related corruption scandal) of the new major steel company, Hanbo, and the bankruptcy and the subsequent nationalisation of the third largest car manufacturer, Kia, battered international confidence in Korea during the first several months of 1997, the financial crisis in Southeast Asia broke out, dragging the Korean economy into the whirlpool. Once the international lenders lost confidence in the economy, it did not matter whether their view was justified or not. International lenders stopped rolling over Korean debts from the fall of 1997, and the country finally had to go to the IMF for a rescue package in December 1997 (for a more detailed chronology of the crisis, see Chang, 1998).

In the face of a most comprehensive and tough IMF programme, with stiff macroeconomic conditions and unprecedented demands for institutional changes (especially regarding corporate governance but also labour and social welfare), the economy contracted to an unprecedented degree. In a country where 5% growth was considered a 'recession', the economy shrank by 5.8% in 1998, recording the biggest contraction in output since the Korean War (1950-53). Industrial production was especially adversely affected and fell by 7.5%.

---

[10]  The World Bank considers countries with debt/GNP ratios under 48% as low-risk cases, and Korea's debt/GNP ratio was only 22% in 1996, and was still around 25% on the eve of the crisis. The corresponding figures at the end of 1995 were 70% for Mexico, 57% for Indonesia, 35% for Thailand, 33% for Argentina, and 24% for Brazil (World Bank, 1997). Also, in terms of debt service ratio, Korea on the eve of the 1997 crisis was well below the World Bank 'warning' threshold (18%) at 5.4% in 1995 and 5.8% in 1996. These figures compare very favourably with those of countries like Mexico (24.2%), Brazil (37.9%), Indonesia (30.9%), and Thailand (10.2%) in 1995 (World Bank, 1997).

The virulence of the 1997 crisis may be put into clearer perspective by comparing it with the 1980 crisis, which had resulted in the biggest fall in output before the 1997 crisis (-2.7%).

Gross fixed capital formation fell by 21.2% in 1998, whereas in 1980 it recorded a 10.7% fall. Particularly hard hit was machinery and equipment investments, which fell by a staggering 38.5% (a particularly large fall, given that it had already fallen by 8.7% in 1997). The corresponding fall in 1980 was 24.6% (and that after very high growth in 1979 – 23.3%). Exports in 1998 fell by 2.8% (in value terms) for the first time since 1958, whereas they grew at 16.3% in 1980.

Unemployment rose from 2.5% just before the 1997 crisis (and from the trough of 2% in 1996) to the height of 8.7% in February 1999 (it is reported to have fallen since March 1999). This contrasts with the much smaller rise from 3.8% in 1979 (or from the trough of 3.2% in 1978) to 5.2% in 1980. Income inequality also worsened as never before following the 1997 crisis. The ratio of the income of the top quintile to that of the bottom quintile rose from 4.49 before the crisis to 5.38 by 1999 (*Joong-ang Daily Newspaper*, 18 June 1999). And the ratio of the income of the top 10% to that of the bottom 10% rose from 7.1 in the first quarter of 1995 to 9.8 in the first quarter of 1998 and 10.2 in the first quarter of 1999 (*Daehan Maeil Newspaper*, 25 June 1999). The worsening of income inequality in the aftermath of the 1980 crisis was not very significant, if at all.[11]

It is not simply its virulence but also the characteristic of its management that sets the 1997 crisis apart from the two previous ones. In the management of the 1997 crisis, the traditional anti-finance/pro-industry stance of the Korean government was abandoned. During the 1997 crisis, credit squeeze was much greater – loans by deposit money banks *fell* by 0.1%, whereas they grew by about 28% during 1970-71 and by about 36% in 1980. Especially important in creating the credit squeeze during the 1997 crisis was the imposition of the BIS (Bank for International Settlements) capital adequacy standard, which seeks to ensure the safety of the banks if necessary at the

---

[11] Of the five estimates of trends in income inequality reviewed in Ahn (1996), two showed a small fall in the Gini coefficient between 1980 and 1982 (from 0.389 to 0.357 and from 0.409 to 0.393) and three showed a small rise during the same period (from 0.386 to 0.406, from 0.356 to 0.385, and from 0.337 to 0.376).

cost of industry (more on this in Section 5). Even the fall in exports following the 1997 crisis, which contrasts with the continued rise in exports after the 1980 crisis, owed significantly to the squeeze on export credits, rather than to an overvalued currency or to depressed world market conditions (the world economy was in a deep recession in the early 1980s, whereas it has remained relatively buoyant since 1997).

As the credit squeeze crushed the economy, the IMF belatedly took a U-turn on macroeconomic policy in May 1998 and allowed the Korean government to lower interest rates and pushed it to increase budget deficits (the Korean government has had a traditional aversion to deficit financing). And largely as a result of this, the speed of contraction of the economy slowed down from the 4th quarter of 1998, and by the end of the 1st quarter of 1999, the economy started to show signs of recovery. At the time of writing (August 1999), GDP growth rates of 6-8% are predicted for 1999. While widely regarded as impressive, this recovery does little more than bring the level of economic activity to the 1997 level and is not as quick as the recoveries from the two earlier crises.[12]

What do we make of this recovery? Does it prove that the IMF policy was a success, as the IMF and its supporters claim? Our contention is that it does not. First of all, the recovery is largely a natural reaction to the easing of the macroeconomic policy that was excessively tight and unnecessarily shrank the economy (and in this sense the original IMF policy has been proven wrong). More importantly, it is questionable whether the recovery is sustainable in the medium term.

The current phase of recovery has been led by consumption rather than by investments. What is worrying is that the rise in consumption seems to be largely fuelled by the wealth effect created by an overly-inflated stock market, which in turn was the result of the excess liquidity created by the easing of monetary policy (since the 3rd quar-

---

[12]    If the Korean economy grows at 6% in 1999, its GDP will be still a fraction lower than in 1997. A 7% growth will mean an 0.8% improvement over 1997, and even an 8% growth will mean a meagre 1.7% improvement. In 1972, the GDP growth rate slowed down from 8.5% in 1971 to 4.8%, but shot up to 12.8% in 1973. In 1980, the economy experienced a 2.7% fall, but recorded a 6.2% growth in 1981, which means that Korea's 1981 GDP was 2.1% higher than that in 1979.

ter of 1998) in the face of a dramatic collapse in real investments. The stock market price index, which fell below 300 (297.9, to be precise) in the 2nd quarter of 1998, went up to 562.5 by the 4th quarter of that year, broke the 1,000 mark in early July of 1999, and is hovering around 900 at the time of writing (August 1999). In theory, the increase in consumption through the wealth effect may eventually lead to an increase in investments, which should make the recovery sustainable, but it is questionable whether the stock market will remain buoyant for a long enough period of time, especially given the imminent large-scale correction (or collapse?) in the US stock market.

What is more worrying, however, than the medium-term sustainability of the recovery is the series of institutional changes, especially in the financial and the corporate governance systems, that the country has adopted following the crisis. In our view, these changes are worrisome because they are likely to have negative effects on the long-term dynamism of the economy – an issue that we turn to now.

## 5.  Institutional Changes After the 1997 Crisis – What Future for Korea?

The policy package that was adopted in order to manage the (still-unresolved) 1997 crisis is not entirely in the mould of the standard IMF package and still shows some traditional Korean streaks. For the most important example, the Korean government cajoled and threatened the *chaebols* into a 'voluntary' industrial restructuring programme involving mergers and business swaps in eight industries (semiconductor, automobile, power-generating equipment, naval diesel engine, aircraft, petrochemical, petroleum refining, and railway carriage) – the so-called 'Big Deal'. Although this programme is not part of a coherent long-term industrial policy as in the case of previous industrial restructuring programmes, it is similar to its earlier counterparts in spirit.

However, in general, the crisis management package implemented since 1997 has resulted in institutional changes that are likely to significantly transform the nature of the Korean economy, in our view, for the worse.

First of all, the 'pro-finance' policy stance, which characterised the macroeconomic policy in the early days of the crisis, was subsequently institutionalised through a series of legal changes in the financial system. To begin with, the role of the central bank was redefined into a fundamentally monetarist (i.e., pro-finance) one. In the old central bank act, the Bank of Korea (BOK) was supposed to maintain the 'soundness of the banking and the financial system' (which can mean a lot of things in practice) as well as price stability. The new Act that took effect from April 1999 specifies price stability as the sole aim of the BOK. This change, while appearing minor, has profound implications for the Korean financial system, as it de-legitimises the kind of pro-investment, pro-growth monetary policy that characterised the Korean financial system until recently. Moreover, the banking law and other financial laws were revised in a way that strengthened the shareholder interest in the running of the banks, thus making it possible and, more importantly, legitimate to defend financial interests at the cost of industrial interests (something that was not allowed before).

The second important institutional change in the Korean financial system after the crisis was the introduction of the BIS standard on capital adequacy ratio into the financial system. The BIS standard has certain merits (e.g., simplicity, transparency), but one important problem with it is its pro-cyclical nature, as proven by the recent Korean experience. During a recession, the increase in bankruptcy and the fall in asset prices shrink the asset bases of the banks. In such a situation, if they were to observe the BIS standard, they will have to withdraw their loans in order to meet the standard, thereby making the recession even worse.[13] Moreover, the very way in which the BIS standard is defined encourages the holding of liquid assets and therefore a strict enforcement of the standard, to which the Korean government claims to be committed, will make the banks reluctant to lend to industrial projects that have long gestation periods.

Also problematic is the demand made on the *chaebols* that they bring down their debt-equity ratio from above 400% to 200% by the end of 1999, which made them cut down on new investments while

---

[13] Thus seen, the timing of the introduction of the BIS standard in Korea could not have been worse – right in the middle of the deepest recession in the country's modern history.

engaging in 'distress sales' of their assets. The short-run effect of this change was to create a downward investment spiral. But more importantly, in the long run, it is doubtful whether the Korean corporations are going to be able to mobilise the funds necessary for the kind of aggressive investment strategy that they have traditionally pursued, if they continue to meet this demand. The hope held by the defenders of this policy is that the deregulation of the stock market will lead to a greater reliance on direct financing, thus making it unnecessary to rely on debt financing. However, given the well-known short-term orientation of the stock market, it is unlikely that the Korean firms are going to be able to mobilise through the stock market enough 'patient' funds needed for investments in large-scale industries.[14]

The fourth type of institutional change that needs our attention is the full-scale capital account opening. Especially notable are the full-scale liberalisation of corporate borrowing from abroad (which makes government regulation of foreign debts much more difficult) and the complete opening of the stock and bond markets to foreigners. These changes are likely to increase the volatility in the financial market (and there are signs that they are already doing so), which is not conducive to long-term investments. This, once again, will have the effect of dampening the country's investment-growth dynamics.

## 6.   Concluding Remarks

In this chapter, we have discussed the causes and the consequences of the 1997 financial crisis in Korea from a historical perspective. We argued that, unlike in the two earlier episodes of financial crisis in the country, which were managed in the interests of industry, the 1997 crisis has been managed in the interests of the financial rentiers (both domestic and foreign). More important are the changes in the institutions of corporate governance, financial regulation, and industrial policy, which herald a transition to a new eco-

---

[14]   It should also be noted that the large Korean firms, together with their counterparts in other developing countries, have in fact relied much more, and not less, heavily on the stock market for investment financing than the large firms in the advanced industrial countries have done. See Chang and Park (1999) for more details.

nomic system (although it is still too early to predict the exact shape of things to come).

Is this transition desirable? Our answer to this question is 'no'. From a short-run perspective, the performance of this new economic system in resolving the crisis itself has been much poorer than that of the traditional system. The recovery, while quite impressive, has been slower than the recoveries from the two earlier crises, while unemployment and income inequality increased as never before. And this was despite the fact that the external conditions were much more favourable than in the cases of the two earlier crises – they had to be managed in the context, respectively, of the First Oil Shock in 1973-74 and of the Second Oil Shock and the subsequent monetarist recession in the early 1980s. From the longer-run perspective, the recent institutional changes are likely to dampen the economy's investment dynamism by making the financial system much more volatile and 'conservative' than before, and consequently making long-term, patient capital much more scarce.

# Bibliography

Ahn, G.S. (1996). 'Trends in Korean Income Distribution: Conflicting Estimates and Their Evaluations', in J.W. Lee *et al.*, *Industrial Relations and
the Lives of the Workers in Korea* (in Korean). Seoul: Seoul Institute of
Economic and Social Studies.

Amsden, A. (1994). 'Why Isn't the Whole World Using the East Asian Model
to Develop?: Review of the World Bank's East Asian Miracle Report',
*World Development*, vol. 22, no. 4.

Amsden, A. & Euh, Y. (1990). 'Republic of Korea's Financial Reform: What
are the Lessons?', Discussion Paper, no. 30. Geneva: United Nations
Conference on Trade and Development (UNCTAD).

Bank of Korea (BOK) (various years). *Economic Statistics Yearbook.* Seoul:
Bank of Korea.

BOK (1999). *1998 National Accounts* (preliminary). Seoul: Bank of Korea.

Brittan, S. (1997). 'Asian Model R.I.P.', *Financial Times*, 4 December 1997.

Chang, H-J. (1987). 'Crisis of Capital Accumulation in South Korea, 1979-
1982', unpublished M.Phil. dissertation, Faculty of Economics and Politics, University of Cambridge.

Chang, H-J. (1993). 'The Political Economy of Industrial Policy in Korea',
*Cambridge Journal of Economics*, vol. 17, no. 2.

Chang, H-J. (1998). 'Korea: The Misunderstood Crisis', *World Development*, vol. 26, no. 8.

Chang, H-J. (2000). 'The Hazard of Moral Hazard – Untangling the Asian
Crisis', *World Development*, vol. 28, no. 4.

Chang, H-J. & Park, H-J. (1999). 'An Alternative Perspective on Government Policy Towards Big Business in Korea – Industrial Policy, Financial Regulation, and Political Democracy', a paper prepared for the project
on 'The Korean Chaebols in Transition: Restructuring Strategy and
Agenda', organised by the Korea Economic Research Institute (KERI),
Seoul, Korea.

Chang, H-J., Park, H-J. & Yoo, C.G. (1998). 'Interpreting the Korean Crisis:
Financial Liberalisation, Industrial Policy, and Corporate Governance',
*Cambridge Journal of Economics*, vol. 22, no. 6.

Corden, M. (1998). 'Sense and Nonsense on the Asian Crisis', The Sturc
Lecture, delivered on 8 November 1998, at the Paul H. Nitze School of
Advanced International Studies, Johns Hopkins University.

Frankel, J. (1998). 'The Asian Model, the Miracle, the Crisis and the Fund',
a speech delivered at the US International Trade Commission, 16 April
1998.

Furman, J. & Stiglitz, J. (1998). 'Economic Crises: Evidence and Insights
from East Asia', a paper presented at the Brookings Panel on Economic
Activity, 3-4 September 1998, Washington, D.C..

Itoh, K. (1982). 'Development Finance and Commercial Banks in Korea',
*The Developing Economy*, vol. 20, no. 4.

Kim, P.J. (1995). 'Financial System and Policy, 1961-79'. Seoul: Korea Institute of Finance.

Kregel, J. (1998). 'Yes, "It" Did Happen Again – the Minsky Crisis in Asia', a paper presented at the conference on the 'Legacy of Hyman Minsky', December 1998, Bergamo.

Krugman, P. (1998a). 'What Happened to Asia?', mimeo., Department of Economics, Massachusetts Institute of Technology.

Krugman, P. (1998b). 'Fire-sale FDI', a paper presented at the NBER Conference on Capital Flows to Emerging Markets, 20-21 February 1998.

McKinnon, R. & Pill, H. (1998). 'International Overborrowing – A Decomposition of Credit and Currency Risk', World Development, vol. 26, no. 7.

Radelet, S. & Sachs, J. (1998). 'The East Asian Financial Crisis: Diagnosis, Remedies and Prospects', Brookings Papers on Economic Activity, 1998, no. 1.

Sachs, J. (1984). 'Comment on C. Diaz-Alejandro, "Latin American Debt: I Don't Think We Are in Kansas Anymore"', Brookings Papers on Economic Activity, 1984, no. 2.

Singh, A. (1998). 'Financial Crisis in East Asia: "The End of the Asian Model?"', Issues in Development Discussion Paper, no. 24. Geneva: International Labour Office.

Stiglitz, J. (1998). 'Sound Finance and Sustainable Development in Asia', a speech delivered at the Asian Development Forum, 12 March 1998, Manila, the Philippines.

Taylor, L. (1998). 'Capital Market Crises: Liberalization, Fixed Exchange Rates and Market-driven Destabilization', Cambridge Journal of Economics, vol. 22, no. 6.

World Bank (1997). Global Development Finance. Washington, D.C.: World Bank.

# Chapter 9

# EVALUATING THE POST-CRISIS CORPORATE RESTRUCTURING IN KOREA

## 1. Introduction

KOREA'S 1997 financial crisis has led to a thorough restructuring of the country's traditional economic system, often known (somewhat misleadingly) as 'Korea Inc.'. This system was based on close collaboration between the state, banks, and the *chaebols*, with the state as the dominant player. The post-crisis restructuring programme attempted to re-mould the system, at least at the formal level, into an essentially Anglo-American one based on a minimal state, arm's-length contractual relationships, and focus on short-term financial profitability.

What is notable about Korea's post-1997 restructuring programme is that, unlike in other IMF-led 'market-oriented' reforms, the private corporate sector, especially the *chaebols*, was identified as the main target of reform. The *chaebols* were condemned as overly-diversified groups of inefficient firms surviving on low profit only because they could borrow more than what they deserved thanks to their collusion with the state and banks and to 'unfair' intra-group transactions.

On the basis of such analysis, a 'broad' and 'deep' corporate reform programme was implemented. It was 'broad' because the close links between the state, banks, and the *chaebols* that had existed meant that a radical corporate reform required reforms in many other areas. It was 'deep' in the sense that it virtually dismantled the group structure of the *chaebols*, although it fell short of forcefully disbanding them. The measures included a ban on intra-group transactions, the imposition of a *de facto* numerical cap on debt-equity ratios, strengthening of minority shareholder rights, improvement in accounting transparency, introduction of outside directorship, and so on. It may be reasonable to say that the scale of the corporate reform implemented in Korea since 1997 is the largest in the world since the forceful break-up of Japanese and German firms by the Allied occupation forces after the Second World War.

In this chapter, we assess Korea's post-crisis corporate reform programme and argue that, while it has introduced some important positive changes, on balance it is likely to reduce the dynamism of the corporate sector in the future. Then we argue that what the country needs is a 'second-stage catching-up system' that reclaims some positive features of the old Korean economic system and combines them with the positive elements of the post-crisis reform.

## 2.    A Critical Look at the Standard Analysis of the Role of the Corporate Sector in the 1997 Crisis

The IMF-sponsored reform programme implemented in Korea following the crisis was based on the perception that the crisis was caused by some deep-rooted structural features of the Korean economy. Often epitomised by terms like 'crony capitalism' and 'moral hazard', these supposed structural features were regarded as having obstructed rational functioning of the economic system. Those who held this view, including the IMF, inevitably called for a 'fundamental' structural reform of the country.

However, on a closer look, this type of diagnosis is theoretically ill-grounded and lacks empirical support (see Furman and Stiglitz, 1998; Chang, 2000). The resulting reform measures, especially the reform of the corporate sector, were consequently misguided. We examine below two of the so-called 'structural' causes of the Korean crisis that specifically relate to the corporate sector.

### 2.1    Peculiar nature of the corporate sector

One of the most popular explanations of the Korean crisis is that the Korean economy got into the crisis because of the peculiar nature of its corporate sector. The most important element in this argument is the high leverage combined with low profitability of the Korean firms, especially the *chaebols*, which was regarded as a sign that these were inefficient entities which were sustained only through persistent borrowing based on cross-loan guarantees among their affiliates and through continuous (and excessive) diversification into areas where they could drive out the existing firms through their superior financial power. It is also said that high leverage was preferred by the 'owning families' of the *chaebols* because they did not want the dilution of control that equity financing would entail.

However, this characterisation of the Korean corporate structure is questionable, and, even if it is correct, it is doubtful whether it can 'explain' the crisis.

First of all, it is not true that corporate leverage was uniquely high in Korea. The average debt-equity ratio of Korean firms, which historically moved in the range between 300% and 350%, is not exceptionally high by international standards. According to a World Bank study covering the period between 1980 and 1991 (Demirguc-Kunt and Maksimovic, 1996), a key table from which is reproduced below (Table 9.1), the corporate sector debt-equity ratios of Japan (369%), France (361%) and Italy (307%) were similar to Korea's. The figures for Sweden (555%), Norway (538%), and Finland (492%) are even higher, at near or above 500%. The ratio for Japan in the 1970s was also around 500%.

Secondly, it is not clear whether high corporate leverage in itself is a bad thing. There is a well-known and still-inconclusive debate in financial economics on the relative merits of equity financing and debt financing, with some people regarding debt financing as offering a more 'high-powered' incentive system (Harris and Raviv, 1991; Brennan, 1995).

Thirdly, the belief that the *chaebols* had high leverage because they eschewed equity financing is also not borne out by facts. The contribution of stocks in investment financing in Korea during the period of 1972-91 was at 13.4%, much higher than that in Germany (2.3%), Japan (3.9%), the UK (7.0%), or the USA (-4.9%) (Table 9.2). Korean corporations had large debts not because they eschewed stock financing, but only because they found even these large sums raised in the stock market insufficient for the aggressive investment strategy that they had pursued with impressive results.

| Table 9.1: Capital Structure of Firms in Selected Countries (1980-91) | | | | | |
|---|---|---|---|---|---|
| Countries | Debt ratio | Long-term debt to equity | Short-term debt to total equity | Depreciation to total assets | Dividend to total assets | Earnings to total assets |
| Australia | 1.248 | 0.563 | 0.653 | 0.033 | 0.025 | 0.064 |
| Austria | 2.696 | 1.121 | 1.495 | 0.051 | 0.017 | 0.075 |
| Belgium | 2.023 | 0.764 | 1.259 | 0.039 | 0.022 | 0.092 |
| Brazil | 0.560 | 0.139 | 0.421 | - | 0.014 | 0.057 |
| Canada | 1.600 | 0.990 | 0.539 | 0.045 | 0.007 | 0.064 |
| Finland | 4.920 | 3.094 | 1.856 | 0.042 | 0.014 | 0.077 |
| France | 3.613 | 1.417 | 2.108 | 0.043 | 0.013 | 0.094 |
| Germany | 2.732 | 1.479 | 1.188 | 0.070 | 0.057 | 0.087 |
| Hong Kong | 1.322 | 0.309 | 0.967 | 0.017 | 0.019 | 0.121 |
| India | 2.700 | 0.763 | 1.937 | 0.038 | 0.014 | 0.132 |
| Italy | 3.068 | 1.114 | 1.954 | 0.041 | 0.070 | 0.080 |
| Japan | 3.688 | 0.938 | 2.726 | 0.026 | 0.007 | 0.067 |
| Jordan | 1.181 | 0.266 | 0.915 | - | 0.033 | 0.073 |
| Korea | 3.662 | 1.057 | 2.390 | 0.053 | 0.008 | 0.100 |
| Malaysia | 0.935 | 0.284 | 0.639 | 0.021 | 0.026 | 0.087 |
| Mexico | 0.817 | 0.375 | 0.442 | - | - | 0.076 |
| Netherlands | 2.156 | 0.710 | 1.297 | 0.043 | 0.020 | 0.094 |
| New Zealand | 1.527 | 0.752 | 0.776 | 0.030 | 0.025 | 0.106 |
| Norway | 5.375 | 3.495 | 1.880 | 0.049 | 0.009 | 0.092 |
| Pakistan | 2.953 | 0.595 | 2.358 | 0.038 | 0.028 | 0.115 |
| Singapore | 1.232 | 0.491 | 0.718 | 0.022 | 0.018 | 0.077 |
| South Africa | 1.115 | 0.597 | 0.518 | 0.013 | 0.062 | 0.206 |
| Spain | 2.746 | 1.086 | 1.649 | 0.040 | 0.016 | 0.095 |
| Sweden | 5.552 | 2.879 | 2.321 | 0.036 | 0.011 | 0.100 |
| Switzerland | 1.750 | 0.878 | 0.872 | 0.043 | 0.016 | 0.073 |
| Thailand | 2.215 | 0.518 | 1.769 | 0.030 | 0.029 | 0.129 |
| Turkey | 1.996 | 1.511 | 1.511 | - | 0.068 | 0.239 |
| UK | 1.480 | 1.065 | 1.065 | 0.032 | 0.025 | 0.025 |
| USA | 1.791 | 1.054 | 0.679 | 0.045 | 0.016 | 0.016 |
| Zimbabwe | 0.801 | 0.187 | 0.615 | 0.031 | 0.028 | 0.028 |

**Source**: Chang and Park (2000). Calculated from the International Finance Corporation's Corporate Finance Data by Demirguc-Kunt and Maksimovic (1996: p. 354).

| Table 9.2: Gross Sources of Finance in Selected Countries (1970-89) (%) | | | | | |
|---|---|---|---|---|---|
| | Germany | Japan | UK | US | Korea* |
| Internal | 62.4 | 40.0 | 60.4 | 62.7 | 29.0 |
| Bank finance | 18.0 | 34.5 | 23.3 | 14.7 | 18.9 |
| Bonds | 0.9 | 3.9 | 2.3 | 12.8 | 5.7 |
| New equity | 2.3 | 3.9 | 7.0 | -4.9 | 13.4 |
| Trade credit | 1.8 | 15.6 | 1.9 | 8.8 | n.a. |
| Capital transfer | 6.6 | n.a. | 2.3 | n.a. | n.a. |
| Other | 8.0 | 2.1 | 2.9 | 5.9 | n.a. |
| *1972-91 | | | | | |

Sources: Chang and Park (2000). All figures other than those for Korea are from Corbett and Jenkinson (1994: p. 9).

Fourthly, whether the Korean firms actually suffered from low profitability, which allegedly led to the debt build-up, is also questionable. According to a study by Claessens *et al.* (1998), where they measure corporate profitability in terms of returns on assets, Korea indeed had the 44th lowest returns on assets among the sample of 46 countries. However, if we use other profitability measures, Korean corporate profitability has not been so exceptionally low. For example, when we use the criterion of 'operating profit', that is the profit before paying financial expenses like interest payments, foreign exchange losses (gains) and so on, Korea actually had a higher rate of profit than the US, Japan, or Taiwan during 1988-97 (Table 9.3). Claessens *et al.* (1998: p. 7, Table 3) also confirm this observation. They show that the 'operational margin' (which is similar to the notion of operating profit)[1] of the Korean firms during 1988-96, at 19.6%, was higher than that in the USA (14.4%) and Germany (14.6%), although it was lower than that in five of the eight other East Asian countries for

---

[1]  The notion of 'operational margin' used by Claessens *et al.* is defined as the difference between sales and the costs of goods sold as a share of sales. This is slightly different from the notion of 'operating profit' that we use, as it does not subtract selling and administrative expenses from the numerator. We think our measure is somewhat superior because the measure used by Claessens *et al.*, by not subtracting the selling and administrative expenses, does not fully reflect the managerial efficiency of the firm.

which the figures were available (Japan, Indonesia, Taiwan, the Philippines, and Thailand; Hong Kong, Singapore, and Malaysia had lower figures).

**Table 9.3: Structure of Profit in the Manufacturing Sector in Korea, Japan, the USA and Taiwan**
(%, average during 1988-97)*

|  | Korea** | USA | Japan | Taiwan |
|---|---|---|---|---|
| Operating income to sales | 7.0 (7.1) | 6.6 | 3.3 | 6.5 |
| Ordinary income to sales | 2.1 (2.7) | 4.2*** | 3.3 | 4.5 |
| Financial expenses to sales | 5.6 (5.3) | n.a. | n.a. | 2.1 |

\* Taiwan's figures are for 1986-95
\*\* Figures in parentheses are for 1986-95
\*\*\* Net profits

Sources: BOK website, BOK (2000), Chang and Park (2000)

Fifthly, given these wildly different results that we get from the use of different profitability measures, it is not clear whether low profitability in itself can 'explain' the Korean crisis. For example, as we mentioned earlier, Korea had one of the lowest rates of corporate profitability in the world if we use the return-on-assets criterion. However, by the very same profitability criterion, the other East Asian crisis economies had very *high* profitability. Thailand and Indonesia ranked first and third, and Malaysia ranked eighth (second was the Philippines, a semi-crisis country). According to this criterion, the other Asian-crisis economies should not have experienced any crisis.

Sixthly, the thesis on excessive diversification of Korean *chaebols* also needs to be re-examined. The *chaebols*, especially the large ones, may have until recently owned 50-60 subsidiaries operating in dozens of different industries, but most of their sales revenues were generated by a few core firms. Between 1988 and 1995, the four largest subsidiaries of the top four *chaebols* generated an average of 79% of their total sales. Especially in the case of Samsung, the four largest firms, two of which were in the same industry (electronics), alone accounted for about 90% of sales – a striking concentration (rather than diversification) of activities given the number of its subsidiaries (55 as of 1995). The same can be said of the smaller *chaebols*, with the reliance on a small number of subsidiaries tending to increase as their size diminishes. For instance, in 1994, the *chaebols* that ranked between 6th and 10th generated 72.6% of their sales from the four largest subsidiaries. In the case of the *chaebols* that ranked between 11th and 20th, the three largest subsidiaries generated 72.1% of their sales, and in the case of the *chaebols* that ranked between 21st and 30th, as much as 72.3% of the sales were generated by the two largest subsidiaries.

## 2.2   The logic of 'too big to fail'

Many commentators have argued that the *chaebols* took excessive risk because they knew that they were 'too big to fail' (henceforth TBTF) in the sense that the government could not afford to sit and watch them go bankrupt for fear of large-scale 'ripple effects' such as large-scale unemployment and bankruptcy of subcontracting firms (e.g., Yoo, 1997; Burton, 1998). They cite the government rescue of some large firms in the past as evidence that the logic of TBTF has been in operation in the country – the most frequently cited example being the nationalisation of the bankrupt third-largest car manufacturer Kia in the build-up to the crisis.

At first, the logic of TBTF seems difficult to dismiss, especially given that it is indeed practised by all governments in all countries, including the ones that claim to be the most market-oriented. The rescue of the US hedge fund, Long Term Capital Management (LTCM), following the 1998 Russian financial crisis, is one prominent recent example, but the history of capitalism is littered with similar examples. In the late 1970s, the country's first right-wing government for over 50 years rescued the bankrupt Swedish shipbuilding industry through nationalisation. In the early 1980s the avowedly free-market Reagan administration rescued the carmaker Chrysler from the brink of bankruptcy. To take the most extreme example, the Chilean government under General Augusto Pinochet, which did not hesitate to use violence to quell opposition to its neoliberal policy, nationalised the entire banking sector in 1982, when the country experienced a severe financial crisis.

The biggest problem with the TBTF story, however, is its conflation of the rescue of a firm and the rescue of its owners or managers who are responsible for making the rescue necessary. To the manager, it is not much of a consolation that his/her firm is saved by the government due to its large size, if the rescue operation involves the termination of his/her contract. So if a manager knows that he/she will lose the job when his/her firm performs badly, there is little incentive for him/her to take excessive risk. The same goes for the owners. If the owners know that the rescue operation will require ceding of their corporate control (as has almost always been the case in Korea – see below), they cannot afford to be lax in management (in case they are owner-managers) or in supervising the hired managers.

In this sense, the rescue of LTCM, which did *not* involve the removal of the incumbent management (although its control was weakened due to debt-equity swaps), has definitely given a very bad signal to the rest of the financial industry and will probably encourage excessive risk-taking (or 'moral hazard') in the future. On the other hand, the rescue of Kia, which involved a change in the top management, could not have sent such a signal to the managers of other large enterprises. In other words, whether government bailout of some large firms encourages excessive risk-taking by the managers of other large firms depends on whether it is accompanied by punishments for bad management.

The evidence in the case of Korea is simply not on the side of the TBTF story. Especially in the 1960s and the 1970s, when the country was going through rapid structural changes, it was not infrequent to see even some of the largest *chaebols* going bankrupt and their carcasses being divided up through state-mediated takeovers. The second largest *chaebol* during the 1960s, Samho, had all but disappeared by the late 1970s after a series of bankruptcies of its core firms. The Gaepoong *chaebol*, which ranked between third and fourth during the 1960s, virtually disappeared by the mid-1970s following a series of business failures. The Donglip *chaebol*, which ranked ninth in the early 1960s, went bankrupt by the end of the decade. The owner of the once-largest car manufacturer in the country, Shinjin, was forced to sell it off to the state-owned Korea Development Bank (which subsequently sold it to Daewoo) in the late 1970s, when it got into trouble. Dongmyung, the *chaebol* built around what was the world's largest producer of plywood around the early 1970s, went bankrupt in 1980.

These are striking statistics. For example, the collapse of three of the top 10 *chaebols* of the 1960s (namely, Samho, Gaepoong, and Donglip) is equivalent in American terms to the disappearance by the early 1980s of Standard Oil (New Jersey), Ford Motor, and IBM, which ranked second, third, and ninth respectively in the *Fortune* US enterprise ranking in 1964. As a result, until the mid-1980s, there was a very high turnover even in the ranks of the top 10 *chaebols*. Only three of the top 10 *chaebols* in 1966 were among the 1974 top 10 and only five of the 1974 top 10 were in the 1980 top 10 (Chang, 1994: p. 123).

After the mid-1980s, and especially in the 1990s, the ranking of the top 10 *chaebols* remained highly, if not completely, stable, but among the lesser *chaebols* there was still a high turnover. Between 1986 and 1996, among the 20 *chaebols* that ranked between 11th and 30th, there were on average 14 changes in the rankings and 2.2 new entries into the group every year (Park, 1998: Table 9). Between 1990 and 1996 alone, three of the top 30 *chaebols* (Hanyang, Yoowon, and Woosung) went bankrupt, showing that there is no substance to claims such as: 'In Korea, none of the *chaebol* had been allowed to fail for a decade before Hanbo steel collapsed in early 1997' (Radelet and Sachs, 1998: p. 42). In 1997, in the build-up to and at the beginning of the crisis, six of the top 30 *chaebols* (Kia, Halla, Jinro, Hanbo, Sammi, and Haitai) went bankrupt, again debunking the TBTF story (Chang *et al.*, 1998).

Of course, all these are not to deny that the Korean government not infrequently injected money into ailing large enterprises through the state-owned banks (especially the development bank, Korea Development Bank). However, these financial injections were conditional, with very few exceptions, on the change of ownership and top management, and were always accompanied by tough terms of financial restructuring. In other words, the rescue of large enterprises by the Korean government should be seen as government-mediated takeovers or restructuring rather than as bailouts in the strict sense (*à la* LTCM).[2]

---

[2]  When the amount of money involved in the rescue operation (e.g., debt write-offs, tax exemption, and other direct and indirect subsidies) was considered too large, the government went for direct nationalisation. The merger and subsequent nationalisation of the four companies in the power-generating equipment industry in the early 1980s is the best example (for further details, see Chang, 1993: pp. 148-9).

In sum, whether government rescue of large ailing enterprises based on the logic of TBTF will lead to 'moral hazard' (in the form of excessive risk-taking) on the part of the managers of other large firms depends on the terms of the rescue, especially whether and how much the existing managers are made to pay for their mistakes (recall our distinction between the Kia and the LTCM types of government rescue). It is only when the managers of the bailed-out enterprises are not properly punished that the logic of TBTF works. There is no evidence that this logic was in operation in Korea to any meaningful degree.

## 3.    Restructuring the *Chaebols*

The reform of the *chaebols* was the main thrust of the post-1997 corporate reform programme. The major benefit anticipated from the *chaebol* reform was the lowering of financial risks in the corporate sector, which in turn would lower the financial risks for the overall economy. In the longer run, it was also expected that the reform would help improve the  competitiveness of the Korean firms by improving their governance. However, these benefits are yet to materialise, and even if they do, they should be set against the costs generated by the same set of reform measures.

### 3.1    Reduction in debt-equity ratio

The drastic reduction in the corporate debt-equity ratio is often claimed to be one of the key achievements in the post-crisis corporate reform. Following the crisis, the five largest *chaebols* were mandated to lower their debt ratios, which stood at 473% on average at the end of 1997, to below 200% by the end of 1999. They 'over-achieved' the target by reducing it to 235% in 1998 and to 148.7% in 1999. The ratio for the 30 largest *chaebols* also went below 200% in 2000 (Table 9.4). The debt-equity ratio of the manufacturing sector as a whole consequently fell from 396% in 1997 to 214% in 1999 and to 210.5% in 2000, the lowest since 1968.

Unfortunately, this drastic fall in debt-equity ratios has not really been translated into a lowering of financial risks in the corporate

| Table 9.4:  Trend of Debt-Equity Ratios of the 30 Largest *Chaebols* (%) | | | | | | |
|---|---|---|---|---|---|---|
|  | 1995 | 1996 | 1997 | 1998 | 1999 | 2000 |
| 5 largest | 297.6 | 344.2 | 472.9 | 235.1 | 148.7 | 162.0 |
| 6th-30th largest | 435.1 | 460.8 | 616.8 | 497.1 | 498.5 | 186.0 |
| Total | 347.5 | 386.5 | 512.8 | 379.8 | 218.7 | 171.2 |

**Source**: FTC website.
**Note**: Figures at the end of the year. Financial affiliates are excluded.

sector. To begin with, the reduction in the debt-equity ratio did not lead to a corresponding reduction in interest payments. In 1999, financial expenses to sales in the manufacturing sector fell from 9% in 1998 to 6.9% – an apparently significant reduction. However, the 1999 figure was still higher than the figure in 1997 (6.4%), the year when the financial crisis broke out, as well as the average figure during 1990-97 (5.8%). This was because Korean companies reduced their debt-equity ratios mainly through new stock issues, asset sales, and asset revaluation, rather than through repayment of their debts. The amount of total debt in the manufacturing sector in fact slightly increased from 389.6 trillion won ($324 billion) in 1998 to 391.2 trillion won in 1999 (BOK, 1999: p. 2000).

The 'financial engineering' that was involved in this process has brought about, on the whole, few benefits. Of the three key measures that the Korean companies used in order to reduce their debt-equity ratios, asset sales contributed to improving profitability of the manufacturing sector by around one percentage point in 1999 (BOK, 2000: p. 16).[3] However, this gain was nearly cancelled out by the costs incurred in asset revaluation, which was another major method taken by the *chaebols* to reduce their debt-equity ratios.[4]

---

[3]   The BOK (Bank of Korea) estimated that the extraordinary income in the manufacturing sector, which it said came mainly from asset sales, amounted to 1.0% of total sales, i.e., 4.6 trillion won (US$4 billion) in 1999.

[4]   The Korean government did not allow revaluation of corporate assets from 1981 for fear that the *chaebols* might leverage on it for real estate speculation. Once the debt level became a critical issue, the *chaebols* persuaded the government to allow revaluation of their assets to get a fair valuation of their financial status since the numerator, the value of their debt, varied with price movements while the denominator, the value of their equity, was fixed in accounting.

Exactly because it was achieved in these 'wrong' ways, the reduction in debt-equity ratios did not raise the traditionally low profitability of Korean corporations, which was ultimately why the reform measures were being implemented.

The ratio of ordinary income to sales (ordinary profit rate) for the manufacturing sector recovered to 1.68% in 1999, from negative figures in 1997 and 1998, but it slipped again to 1.29% in 2000 and further to 0.4% in 2001. The average ordinary profit rate for the two years of vigorous economic recovery in 1999 and 2000 was only around half of the historical average before the financial crisis (2.8% during 1973-96). If we include the figure for 2001, a year of sharp economic slowdown, the average is even worse at 1.12%. The corporate sector with 'high debt plus thin profit margin' has been transformed into something possibly even worse – namely, one with '*lower debt plus even thinner profit margin*' (Figure 9.1).

**Figure 9.1: Trend of Profitability in the Manufacturing Sector in Korea**

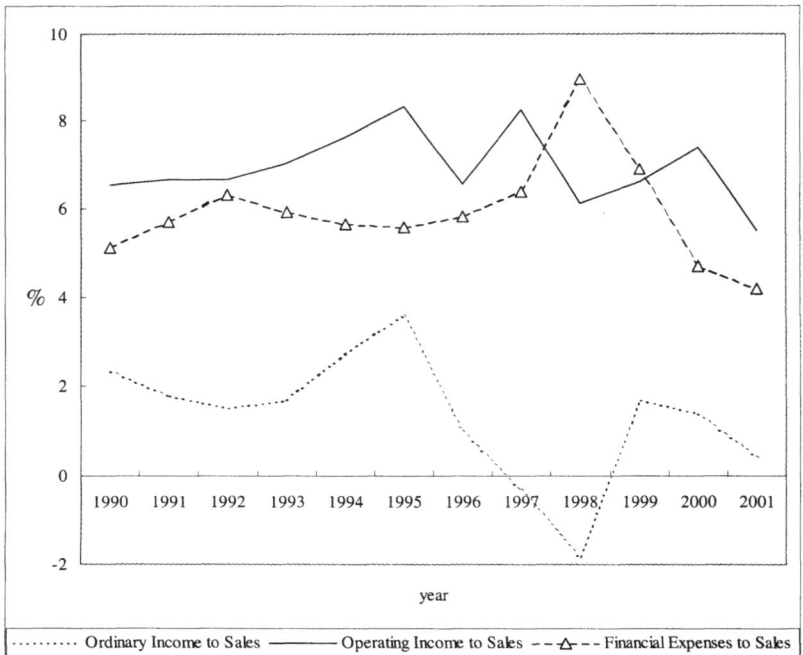

| | |
|---|---|
| ·········· Ordinary Income to Sales | ——— Operating Income to Sales    - - -△- - - Financial Expenses to Sales |

**Source**: BOK website

Moreover, there was no improvement in operating profit or sales, which in our view are better measures of corporate competitiveness than ordinary profit. In fact, their post-crisis figures show deterioration. The ratio of operating income to sales (operating profit rate) for the three years of recovery was 6.5% on average – lower than the 7.2% average for 1990-97.

These profit rate figures are even worse than they may appear at first sight, when we consider that the denominator (sales) was not growing during this period as fast as it used to. The sales growth rate in the manufacturing sector in 1999 and 2000, the years of sharp macroeconomic turnaround, was 11.6% on average, much lower than the average during 1990-97, which was 14.5%. The average sales growth rate during the three post-crisis years (1999-2001) was only 8.3% on average (the sales growth rate in 2002 was only 1.7% – the lowest since 1961, except for 1998, when it was 0.7%).

If the benefits of the radical, policy-driven reduction in the debt-equity ratio are difficult to find, if not non-existent, its costs were significant.

Above all, companies with high debts were categorically regarded as non-viable regardless of their short-term efficiency or long-term prospects. Financial institutions, facing stiffer supervision standards and preoccupied with their own survival, called in or stopped rolling over their loans to those companies with high debt-equity ratios, driving them into bankruptcy (more on this later). This was a major reason why the credit crunch in the Korean financial market persisted well into 2000, when the interest rate was at a historically low level.[5]

The debt-equity ratio reduction policy also drove the Korean firms to sell their assets at bargain prices. Although what exactly constitutes a bargain price can be debated, considering the asymmetry of negotiating power between sellers and buyers in times of financial crisis, it seems reasonable to suppose that those assets they sold were mostly sold at heavily discounted prices.

---

[5]  Thus seen, a large part of the build-up of non-performing loans (NPLs) after the crisis was due less to the inherent inefficiencies of the Korean corporate sector than to an abrupt change in the financial environment in a way that excessively punished high debt.

## 3.2    The 'Big Deals' and the 'workout programme'

In dealing with *ex post* adjustments of industrial capacity and financial problems, the Korean government adopted different approaches between the five largest *chaebols* and the smaller ones. For the five largest *chaebols*, which were regarded as having sufficient financial and managerial resources to restructure by themselves, the government 'encouraged' the 'Big Deals', that is, business swaps among the *chaebols* in industries with over-capacity. For the 6th to the 30th largest *chaebols*, which were considered too weak to restructure by themselves, the government devised the 'workout programme', a bank-sponsored restructuring process. In July 1998, it was announced that eight major business sectors that included 17 companies of the five *chaebols* were going to be subject to the Big Deals. One hundred companies were also put under the workout programme.[6]

Unfortunately, these programmes have not been very successful. Among the eight Big Deals proposed, none proceeded in the form of business swaps. Most of them ended up as one-sided takeovers or as simple mergers. Even worse, some proposed deals were simply not made. Also, among those deals concluded, many projects do not yet show signs of turnaround.

Likewise, despite a substantial debt restructuring, the majority of the 'workout' companies have not been turned around yet. Creditor banks rescheduled 86 trillion won in debts and provided 4.5 trillion won in fresh money to these companies by May 2000. Of the 100 companies selected for the workout programme, however, 29 companies went bankrupt and 35 companies were still under the programme as of June 2001. The 36 companies that 'graduated' from the programme are mostly small and medium-sized enterprises (MOFE, 2001; SERI, 2001).

One achievement of the Big Deal programme and the workout programme has been to reduce the number of affiliates in the *chaebol* groups, thus possibly reducing their 'excessive' diversification. The average number of businesses run by the five largest *chaebols* was

---

[6]    The programme soon expanded to smaller conglomerates and medium-sized companies, and later included the 12 Daewoo affiliates after the group became technically bankrupt in August 1999 (MOFE, 2001; SERI, 2001).

reduced from 30.0 in 1997 to 23.2 in April 2001. The total number of affiliates of the 30 largest *chaebols* also fell by 22.3%, from 804 in April 1998 to 624 in April 2001 (MOFE, 2001).

Was this a good thing? Apart from the fact that the number of affiliates *per se* does not necessarily indicate the degree of diversification (see Section 2.1 above), there is no empirical evidence that diversification of the *chaebols* had been a negative thing. To be sure, there have been some corporate failures due to ill-managed diversifications such as the cases of the Kia Group or the Hanbo Group. However, the diversified business structure provided the *chaebols* with a better ability to spread risk. The point is that there are both pros and cons for business diversification, and there is no such thing as an 'optimal' degree of diversification that fits all business groups. And therefore reduction in diversification in itself cannot be judged positive or negative.

### 3.3    Reforming the governance of the *chaebols*

If the radical reduction of debt-equity ratios, the Big Deals, and the workout programme were intended to deal with the symptoms of the *chaebol* structure, there were also attempts to change the very structure that was supposed to have caused these symptoms. Towards this aim, far-reaching changes have been made in relation to fair trading regulation, accounting, financial institutions, mergers and acquisitions, and internal corporate governance. Table 9.5 provides a summary of these measures.

### A.    Fair Trading Regulation

A major strength of business groups like the *chaebols* lies in their ability to make internal resource transfers *at prices designated by the centralised decision-making authority within the group*. Accepting this logic, before the financial crisis, the Fair Trading Commission (FTC) in Korea focused on restraining the concentration of economic power by the *chaebols* without denying the desirability of business grouping itself. As a result, it was lenient in regulating internal transactions among affiliates of the *chaebols*, although its attitude slowly but continuously hardened from the early 1980s.

However, the post-crisis corporate reform was carried out on

| Table 9.5: System Changes in Governance of the *Chaebols* | |
|---|---|
| **Classification** | **Main Contents** |
| Fair trade regulation | 1. Strengthening punishment for 'unfair' internal transactions<br>2. Revival of regulation on the amount of investment in related firms to 25% of net assets of a business group<br>3. Abolition of debt guarantee among affiliated firms |
| Accounting standards | 1. Introduction of consolidated financial statements<br>2. Obligation of establishing election committee for the assignment of outsider auditors for listed companies and affiliates of the *chaebols* |
| Financial market discipline | 1. Regulation of bank loans<br>– Debt-equity ratio of 200% became a *de facto* limit in provision of loans<br>– Prohibition of new loans with guarantee by affiliated firms<br>– Establishing a system for constant assessment of corporate credit risk, including introduction of forward-looking criteria (FLC)<br>2. Liberalisation of the merger-and-acquisition (M&A) market<br>– Permitting hostile takeovers<br>– Abolition of regulations on foreigners' shareholding |
| Internal governance | 1. Outsider director system<br>– ¼ of the board of directors should be outside directors<br>2. Responsibility of major shareholders<br>– Registration of the controlling shareholder as the representative director of leading affiliates<br>– The removal of the 'Chairman's Office'<br>3. Right of minority shareholders<br>– Loosening conditions for derivative suits, inspecting accounts, and request for the dismissal of directors and auditors by shareholders<br>– Introduction of a cumulative voting system when appointing directors<br>4. Right of institutional investors<br>– Allowing voting rights for shares in funds managed by investment trust companies and bank trust accounts |

**Source**: MOFE website, SERI (2001)

the assumption that transactions among *chaebol* affiliates that do not use market prices are 'unfair'. Consequently, in the three-year period 1998-2000, the FTC embarked on unprecedented investigations on 'unfair internal transactions' by the *chaebols*, and levied 234.3 billion won (US$195.2 million) in fines on the 30 largest *chaebols*, most of which were on the five largest *chaebols*.[7]

Another pillar of intra-*chaebol* transaction, i.e., debt guarantee among affiliates, was also completely abolished. Debt guarantee was singled out as an important factor that allowed 'unfair' expansion of the *chaebols*. It was also seen as increasing financial vulnerability at the group level, as it could lead to 'chain bankruptcy'. Thus, the abolition of debt guarantee was undertaken not only as a fair trading regulation but also as a measure to strengthen financial market discipline over the *chaebols*. The size of debt guarantee of the 30 largest *chaebols* stood at 26.9 trillion won as of April 1998, an amount equivalent to 39.5% of their total loans at the time. Under joint pressure from the FTC and the Financial Supervisory Commission (FSC), this was reduced to 9.8 trillion won by April 1999 and became nil at the end of March 2000 (Table 9.6).

| Table 9.6: Removal of Debt Guarantee in the 30 Largest *Chaebols* (trillion won) | | | | |
|---|---|---|---|---|
| | Apr. 1998 | Apr. 1999 | Dec. 1999 | Mar. 2000 |
| Loans with guarantee | 26.9 (39.5%) | 9.8 (9.7%) | 4.3 (4.3%) | 0 (0%) |
| Number of firms with debt guarantee | 216 | 127 | 68 | 0 |

**Source**: FTC website

---

[7]    During this period, the FTC conducted four investigations on the five largest *chaebols* and one investigation on the 6th-30th largest *chaebols*, and imposed 216.2 billion won in fines on the former and 18.1 billion won on the latter (FTC website).

## B.    Accounting Standards

As a measure to increase transparency and thereby accountability of the *chaebols*, the Korean government revised the corporate audit law and made it compulsory for the 30 largest *chaebols* to produce 'consolidated financial statements', that is, accounts for the business group as a whole, and not just for the individual affiliates.

With the introduction of the consolidated financial statement, it has become possible for outsiders to see the 'true' financial situation of a business group (including the size of internal transactions and interlocked shareholding), which used to be 'insider' knowledge. As a result, it has become impossible for the *chaebols* to inflate the value of their sales and assets through internal transactions and 'circular' or 'roundabout' holding of shares, which was a typical way of overcoming lack of financial resources.

Apart from the introduction of the consolidated financial statement, the Korean government has also made it obligatory for the *chaebol* affiliates and all listed companies to establish an election committee for the appointment of outside auditors in order to ensure the objectivity of the auditing process.

## C.    Regulation of the *Chaebols* Through Financial Regulation

Since the accumulation of non-performing loans (NPLs) in the financial sector was an immediate cause of the financial crisis, the restructuring of the financial sector itself was a major item in the reform agenda. The financial sector therefore underwent the biggest reorganisation in its history. The details of the financial sector restructuring programme are set out in Table 9.7.

As a result of this programme, 572 ailing financial institutions (27.2% of total financial institutions in existence at the end of 1997) were closed down and several major commercial banks were nationalised as they were recapitalised with public money (see Table 9.7). Other financial institutions that survived the financial crisis have undergone or are undergoing voluntary or government-induced mergers and acquisitions (M&As). In addition, the Financial Supervisory Commission (FSC) was established as a comprehensive financial watchdog, the functions of which had been previously divided between the Bank of Korea and the Ministry of Finance and Economy. Financial supervision standards were also significantly strengthened.

| Table 9.7: Major Measures Taken for Restructuring the Financial Sector | |
| --- | --- |
| Classification | Main contents |
| Strengthening financial supervision | 1. Established the Financial Supervisory Commission in April 1998<br>2. BIS ratio strictly applied as a deciding indicator of soundness of financial institutions (8% for commercial banks and 4% for small financial institutions) along with introduction of prompt corrective action measures<br>3. Introduced forward-looking criteria (FLC), conforming to 'global standards', in December 1999 |
| Disposal of insolvent financial institutions and consolidation | 1. Disposal of 572 ailing financial institutions by end-April 2001 (27.2 % of total financial institutions in existence at the end of 1997)<br>2. Injecting 137 trillion won of public funds into the sector<br>3. Consolidated four commercial banks and one merchant bank into the Woori Financial Holding Company |
| Partial Deposit Guarantee System | 1. Changed the previous Full Deposit Guarantee System into a Partial Deposit Guarantee System (when a financial institution enters bankruptcy, only up to 50 million won of deposits is guaranteed) |
| Governance | 1. Introduction of the outsider director system<br>2. Introduction of a committee for recommending appointment of bank presidents<br>3. Credit is assessed by an independent credit assessment committee |

**Source**: MOFE website

What is notable is that many financial reform measures were designed in close coordination with the corporate reform programme, because the NPLs after all came mostly from the corporate sector. For instance, the prohibition of loan guarantee among *chaebol* affiliates was not simply a change in financial supervision criteria but also a change in fair trading regulations over the *chaebols* (see above). New financial supervision criteria, such as the forward-looking criteria (FLC), were introduced at the end of 1999 as a way of restraining possible over-investment by the corporate sector. Under the previous standard, financial institutions were required to set aside provisions only against those loans on which interest had not actually been paid.[8] But the FLC require that financial institutions set aside provisions even against loans on which interest is regularly paid, if borrowers' management conditions, financial status, future cash flow and so on are regarded as inadequate. In judging a borrower's future business prospects, the corporate debt-equity ratio is again seen as one of the key considerations (FSC, 2000).

Moreover, other financial reform measures that are not directly related to the corporate reform programme, such as the strict application of the BIS minimum capital adequacy standard (the so-called BIS ratio), also have had significant indirect impact on the corporate sector.

For instance, the Korean government instituted a system to automatically force the liquidation or merger of financial institutions when they do not maintain the BIS ratio. Given this, financial institutions came to reduce, or even altogether stop, corporate lending, even when it was evident that a further provision of loans to the corporate sector at the expense of lowering the BIS ratio in the short run would increase their profits and soundness in the long run (more on this in Section 4). This, in turn, has substantially increased the need for corporations to maintain a higher level of liquidity, reducing the volume of financial resources available for long-term investment.

It seems to us that one of the most serious problems arising from applying rigid criteria of financial regulation, such as those relating to the BIS ratio or the corporate debt-equity ratio, lies in their pro-cyclical nature. In a recession, an increase in bankruptcy and fall in asset prices shrinks the asset base of the financial institutions, which induces them to withdraw their loans from the corporate sector in order to meet the BIS standard, which makes the recession even worse.

---

[8]   With the introduction of the FLC, the very definition of NPLs itself became more stringent. Now loans are to be automatically classified as NPLs if borrowers do not pay full interest for three months. The period was six months under the previous regulation standard.

Also, in a recession, firms need to increase their borrowing in order to maintain their cash flows, as their sales decrease and raising money through stock issuance becomes difficult. However, the debt-equity ratio regulation precludes the possibility of riding out a short-term liquidity problem by increasing debts. Indeed, we believe that this pro-cyclical nature of the new financial regulations is behind the pro-longed credit crunch during the period of crisis, as we shall elaborate later (Section 4).

## D.  Liberalisation of Mergers and Acquisitions (M&As)

Another element in the corporate reform programme was to in-stitute a fuller liberalisation of the M&A market, which was supposed to introduce harsher discipline on the corporate sector. The Korean government removed the acquirer's obligatory tender offer of shares up to 51% of total shares outstanding and abolished restrictions on the total amount of shareholdings a company can have in other com-panies, which used to be powerful obstacles to hostile takeovers. Abolition of the regulations on foreigners' shareholding in domestic companies also meant that the M&A market was now fully open to foreigners.

Although the M&A market was liberalised, hostile M&As are rare as yet. This is partly because hostile M&As are still frowned upon by the majority of the population, but also because domestic institutional investors, who would be the main players in the M&A market, are still cautious about their participation. Legally, however, there are no obstacles to hostile M&As, and it may only be a matter of time before the M&A market becomes active (although this is not a foregone conclusion). And knowing this, the 30 largest *chaebols* in-creased their internal shareholding from 43.2% in 1997 to 50.5% in 1999 (FTC website) in order to safeguard themselves against hostile takeovers, despite the fact that this was a period of severe liquidity constraints and therefore that such a move would cost them dearly.

## E.  Internal Governance Reforms

Internal governance reforms were directed at improving the managerial transparency and the accountability of the *chaebol* own-ers.

Firstly, the 'Chairman's Office', which had been the nerve centre of coordination within the *chaebols*, was abolished. At the same time, legal responsibility of the *chaebol* owners was strengthened, as they were forced to register themselves as representative directors of their leading affiliate firms, which makes them liable for public prosecution and civil lawsuits for managerial misconduct.

Secondly, the government revised the commercial law to make it obligatory for listed companies to appoint at least one quarter of directors from outside the firm. People who share interests with major shareholders were also banned from being elected as outside directors.

Thirdly, the rights of institutional investors were significantly enhanced. Investment trust companies and bank trust accounts were given voting rights. Although institutional investors are required to get approval from the FTC when they are involved in takeover activities, they have come to acquire almost all the rights of other shareholders.

Fourthly, the rights of minority shareholders were strengthened. The minimum proportion of shares that is required in bringing a lawsuit against misconduct of managers was reduced from 1% to 0.01%. The minimum requirements for inspecting the accounts were also weakened from 3% to 1% of shareholdings (0.5% in the case of listed companies with more than 100 billion won worth of equity capital). A cumulative voting system was also introduced in order to make it easier for the minority shareholders to appoint board members representing their collective interest.[9]

## 4.    Assessing the Governance Reform Programme

There are certainly some positive aspects in the governance reform programme implemented since 1998. For instance, the strengthening of regulations on auditing and accounting is important in pro-

---

[9]    This system lets shareholders vote on *all of the directorships*, not on individual directorships separately. In a system where shareholders vote on individual directorships, minority shareholders cannot win any single directorship against majority shareholders. However, in the cumulative system, they can concentrate their votes on one or a few directors and elect their own candidates.

viding concerned parties with objective and reliable performance indicators of companies, especially when the number of concerned parties becomes large as companies diversify and broaden their sources of finance. In the same vein, it is desirable to strengthen the rights of minority shareholders to defend their interests from possible neglect from the managers, who tend to cater for the interests of major shareholders. However, other measures in the programme have had negative effects on the national economy.

In the short run, many reform measures created, or at least intensified, a credit crunch because they made it necessary for the corporate sector to maintain a high level of liquidity and for the financial sector to withdraw liquidity from the corporate sector. This, in turn, increased non-performing loans in the economy and consequently the public burden for adjustment after the crisis.

In the long run, the governance reforms put the *chaebols* under serious constraints in operating as business groups, especially through the ban on internal transactions. To be sure, there can be negative effects of internal transactions, but they also have positive effects. Previously, internal transactions were a major source of a *chaebol*'s strength in supporting new large-scale ventures, as evidenced by Samsung's entry into the semiconductor industry or Hyundai's entry into the shipbuilding industry. Coupled with the stringent regulation on the corporate debt-equity ratio, the restriction on internal transactions has substantially reduced financing options for the *chaebols*.[10] As Table 9.8 shows, a remarkable trend in corporate financing after the crisis was an abrupt depletion of external funds available for the corporate sector. The total amount of external financing of the corporate sector dropped from 118 trillion won in 1997 to less than a quarter, i.e., 27.6 trillion won, in 1998. Even during the period of vigorous economic recovery in 1999 and 2000, the external funds available for

---

[10] Regarding this, a leading businessman in Korea, in an interview with one of the authors in August 2000, said: 'It has been possible for major *chaebols* to mobilise a large amount of investment funds through internal mechanisms without letting foreign competitors or foreign financial institutions know about their plans. The size and the speed of mobilisation of those resources were what foreign competitors feared most. But now, even the major *chaebols* (the five largest ones) have to go to the international financial market if they need to make an investment of over 1 trillion won (US$870 million).'

**Table 9.8: External Financing of the Corporate Sector**
(billion won)

|  | 1996 | 1997 | 1998 | 1999 | 2000 | 2001 |
|---|---|---|---|---|---|---|
| Total | 118,769 | 118,022 | 27,664 | 51,755 | 66,531 | 51,939 |
| Indirect Financing | 33,231 | 43,375 | -15,862 | 2,198 | 11,391 | 1,185 |
| From Banks | 16,676 | 15,184 | 259 | 15,525 | 23,348 | 3,381 |
| From NBFIs | 16,555 | 28,191 | -16,550 | -13,267 | -11,997 | -2,377 |
| Direct Financing | 56,097 | 44,087 | 49,496 | 24,792 | 18,996 | 36,838 |
| CPs | 20,737 | 4,421 | -11,678 | -16,116 | -1,133 | 4,210 |
| Stocks | 12,981 | 8,974 | 13,515 | 41,137 | 20,806 | 16,504 |
| CBs | 21,213 | 27,460 | 45,907 | -2,827 | -2,108 | 11,761 |
| Foreign Borrowing | 12,383 | 6,563 | -9,809 | 11,537 | 15,765 | 2,283 |
| Others | 17,059 | 23,997 | 3,839 | 13,228 | 20,380 | 11,633 |

**Source**: Flow of Funds, BOK website
**Note**: CP is corporate paper. CB is corporate bond. Others include corporate loans, government loans and so on.

the corporate sector were only around half of that available in 1997 and the situation became worse in 2001.

The major culprit here was the fall in the borrowing from financial institutions, i.e., indirect financing. In 1998 when the country was in the depth of the crisis, financial institutions *withdrew* 15.8 trillion won of loans from the corporate sector in their attempts to raise their BIS ratios and to reduce their risk exposure – in other words, it was actually siphoning money out of the corporate sector! Although indirect financing slowly began to recover from 1999, its level fell far short of the pre-crisis level, even if we accept that there may have been a certain amount of 'excessive' lending before the crisis. The amount of indirect external financing available in 1999, at 2.2 trillion won, was only about 5% of the 1997 level (43.4 trillion won). In 2000, it was, at 11.4 trillion won, still only 26% of the 1997 level. As the economy began to slow down sharply along with the recession in the world economy, indirect financing shrank dramatically again in 2001. In that year, indirect financing shrank back to just under 1.2 trillion won, or down to 2.5% of the 1997 level.

The corporate sector has tried to survive this severe credit crunch by increasing the issuance of stocks and corporate bonds. However, they were far from sufficient to compensate for the total collapse in indirect financing. Even with more than a doubling of equity financing (from 10.978 trillion won in 1996-97 to 22.991 trillion won in 1998-2001), total direct financing fell to less than 2/3 of the pre-crisis level (from 50.092 trillion won in 1996-97 to 32.531 trillion won in 1998-2001). Given the total collapse of indirect financing that we talked about above, the total amount of external (direct and indirect) financing available for the Korean corporate sector during the post-crisis period (1998-2001) was only 42% of the pre-crisis level (49.472 trillion won, as opposed to 118.396 trillion won for 1996-97).

Moreover, the option to issue corporate bonds or new stocks was available only to the largest companies which had established their credibility in the securities market. For example, when excluding asset-backed securities, the share of big firms in the corporate bond market reached 99% in 1998 and 95% in 1999 – the corresponding figure was 72% in 1991 and 87% in 1994 (Crotty and Lee, 2001). All these mean that the smaller firms had virtually no access to external financing.

As a result of the collapse in external corporate financing, there was a collapse in investment in the years following the 1997 financial crisis. The gross investment ratio in the national accounts fell from an average of 37.1% during 1990-97 to a mere 25.8% during 1998-2001 (27.3% if we exclude 1998 as an exceptional year) (the figures are from the BOK website).

Overall, it is certainly true that the *chaebols* had some negative features – some inherent in their structure, others more incidental. However, by altogether banning internal transactions and other features that allowed them to operate as business groups, the reform programme has destroyed the positive aspects of the group structure as well – a classic case of 'throwing the baby away with the bath water'. It is vital that these and other positive aspects of the old system are revived in a way that minimises the negative features of the old system and preserves the positive aspects of the recent reforms. In the next section, we explore how this may be done.

## 5.     The Need for a 'Second-Stage Catching-up System' for the Korean Economy

In our view, what was needed for Korea after the crisis was not to try a transition to an idealised Anglo-American system but to build what we call a 'second-stage catching-up system', which the country had failed to do before the crisis.

Our position starts from the recognition that Korea's catching-up still has a long way to go. The country may have spectacularly succeeded in the first stage of catching-up but is still only a middle-income country with a per capita income of $9,628 in 2000, around one-fourth that of the US. According to Lee's (1999) estimate of 'relative backwardness', Korea in 1995, when the country's per capita income reached $10,000, was approximately where Japan was in the middle of the 1960s, when the Japanese catching-up system was at its most spectacular in its success.

The reformers believe, at least implicitly, that Korea's transformation into a high-income country would be more or less automatically achieved only if the 'global standard' institutions in finance and corporate governance they have recently introduced can be made to stick. However, as we pointed out above, the reform measures were principally geared towards reducing financial risk of the system, even to the extent of 'over-killing' the economy in the short run. Nowhere in the reform programme was the question of long-term growth and catching-up considered. Indeed, we would argue that many of the 'global standard' financial and corporate institutions that the reform programme has introduced are likely to damage the future growth prospects for the Korean economy.

An important case in point is the BIS capital adequacy ratio. The BIS rule requires that the capital base of financial institutions should correspond to the weighted risk of their assets. The problem is that this is an 'unfair' rule from developing countries' point of view, as they have relatively scarce financial resources but are required to maintain the same capital base per lending. Moreover, the pressure on developing-country financial institutions to adopt the BIS standard more or less overnight forced them to expand their capital base very rapidly, thus creating a severe credit crunch, as seen in the case of Korea.[11]

This is not all. If the logic behind the BIS ratio is fully applied, the latecomers will be put in an even more disadvantageous position. Financial risk for assets in developing countries is normally higher than that for assets in developed countries, which means that financial institutions in developing countries should maintain a larger capital base for the same amount of loan exposure, compared to their counterparts in developed countries. In fact, the 'New Basel Accord' announced by the Basel Committee in January 2001 requests that financial institutions should apply different weights to corporate lending according to the ratings given to the borrowing company by international credit rating agencies. So, for instance, if a company has a credit rating between AAA and AA-, a 20% risk weighting is applied whereas a 150% risk weighting is applied to a company with a credit rating of BB- and below, into which most Korean companies were classified in 2001 (SERI, 2001).[12] From the viewpoint of the companies or financial institutions in developing countries, this is a major blow to their ability to attract or provide investment financing.

The same argument applies to other 'global standard' institutions. For instance, if equity financing is considered the global standard for corporate financing, this will have particularly adverse effects on countries that have been heavily relying on debt financing. In the Korean case, this idealised preference for equity financing created far too negative a perception about its relatively high corporate

---

[11] This kind of credit crunch happened even in Japan in 1997 and 1998. One reason why the Asian financial crisis was exacerbated was that, according to the Basel accord, Japanese commercial banks had to meet the 8% BIS ratio by March 1998 when the quality of their assets substantially deteriorated due to the spread of the Southeast Asian financial crisis and the prolonged recession in the local economy. As a consequence, they had to withdraw existing loans to raise their BIS ratios (MOFE, 1998).

[12] Even according to the old BIS rule, there are some differences between the OECD member countries and non-member countries in the application of the BIS rule. For instance, loans to commercial banks receive the risk weight of 20% (compared to the 100% risk weight that corporate lending has) in the OECD member countries, while they receive a higher weight in non-member countries. But the risk weighting was the same within OECD countries, or within non-OECD countries, according to the old rule.

debt-equity ratio and brought about the policy aimed at its radical reduction, which resulted in a severe credit crunch and the 'fire-sales' of corporate assets. For another example, if the 'global standard' condition for 'fair' competition is that each company operates as a standalone unit, those companies which have been growing through business grouping, such as the *chaebols*, are suddenly put into a disadvantageous position.

As an economy that is still catching up, Korea needed, and still needs, to devise a new economic system which is suited to a second-stage catching-up. In our view, this new system should be built on the strengths of the traditional system, and not based on a complete abandonment of it. We sketch below how this new system may look like.

The most important lesson from the experience of the post-crisis reform in redefining the role of the Korean state, in our view, is that the state should act as the 'mediator' between the homogenising forces of globalisation and the unique characteristics of the local economy. The economic reforms in Korea were designed and implemented in the belief that the country should adopt 'global standard' institutions. The unique characteristics of the local economy were regarded as outdated, or even pathological, and thus were destroyed or allowed to languish. As we have repeatedly pointed out, however, the 'global standard' institutions have not only imposed unnecessary costs but many of them are currently functioning more as obstacles to, rather than spurs for, further development of the economy.

Of course, in the present international environment, it will be difficult for Korea to completely resist the introduction of certain 'global standards'. However, it does not mean that it should follow them blindly, regardless of their consequences for the national economy.

A case in point is, once again, the adoption of the BIS capital adequacy ratio. Given that the BIS rule is now a 'global' norm, there was little that the Korean government could do in changing the rule itself. However, it could still have applied it more flexibly, in a way that promotes national interest. For instance, rather than applying the rule to all commercial banks, it could have made it obligatory only for those that have high international exposure, whilst applying less stringent standards to those that have limited exposure to international financial markets.

A similar kind of creative response is required in relation to industrial policy. Outwardly, the Korean government has almost totally given up on industrial policy. However, there still exist important *de facto* industrial policy measures, especially the regulations on corporate lending. The problem with this approach is that, if industrial policy is implicitly conducted through the financial supervision system, it is likely to be geared towards the needs of the financial sector, rather than those of the whole economy. Therefore, if it is felt necessary to control the financial risks from investment competition between major firms, it should be dealt with by explicit industrial policy measures tied to a long-term development strategy, rather than through indirect intervention through financial regulation, which is too blunt an instrument for the job.

In a similar vein, the state should find a way to regain control over cross-border capital flows. While open capital markets can allow developing countries to have access to larger and cheaper funds, this has to be set against the costs of open capital markets. Firstly, a large part of foreign funds comes from entities for whom the maximisation of short-term financial returns is paramount (e.g., pension funds), and therefore they tend to demand corporate practices that are not conducive to high investment and rapid growth (e.g., demands for high dividends rather than retention of profit). Secondly, the access to foreign funds is subject to very quick reversals, as Korea has learnt from its bitter experience in the 1997 crisis. Thirdly, if the possibility of such reversal is to be minimised, foreign exchange reserves have to be kept, as is the case with Korea now, which means that the country has to forgo the financial returns that could come if this sum was kept in less-liquid, higher-yielding assets. Fourthly, should a currency crisis happen (as even huge reserves are not an absolute guarantee against a currency crisis for a country whose currency is not one of the major settlement currencies), open capital accounts make it necessary to keep interest rates high, thus driving otherwise healthy enterprises into bankruptcy (as happened in Korea in the first six months of the IMF programme).

Of course, the degree of external financial liberalisation is basically a result of international negotiations, and therefore there is certainly a limit to deciding on the degree of financial openness purely on the basis of domestic considerations. However, the state should at least maintain some policy tools to guard the economy against disruptive forces of cross-border capital flows, given the costs that they can impose.

Similar kinds of policy pragmatism and flexibility in the implementation process are required in relation to the reform of the *chaebols*. As a middle-income country, Korea still needs to utilise this positive aspect of business grouping, such as its ability to take greater risk. The possible abuse of internal transactions can be checked by increasing transparency of corporate management and strengthening the right of minority shareholders, rather than by an outright ban on internal transactions. A reformed industrial policy, more explicit and direct than the *de facto* industrial policy of recent years but more transparent and indirect than the traditional one, can also contribute to checking excessive risk-taking in the corporate sector.

## 6.    Some Final Thoughts

The corporate reform programme implemented by the IMF and the Korean government following the 1997 financial crisis set out to dismantle what remained of the traditional economic system of the country after the liberalisation exercise in the 1990s and replace it with an Anglo-American-style system. In our view, however, what the country needed was a re-invention of the traditional model, and not a total break with it.

The new system is mainly geared towards ensuring the stability and the profitability of the financial sector. It is, therefore, not a big surprise that corporate financing has dried up, significantly reducing the investment capability of the corporate sector, as shown in the dramatic fall in national investment figures. However, the new system has failed to reduce financial risk of the corporate sector, has imposed significant 'transition costs' on the economy (in the form of 'unnecessary bankruptcy', etc.), and is likely to reduce the dynamism of the country's corporate sector in the long run.

The biggest challenge for the country will be whether it can figure out a way to forge a second-stage catching-up system which revitalises investment dynamism while managing financial risk properly in the economy. We have tried to outline some elements of this new strategy in this chapter.

# Bibliography

Bank of Korea (BOK) (1999 and 2000). *Financial Statement Analysis* (in Korean). Seoul: Bank of Korea.

Bank of Korea (BOK) website, http://www.bok.or.kr

Brennan, M. (1995). 'Corporate Finance Over the Past 25 Years', *Financial Management,* vol. 24, no. 2.

Burton, J. (1998). 'Boxed Into a Corner', *Financial Times*, 23 November 1998.

Chang, H-J. (1993). 'The Political Economy of Industrial Policy in Korea', *Cambridge Journal of Economics*, vol. 17, no. 2.

Chang, H-J. (1994). *The Political Economy of Industrial Policy.* London and Basingstoke: Macmillan.

Chang, H-J. (2000). 'The Hazard of Moral Hazard – Untangling the Asian Crisis', *World Development*, vol. 28, no. 4.

Chang, H-J. & Park, H-J. (2000). 'An Alternative Perspective on Government Policy towards Big Businesses in Korea: Industrial Policy, Financial Regulation, and Political Democracy', in S-H. Jwa & I. Lee (eds.), *Korean* Chaebol *in Transition: Road Ahead and Agenda.* Seoul: Korea Economic Research Institute.

Chang, H-J., Park, H-J. & Yoo, C.G. (1998). 'Interpreting the Korean Crisis: Financial Liberalisation, Industrial Policy, and Corporate Governance', *Cambridge Journal of Economics*, vol. 22, no. 6.

Claessens, S., Djankov, S. & Lang, L. (1998). 'Corporate Growth, Financing, and Risks in the Decade before East Asia's Financial Crisis', Policy Research Working Paper, no. 2017. Washington, D.C.: World Bank.

Corbett, J. & Jenkinson, T. (1994). 'The Financing of Industry, 1970-89: An International Comparison', Discussion Paper, No. 948, Centre for Economic Policy Research, University of London.

Crotty, J. & Lee, K-K. (2001). 'Economic Performance in Post-Crisis Korea: A Critical Perspective on Neoliberal Restructuring', mimeo. Amherst: Department of Economics, University of Massachusetts.

Demirguc-Kunt, A. & Maksimovic, V. (1996), 'Stock Market Development and Firm Financing Choices', *The World Bank Economic Review*, vol. 10, no. 2.

Fair Trading Commission (FTC) website, http://www.ftc.go.kr

Financial Supervisory Commission (FSC) (2000). 'The Direction of the Development of Financial Activities After the Introduction of the Forward Looking Criteria' (in Korean), Seoul.

Furman, J. & Stiglitz, J. (1998). 'Economic Crises: Evidence and Insights from East Asia', *Brookings Papers on Economic Activity*, 1998, no. 2.

Harris, M. & Raviv, A. (1991). 'The Theory of Capital Structure', *The Journal of Finance,* vol. 46, no. 1.

Lee, J-M. (1999). 'East Asian NIEs' Model of Development: Miracle, Crisis, and Beyond', *Pacific Review*, vol. 12, no. 2.

Ministry of Finance and Economy (MOFE) (1998). 'Causes of, Responses to and Consequences of the 1997 Economic Crisis', unpublished internal report (in Korean).

Ministry of Finance and Economy (MOFE) (2001). 'An Assessment of Corporate Restructuring until June 2001 and Future Plans', unpublished internal report (in Korean).

Ministry of Finance and Economy (MOFE) website, http://www.mofe.go.kr/

Park, H-J. (1998). 'Strategy, Competition, and Organisational Structure of the *Chaebol*', mimeo., School of Oriental and African Studies, University of London.

Radelet, S. & Sachs, J. (1998). 'The East Asian Financial Crisis: Diagnosis, Remedies and Prospects', *Brookings Papers on Economic Activity*, 1998, no. 1.

Samsung Economic Research Institute (SERI) (2001). 'Three Years After the IMF Bailout'. Seoul.

Yoo, S.M. (1997). 'Evolution of Government-Business Interface in Korea: Progress to Date and Reform Agenda Ahead', Working Paper, no. 9711. Seoul: Korea Development Institute.

Milton Keynes UK
Ingram Content Group UK Ltd.
UKHW040147031123
431715UK00003B/79

9 781842 771419